THE SELECTED LETTERS OF FREDERICK MANFRED

Frederick Feikema Manfred, 1980
(photo by Larry Risser)

Edited by Arthur R. Huseboe and Nancy Owen Nelson

The Selected Letters of

Frederick Manfred

1932-1954

University of Nebraska Press: Lincoln and London

Publication of this book was assisted by a grant from the South Dakota Committee on the Humanities. Opinions expressed in this book are not necessarily those of the National Endowment for the Humanities or the South Dakota Committee on the Humanities.

Manufactured in the United States of America

The paper in this book meets the minimum requirements of American National Standard for Information Sciences – Permanence of Paper for Printed Library Materials, ANSI Z39.48-1984.

Library of Congress Cataloging in Publication Data
Manfred, Frederick Feikema, 1912–
The selected letters of Frederick Manfred, 1932–1954.
1. Manfred, Frederick Feikema, 1912-   – Correspondence.   2. Authors, American – 20th century – Correspondence.   I. Huseboe, Arthur R., 1931-
II. Nelson, Nancy Owen, 1946-   III. Title.
PS3525.A52233Z48   1988   813'.54   [B]   88-4798
ISBN 0-8032-2344-7 (alk. paper)
ISBN 0-8032-7237-5 (alk. paper: pbk.)

Contents

ILLUSTRATIONS

Frontispiece:

Frederick Feikema Manfred, 1980

Following page 314:

Letter to Helen Reitsema, May 1933

Helen Margaret Reitsema, 1936

John Huizenga, 1936

John DeBie, 1934

Peter De Vries, 1931

Frederick Feikema, 1934

The Feikema boys on the farm east of
Doon, Iowa, fall 1934

Herman Van Engen and Frederick
Feikema, summer 1938

Frederick Feikema at the sanatorium,
February 1942

The first autograph party for
The Golden Bowl, 28 September 1944

Frederick Feikema writing *Boy
Almighty,* 1944

Frederick Feikema and Eric Sevareid
at autograph party for Sevareid's
Not So Wild a Dream, 1946

Herbert Krause and Frederick Feikema
at party for *This Is the Year,* April 1947

Frederick Feikema Manfred, 1952

Frederick Manfred and his family,
December 1954

He can tell a story—start it and keep it rolling

like a runaway stagecoach in a horse opera until

it crashes in whatever canyon or against whatever

cliff he has prepared for it.

Wallace Stegner

Introduction

The present selection from Frederick Manfred's early correspondence sets out for the first time the richly detailed inner and outer life of one of America's most versatile, productive, and independent novelists, regarded with respect and even awe by some comtempory writers and critics but with suspicion and even distaste by others. Perhaps an obvious reason for the conflict between Manfred and a number of critics is that the prairie novel has not yet become a respected genre in American literature. Despite such successes as Willa Cather's *My Ántonia* and Ole Rölvaag's *Giants in the Earth,* the novel of the prairie has often been looked upon—particularly by the East Coast critics—as unimportant, if not irrelevant, to the total American experience. Nevertheless, Manfred has written two best sellers in *This Is the Year* and *Lord Grizzly*—the first of these also the Associated Press editors' choice for best novel in 1948 and the second nearly winning the National Book Award in 1954—and with twenty novels and five books of poems and stories he has created in the heart of the northern prairies and plains a sprawling literary republic that he calls "Siouxland." Manfred's vast and powerful vision has not, to date, received its just appreciation. The letters in this collection will help to right some of the imbalance that exists between Manfred's present reputation and that accomplishment.

As a record of Frederick Manfred's life and literary career, the letters are valuable enough, but the 161 printed here give particularly deep insights as well into the troubled decades of the Great Depression, the Dust Bowl, and World War II and the first decade of the atomic age. Among them are lively missives from Manfred to many of the leading literary figures of the period, including Sinclair Lewis, Robert Penn Warren, Peter De Vries, Henry Miller,

Wallace Stegner, David Cornell De Jong, Herbert Krause, Earl Guy, Van Wyck Brooks, H. L. Mencken, William Carlos Williams, William Van O'Connor, Malcolm Cowley, Nelson Algren, Eric Sevareid, Meridel Le Sueur, Bernard DeVoto, Mark Schorer, and John Crowe Ransom. Yet these letters are only a sample of a vast treasure trove of Manfrediana. The complete collection of Manfred's correspondence from 1932 to 1984, now in the archives of the University of Minnesota, consists of approximately five thousand single-spaced pages. With them are Manfred's journals, the manuscripts of all of the twenty novels, the short stories, the poetry, and the essays. All of the collection is accessible to scholars, except for some packets of sealed materials to be opened only after Manfred's death.

One need not be a scholar of Manfred's works, however, to find pleasure in this present selection. Manfred's letters from 1932 to 1954 read like a cross section of belles lettres and autobiography: there are familiar essays, short biographical sketches, jeremiads, poetic outbursts, models of argument and persuasion, and even passages of brisk dialogue. In them one meets Manfred as a young man and as a young artist; the reader sees him begin to flesh out his aesthetic theories and, depending on the correspondent, take on various personas—sometimes irascible and stubborn, sometimes compassionate and gentle—as he reports his early experiences as a wanderer, a rubber-factory worker, a journalist, a politician, and finally a committed writer. One also meets persons who are important in Manfred's life and career but who virtually take on lives of their own within the letters, appearing and reappearing throughout the two decades. For the first eight years of the correspondence, the only known letters are those written to Helen Reitsema, John Huizenga, and John DeBie—all of them close friends from Calvin College and all essential to Manfred's emotional and intellectual life.

Without question the most powerful of these early associations was with Helen Reitsema. Her rejection of him and her marriage to someone else in 1937, after Manfred's years of hoping and waiting, was a devastating emotional blow from which he only slowly recovered. She was, and continued to be for more than thirty years, a source both of inspiration and deep frustration. A short time after her engagement he wrote, "There isn't such a thing as love for me anymore. The loss of Helen forever killed that in me." Five years later he wrote to Peter De Vries, "There was the sharp, tendon-cutting, almost eviscerative breakup between myself and The One." In the novels Helen appears again and again, especially as the idealized Hero Bernlef in the trilogy; and as recently as 1962 Manfred dedicated the revised one-volume version of the trilogy, *Wanderlust,* to her. The present edition of the letters will provide scholars with new sources and a new stimulus for interpretation and understanding of Manfred's female characters and of his place as a character in his own work.

From John Huizenga, another early correspondent, Manfred received much emotional and intellectual strength, especially in the years of wandering before his marriage to Maryanna Shorba. The two men had many college friends in common, and to Huizenga, Manfred wrote long letters of bragging, complaining, and dreaming. Unlike the letters to John DeBie, the other close college friend, the letters to Huizenga are very personal records of Manfred's developing philosophy and psychology, his flirtation with socialism and communism, and his pursuit of a career as a writer. On 13 April 1935, for example, Manfred wrote, "The other day, I had this irresistible and likable thought. You and I live but once, don't we? Why should we be separated as much as we are? There's no sense in it, is there? The idea of finding someone to replace you is repellent and unnecessary—for one needs constantly someone who is a friend such as we've been to each other." And he signed it, "My earnest love to you, Fred." At the same time, Manfred admits, his admiration for Huizenga sometimes made him feel "confoundedly ill at ease," made him try too hard, made him write those polysyllabic epistles that he characterized years later as "looking up" letters. To DeBie, on the other hand, he wrote more prosaic "looking down" letters. Manfred returned Huizenga's inspirational friendship by fictionalizing him as Huse Starringa, the eloquent opponent of the institutional church in *The Primitive* (1949), the first volume of the trilogy *World's Wanderer,* and again as Howard Starring in the revised version of the trilogy, *Wanderlust* (1962).

With John DeBie, Manfred was on comfortable terms. The two had become acquainted at Western Academy in Hull, Iowa, where Manfred was two years ahead. After Manfred stayed out for two years to work, the two men traveled together to Calvin College with a carload of friends, and they remained close for years after. The letters to DeBie tend to be more reportorial than emotional, but in them Manfred shares many of the same concerns that he expressed to Huizenga. He uses both men as sounding boards for his liberal ideas in politics and religion, for example, and for his many unfulfilled love affairs, and he experiments with new images and coined words in a way that foreshadows his later experimentation in the novels.

To DeBie, Manfred reports the first serious encouragement that is given to his writing. A long conversation in New York City with Floyd McKnight, a poet, and with Gordon Melvin, author and faculty member in the education department at City College of New York, seems to Manfred a confirmation of his high hopes for a literary career. He writes to DeBie in May 1935, "That is the only happy feeling I have, Debby. That feeling I had in college that I was destined to do something of merit and that confidence I had in myself was not unmerited. To jump out of my class now, Schopenhauer and Shakespeare both had a great respect for their work. They said it was permissible. Could I scurry under such a cover also?" Manfred hoped in 1935 to use a volume of poetry as a way of interesting a publisher in the novel he was writing, but none of his gambits with publishers was to succeed for many years.

The development of Manfred's first published novel can be traced through the letters of the next eight years. The idea for a story had come to him when he hitchhiked to Yellowstone National Park in the summer of 1934. From that time on he had been taking notes, writing plot outlines, and recording conversations until mid-June 1937, when he began seriously to write the story of a young man and woman who were hitchhiking for their honeymoon. Manfred is fond of telling how he regaled the party guests at Jim Shields's one night and then went home to write out the first draft of what would eventually become *The Golden Bowl*. Encouraged by author Meridel Le Sueur, who told him the novel would "outrank and outsell" Steinbeck's *Of Mice and Men,* and disciplined by writing for the *Minneapolis Journal,* Manfred sent *Of These It Is Said* (the earlier name of the novel) to Random House in the fall of 1937. It was rejected, and subsequent efforts to find a publisher were equally unsuccessful until Webb Publishing finally accepted it, after several rewritings, in 1944.

From this point on, the most persistent and powerful theme in the letters has to do with Manfred's efforts to win a publisher and a public, often in the face of his fierce determination to compromise with neither, to tell instead his own stories in his own language. The letters in the present collection trace that struggle through the early success of the prairie novels *The Golden Bowl* and *This Is the Year,* the moderate success of *Boy Almighty* and *The Chokecherry Tree,* and the critical decline among influential New York critics with the *World's Wanderer* trilogy. The letters take us to Manfred's important decision to change his pen name from the Frisian Feike Feikema to the American Frederick Feikema Manfred, and to his phenomenal national success with the mountain-man novel *Lord Grizzly.* Critical response in this period was conveyed through book reviews ranging from magazines and papers of national influence, such as the *New York Times Book Review,* the *Los Angeles Times,* and *Kenyon Review,* to such lesser-known newspapers as the *Milwaukee Journal,* the *Boston Herald,* the *Grand Rapids* (Michigan) *Press,* and the *Meriden* (Connecticut) *Record.* The criticism reflects, though may not fully explain, what is considered by some to be Manfred's roller-coaster reputation. Once asked in a meeting of Minneapolis and Saint Paul booksellers why his work (*Golden Bowl* and *Boy Almighty*) was so spotty, Manfred offered this testament to his unfailing conviction about his life's work: "Spotty is it? Well, it all depends on where you sit. Now, from where I sit, it's all pretty good, but some of it's better."

After the success of *The Golden Bowl,* praised by Andrea Parke in the *New York Times Book Review* as a "simple, powerful picture of human experience," Manfred wrangled *Boy Almighty* (1945) into print, giving Webb Publishing its second success with a Manfred novel. The story of Eric Frey's struggle with the malevolent Whipper encountered mixed reviews, most of the reviewers praising it for its remarkable honesty and realism but finding its style difficult. For instance, Jennings Rice of the *New York Tribune Weekly Book Review* found that the book contained "vigorous realism and delicate sensitivity," but he took issue with Eric's atrocious grammar. Both Nona Balakian in the *New York Times Book Review* and the reviewer for *New Republic* found the book to be the work of an impassioned young artist. Despite the "clumsiness" of style, *Boy Almighty* was seen as evidence of a powerful young midwestern writer whose realistic prose mixed bitterness with the beauty of love.

Manfred's national reputation reached an early peak with the publication by Doubleday of *This Is the Year* (1947), an expansive novel of the soil that went into two printings. The unanimous Associated Press book reviewers' choice for Novel of the Year, *This Is the Year* also brought praise from Sinclair Lewis and Van Wyck Brooks. A *Time* reviewer found it a "unique regional novel." John

Farrelly in *New Republic* wrote of it as a "large, expansive, preten-tious and sincere novel," and Harrison Smith of *Saturday Review* praised its "vitality of an epic narrative." One critic who disliked the novel attacked its lack of control or its failure "to differentiate subject from experience, . . . to extract theme from subject" (Mark Schorer in *Kenyon Review*).

The Chokecherry Tree, in 1948, received a more mixed response. Negative reviews of the novel found it lacking in control of charac-terization and style. Robert Heilman in *Sewanee Review,* for exam-ple, thought it a "farce-comic observation of details" that takes the reader nowhere by means of a superficial, clichéd, and journalistic style. Most reviewers, however, thought Manfred's examination of the unheroic little Elof Lofblom both endearing and sensitive. Richard Sullivan in the *New York Times Book Review* pointed to the novel's strength in humor and sincerity, and Nash Burger, also writing in the *Times,* considered it "moving and persuasive."

With the writing and publishing of the *World's Wanderer* tril-ogy, Manfred's disagreements with Doubleday intensified until, in 1953, he left the company. He contended that Doubleday's editors were rushing him into print while being niggardly with advances; Doubleday, meanwhile, had gradually been growing disillusioned with Manfred as a potential best-selling novelist. With its rejection of *The Rape of Elizabeth* in late 1952, Manfred finally made up his mind. The parting between author and publisher came after a nearly unbroken succession of negative reviews in the East, begin-ning with *The Primitive* (1949). Although Edward A. Laycock in the *Boston Globe* found it "more exciting and enjoyable than the most sensational best seller," Walter Havighurst in *Saturday Review* described it as a "book of grotesques" and "no novel at all," while George Stewart in the *New York Times Book Review* found the book's language to be "mediocre poetry." Even the more favorable eastern reviews gave only qualified praise to the novel. It had at best, said the *New Yorker* critic, an "impassioned, headlong style" and "im-mense detail." Riley Hughes in *Commonweal* found *The Primitive* to be fraught with "thin intellectual, emotional, and stylistic equip-ment" and ominously warned that the rest of the trilogy could be no better.

Most influential reviews of *The Brother* (1950) and *The Giant* (1951) were similarly negative or at best only lukewarm. Ruth Chapin in the *Christian Science Monitor* praised *The Brother* for its "sense of purely physical atmosphere and scene" but found the novel inept in wit. Hal Borland in the *New York Times Book Review* said it was juvenile, ranting, and had no clear purpose. *The Giant* faced a fate that was little better, in spite of Manfred's assertion in a postscript that the trilogy belonged to a new genre of auto-biographical novel that he chose to call the "rume." Harrison Smith in *Saturday Review* found *The Giant* an effective picaresque novel but full of confusing detail, while Sterling North in the *Washington Post* called *The Giant* a "third-rate piece of adolescent caterwauling by an alleged novelist . . . who has failed to master even the most primary essentials of storytelling."

This low point in the responses of influential critics marks the end of the first phase of Manfred's writing. Although some scholars, such as Joseph Flora, have assumed that the writer's pen name change from Feike Feikema to Frederick Feikema Manfred in 1952 represented his rejection of the earlier work, the letters before 1952 prove that Manfred had been considering a new name off and on for a long time. Although the period beginning with the pub-lication of *Lord Grizzly* in 1954 suggests a significant change in focus to western historical material, the letters demonstrate that Manfred was interested in the Hugh Glass—grizzly bear material as early as 1944 and show a remarkable consistency of vision: very early in his career Manfred had determined to write a multivolume series of novels about the northern prairies and plains. *Lord Grizzly* was merely the next step in a plan already under way, the first novel to explore the century before his own.

Thus the name change represents a change in direction rather than a denial of his earlier work: before 1951 all of his novels had grown directly out of his own rural and urban life experiences and were set in his own lifetime. After 1951 and for the next fifteen years, all but two works of fiction (*Morning Red*, published in 1956, and *The Man Who Looked Like the Prince of Wales*, 1965) were deeply re-searched historical novels and stories about the American West: *Lord Grizzly, Riders of Judgment, Conquering Horse, Scarlet Plume, King of Spades*, and *Arrow of Love*. The first five of the six, in fact, comprise the Buckskin Man Tales, Manfred's highly successful grouping of novels about the Northern Plains from 1800 to the turn of the century.

A great deal of thought had gone into dropping his pen name and changing his legal name from Frederick Feikema to Frederick Feikema Manfred. His father's given name was Feike, later Ameri-canized to Frank, and Manfred had been baptized Frederick

Feikema. As early as 1937 he had considered a combination of these as a pen name—Frederick Franks—for he had been unhappy all along, he says, about his surname. Manfred was attracted to the idea of finding an easily recognized name but repelled by the thought of losing any part of a name identification that kept him tightly tied to his Frisian-Saxon heritage.

He had been aware for a long time that his pen name caused difficulty wherever he went. When he was introduced to people at parties, they invariably stumbled over the pronunciation: he would hear Fee'-kee Fee-kee'-ma, Fee-Kuy'-ma, and other variations, when the proper pronunciation was Fy'-ke Fy'-ke-ma. Then, in 1951, there arose the dark suspicion that the implications of mispronunciation went far beyond mere embarrassment: he was losing critical book sales at a time when his financial situation had him nearly at wit's end. In mid-June he was forced to sign county pauper papers so that he could be admitted to the University of Minnesota hospital for surgery. For months his relationships with his agents and his editors at Doubleday had been growing increasingly strained because of the poor sales of the first two volumes in the trilogy and because the publishers had become ever slower in their payments. The catalyst for a name change seems to have come from publisher Dennis Dobson in London, who told Manfred booksellers complained that he was "an unknown author with an unpronounceable name." Behind all of these concerns was the painful recollection that as a child he had been teased with "Frycake" and other coarse takeoffs on his family name.

Manfred's interest in etymology and in foreign languages—especially Frisian and Old and Middle English—led him to experiment with a variety of interesting variations for a new name: Frederick Friskner (unanimously liked by his friends in an informal telephone survey), Frisk (unanimously disliked), Frisham, Freyson, Freysham, Frishingham (admittedly "odd"), Frederickman, Fredman, Fredeman, and —finally—Manfred, gotten by flipping Fredman end for end. Manfred, as it turns out, is really a translation of Feikema: "man of peace." By coincidence, or more than coincidence, Thurs Wraldson's true father in the third volume of the trilogy (1951) proves to be a Christian College professor named Menfrid; and Thurs's own middle name is Manfred. Convinced that he had hit upon the right meaning and sound at last, Frederick Manfred wrote to Alan Collins and George Shively at Doubleday that "*Manfred* lends itself to 'epithet' making . . . of a distinguished sort: 'the Manfredean prose,' 'Manfredia,' 'the Manfredians or Manfredeans.'" By 21 August 1951 Manfred had been chosen as the last name, with Frederick, already his christened name, as his first name. By 8 September he had completed a survey among his most trusted and liked friends, and their vote was thirty-three to seven in favor of the new name. Even the Feikema clan, at its Sioux Falls reunion the previous Labor Day, had approved of Manfred, although the old pioneers regretted the loss of Feike Feikema. And so in 1952 the name became Frederick Feikema Manfred, really his legal name with Manfred added. It appeared in print for the first time on the cover of *Lord Grizzly*: FREDERICK F. MANFRED.

The success of this new novel, with its three printings in hard covers and its appearance on the *New York Times* best-seller list, helped to reestablish in the East and nationally Manfred's reputation as a writer of merit, and in fact raised it well above all previous levels. *Lord Grizzly's* publishing history itself verifies Manfred's achievement: three printings in hardback totaling more than eleven thousand copies; four paperback editions (two outside the United States), one of which sold nine hundred thousand copies. High praise for *Lord Grizzly* was forthcoming from William Carlos Williams, who stated, "I have never in a lifetime of reading about our west met with anything like it." Walter Havighurst in the *New York Herald Tribune Weekly Book Review* found *Lord Grizzly* a "hair-raising novel" with "strong, clear characterizations. . . . the most physiological narrative ever written." Victor Hass in the *New York Times Book Review* contrasted the old novelist of *World's Wanderer* with the "new" novelist, whose "ranginess, . . . free-wheeling robustness, . . . engaging lustiness of style and expression" indicated new directions. J. Donald Adams in a later *New York Times Book Review* commented on Manfred's important contribution to a more positive view of the "Indian's inner life" much needed in western fiction.

With this novel Manfred almost won the National Book Award. The story of that near miss, one of the one-hitters that Manfred lost, is sketched out by Manfred in a 1984 letter to the editors of this collection. In 1955 Robert Penn Warren encouraged Manfred with a postcard, telling him he had read *Lord Grizzly* and was voting for it for the National Book Award. Some months later, after William Faulkner had won with *A Fable,* Manfred learned from his McGraw-Hill editor that Malcolm Cowley, chairman of the three-member panel, had made sure that *Lord Grizzly* did not win because it was a historical novel and he believed that a novelist should write only about his own generation. What Cowley did (said the editor) was to cast five votes for *A Fable* but no votes for second or third place. Had he given even one vote to *Lord Grizzly,* that novel would have won the National Book Award for 1954.

Although Manfred has reservations about the accuracy of the story, there is no doubt that the near miss was a disappointment. With *Lord Grizzly,* however, he created the first of what was to become the Buckskin Man Tales, a series of five western novels that today have made him better known and more widely admired than many National Book Award winners.

The letters in this collection present a remarkably full picture of the genesis of *Lord Grizzly* and of the Buckskin Man Tales and indicate as well connections between those novels and the earlier and more recent farm novels. Long before his first novel appeared in print in 1944 (*The Golden Bowl*), Manfred had in mind a cycle of six to ten books about the farming Midwest. In a 1940 letter to a Macmillan editor, he complained bitterly about the rejection of an early version of *This Is the Year* and reported that he was in the middle of a new novel about people "who didn't migrate from South Dakota." In closing, he announced that over the next ten to twenty years he would complete a cycle of novels about himself and his people, and, he said, "I can't be stopped." Not until 1947, however, did he refer again to the idea of a group of related novels, in this case the trilogy *World's Wanderer*. In the meantime he had published *The Golden Bowl, Boy Almighty,* and *This Is the Year* and by mid-1947 had finished *The Chokecherry Tree*. Once the last-named was in the publisher's hands, Manfred turned to *World's Wanderer*. By 26 July he had it sketched out, and in November he sent an outline to George Shively, his editor at Doubleday.

Before the Buckskin Man Tales had been conceived, then, Manfred had in mind the writing of a series of works, even more than one series. He knew, of course, of the popular success of such writers as Dos Passos, whose sprawling trilogy *USA* had won acclaim and wide sales in the 1930s, and he wanted that success for his work. He continued to ruminate about the possibilities for writing long, related works and in 1950 wrote about a "duology" to be called *Wings,* a trilogy to be called *Sons of Adam,* another trilogy to be called *A Child Is Born,* and a decology to be called *Siouxland*

Saga. None of these materialized, however, at least in the form originally contemplated.

Not until 1952 did the story of Hugh Glass show up in Manfred's letters as the topic for a novel, although he had first read about Glass in mid-1943 and in his copy of *South Dakota Guide* had written, "1st read in summer of 1943." As he has said on many occasions, he was struck immediately by the epic qualities of the story, by Glass's wounding, his crawl, and his forgiveness of the two men who had deserted him. Later in 1943 Manfred began to collect items about Glass in preparation for a story about the mountain man.

If we turn to the correspondence in order to trace the idea further, we discover an August 1943 letter that tells of his intention to visit his home territory again after a long absence: "I aim to spend three or four months down through the Missouri valley," he writes, "studying, listening, absorbing (I wrote the book *This Is The Year* after I left and I've never been back and so I've never really looked at the community close at hand for the purpose of writing about it)." By May of 1944 his "three or four months" had shrunk to weeks, but it was an important visit to the Missouri Valley.

In preparing to write Hugh Glass's story, Manfred learned how to conduct historical research, for he knew very little about Indians or mountain men, and during the next eight years he amassed, in dilatory fashion, dozens of pages of notes. On 10 September 1952 while he was out walking, it came to him just how to write the Hugh Glass novel, "all the way from the working out of the plot to the exact tone and drift of it." On 24 September he asked Doubleday for an advance so that he could do serious research in the Badlands and the Black Hills. The plot outline he already had in mind: the wrestle, the crawl, and the showdown. Despite Doubleday's rejection of his request, in October Manfred was busy writing to promising sources, including Archer B. Gilfillan, a South Dakota sheepherder and the author of *Sheep,* for information about Glass.

In January 1953 comes the first word in the letters that Manfred has in mind a series of books that will includes his planned novel about Hugh Glass. In that month he wrote out an application for financial support to the Minnesota Historical Society, proposing a trilogy to be called *The Far Country.* It would be made up of *The Golden Bowl,* he said, a novel to be called *The Lone Prairie,* and *Old*

Hugh Glass. His purpose would be "to recreate by means of imaginative fiction, a very important phase of early American frontier history, of the American fur trade and of the exploration of the Far West." The second novel of the trilogy, *The Lone Prairie,* was to "depict the second phase, the day of the cattle kingdoms, in the High Plains area." The third novel, *The Golden Bowl,* already published, "depicts the third phase, the homesteader invasion and near defeat by the Depression and Drought." Manfred thought of the trilogy as "the first such creative work of historical fiction of the High Plains area." His request was turned down, but on 21 March Manfred wrote to Van Wyck Brooks about a long decology to be called *Siouxland,* thus returning to an idea he had developed in 1950. The decology would include his latest novel, now given its most recent—and final—name, *Lord Grizzly.*

The idea of a series of related novels was now firmly in place, even though the novels that would end up as the Buckskin Man Tales were not yet written.

The letters of 1953 reveal with clarity Manfred's emotional state during the writing of the first of the tales, *Lord Grizzly,* and thus help to explain why *Lord Grizzly* had more power than any of its predecessors. Because most of the relevant letters have been omitted from the present collection in order to preserve the privacy of a family, the outline, at least, of the events of that spring needs to be presented. Throughout the months of writing the novel, Manfred was caught up in a family crisis brought on by a false criminal charge against a relative. As soon as he heard of the charge, he flew to the West Coast to provide moral and financial support, and when he returned to Bloomington, Minnesota, he began firing off barrages of letters: to the California newspaper that had carried the story, to the family attorney, to the arresting officer and the judge in the case, and to friends and members of the family who could be of help. The two months, April and May, between the arrest and the preliminary hearing accord exactly with the two months during which Manfred wrote the first seventy-thousand words of *Lord Grizzly,* and the sense of outrage at injustice in the novel most certainly is heightened by the emotions he felt during the time of its writing.

No other Manfred novel is more directly influenced by events of the immediate present. In April he wrote to his brother Henry: "Yesterday I finished a scene where a man wrestled a grizzly and I dreamed all night about it besides feeling sick after it was done."

A few days later he wrote to an editor at Doubleday: "I've never written better. It's as if I actually lived back in 1823–24 and actually was Old Hugh Glass." In later years Manfred told friends that he was able to understand Hugh's forgiveness of the two men who had betrayed him because the above-mentioned relative had forgiven those who had falsely accused him.

Months before *Lord Grizzly* appeared in print and was swept aloft by storms of critical acclaim, Manfred was convinced that it would prove to be his greatest work and would rescue his reputation, particularly in the East, and make him famous. On 22 September 1953 he wrote to Scott Bartlett, his editor at McGraw-Hill, that the firm should buy up the rights to all his books on the theory that when *Lord Grizzly* took off, those books would become valuable property.

Manfred's certainty that *Lord Grizzly* would be a critical success helped to focus his attention once again on the frontier West. He wrote on 19 January 1954 that he had two more novels brewing. One about the early 1800s and tentatively titled *Green Earth* would become *Conquering Horse*; the second, titled *Wildland,* eventually would become *Riders of Judgment.* "This work," Manfred said, referring to the trio, "will tie my present day Siouxland back through all the stages into that green pristine past of pre-white times." It is a vaster vision than the one that organizes the present Buckskin Man Tales, for it encompasses all of Manfred's work, tying the frontier tales to the prairie novels and to the rest of the Manfred canon. "I hope to have written or printed a long hall of fictional history from 1800 to the day I die," he said. "Of the Midlands. Or the West." The Sioux Indian would have an important place in it, and so would the white frontiersman, for Maury Grant, Pier Frixen, and the rest are "descendants of Hugh Glass." In his most ebullient moods Manfred thought of himself as an American Homer writing an *Iliad* in *Green Earth* (*Conquering Horse*): "I want to write the 'first' classics of our Homeric culture," he wrote to his editor, "if it is at all in my power." Several years were to pass, however, before he finally hit upon the combination of five novels that would make up the Buckskin Man Tales.

The tales have been widely and favorably reviewed throughout America and abroad in the years since, and subsequent republication of the entire series in the 1980s by Gregg Press in hardback and by the University of Nebraska Press in paperback attests to their continuing popularity. The second novel in the series, *Riders of*

Judgment (1957), was lauded by Robert Wright for its "high serious-
ness, for authenticity and vivid sense impressions, and for its grip-
ping narrative powers"; S. P. Mansten in *Saturday Review* praised it
for its stylistic superiority. *Conquering Horse* (1959), considered by
some as Manfred's most impressive achievement, was called "vi-
sionary" by Paul Engle in the *New York Times Book Review,* while
Irwin Blacker described it in *Saturday Review* as a realistic account
of Sioux Indian culture. The fourth novel in the series, *Scarlet
Plume* (1964), though judged brutal and needlessly sensual by
some, was seen by Victor Hass as a book of "great skill and percep-
tion" (*Chicago Tribune*). *King of Spades* (1966), the last of the tales,
received one of its most sympathetic reviews in the East: Brian Gar-
field in *Saturday Review* characterized it as "one of the tallest of all
possible tall tales" with its "defiant boldness, its spirited freshness,
its outlandish tongue-in-cheek unbelievability." On the whole,
however, the novel has been less warmly received because of its violence, melodrama, and explicit sex.

A different criticism was voiced in 1975 by Madison Jones in a
New York Times review that marks the high point in Manfred's popularity: *King of Spades* is the least successful of the five tales because
it "lacks the dramatic realization that is so complete in Manfred's
best work." Yet the Buckskin Man Tales, says Jones, taken as a
whole, represent the high point of Manfred's storytelling powers.
"The whole world is alive for him," says Jones, and "his gift for
portraying the eloquence of purely sensuous experience" is
reminiscent of no less a master of epic detail than Homer.

Madison Jones titled his review, as a matter of fact, "Frederick
Manfred—Parallels with Homer." It was a bold claim, especially at
a time, as Jones points out, when Manfred was little known outside
the West. But it also came at the moment when all five of the Buckskin Man Tales were in print at the same time, published by New
American Library–Signet in paperback editions. It was a claim, curiously enough, that Manfred himself had hoped would be made
for his "first classics of our Homeric culture."

The tracing of Manfred's later career, of course, belongs with
the next volume of letters, which will contain the correspondence
from 1955 to the 1980s. The present collection is rich enough in new
insights into the life and times of a creative artist to interest a wide
readership. What must have the most peculiar fascination of all,
however, is the fact that an author who in eleven years published
eight novels should have written so many hundreds of pages of

forceful correspondence. Even in the face of a warning against the waste of letter writing from no less a literary great than Sinclair Lewis, Manfred continued to take a special delight in writing to friends. One of his notes to Lewis assumes a properly obedient tone, to be sure. In it Manfred begs Lewis not to respond, to save his energies for another paragraph of fiction. But in Manfred's own case, as he wrote to Harrison Smith (17 November 1952), composing letters was a spur to his creative energies and a kind of discipline: "I like to write lengthy vernacular letters to dear friends, mostly because they often help me unlock or loosen a word jam, as well as help me cut down on the polysyllabic style that likes to creep up on me."

When asked to read through the present collection, Manfred reported to the editors his surprise at discovering how much correspondence he had written in those years. At the same time he was pleased to find ringing throughout nearly every letter his entire commitment to writing as a career and his conviction that he would prevail, no matter how many rejections. Slow but certain, too, he noted, was his development as a letter writer, from overeager and fumbling to "sharper, more poetic, warm and friendly."

If the letters in this collection also convey to readers the many aspects of Manfred's life and career as an important American novelist, they will have served its purpose. Scattered among the essays on literature, politics, and social conditions are epistles reflective of Manfred's personal dilemmas and triumphs, including his flirtation with socialism and communism, his loss of the ideal woman, his apprenticeship as a newsman, his two-year stay in a tuberculosis sanatorium, his ardent courtship of and marriage to Maryanna Shorba, his campaigning for Hubert Humphrey, and, in particular, his early struggles with publishers to get his works into print. What his friend Wallace Stegner has said of Manfred's novels in the introduction to *Conversations with Frederick Manfred* is true of these letters: They are like the fairgrounds on the Fourth of July. "Everybody is there, wide awake and alive."

Frederick Feikema Manfred has lost a good many one-hitters in his career, and when his team has scratched out an occasional victory it has been by virtue of deft base running and sharp fielding rather than by means of spectacular home runs. The baseball analogy is more appropriate to Manfred as novelist than any drawn from either of two other sports at which he has excelled, basketball and boxing, and it is an analogy he has often applied to himself. Whether missing out on a National Book Award by a vote or two or narrowly losing a film contract for one of his novels, Manfred has continued to play each game out to the end because he believes in the inevitability of the tales he tells. More than anything else the letters in the present collection confirm the intensity of Manfred's dedication to the ancient and honored art of storytelling.

It may be that the baseball analogy is Manfred's particular favorite because that game emphasizes skill, craft, patience, and intelligence much more than the other sports of his youth. As a college basketball player in the 1930s, Manfred simply overwhelmed the competition. At six-foot-nine he was taller by a hand than nearly all of his competitors and was told that he was at that time the tallest player in America. At Calvin College he was the starting center for three years. In 1936 while playing for Nettleton Commercial College in Sioux Falls against Freeman Junior College, in one game he scored fifty-seven points. And in 1939, in his lone venture into boxing, he knocked out his 260-pound opponent—a sparring partner of Joe Louis—in the first round and with one blow. Despite the urging of the promoter who had arranged the match, Manfred refused to fight again, in part because of the danger of injury but also because once again he would be relying on his height and strength instead of his wits, on the gargantuan size that in those days was a perpetual embarrassment to him even while it had its occasional advantages. In later years, in fact, Manfred came to suspect that his huge size had frightened away the one girl he had hoped to marry, and he continues today to be irritated when critics call as much attention to his physique as to his writing. Yet Manfred's size is as much a part of the man as is his rich mind and expansive personality. And the letters are like the man as they are like his fiction—all three brim with energy. Just as Wallace Stegner finds the stories to be like a runaway stagecoach, so the letters possess a compelling urgency and have for the spectator the same power to entertain.

It was Sinclair Lewis who first suggested, in 1946, that the University of Minnesota library should lay claim to the Manfred correspondence and other papers before they left the state. Lewis already had made plans to deposit his own manuscripts at Yale University's Sterling Library; but here was a young Minnesotan (Lewis pointed out) who was beginning to make a name for himself as a novelist, and the university ought to move with dispatch. Manfred was pleased when the request came from librarian E. W. McDiarmid, especially because it had been initiated by Lewis, and he began a practice that continues to the present of depositing copies of his letters and other papers at the Manuscript Division of the University of Minnesota Libraries.

Early in 1982 Manfred decided to place, temporarily, a duplicate set of his correspondence in the Center for Western Studies at Augustana College in Sioux Falls, South Dakota. His long-standing fear of atomic destruction, expressed in a number of his letters, had led him to seek a second repository, one less likely than the Twin Cities to be destroyed in a nuclear attack. The Center filled the bill, located as it is more than two hundred miles from Minneapolis-Saint Paul and almost as far from Omaha. The staff offered Manfred a safe in which to house the collection, and that cinched the matter. A suggestion from Arthur Huseboe, member of the Center board and professor of English at Augustana, led to the decision to publish the correspondence. The idea already was in Manfred's mind, and his response to the suggestion was cautious but prompt.

In a letter of 27 July 1982 Manfred gave his permission to publish the correspondence that he had been depositing at the University of Minnesota for more than thirty-five years. After all, the letters would be of value to students of his work, and he himself could provide useful explanations. To Huseboe he wrote:

I hereby with this letter authorize you to do an edition of the Frederick Manfred letters. For the moment let's call the work THE SELECTED LETTERS OF FREDERICK MANFRED. . . . *I will help you as you need me.*

I give you full right to look into all letters written by me, except those that have been sealed until some time after my death. There aren't many sealed letters.

The help that Manfred subsequently provided was very extensive, for during the summers of 1983 and 1985 the two editors were able, with his assistance, to index nearly the entire collection from the early 1930s to the mid 1970s and with Manfred's aid to identify the persons, places, and publications in that index.

More than 3,000 letters written by Manfred are included in the collection at the Manuscript Division and in the Center for Western Studies. Of these, as might be expected, the early years claim the smallest number. For 1932, for example, only one letter is extant. For 1954, by contrast, there are 117, and some of these are two or more pages long, typed and single spaced. Consequently our process of selection for the period 1932–54 has been a good deal simpler than that for later periods. We have left out mere notes, most of the letters that deal in minor matters of daily life, letters that seemed repetitious of those selected for publication in this edition, and a handful of letters from 1953 that Manfred has sealed to avoid hurting the feelings of living persons. Thus more than 800 pieces of correspondence dating from 1932 to 1954 have been set aside.

Manfred did not begin to keep copies of his correspondence until 1939, when he retained a carbon copy of a letter to Jean Danielson, and 1940, when he saved a copy of the long letter of complaint to Macmillan following the rejection of *This Is the Year*. Before that time the only extant correspondence in the Manuscript Division consists of letters to Helen Reitsema, John Huizenga, and John DeBie—all of whom returned the originals to Manfred for photoduplication. Manfred says that after his two-year stay in the sanatorium (1940 through 1942), when he wrote little beyond the dozens of love letters to Maryanna Shorba, he began to keep carbon copies of first drafts of every important letter.

The 161 letters selected from the collection for the present edition have been transcribed in their entirety, with the exception of less than a dozen in which words or short passages have been deleted at Manfred's request to protect the privacy of living persons. Our principal effort has been to present the letters as Manfred wrote them, with only trifling silent corrections. These have been limited to instances of incorrect, omitted, or inconsistent punctuation; failed capitalization; grammatical slips; misspelled words; and the like. One of Manfred's favorite misspellings, however, we have been tempted to retain: *similiar* for *similar*. He has been consistent during the thirteen years represented in this collection in spelling it with the third I. We have, however, corrected it throughout. On the other hand, we have been careful to preserve those words that illustrate Manfred's oft-noted tendency to pun, to play with established words, and to create new words.

We have had to do very little in order to standardize the format of the printed letters. Except when the information is not known, each letter is headed with the name of the recipient, the place of origin, and the date. Manfred rarely used inside addresses, and we have virtually omitted these altogether, relying occasionally on notes to provide information about a particular correspondent. When the original letter has supplied a return address, we have retained it, providing in a few instances additional information within brackets. It has seemed preferable to us to rely as little as possible on brackets for editorial comments, for we wish the reader to find as few impediments in his or her path as possible. Sidenotes, too, are supplied with restraint and for the same reason. A few of them have been provided by Manfred himself and are duly noted as by FM, the abbreviation we have used for Manfred. On the other hand, we have endeavored to supply extensive clarifying information in the index. There we have added given names in virtually every instance when only a surname has appeared in the text, and we have supplied a brief identifying phrase with the name of each person of importance to Manfred's life and career.

We have been much helped in the work of editing by a number of friends. John R. Milton, whose *South Dakota Review* has been for more than two decades a vade mecum for western writers and critics, gave valuable advice during the selection process. John O'Brien and Kathryn Welter helped in transcribing Manfred's handwriting and in tracking down dates, names, and places. Typing of the text was done by Glenna Swier, Marilyn Berry, Chris Olkiewicz, Carol Burcham, and Pat Neubacher.

Allan Lathrop of the Manuscript Division of the University

of Minnesota Libraries generously granted permission to use the collection, offered advice, and answered questions. We appreciate his support.

Without the assistance of certain correspondents, this collection would have been much impoverished. We are grateful to Helen Reitsema Vander Meer for supplying a number of the letters sent to her by Manfred in the 1930s and to the late John DeBie and to John Huizenga for returning their collections of Manfred letters.

A number of grants have made much of the work possible: two small grants from the Bush Committee at Augustana College, a one-semester leave for Arthur Huseboe, and a faculty lecture grant for Nancy Nelson from Henry Ford Community College. We are grateful to our institutions and to our colleagues for making this support possible.

Our greatest debt is to the South Dakota Committee on the Humanities for a grant of eleven thousand dollars to support the publication of the letters.

THE SELECTED LETTERS OF FREDERICK MANFRED

1932

In this first year of Manfred's correspondence, the only extant letter is to Helen Reitsema, his idealized woman. At the end of his sophomore year at Calvin College, he works as a hired hand for farmer Louis Van Leeuwen; the crops fail and Manfred settles for a new nineteen-dollar suit rather than the ninety dollars promised. That fall he begins his junior year at Calvin.

To Helen Reitsema

Calvin Dorm
Sunday Afternoon
Dec. 4, 1932

Miss Helen Reitsema,

I believe that I owe you an apology. When I pondered, after-wards, on what I had said, I came to the realization that I had offended your Goodness, Honor, and Virtue. Sounds strange, doesn't it? Listen. My attitude implied, if one looks at it in one way, that I was foolish for calling on a person who does not live up to the above named three qualities. Really, you know, such a thought had not entered my mind at all:—nor ever will! The actual motive for conveying such a detestable attitude was to this effect: you were so far above me that it was impossible for me to ever be a possible friend of you.

And here is something that had not dawned upon me to the fullest extent. I had made this horrible and almost unforgivable mistake, that you owed me an explanation because I egotistically did not want to be considered a fool.

However, we must remember this too. Everyone should choose friends with care. I usually choose my lady friends with certain considerations. Among these are the following.

First, this ill-fated scribbler can continue school through the financial help of some gratuitous friends. I am obliged to give an account of every "red cent." Then, I wish to choose friends that are of the best. I wish to choose friends that will try to appreciate, or rather, understand my idiosyncrasies and eccentricities. Then too, I wish to choose those who, I think, will have in certain phases of life an affination of spirit or soul.

Such things, at least, are thought of when I carefully "call-up" a lady friend.

Undoubtedly you know that young fellows hate to be turned down though there may be a perfectly legitimate reason. It's a sort of metaphysical slap in the face. Add to this a sensitive nature and an over-suggestive imagination! Moreover, when the same young fellow is turned down, say more than a few times, things do look black. A sort of mental reflection is sure to follow. He'll ask if the fault lies in himself and not in her. In my case, I thought the fault lay in me and I thought you considered me foolish. And that hurts.

Perhaps I listen to gossip too much. Do you know what Dame Gossip whispered to me? Your thoughts concerning me were to the effect that I was anything but a clodhopper and a fool from the West, incapable of becoming civilized. I'd never acquire the finesse of permissible drawing-room manners. I gave her a cold shoulder—yet she was there!

I see now that you do not owe me any explanations when I call up. I have, so to speak, no string on you. I guess that must be a woman's right. I see that I have many things to learn. I'll get there, though! I sincerely and humbly apologize and see my "silliness." Now I have actually become a fool.

I wanted, however, to tell you how things looked on my side of the fence. I can readily understand why you would not care to be a friend of mine from now on.

This perhaps explains why I did not send you a letter of condolence last summer. Maybe unspoken words convey deeper sympathy than spoken words.

Pray do not take this method of message-conveyance too ill of me. But, is my apology or explanation accepted?

Burn or destroy this, when you are through!

That is, if you will.

Sincerely,
Although humbly,
Frederick Feikema

1933

In the spring of 1933, Manfred decides to stay in Grand Rapids for the summer with John DeBie and John Baker. He works on the campus and reads widely in Tolstoy, Whitman, and Shelley, storing in his mind some valuable literary experiences.

To Helen Reitsema

[Calvin College]
May 1933

1. Helen had lent money to FM.

My Lady,

Since I am not allowed to do nothing more than write a letter, may I then have two dates, Wednesday to the *All School party* and *Sunday Again?* I'll try to write a *"real"* letter. I still have, by the way, some of your money.[1]

Here's the joke I couldn't think of the other day. Why is a senator called a mugwump sometimes? Because he has his mug on one side of the fence and his wump on the other side!

My pretty one, I am more fond of you than ever. I feel as though I could be happy with things just as they are!

I read some poems, sonnets, in the May issue of *Harpers*. You must read that. Also the short-story, *Natural Enough*.

Isn't everything wonderful? Spring is *coming! You're here! There is music!* You are always free to turn me down, you know. Let me know to-morrow.

Your, Fred

1934

The few letters of this year are particularly important in revealing Manfred's personality, ambitions, interests, and general directions. He writes to the three people most important to him at this time: John Huizenga, John DeBie, and Helen Reitsema, all Calvin College friends. After graduation and a summer of hard farm labor shocking grain and shelling corn, Manfred hitchhikes to Yellowstone National Park. The trip will later be the inspiration for his first novel.

To Helen Reitsema

My dear Helen,

Lest you receive or conceive the wrong impression or thought, I wish to assure you of a few things. Perhaps an evaluation or an appreciation will surfeit the situation, nevertheless, you'd like to have me do so. Maybe you'll smile a little, if not with your lips at least in your mind.

My dear, believe me, I enjoyed myself as much Sunday night as I did Friday; because the evening passed without any unnecessary procedures or things taken for granted. We both felt, at least that was my diagnosis, that was the sort of evening it should be,—and it was. Once when I left, though, I almost said, "Oh, Helen!"

I can never become tired of repeating, "Helen, you're marvelous, and beautiful, and pleasing, and lovely,—the kind of woman who, once she gave her word, would always be a comarado."

And if you have a feeling of compunction about such delightful evenings, such as Friday night, why tell me. It was "dizzy-like" for me, despite the jolting and rolling of the car. It didn't give me much chance to render my ideas of artistic, hesitant, and rapturous advancer. I still wish sometime for an opportunity of that sort. And please remember, I'll never do anything indiscreet, even if you should be artistic, which I wish you, too, to be, sometime—?

If you should happen to come back before Friday night or Saturday morning, I'd like very much for you to call me at 51771 (Butler Hall) or the college. I don't know how long I'll stay, and I like to be with you as much as is decently possible.

I hope you like the book, although the guidelines may detract from the worth of it. You see, I wanted to buy a copy of Walt Whitman for you, but the drain on the revenue folder was a bit too persistent and forceful. I intend, however, to purchase that slight token—it will be a belated graduation gift.

I know I can safely say, judging from past experiences, that I'll be seeing you, your eyes wherein love lies slumbrous and unbidden, your mouth, your high, white forehead, violet-veined—all these—all my short tragic-freighted life. Whenever I peer at an object, I'll be seeing that through the hazy, dim image of you.

I hear now in my mystical mind's eye the silver of your low murmur next to my ear in the crescendo of a violin. I anticipate the affinity of my soul to yours in the swing-like sway of the "Blue-Danube Waltz" and the half-tragic and half-delirious undertone and thematic blending of César Franck's 1st Symphony. I feel the brushing of your hair on my face when I hear the loving waves playing upon the sands of the beach. I feel the soft splash of your low words against my ear when the wind of night rustles and susurrates but softly through the pine bristles in the full saffron moonlight, and everywhere in the lighting glimmer and dulling glow of street lights and signs I hear the sound of your voice calling, "Fred," and I see your tresses lift from your white, light shoulders in your swift rush to me.

Helen, perhaps you think you peeve me when you pliantly resist my wishes (That's life), but there is a pleasure in your pure hesitation and your legitimate reluctance, shy and good. It makes me feel the worth of you increased to the unassailable heights of whiteness, it makes what I receive, so graciously from you, the gift of a goddess—free given as if from her unselfish lap.

Many of my friends would think me deranged, writing thus, and foolish to kneel in golden-worded rapture—but I do not—for do I not plead for my happiness which I wish to live in, and in this case, unshared in and with?

I am sorry I met you in the hall to-night. It'll spoil my rest. And isn't this beautiful?[1]

And if you can answer once to every ten letters of mine, and if you will kindly write one page to every ten I write (long letters), I'll perhaps be satisfied somewhat.

> Your comarado, your cuz, &
> your assiduous Dantized (but
> I hope not tragedy transfixed)
> Fred

1. Twenty-eight lines of Swinburne's "Chorus" from *Atalanta in Calydon* are omitted.

To John Huizenga

Doon, Iowa
July 29, 1934

Dear John,

A few weeks have passed since we last guggled with the Decker [Dekker] culinary efficiency. And with the passing of time, a passing moment brought an equally transient mood—which mood indicated that a few tedious, uncharming strands of gossip be written to you.

A few facts about myself: I have been working on the great, salubrious plains of Iowa. Shocking grain, shelling corn, dropping and hearing a few risqué anecdotes, avoiding trouble, and feeling damnably lonesome for some city light, with all the appurtenances and phantasmagorias that accompany it.

A few golden nuggets, or worthwhile humans, are to be found here. I found one ardent socialist or mildly radical communist here. And he, surprisingly read much, spoke logically,—and with a purpose. He told me much concerning the inside information on farm politics. He almost has me persuaded to enter the arena of compromise and "fat-checks"—politics.

I am working in the harvest fields on the congenial farm operated by A. Feikema.[1] Not being accustomed to strenuous farm work, my inclinations to write an interesting letter are very flagging.

1. Andrew Feikema, FM's great-uncle.

You received my card, didn't you. I really wanted to get into Chicago early that night, but I had "tuff" luck.

The more I drift around, the more transient any form of living or any purpose of living seems to me. The more I try to formulate something, the more my ideals and so-called original issues fall asunder and cascade into ruin. Sometimes, John, I believe there is more evil or bad in this [canceled] (damn) fragilely spun universe than good. I wonder if we do not make the mistake of trying to formulate an idea out of manifestations around us. There perhaps isn't any one or two principles in this world—all is flux and blind drifting of either physical or spiritual force. Man's attempts, man's rudimentary artifices, become spicy humour for whatever malignant gods that be. I envy people who believe in an unfounded "loving god." Not their god, perhaps, but their damnably irritating placidity. Sometimes—and perhaps more often than I think—I do believe in that sort of thing.

However, today I did not attend any services of ecclesiastical fervorism. And attendant with it, came many loud-voiced, religion-infested remarks. They fell off as does water from the oily back of a complacent duck.

I have no idea of the future: that is, what I am to do. There are some tentative gestures, such as, a position as Eng. prof. at the newly reorganized Western Christian High at Hull, or a year at Iowa City. Apparently I have a chance to get a Tuition Scholarship or a Fee Exemption from the U. of Iowa.

Otherwise, I am due to drift around. I have about fifteen dollars on hand. But, today I received a bill of $5.70 which I must pay, it seems.

To-morrow I intend to go swimming, perhaps play some tennis

if my hand doesn't hurt too much. I fell from a corn crib wall and to protect my "behind-that-follows-the-before," I put my hand behind me;—with the result that I doubled my palm back, hurting my wrist badly.

God, I almost hate this living now. I haven't polished my nails, nor shaved, nor combed my hair decent for many days. I long to get back where there is at least teeming life and where people dress decent. Perhaps, I never did, but at least I like to look at other well-dressed people.

If one of the kindly muses who rest in eternal blissfulness and charming insouciance upon the equally undisturbed Mt. Parnassus descend upon thy spirit,—why write me a line.

They'll be accepted with eagerness.

And now—yes, oh yes,

Your comarado, despised,
despondent, destitute, and
depressed,
Frederick.

To John DeBie

Calvin Dorm
Dec. 5, 1934

Dear Debbie,

Quite weary, yet with a sense of peace that follows severe physical action, I herewith begin the composition of this letter while the subtle musical effluvium of Wayne King's chorus deliquesces into myself. Usually such a situation, or predicament, results in the perennial outthrust of the human heart, the call of love. But, strangely there is no urge or pull of that sort. I just happened, in my careless mental trundling, to encounter the fact of you.

I have been wondering, it may be strange, if you still have inner peace, or just peripheral peace? And *vice versa* with [canceled by DeBie]?[1] I used to watch you closely, not so much your words, but your eyes, your face with its manifestation, but most important of all, your general tenor of soul when encountering those "inscrutable facts" that Carlyle also stubbed his intellectual tornquist nose against. And however much I verbally "chided" and rebelled against that, I admired you. But for the sheer sake of copying— no, I saw no virtue in that, for after all, I wanted complete honesty.

Debby, seriously now, I have a problem. I don't expect you to answer it, nor do I want you. It's a fact,—and too, about a brute.

1. A woman's name.

We used to be facetious about sexual urges and their releases,— as though the things were necessary. In those days, I do not believe that they were conjectural *for me,* for I did not actually at all times feel them. Now, I can definitely identify a certain tension in myself of a strained sex impulse which needs expression (of some sort). First, however, I don't seem to have either enough girl friends, or the right ones. But were the case true that I didn't have any, I could get them. And here's the piquant irritation—I don't care to go after girls. I wonder if these tendencies, this tension of mine is not taking a "queer twist." I am afraid of that!

2. FM was center for the Universal Carloaders.
3. Michigan.

We played basketball[2] tonight! Beat the best team in the league 26 to 22. I made 9 points. by the way, Calvin gave [canceled by De-Bie][3] a near drubbing the other day.

4. For the Plato Club at Calvin College.

I am writing a Paper on Will James' Radical Empiricism *vs* Absolutism and Natural Positivism.[4] Will James' idea is alluring and somewhat exclusive.

I read much, and think much about my reading while I work. I have one major objection to my work—I must get up *too early*!

And as for writing those great poems and novels so soon; why I believe I must absorb some hard experiences and do some thinking for a while yet. Quiet procedure! Of course I practice a lot. Write, write please Debby.

Your pal,
Fred

To Helen Reitsema

[Calvin College]
Thursday Evening, alone
Dec. 7, 1934

Helen, dear,

Are you still really in love with him? My dear, I ask that only because I've become so profoundly lonesome. I do not ask for a mutual sharing of comradeship because I'm inherently weak, or lack maturity as you once hazarded, or because I'm selfish. It's more because I feel more trenchantly than ever that only one woman in this world embodied the nearest and the completest prerequisite of my idea of the ideal lover.

Perhaps you can obtain some sort of conception of what I had to offer in the cinema *The Painted Veil.* The scientist was the symbol of what I discovered to be the cue to true love. It's so utterly different from the common conception of "true love." I believe that my conduct with you has borne out the too unintellectual attempt of mine in the past to carry out the greater program of love.

The sentiments expressed by my acquaintances and "thrown-together-withs" has driven home the idea that people are demanding rather than sharing with the force of unalterable logic. And since I have orientated myself in this new world in which I am tragically happy, I cannot step down again. That is why I am not so eager to contact new relationship so essential to empty hearts. I wonder if this attitude hasn't made me more likable, but less lovable. I have that impression. I haven't flairs, or complacent social graces, or quick wits, or hardly the hard metal-like maturity of some, but I believe I have the nascent beginnings of what some will call a negative character.

With your love, ah, with your love I will not, in all probability, storm the literary or the social world with quickness, but, since I have much to learn by hard experience (something of what I am acquiring now) I need the background of love for the foreground of procedure. And, my own, a man in love can do much; his work proceeds and reflects a mellow goldenness in scrutiny and sympathy. A man that has not learned that love must be wasted and unreturned at times usually regards and reflects in a yellow, jaundiced spirit.

The last time we spoke of ourselves, you made the remark, "Dear Fred, I believe you don't know what *is* good for you. Someone else, me, must tell you what is good for you." Since then, that sentence has haunted me when I rode streetcars, when I went to concerts, during the rest periods of a sweaty, unintelligent basketball game,—and when I try to make the unwilling eyes of your portrait face me. For dear, I do know what I want. With all the astuteness I am capable of, I have known always that I needed your companionship. That companionship was possible because you were living on the same terrene I was, that you looked at the same moon I did, that you listened to the same music that I did. Am I foolish if I do not wish to throw that away? That, I believe, is the unpardonable sin!

Darling, my darling, I do not believe that I ever have been so lonesome for the love that you are capable of. The only kind of love I can give myself wholeheartedly in, is the kind I know I can and shall share with you! Do you know that all this interminal agony has been alleviated somewhat in anticipation of reading your return letter, whatever it may auger. I shall not open it immediately, for I shall first think of the fingers that have touched it, the tears that should have made the writing unintelligible, the charming blue eyes that have seen it, and the good, good heart that has prompted to write the truth—however much it may sear mine. What would I do with love? Ah, dear, it shall restring my heart's bow for my mind's arrow!

I have written my letters to you since I left you that night—and as many have I burnt. And all of them have asked, as this one is asking now, what could have occurred to you when I left last summer? The agony that a lover finds himself in when he discovers infidelity, is as nothing compared to mine!

I wish, whimsically and poignantly sometimes, that some Imperial power could unveil my heart structured now in my love for you. So impressed would you become with the revealments there, that you would unashamedly, with your head thrown back, with your soul standing perfect in self ready for any experience that was coming with me, come to share in a possible part the great love that is great enough to equal the love of two. Cannot you see the marble shaft built by my strength and your reluctance lighted only on my side and which waits for the light from you to bring it forth in the full glory of the sunshine of our love. That marble shaft wants no shadows or half-tones. It wants the sun to be in the highest faith overhead!

When you smile, it is enough for me to know I am an individual apart from all others, because I love you with *this my love*.

Your patient one,
Fred

1935

The 1935 letters encompass Manfred's travels to both east and west coasts: he works at the U.S. Rubber Company in Passaic, New Jersey, and on the farm in Iowa; in the fall he travels to California with his father and stepmother. Manfred's determination to become a writer is evident in his efforts to break into journalism, in his admiration for writer and critic Floyd McKnight, and in his reading and writing of literature with socialistic themes.

To John DeBie

609 Burton St. S.W.
[Grand Rapids, Michigan]
March 10, 1935

Dear Debbie,

Grand Rapids is awakening in a mist-draped atmosphere this morning. Strange, however, I feel no depressive mood upon me, even though I am smoking my first cigarette and am beginning to feel the first faint ache of the day in my corn-capped toe.

Sundry things have happened since your last letter. This forthcoming Tuesday I intend to leave town for New York. I am leaving via the transportation trucks lines and expect to be there about Friday Evening.

These then are the circumstances: Howie Hoving had written his father about my plight and my dubious ability to pen my ideas. He in turn communicated them to certain individuals in New York, the result of which was that there may be a job open for me in the journalistic line. And to make the venture more than an adventure, I am assured at least of a labor job that shall pay me more than I am saving now.

Meanwhile, more was transpiring. One of the critics who examined my work accomplished in the Calvin *Chimes* (for that was the only available material for Howie's dad to show these men) wrote me a personal letter and supervened it with a gift volume of a certain Miss Branch's poetry. And since then this critic, Floyd McKnight, and I have written each other. He believes that I show undoubted literary ability, more so in my prose writing than in my poetry. I've also written Miss Branch (President of the Poet's Guild of New York).

Mr. McKnight has invited me to stay at his house a few days and has also extended an invitation to give a talk for a meeting, the purpose of which is a discussion on poetry.

Thus all in all, a combination of events point to future happiness.

The more I read of economics and *history* and politics, the more I am convinced that communism is the only solution for the total people's happiness. The inherent fallacy of capitalism can never be eradicated nor alleviated (unplanned market)—but with the prowlike force of history forcing us onward, we are headed for the inevitable—communism. Although Strachey's book[1] is somewhat hasty and over-simplified, yet he pictures freedom of religion (although formerly it was merely an outgrowth of man's fear of what he knew nothing of) freedom of national cultures, and freedom

1. *The Coming Struggle for Power* by John Strachey.

from wars (once it has been started). Russia's beginning was in the midst of the direst straits; but if America were to turn communist, what a wonderful heritage of machinery, science, skilled workmen, distillation of culture, and natural resources they would have.

Yours, fondly,
Fred

[margin] P.S. I shall drop you a card as soon as I arrive there to advise you of my address and fortune!

To John Huizenga

83 Midland Ave
[Wallington, New Jersey]
Sunday Aft. 4:30
March 18, 1935

My dear John,

I must haste to write you, before this Sunday fleets by. I have spent most of this day sleeping, listening to "good" music, and reading *The Nation* and *The New Masses*. Right now, Toscanini has almost completed his attempt to weave a spell of sentimentality into me.

Somehow, I find this penning hard to do; mainly because there are so many unutterable things to convey to you, and because any attempt to write somehow smacks of exhibitionism. No doubt the over-trampled platitude can be made, all persons are more or less victims of this intellectual as well as friendly disease.

With regard to the trip, there isn't much to say. I believe I've now an insight into the truck-driver personality. I can easily understand that the foremost pleasure in their lives is to "make women": not their few chosen and romanticized women, but plain women with wiggling hips and painted "boobs." Driving mainly under a strain, with no regular sleep, living in grease, stuffy hotels, snowstorms and rain-storms; in disfavor with bosses, and constantly under the omnipotent pressure of the "*Schedule;*"—they have no time for books, for inspiring thoughts, continued friendship with women who can be more than bodies, and comradely "criticism" and approbation. I felt sorry for them; for I too was beginning to act, to feel, to think as they. Circumstances can influence so much! And I'm frightened they'll disrupt something I hold dearly;—whatever it is that strikes fire between us.

I secured rides fairly easily until I arrived in Rochester, N.Y. There by sheer luck, Oh don't scowl now, John, I secured a ride to New York with Mr. Ball driving a truck having about 30,000 lbs. of raw silver in it. We were, then, in danger of hijackers.

We traveled via Utica, Amsterdam, Albany, across the River Hudson along the trail that was used by General Herkimer's straggling band, the Mohawk Valley Trail. From thence, we traveled southward, towards Poughkeepsie (home of the oarsmen's regatta). Near Hyde Park, directly opposite Roosevelt's hoarded and ancestrally acquired estate, two of the traction wheels left the truck. At the time I was near the act of copulation with dear Marion Dekker, alas and alack, not because she was so desirable but out of the feeling that once I missed an opportunity. Suddenly the truck began to weave and to bobble so much, I began to think I might either be on Fulton's old Clermont or the new Airship "Macon." Perilously we came to a stop. A car coming towards us made a complete turnabout in sheer terror and avoidance upon the slippery pavement. My driver, a mental-moron, was impelling the truck along at a 40-mile-an-hour rate.

He left me about seven in the morning to guard the machine, while he went after repairs.

I cursed everything roundly by 2 o'clock for he didn't show around by then. I was hungry. I vented a doubtful spite by spitting over Roosevelt's paltry slate fence and hydraulisizing his favorite cherry tree with human fluid. The repercussions were no doubt felt in Washington.

Finally, about four, I became so desperate, I changed clothes, washed my face in snow, and hitched to Van Courtlandt Park with the secretary of the Commercial Credit Corporation—one of the largest concerns in the world. He indicated points of interest. His mind was clean morally, fairly thoughtful, to a certain extent beyond the fringe of smugness. I believe he liked me. He lived near the Vanderbilts. I have an invitation—but it was mere politeness.

1. Howard Hoving.

Tomorrow I'm to see Mr. Brown. He told Howie's[1] Dad I needn't fear coming East. He could get me a job on the Passaic *Herald-News* (120,000 circulation).

It is so funny, John. Now I'm pellmell into the same kind of religious people I was before. And I wanted to start N.Y. away from such—and with others of my and your type. And my job depends on the membership of some reporter in the *Newspaper Guild*—an organization I'm in favor of. I'm a "*scab*." What to do?

Once poor, once in a mess, always so.
Fondly,
Fred.

[margin] P.S. Howie has swell folks, though religious. His dad is slow but swell. The women here in the East are poor, except one. But she's engaged! Maybe she isn't so hot afterall!

To John Huizenga

[Wallington, New Jersey]
(In a manner by the river)
April 13, 1935

My dear John,

I trust you understand the negligence in regard to my answer. I delayed until I knew exactly what I was to do next. Finally, I landed a job yesterday. By means of pull, and a little dexterous handling of the personnel man, the employment agency, and the boss of a new project, I and a friend (new and hardly acquainted) got this job at U.S. Rubber Co.

The nature of it? Well that depends. The first week I earn $16.00 ($.40 x 40 hrs) but from then on the plant works on a bonus-basis, sometimes and usually amounting to $.60. Occasionally, up to $.70. This new project? The Navy has sent in an order for rubber hose. I must handle the compressor. If I show a combination of brains, brawn, and tact I may be promoted to "Boss." That is what this new acquaintance of mine indicated—and he has quite a lot to say. Every promotion means a doubling of salary. Anyway John, it means a livelihood for a while. Howie's folks were swell, weren't they, in keeping me around so long—especially to tolerate my "black" disposition augmented by reading *The Nation* and *The New Masses*.

As to some other connections—which follow: McKnight seems to be authentic in a small way. But, he can't do much except advise and introduce me to people. He is a member of the Poet's Guild of which Millay, Branch, Frost, MacLeish, and Robinson (was) are members. I shall meet them in due time—and have been invited to speak on the nature of poetry among people (farmers & laborers—their intrinsic tight-lipped, taut-word formations) and the atmosphere a wide plain has for a sensitive person. Then too, he is a good friend of Scottie Downs—president of the Am. Historical Society. That'd be good.

1. Cornelius (Case) Fortuin.

Continuing, Fortune's[1] father has a tentacle clawing the private rooms of a new insurance Co. You see, he is an insurance man. This new Co. is of this nature. By actuarial mathematics certain men came to the conclusion the normal family spends less than $10 a year in a hospital or in the hands of a doctor. (perhaps very *much* less) So they proposed a scheme whereby each family pays 3¢ a day for an insurance policy—and that family if sick collectively or individually goes to a designated hospital and doctor (moderately good).

These men, if they take me, advance me $200 for the first month. If I don't sell enough to make up this amount by the commission I should get—I lose the job, but keep the $200. If I sell more, I keep the $200 and the extra I make. The project was so successful in Newark that they've set up an office in New York and are to give $10,000 to the manager there. He's a cousin of Fortuin's. Lots of experience can be obtained in this one.

The newspaper job fell flat. There was a position open. He had to know local and national politics. He had to report on Dem. policies and practices—favorably. They [Democrats] picked their own man!

I've sent some revolutionary poems and stories to *The New Masses*. They made comments that were very inspiring and helpful. In connection with the last point, they said that "the thought confuses—seek cleanness and directness—and the natural limpidness of your word-choice will make the poems compact and lyric—that holds for your prose also." That's what you told me, too, remember?

So I've sent them some more. Just now I'm occupied with two projects. I'm editing some poems and a preface preparatory to a possible publication. McKnight said there's no money in it but they were good—he likes revolutionary poetry. He added further that Millay, Robinson, and Frost live on miserable pittances.

And then, the Houghton Mifflin Co. has an offer I've told you about. For two new writers of promise they offer $1000 a piece outside of the regular royalty. The choice is to be determined by recommendation, proposed plot, and a few exemplary chapters. This looks good to me.

Yesterday and a few days previous I received *The Human Mind* by Karl Menninger, *The Human Body* by L. Clendening, *Facts and Theories of Psychoanalysis* by I. Hendricks. These look good to me: anyone that wishes to write and understand modern (proletarian) literature must know something about that. Don't miss that course in ab. psycho. next year.

I've written about 5 stories and innumerable poems and an essay (which I'll send you). It states my theory and analysis of literature—especially poetry.

I've finished, while here, *Freedom Organization* by Russell; *Magnificent Obsession* by Douglas; *State Fair* by Phil Strong (brief and good); and I'm almost finished with Dewey's *A Common Faith*. And then I've been reading Whitman. May I recommend to you

The Prairie Grass Dividing pp. 131–2
Sometimes With the One I Love p. 136
O you whom I often and silently come pp. 137
Among the Multitude pp. 137
Thought pp. 458

Now to some of my adventures. I believe that I've been in New York about five times; three being uninteresting, so we'll discard them.

The first night, or days there, were with Floyd McKnight. Previous to that I hadn't met him so we arranged by mail to meet at the 23rd St. Ferry. We found each other and proceeded to a French Restaurant—Jean and Pierre. Everything Fr. Even the women. They seemed to have a multitude of delicacies, a hodge-podge of soups, a devil-may-care potato, a puny dab of *iced cream,* and capped the whole glomeration of french-titled absurdities with an equally absurd demi-tasse.

Then we saw, after the two hours of eating and getting acquainted, *The Distaff Side,* in which the English actress Sybil Thorndike performed. Exquisite and sadistic!

We slept side by side; I watching for those tendencies you talked of and warned about with an equally eager and horrified open eye all night. Next day he went to work—and so alone, I went to the Art Museum and Museum of Historical and Natural History. I spent considerable time looking at the pictures mentioned by Craven, in both books. I liked particularly in toto *November Evening* by Charles Burchfield and the sculptoring by Benton entitled the *Two Natures In Man—Struggling.* Marvelous.

Then went to Radio City; saw the *Little Colonel.* Heard the Symphony Orch; Saw *El Amor Brujo* (The Phantom Lover), a Ballet with *Vincente Escudero,* and the pictures or murals of Rivera. Marvelous again—but too big to be artistic, I mean the building.

In the Evening saw *The Black Pit,* a startling play, both well acted and conceived for communism.

Howie can tell you about the other trip. Oh yes, that evening after the play, entered Greenwich Village. Wild characters and scenes if one knows where to find them. With Howie, we couldn't find them.

Last week went out with a girl Fortuin knew. I "necked" fiercely, but when she seemed to beg for *it,* I quit. *Heil* virginity!

I hope this letter is the sending of love to you.

Feike

[margin] P.S. Interested to read Helen's to be married. Must not be frigid afterall.—Well, I shall take proper measures soon for a real sex life. What do you think? Write please!

P.S.S. Later at night.

I forgot to mention that some of the local boys escorted me around a couple of nights. In one night we visited about four high-class nightclubs. We remained at one for about two hours. Stimulated by a number of *Tom Collins*'es, I finally acquiesced to an insistent plea to dance. For two hours I waltzed and swung around the floor with what the "boys" call "broads"—who work usually in Broadway burlesques and elsewhere and at night seek to fill their empty coffers with money gotten by "evil practices." One girl I liked somewhat and danced with much seemed to have brains—but life had battered her curving shell quite hard until she was forced to accept the inevitable!

John, there's something deeply urging and compelling about the crossing of the ferry. And the skyline against a dawn beyond demands limpid prose and quick poetry in spite of the actuality lurking there—the kind of writing I can't command.

The other day, I had this irresistible and likable thought. You and I live but once, don't we? Why should we be separated as much as we are? There's no sense in it, is there? The idea of finding someone to replace you is repellent and unnecessary—for one needs constantly someone who is a friend such as we've been to each other.

Shall we then, after your matriculation, seek some way or make a plan mutually acceptable?

How's Katherine?[2] Actually, John, I have a vague, yet nevertheless strong intuition, that she is capable of the kind of understanding Judith had with Lewis in *The Fountain*. It is before the possibility of a comradeship she, or any other woman, has to offer that I feel humble.

Merely look at my background, my boasting, my haste, my jeal-

2. John's sister.

ousies, my betrayals of trust, and lack of allegiance to the ideal life
I sometimes want to live.

Again, then, John, as you say,

My earnest love to you,
Fred.

To John DeBie

83 Midland Ave.
Wallington, N.J.
May, 1935

Dear Debbie,

Since the last time I wrote you, I began working for the U.S.
Rubber Co. It's a menial task, and a rather thankless one at that. At
present, I slice rubber with a paring-like knife that has to be sharp-
ened between runs. I stand on my feet all day, and in the evening,
like this evening, I am as a result very tired. The gang is a terrific
mixture of illiterate Dagoes and equally untutored Italians, Wops,
Slavs, and Polish. And I am the only educated fellow around there.
Many of them are Red in thinking and wishing but Hearst in expression—taught no doubt by the raucous journalism that exists
today.

If the boss is not around to urge me alternately with promises
of better wages or a swift kick executed in a definite way with the
flourish of jocularity, then some sub-boss or pigeon-stool hounds
the very backward glances of myself. The wages? Oh, yes, I receive
for forty (40) hours of work the inexplicable sum of $16. However,
there are two alleviating factors. It keeps me for a while and it is
an experience that I shall not regret. The latter fact will come in
handy for argument's sake.

All of those things we used to advocate for the laboring man
have weight for me now. I know what it means to work in the factory; and this factory incidentally is the best around here, by the
consensus of all workers in and out. All of the workers are suspicious of each other, for if any one of them perpetrates an act that
might by the slightest bit of imagination be construed as not in
accordance with the fascist-run factory, then it is reported to the
boss; he naturally does not have much respect for the tattler for
he knows not only that the fellow is trying to get a raise but also
is subject to such cheating; if on the other hand you do not report
such things you are suspected also, for obvious reasons. Therefore
the factory man is in a hell of a puddle.

And on Sunday, I go to church, no matter how much I hate it.

I believe that churches and doctrine are a detriment to religious feelings. I'll explain that later on, but just now I want to tell you why I go to church. You see, these people I stay with are religious. They, contrary to that fact, have been very kind to me; keeping me here for a number of weeks without cost and so on. They want their children to go to church, and since they're not mine, I cannot be an example of the sort that does not go to church. So I go, not to cause them grief and to hurt their opinion of me. It's a case where I cannot be recreant to my obligations. So with the idea of going to movies or mentioning some things that are good, but might be interpreted as wrong with them. If I do such things, I am very wise not to tell them.

Now about the church idea. The religious feeling is definitely the outgroping, wide-flung endeavour of mankind to grasp reality and its meaning. It is never conclusive, never arbitrary, never dictatorial, never absolute; only relative, for-the-present truthful. Since it is hard for intellectual people to believe in the myth that supports the whole close-knit, logical fabrication, we must overthrow the adscititious addendum. The moment one dictates, from an Absolutistic standpoint, he becomes a snag in the stream of humanity marching down the hall of time. His positive truth becomes upset because his thesis is constantly disproved. Take for example the idea of maternal impressions, that has been proven false. Also the idea that thunder is the voice of god—when it is the crackle of fickle electrical charges that flitter back and forth between two surcharged objects.

The religious feeling is that part of man's expression or the whole of it that gazes and scrutinizes the world for the advancement of knowledge and man's ease.

And along the same lines, we can argue communism. Before industry had its beginning, it was fairly safe for mankind to be free to do what ever he wished. But machinery means greater control and power, and lest we allow these to fall in irresponsible hands, we must put them in the hands of the government elected by people and serving the people. In other words, no man is allowed to pile up enough power either by money or property to influence such government.

A simple illustration will bring that home to us. Scientists claim, and no one can doubt it, that man by his ingenuity through machinery can provide enough for all men to live happily by the low requirement of two hours work each. If the wages remain the same as now, what will happen to the laborer who performs all of this, or those who will not work because a small group work more than their share? Capitalists have been known to be adverse to give work or money to those who do not work for their wealth. Therefore, many people will have to die or a new system will have to be put into action. Fascists have a remedy, as has Hearst, so has the Hearst-supported, elected, and advised Roosevelt; that of war. Let the poor bastards die!

For that reason, I am in favor of communism. Socialism cuts the ice only half way. It will revert to either capitalism or communism. The latter only if it follows its premises. And today, the money of the land is in the hands of the few or monopolies; that is also true of the world; and in opposition to the world in order to maintain nationality, monopoly will have to stay. Socialism will not come to pass. Read John Strachey in both his latest books which I've read:

The Nature of a Capitalistic Crisis
The Coming Struggle for Power.

I am somewhat interested in Tevie [Johan TeVelde]. Show him this letter. And if he thinks I might be interesting enough to write to, let him argue against these tenets or suggestions. I like the little jigger.

Last Saturday, Floyd McKnight and A. Gordon Melvin took me out for a ride, both, to nature and my poetry. The former is this man I've become acquainted with and he is recognized by Miss Branch and Robinson, and Frost, and others as a master in sound and rhythm. He cannot get his poetry published for the following reasons: the poetry that is published is of some famous celebrity or of some waddling matron of the 400 or her son, the latter two paying the cost of publication. These are facts Debbie. The Melvin fellow was a former teacher on Columbia staff, and is now a teacher on the CCNY (CITY COLLEGE OF NEW YORK) and has published three books and is a Doctor of Philosophy. I hardly dare tell you what they said in the Columbia Faculty Clubroom, built and furnished by Rockefeller, but the essence of it was that I had a new idea in my preface and in my poetry. It, they said, was the best they had read for the last 10 years and for a young fellow like myself, was remarkable. They predicted a good future without money for me.

That is the only happy feeling I have, Debby. That feeling I had in college that I was destined to do something of merit and that confidence I had in myself was not unmerited. To jump out of my class now, Schopenhauer and Shakespeare both had a great respect for their work. They said it was permissible. Could I scurry under such a cover also? And I want to thank you for your friendship. You and others I have as friends are the true ones, and made me what I am. I feel that after such efforts I have earned my way into your friendship.

Yours,
my earnest respect to you,
Freddie.

To John DeBie

[Wallington, New Jersey]
June 15, 1935

Dear Debbie:

My natural impetus which usually flows or torrents violently through the many channels of life during week days has reached the plains of inactive Saturday, spreading softly out like a huge fan, dropping its sediments (sorrow, joy, sleepiness, laziness, hope, activity) indiscriminately,—in fact I'm a plain chaos just now.

I slept until 10 o'clock this morning—from ten last night. I spent most of the day fixing my new suit (grey, dark, checked, trim, and yoke-backed), reading E.E. Cummings' *Enormous Room* (World War Prison Scenes), rereading *Strachey*, Beard, and plowing through *Story, Nation,* and *New Masses.* I was going to rewrite a story and write another chapter to my novel to-day—but haven't as yet. Most likely I won't though, for writing letters usually dissipates a lot of energy actually convertible for artistic enterprises. Hence, you're privileged, Debbie.

I hear that Dr. Stob has been reappointed for four years and that philosophy is not to be taught by a regular prof.—but most undoubtedly will be taught by other members of the now present staff. TERRIFIC!

Most likely I shall see you then this summer, Debbie. And I believe that I can interest you in something truly stirring and gigantic. I met a man through an on-the-face innocuous advertisement in *The Nation.* We corresponded a while—apparently our letters exact opposites of each other. You see, he wanted young, eager, intelligent men to band to-gether for purposes of forming a third party. To my surprise, he wanted to meet me despite my Stracheyist theories of living. So I went to N.Y. a week ago. We met in a German-owned (that is, the owner is an ex-communist escaped from Hitler) Restaurant and Bakery. There I met many escaped Socialists and Communists from Germany. How proud, self-possessed, scintillatingly interested they seemed to be. At first he was hesitant to introduce me to them, for he didn't know how I stood in regard to affiliations.

His name was Ernst Wilke—a former lieut-general for Hindenburg in the W.W. He was 35 years old, had an intense, preoccupied expression, with light blue eyes that were mirrors of alternating complacent sage-like Olympianness and Mephistophelean fire, and sandy hair.

For three unregarded hours I combated, cajoled, twisted, retorted, resisted his arguments and presumptions. At every step, however, I noticed his ideas clicked precisely with mine. Whenever I noticed an unclear point or a point not compatible with (of course) both our systems I used every device of sophistry, logical, emotional appeal capable of a Feikema. Thus to-gether, we convinced ourselves about the thing. So now I'm in on the Inmost Inner Sanctum of the Constitutional Progressive American Party. Look at that title. It tells a lot and hides a lot.

Now, I've found a lot of things to quarrel about, but the idea is daring—and if successful, and it seems possible even to my late un-aspiring mind—and so I want to talk to you.

Even Communist E. Meima likes it.

Keep your mouth closed, Debbie, for I've told you more than I'm supposed to, but I know your mind and your capacity for secrecy to some extent.

Please write.

Fondly,

"Feike."

To Helen Reitsema

[Wallington, New Jersey]
June 26, 1935

My dear Helen,

Many apologies for those winces you underwent—and especially for the largest, the one occurring when the blank missive found its unobtrusive way into your cognition.

I'm reclining with my back to the window which opens upon a wide, deep river (Passaic) on the other side of which is a factory. It clicks "the whole night through" turning out many bolts of cotton cloth. It's opened full speed ahead for the first time in five years. Reports say owners received a large order from the Navy and Army headquarters. While this is being written Howie's using a hammer in another room. Another disturbance—really two— is this: I just discovered I lost my wallet, in which was five dollars, miscellaneous receipts, and a small photo of you (the last is not so important); and Mr. Voss claims via p. office that I still owe him $15 for my notorious stay in the Dorm. To the best of my knowledge, I don't. I don't understand them at all.

News flash—Jesse DeBoer has just been appointed to teach Intro. Phil. next year—horror of horrors—he was the most easily vanquishable member of the Plato Club—I personally having held him quivering in abeyance very often.

Mildred[1] wrote in a sonnet, "Fools, not to recognize merit"— I would say much more abrupt and exact. "Damn Them." I started to write an "Ode on the Departure of Dr. Jellema," but the vitriolic, philippic, hydrochloric-acidity, and venom dripped so profusely that the pen decomposed in my hand—as did the ink, which vanished entirely.

It seems that both Jellema and Cornelisse have gone to their long awaited "reward"; the one to a deserved post and the other to the happy-hunting ground of basketball warriors—while Stob, too, "Lest we forget," should have gone to his reward. I believe that if I had written The Ode—, I would not have had the damning skill of Dante. Perhaps that's the reason Dante is greater than me. Still, he was unreasonably silly to love Beatrice in the abstract while taking it out (erotically) on his own wife. Wait a minute, Fred— your record may also reveal a Beatrice.

Yes—But not a wife.

Having disposed of that tit-for-tat, we can venture to expose other Super-Ego repressed ideas and instincts. (Time out, cigarette. Thanks for the light, dear. You're so profoundly kind.)

For instance, I've met two girls who deserve my attention (I, that is, as a normal representative of the male *homo sapiens*).

The first potential soubrette, is, see here, it's true, is, as I was going to say, a very nice girl. Her name is Nella. Dutch. Tall, mobile mouth. Arching back. Has borrowed the measurements of Venus with regard to legs and that which they are affixed onto. Splendid possibility for divan sport. (Assumption, I don't believe in "love" in the old way, but in the new way; the love of Maxim Gorky and Logan Clendenning and Ives Hendricks—followers

1. Mildred Reitsema, Helen's sister.

of the almost socialist Freud [no, still a capitalist].)[2] However, the limiting obstructions exist. She's engaged to a H.S. grad—even though she is a col. coed and brilliant in literature and social questions. However (what, again?) she's made advances.

No. 2

Dark, dutch, name's Ruth. Attractive, liberal, moves her Long (remember?) and further amendments acquired from life. In fact, rumour is, she's been married, had an abortion, and is generally an ostracized individual in our group. And since I want to make good connections for betterment economically and pleasurably, a Taboo.

So I haven't gone out.

So I would like to.

Who would I nominate?

You can answer for yo'self!

After the first of the month, I'll be adrift again. I don't know where I'll go—even though I have some excellent connections for writing. But they won't do me any good just now. And certainly won't after I leave; perhaps would not if I stayed.

Thanks for the offer of help. But I would not take it. You'll need soon yourself; I hope not.

So far I have been acting like a sulky child. A communist in fact!

Yes, I've read *The Defender*. If, however, you knew who wrote it, and supported it, you wouldn't think of reading the false thing. The most salient argument is, "In the last analysis, it is not Christian." Since most of the world isn't, it falls flat. Still it may be salient.

The best way one can discover who holds the truth, is to discover who quotes the facts and intelligent arguments. There can be no argument then. Merely for Hearst-like people to say, "It's unconstitutional," doesn't prove much. And the best plays, Krutch and capitalist and conservative writers will admit, are those of revolutionary calibre. I've seen both. The former, revolutionary, are now showing, which I've seen:

Awake & Sing–Clifford Odets
Till the Day I Die–   "   "
Waiting for Lefty–   "   "
The Black Pit–Albert Maltz
Tobacco Road–Caldwell

If you really wish to read favorable arguments for Russia read:

Fascism–John Strachey
The Coming Struggle for Power–John Strachey
The Nature of a Capitalist Crisis–　"　　"
Dialectical Materialism & Lit.–　"　　"
The Nation
The Rise of American Civ.–Beards
Political Economy–Leontiev
Writings of Marx
Writings of Lenin
Writings of Engels
The New Masses
also *Organization vs. Freedom*–by Russell

I read both sides equally much. Especially *The New York Times*
which contradicts itself every day; one fellow says this, another
news bulletin says that in it.

The point is, Helen, I don't appeal or argue from sentiment,
"patriotism," and dogmas, what the papers say, but from an eco-
nomic-political standpoint. Economics gives the key. And mere
opinion or mental partiality will not do. One must weigh every
word, sentence, paragraph, and structure.

Moreover, thousands are dying in Ukraine, eh? First, it was true
in 1933 and before. But the peasants would not plant nor harvest.
So Russia, not succeeding by persuasion, said, "All right, if you
want to go your way, swell." So they used the old Feudal-Capitalist
method of living. They died. There is no famine there now. Even
The Times admitted that apparently men were using 1933 news in
1935. And pictures of 1923 were used in 1935 — it also says, Andrew
Smith, who claimed he was a former Communist, wrote articles
about butchery, starvations, and licentious feasts of Stalin et al.
One paper, *The Nation,* read the Russian print in an affidavit published by Hearst for authenticity, and found that Smith had been
expelled for loafing, not for telling the truth. Hearst taken for a
ride! Many have raised their arms in holy horror of the Kirov Execution. Some 107 were killed. How about the poor strikers, union-
ists, and farmers in America? Gov. Fed. Relations Board estimated
that 1000 were killed by hired thugs, gunmen, and policemen since
Jan. 1. I've seen some of these "reds." Honest men, who don't know
what communism means and hate it themselves. That is all fine,
say patriotic Americans. Moreover, three attempts were made on
Stalin's life. There was a vast plot to overthrow the government

as told by Louis Fisher in *The Nation* last month. I'll send the sheets to you next time.

And I know what goes on in industry. I have unobtrusively examined open and legerdemain ways of robbing workingmen.

It will be ten years yet before I've really grasped Marxism, but what I know of it sounds good. I have a merry time with everyone here—they don't know I'm a communist, but I upset every argument they have. It's too good.

I see a lot of Meima and Fortune [Fortuin].

Fortunately they haven't tempted me to give my first manly gift, but they're contemplating my sanctity. So you see, I'm still a good boy—although immature!

Fondly,
Freddie

Oh yes, do you know Anette Ritzema? I met her and she has done in Broersma. However, I told her that whatever my love-hunger may have wanted, it wasn't love. So I may have an interesting meeting when I see her. I don't [illegible].

Write very soon! Before July 4. And please, please, please send the unsent letters of 9 and 7 pages you wrote. Do you still go with Ray? Or are you available again?

To John Huizenga

[Doon, Iowa]
August 24, 1935

My dear John:

Saturday evening nostalgia prompts me to pen you a few lines. I have spent the last few weeks soaking my body and my soul (personality?) in rural domesticity and contentment. I liked the change so well; the smell of fresh milk, tasseling corn, long hours on the grain fields, interminable hours in cool beds, soaking hours beneath the clear-eyed Iowa moon, the long wait and vigil for and delight in phosphorescent fireflies, the half-doze midst family gossip and superfluous repartee—all there—that I had no desire to read or talk in "a direct line" or much less write.

I have a few moments now before I go to town to imbibe some more local color. And, moreover, I must write *some* letters before Monday, when I expect to begin work on my novel. No doubt it does sound presumptuous to you; you, who are so careful and so reconsidering before attempting a venture. However, John, what

have I to lose? Nothing to do but read and lie around, with board
and room always assured. My uncle Herman [Van Engen], one
of those persons who penetrates to the core, no matter how ill-edu-
cated, re-extended an invitation to stay at his home. I must perform
the morning and evening chores and in return I get a room over-
hung with tall shady ash-trees and pine. There are no children, and
upon occasion, for there are good classical programs here, I can
use his radio. That means eight hours a day to myself, a clean bed,
early hours both morning and evening, and a chance to straighten a
few moody turns of the mind and soul by leisurely brooding and
pondering.

Sunday, August 25, 1935

I went to the usual Sat. Eve. jamboree here, a local and national
custom I suppose. In so much as I wasn't so particular, I enjoyed
the three strains the band played; three strains played here since the
prairie grass and cottonwoods were swept under the capitalistic
propelled frontier. The same old people, the same crude girls, the
identical cumbersome swains, the selfsame beer—spigoting, the
never-ending cycle of picnic mouths. The boys sit in groups on car
fenders and fly-specked sidewalks telling the latest foul pun or discoursing eloquently on a dappled grey team's prowess or esti-
mating the potential cohabitating ability of some hard, full-
bosomed lass. The latter parade up and down, up and down, up
and down,—arms locked, out of stride, heads together giggling,
hips and buttocks in awkward rhythm—muscles rigid, extended,
loosened, falling, resting, and rising. My fly-by-the-second observation went as follows: girls have more of a propensity to homo-
sexuality than boys. Right?

Eddie Meima arrived here a few hours before I did. Naturally
he stayed, for I made him welcome. We had a fairly "good time"
(ah, great phrase, a help in the time of need). After inveigling the
folks to visit some relatives in Hawarden, we used the occasion
to visit John DeBie. He was pitching bundles. Hearty, and more
realistic than before. He said he had a chance to teach in a local high
school near here. I haven't heard if the appointment was given him.

P.S. Just happened to remember something about Will Rogers.
I read the pros and cons of his case. I have heard people extol him
here, farmers, bankers, businessmen, etc. One of the authentic,
it seems, things said of him runs as follows: he was liked by every-

body. Now if that be true, I cannot believe his mind and learning was respect demanding. Now, to get personal. I know a lot of people like me. I feel that if I go out of my way a slight bit, I don't believe I'd have a single enemy. I tried that once, but that was before I began to dovetail ideas and beliefs, and before I employed acid criticism in the dovetailing process. Now, I know some people do not like me because I disagree with them. Either they are small-souled or I am bumptious. However, to get to the question I wish to pose before our consideration, can a man have "brains" and still be liked by everybody, is a man living with a soul so big and a mind so leveled? To seek the golden mean, to weigh things, to hold the conclusion in abeyance 'til all evidence is in (in which case, no case is ever complete), to be a liberal, is that possible and still be nearest the state of being ultimately good, right, true? Somewhere in the Bible there is a statement to the effect that God does not like lukewarm people. That statement stings with truth! Perhaps that's why John Strachey can believe and know as he does—as I?

Comrade Fred.

To John Huizenga

[Doon, Iowa]
Sunday, Nov. 17, 1935

Dear John:

The last long stretch across eastern flats of Colorado, barren Nebraska, and off-again and on-again fruitful Iowa was interminably long yesterday as we sped homeward. I knew a letter from you would be waiting for me.

I did request my brother, Floyd, to forward any important mail, but undoubtedly he forgot. Thus this morning, despite the noisy children and some preaching over the radio, I'm writing a letter.

This is a vast America. I wanted to stop at innumerable places. The folks were interested in getting to two places: Los Angeles, point of destination; Doon, home. Occasionally, the vehemence and eloquence of my persuasion prompted them to stop at places. I have every reason to believe that the lesser known pine forests, brooks, and crags were what I should have seen.

We left home on a Tuesday morning and arrived in Cheyenne, Wyoming, that evening, 675 mi. That's about all there was to that day. The next morning though, after a few hours climbing through the foothills, we emerged above the snow clouds at the summit of the first range. Those were the first mountains for the folks. Towards evening, after traveling all day across the Wyoming mesas and molten lava beds, they got their first experience of crags and canyons. We traveled 20 mi. and in that space we dropped about 5000 ft. into the fairyland of the Mormon Salt Lake Valley. The folks wanted to stop a full day. They were quite interested in the Mormon Temple. I wanted to walk into woods, but since they had unconditionally accepted me as chauffeur of our new Dodge in the Cities, why, I couldn't go. Besides, they couldn't understand why I wished to be alone or wanted quiet, pungent pine, cold mountain water, talk with natives, and an hour or two to absorb all of that quiescent beauty seemingly waiting for a moment to fall or explode.

However, we left Salt Lake City Thursday about 2 p.m. and from then on we traveled over glistening, immaculate salt beds. Peaks and crags peered unbelievably far away along the horizon, reminding me we weren't traveling in make-believe land but in reality. We landed in Elko, Nevada, and there saw the roulette wheel, silver dollars, cowboys (who didn't carry six-shooters or rope women), and foul hotel rooms. The next day at 12 o'clock, at Reno, Nevada (where at the time Barbara Stanwyck was divorcing Frank Fay), we ran into a snowstorm. It was a case of do or die, for the snow began to fall over the Sierra Nevadas, 14,000 ft. up. On the other side was Calif. Thus from 12 o'clock til 6 o'clock we traveled but 80 mi. through a blizzard-bound range of immeasurable heights, straight pines crested with white snow, red sand, dull-orange and grey rocks. Occasionally, the snow came over the fenders of the car, occasionally the road disappeared and we had to stop, often we could see neither the land below or the peaks above. Suddenly, it began to rain as we were almost down, and then the road straightened, and we were in Sacramento. The next day, we made Los Angeles, where my step-sister [Gertrude Faber] lives.

You've heard enough of Calif. I visited Herm De Jonge and his sister, Margaret. The former showed me points of interest: Hollywood, Long Beach, a navy cruiser, pomegranates, orange groves, theatres, the opera *The Countess Maritza,* the homes of some of the movie stars, delightful bars and evening clubs, etc. In this land of waving palms and green-waved eucalyptus, the newspapers apparently are interested only in sex acts of Harlows and Dietrichs, divorces, Hearst gasconades, Americanism, success stories, and underground Reds (workers who merely strike for decent wages).

I saw thousands of men walking the roads because they know,

like the birds and geese do, that one can at least sleep in the open during a winter of Calif. I talked to many of them. Despair and disaster haunt their words and faces: these college and high-school men and women. Aimee Semple McPherson chants the four-square gospel through a shimmering gown of gold and silver: "My eyes are turned to Heaven's door! I don't care to live on earth anymore!" And while other eyes are turned away and hands re-empty empty pockets, gigolos fondle her paps and crush her pelvic bones. Hearst tells 'em to wait for the "break" and trust in Americanism—while he raises three bastard children by his concubine Marion Davies and stores away another year's profit—$8,000,000. Oh, it's a hell of a world. But a world or an America with potentiality: distrustful, wild, lying, hospitable,—completely unorganized. Those men on the road made me want to live—after the first vomiting taste of them.

Perhaps you're wondering, if that's all that inspired him, why, he's nothing better than the opposition. It was the sight of Boulder Dam, mighty mound of man's achievement over nature (but his thieving of mankind when the government money built it, only to give it back to some potentate for a lease propitious to his coffers) that convinced me. It was the watching of men crawling like ants over the mass, the thousands of acres of desert to be turned into fertile territory, the transmission of electricity for hundreds of cities a thousand miles away.

And soberness was taught by the Grand Canyon. It is an inconceivable gap in the earth with every imaginable color either bright, soft, or shadowed. One's eyes fail to grasp. I wish I could have stayed there for weeks.

The painted desert was smaller, a feminine sort of thing beside the Grand Canyon. (Dammit, some relatives are here just now, and Ma and Pa are vying with each other to tell the most.)

As I see it, the Indians are getting a tough break. And our church is caring for the Navajo souls, while trachoma and syphilis wrack their bodies and decompose their guts.

And now in a quieter vain. I intend to see you soon, in a month, but I shall want another letter.

The folks were nice about taking me along. But they had an idea that they should instruct me about every curve and hole and stop signal along the way. I believe that I learned more about the human soul from them, since they're open and simple. The nervous system in them with its hatreds, beliefs, doubts, fears, prejudices lies exposed to a discerning eye, more so than many intellectuals and other higher up people. I liked you from the start of my knowledge of you, for this reason: mentally you were straight, and when yourself was exposed to me as a comrade, I found the type of inhibitions and drives I always wanted my friend to have.

> Adios, and fondly,
> Fred.

1936

The year 1936 is one of job frustrations for Manfred. As in 1935, he hitchhikes between East and Midwest, holding jobs at the Prospector *newspaper in Paterson, New Jersey; at the Feikema gas station at Perkins Corner, Iowa; with the Jewel Tea Company as a salesman; and with the Hartford Insurance Company in Sioux Falls as a clerk. He also explores the possibility of work at the* Argus Leader *newspaper and a radio station, both in Sioux Falls, and of graduate study at the University of Iowa.*

To John Huizenga

[Prospector
Printing Company
letterhead]
[Paterson, N.J.]
Jan. 10, 1936

Dear John:

This letter I hope will fill in the vast gaps left by those fragmentary cards. We'll start from the beginning.

After I bade you good-bye, I walked to Robinson Rd. The very first car I hailed stopped, and after a bit of fencing, I discovered that I could ride to Detroit. This was not in my plan; I intended to go over Jackson and miss Toledo. However, this was too good to miss. Well, when we arrived in Detroit, he offered me a steak dinner. About 12:30 I stood out on the road to Toledo. For two and a half hours, I stood in the rain until I was almost drenched. But, I needed rides and finally one did come. Then, again I stood for a while in that damn, grey, cold, dismal, slithering rain. The whole world was grey and unlivable. My bags were wet, my back was wet, my shoes and feet were wet, everything connected with me seemed irretrievably soaked and unlivable.

That night about eight in the dark, a graduate of our Naval Academy picked me up and brought me to Akron, Ohio. His name was Jimmy Bentley, formerly a backfield star. He was quite friendly and with his initiate intelligence he had a fine sense of humour. I bought a meal there and slept in a fine private home for $.75. The next morning about eight in another drizzling rain, I ventured forth considerably heartened by a sleep in soft bed much like the bed you had last summer. I washed my entire body with warm water; moreover, my shoes were dried and my socks were cleaned again.

Immediately, an agent (a big blustering fool who believed that 1936 was going to be a millenium of gold-filleted prosperity) picked me up. He dropped me at Youngstown, Ohio, about 9 o'clock. The rain was letting up. I walked into a Cafe for a small breakfast. When I came out again, it was colder but drier. Ice began to form on the roads. I waited there for three hours. At 12 a fellow came along by the name of Spencer Brown, graduate of Iowa U. and now an Ass. Prof. at the U. of Maine. He an ardent Communist, very well read, rather wild in his jurisdiction over such mundane affairs as love, sex, lesbianism, strikes, literature, art, and all the other things God forgot to handle. In fact, his providence included a fine meal for me in return for driving his car while he slept. Buying some sandwiches, we drove intermittently (gas stops) into Philly where I pulled in about 10:30.

I got in touch with Billy Swets and Ed Herrema. They found a bed for me in the Gladstone Hotel which the prospective servants of God have appropriated much in the manner that the multitudinous offspring of Jacob lived in the land of Palestine. A longing for gossip and a sentimental memory prompted them to give me a few free meals.

With crocodile tears, I bade them Godspeed and took up my journey into the future where only prayer would be of any material help. A fellow imbued with the delightful charm of erethism deposited me in Trenton, N.J. There, two seeming sailors from Georgia in a wrecked V-8 kindly asked if they might take me to New York. After expressing a shade of politeness, I gurglingly retired into the back seat. Later a cop stopped us. The boys had 1935 license. In the course of the investigation, which looked black for those boys since they didn't have a license card or owner's card, he turned his ambitious anger upon me. Could I explain what I was, who I was, what I was doing to live, and if I carried a gun? Oh, yes. Pressman, son of the soil, affable, and the owner of a driver's license. Beams. Smiles.

When the gentlemen were allowed to go only for the reason that they had a release from their base at New London, Conn., they tried to get away without my indispensable services. The cop assured them that I was the only good guy in the car and "why 'n hell don't you take him along or else by Christ and his balls I will bring you in after all." Quite a bally old scene, y'know. They dropped me off in the lower teat of Manhattan. From there by subway I finally landed at Floyd McKnight.

They treated me swell. I remained there till Monday morning. By the way, the book he has turned out is one of the finest books of poetry printing that I have seen. Actually, the physical qualities are really beautiful and artistic. The contents too I believe you'll like very much. The poetry is quite sober and written somewhat like Whitman's and the old Greek epics. You should send for a copy. 100 Highland Ave., Yonkers, N.Y. $1.00. It is to be reviewed in the *Forum* of Feb. It is to be named the Poetry Book of the Month. Last week it was mentioned by the *Times,* and later, in a few weeks, is to be reviewed. Favorable notices are appearing in most newspapers. If you bear in mind that he edits, composes, directs, sells, and advertises it himself, he has done a fine job. Out of the 500, he has sold 300.

Monday I visited his boss of the American Historical Society. Mr. Downs assured me that after he had settled down somewhat from his unsettled nerves due to the death of one of his employees and his friend, he'd let me know if a vacancy was open. Pay is from $25 to $35 a week. Then I visited *The New Masses,* but they have a front office blind. One can't get to see the Steno of the sec. of Earl Browder who is a Sec. of the Com. Party. Later I dropped in on the John Day Co. I left my fragment of a novel there. Walsh assured me that he'd give it to his wife, Pearl Buck. (She is his chief editorial advisor.) They are reading it now. He has assured me by letter that he can not finance me before the thing is finished.

I arrived here about five, and the entire force of the *Prospector,* including Meima, welcomed me with Huzzas. They had been waiting for me. They gave me the job of Business Manager and Editorial Chief. Since then I have been very busy. My salary has not been spoken of, but I have been assured that I shall get expenses for a while until April when we can get legal ads. Then the paper will be legally recognized after a year of existence. Right now, I have been to see the Democratic Big shot of Passaic county. And I'll be damned, he has taken to me, and there is a good chance to land all of his legal work and that of his friends; best of all the printing of the ballots may be done by us. That will mean about $3500 clear money, after we split with him. He is to enter a blank entry, and when the drawings come in the bidding, he may promise to fill ours out lower than any other. I am damnably surprised that I can be such a traitor. We must live, though. These contacts of mine, initiated by Cornelius Fortuin, who has a potent drag here because he knows how to crap the secs and the stenos of these men not only but also these overpuffed servants of the public, give me a good insight into a small party machine.

Moreover, these men I contact for ads like me also. (Sotto Voce, perhaps I'm a hypocrite.) My height, hitherto a stumbling hurdle, has turned to an advantage. And this place bustles with activity. The only trouble is, I and Meim are the only ones with decent ideas, and you know we aren't much. However, this is fine training. Especially the proofreading.

Last night Meim and I went to an Italian Red Cross meeting. The name suggests the purpose. Mussy is running low in funds. We also knew that many Itals were sore about him and the tactics of the fascists here. Papers hinted a fiasco. Coming there, we noticed about 50 cops. Then I noticed a sign: $.40 admission. Swaggering over to the head cop by the door, Meim in tow, I said coolly (if that is possible), "We're from the press. Where is our door?" He called an usher. Before a few minutes had elapsed we were introduced to the main speaker and all the great Italian dignitaries of this land. We had told them that we were to leave at nine since our paper went to press at 9:30. Thus we wanted a copy of the speech beforehand. (Got that from you; you used to save a lot of time by getting the copy instead of attending.) The fact was, at nine, we had a billiard engagement downtown.

When the meeting started, the thirteen bands started off with the Italian Fascist Anthem, *Giovenezza*—a leg-thumping, arm-extended, heart-surging blazoning. Everyone stood up, on chairs and any high object available. White nurses spotted the arena. Passionate faces sweated and jawed. I was stirred myself. I was afraid of that 8000, of the force there is in the mass; exultant in its response to something they ignorantly thought was good.

Why did the Democratic party allow this? Because the Italians are very numerous. They are merely talking about Italy and that does not prevent them from voting Dem. Moreover the watches and gold and earrings etc., is a loss, but not as great a loss to the party if the election were lost. Politics.

Tomorrow night I shall go to Emily [Krug]. Later I'll write and send the money. Yes, I landed here with 78 cents. I needed this help I get here. Please write soon. This letter is jangled, but I had only 3 hours sleep last night, too many high balls, and I have worked like hell today.

Affectionately,
Fred.

P.S. Send all my stuff *collect* to the above address. Get it all together. Especially the little redbook.

P.S.S. I miss you immensely!

Mr. Brandes[1] suggests that perhaps you can get us an exchange for our weekly; especially since you may have a pull. Could you work it? Give us the word, and we'll put 'em on the mailing list.

1. H. Brandes, owner of Prospector Printing Company.

To John Huizenga

[Prospector Printing Company letterhead]
[Paterson, N.J.]
March 1, 1936

Dear John,

I've spent most of the day with my boss [Brandes], eating his food, listening to his radio, and enjoying the company he had. I suspect that you remember Edward Bierema, the old room mate of Debby? He is an old friend of the Brandes family and he and I were friends more or less of the past. During the afternoon we happened upon your name. At the time we were discussing personalities and one's reaction to certain individuals.

"From all evidence I gather about this Huizenga fellow, he must be an interesting lad. And yet, you know, there was a case where two people who had things in common to some extent, at least enough so that we could be somewhat friendly, never became friends. Why? I don't exactly know. But, he just didn't take a liking to me."

Not that this remark is unduly important in itself, but the mention of your name started a train of thought that finally set me before this typewriter.

Your letter, particularly some of the contents, brought a number of movements in my brain to a definite head. You asked about the monetary end of my job, and you gathered that it wasn't so hot because I didn't mention anything about it. You're right. My wages have amounted to an average at the most to $8.00 for approximately 45 hours of work: physical, mental, etc.

On Monday, Tuesday, Wednesday, part of Thursday, I am supposed to get advertisements. If you know me at all, I am not the man to be interested in convincing another fellow to spend money in something that is not giving him his money's worth. We have only 362 Subscribers, besides a few papers we sell on the street. Not only that, the basic idea behind advertising is inimical to my personal beliefs. It is part of the capitalistic scheme of organized production and unorganized distribution. Then too, to spend thirty hours dicky-dallying around with those fools who haven't one idea in common with me, it is just devilish. I hate it like hell. To me personally, it is a waste of time. [Margin] (The worst is, one must say, "We have 5,000 subscribers." Otherwise they laugh in one's face. Too many of these rags!)

1. Cornelius (Case) Fortuin.

Fortune's[1] brother has been trying to convince me that I have all the talents to become a great high-pressure salesman. I have distinction, geniality, appearance, knowledge, good-looks, etc. And he thinks I'm a damn fool when I hate this idea. He believes that I'm throwing opportunities to the winds. I could make a living selling my-self. Then the fact that I believe in revolution further disturbs him. (He writes for the paper, he gets some business for us, gives us liquor, and in general is a good fellow, all for no price at all—although I suspect that he is seeking revenge on some Democrat who slighted him. He wants eventually to become a power in the Democratic organization. Incidentally, he reads some and intellectually admits we need reform. He hitches his progress with the Democrats.)

After Thursday noon, I'm suddenly supposed to contribute all of my writing. They have an idea that I can cough some of that stuff out of my sleeve. I want to be honest and intelligent about that too, and I claim that I must have time to digest that stuff, and then some more time to create. All right. Do that at night. But, hell, that is my time. More than that. I must do all the corresponding, write and rewrite all the names, file all the business, wrap up all the papers, mail them, clean the shop, and God knows what not.

More than that! I sleep on a bed in the rear of the shop. I haven't slept between sheets since I have been here. And my clothes in a dirty commode, my shoes on a dirty floor, the air smells of burnt gas; sometimes the gas is left on all night because they want to work early in the morning, and that too again robs me of some privacy; the washbowl is always dirty because they use it too; they sit on my bed whenever they want to; they wake me up whenever they want; they rob me of a nap after supper when I want to recuperate, and almost every evening there's always some one bothering around. So I read late after they are all gone. Not much, but some. I get so goddamn disgusted I feel like throwing myself in the river at night.

My meals are pretty good. That is the only money they spend on me, besides my cigarettes and 1 dollar a week when I see Emily [Krug]. More of her later. The room is free. This is what they hold out to me. If you get good ads, the paper will succeed and if you stick with us, later you can get what you want. And there's where I begin to think. What are the chances of this paper becoming successful, and what will it mean to me if it does? Will it rob me of five years? Is my reading to be curtailed, when it is shabby and irregular as it is? Don't I owe them something for taking me in when I had only $.75 in my pocket? What chance have I to get another job?

There is something to their argument that it may mean something. There is no Democratic organ in this county or other counties around here. And these people will buy a paper like that. But to get the thing started, one needs capital. The boss hasn't that. I've looked into this political game quite a bit, and I know many Demo. State Committeemen. But it will mean a hell of a grind for me. With a probable end.

Next, can I get a job? Well, after this argument with Case Fortuin, I began to see that I can capitalize on my height. Walter Duranty, in his *I Write as I Please* says that any mark that will set one off from a crowd, plus good brains, and geniality, are three very strong prerequisites for a correspondent of note. Have I those? I meet some big shots here and I notice very soberly that they take to me quicker than they do to Case, and he has quite some pull, but he's worked so long on it that almost any man could get where he is now. Thus the next few weeks I am slyly going to strike out for the big.

Moreover, Case and others here believe that I have a real opportunity in the political field. People never forget me. I meet easily. I inspire confidence. I am idealistic. I promise things easily. I am honest. (Their sayings!) I am also a tolerable speaker, with chances to become great because I have a strong voice and a sense of balance and nicety of language choice. But I know that it takes a lot of money to be somewhat independent, and if one has no money, there is no independence whatever. I could never stand that. Thus that is dismissed for the present as impractical and totally averse to my personal beliefs.

This is what grips me. I can never be alone with myself in a room, with a good book, a glass of wine, with a radio, with some money in my pocket, with decent clothes. I wake up right in my job. One needs to get away from the business after the office hours.

About my love affairs. Well, in the first place there isn't such a thing as love for me anymore. The loss of Helen forever killed that in me. I am rather sure of that. I can get along without her now. I have made myself believe that at last. But her going, or rather my leaving there forever robbed a great part of myself. She has that. She took the mold and the contents.

But sexually, I have all the drives; perhaps developed or stimulated to a greater intensity. This Emily Krug woman is nice. She reads, likes good music, tries to think but can't compare with myself, has a good body, a fairly good face, ordinary folks, a damnably attractive sister who I'd like to sleep with sometime, and an atmosphere in the house where a lot of tough talking goes on, but when it comes to actualities, a cowardice or an inhibitory defense arises.

I visit her once a week by train. She usually has company of the pedantic high school rah rah home type. They sit around until 12 or later, and if I want to get in a little petting or sadistic crushing, I must miss the 1:39 train. That means that I can't get another until 5. That happened twice. Those two times I tried to screw her, but no go. I like her well enough to enact such a delectable pleasure. She is a good kid! I have told her that I'd never fall in love, that eventually, if I like her well enough, I wanted to release some of the pentup steam. I rather suspect that I may let her go in time.

But then, where to? I don't like to pick up cunts on the street. That is what I believe and think.

Ideally, I like to find a girl again in whom I could build and with whom (I guess that is more accurate) I could construct a relationship most nearly approaching true love.

I have come to the point now where I know it best to build up from the ground, rather than have an idea of love and an idea of a girl for me, and then fit the girl into this idea, later assuring myself by smothering her with kisses, clumsy fumbling over her abdomen, that she is that idea. That will lead to disaster.

(By the way, my eyes are so bad, that I had to get glasses. So

2. Although he had 20/20
vision, FM's eyes were light
sensitive.

I got an ad with an optometrist. We get all our glasses and service
for this ad. So today I am wearing glasses.[2])

Wednesday Evening.

Three days have elapsed since I sat with bursting blood vessels
before the typewriter and drooled that pathetic little tale on paper.
Mrs. King, the lady who cooks my meals, has been very kind.
When she heard that I had to sleep in our new quarters in the paint
smell arising from the truck factory on the first floor, gave me permission to read and write in a little, neat room to the rear of her
luncheonette. That is an excellent thing. She also advised me to quit
them.

Take for instance last night. I read the paper and a book here
until 8 o'clock, played basketball until 10:30, and walked over to
Brandes' home to get the key for the plant. They were in bed.
There were no lights in our new place, but I didn't feel like going
to bed. Where to go to read? Finally I went to a German's
lunchroom (open all night) and read until 1:30. Just as I was leaving
(for I went in there without a penny) he offered me a cup of coffee
and an apple turnover. That was the straw that almost broke the
camel's back. The humiliation!

Thus today I went to the Paterson *News* and the Paterson *Call*.
The former gave me the run around. The latter—well I met the
boss next to the big boss. I shall meet his super-boss, Fredericks,
sometime this week-end. They pay good and they appear to be a
friendly lot.

Eddie Meima and I sob out our stories to each other. He too
is looking for work. He has trouble at home. Something like you
had with your father at one time, if I remember right.

Conditions are sore indeed. Thousands of boys, and men, and
women going along the street—searching, searching, searching.
Some spend their last cent, yea, steal, to buy a gossamer chance at
the Irish Sweepstakes, or some other absurd absinthe. Truly, a marvelous acid-like, sardonic reflection on culture.

Man going out of business, while the octopusian chain-stores
gradually fill the street front and habitate them with harried clerks
and managers. Sycophants of parasites of humanity!

A librarian said to me the other day, "You'll have to reserve this
number *330 M 20* if you want it. Karl Marx is an awfully popular
man these days." She looked at me as if she were a scientist watching a guinea pig. Shall I mention the books I read?

I Write as I Please—Walter Duranty.
Growth of the Soil—Knut Hamsun.
Moby Dick—H. Melville (powerful)
Brave New World—A. Huxley (marvelous)
Solomon, My Son—John Erskine
Arrowsmith—S. Lewis
A Sign for Cain—Grace Compkin
A Book on News-Reporting
Essays—W. Hazlitt.
Numerous magazines, papers, stories, and other slush.
Poetry of Whitman.

I am going to buy a new Modern Library Edition of Karl Marx's *Capital*. This is a good buy: large type, the best edition, with contributions by Friedrich Engels.

As for my novel? Every thought and image of it has been banished—which I needed so much to actually make it write itself. And why? No time!

Keep your eye open for a job there—especially with the *Press*. You say, "I'm sorry your career took you East." Hell! Career?*?! I took whatever I had east!

At any rate, John, lest I become too impious, *I shall finish,* "for I and my church papers have gathered to-gether," (yes, they sent them to me personally!). Write soon, for I may sail with the next tide.

Ever, fondly,

Frederick.

To John DeBie

1337 Valley Place, S.E.
[Washington, D.C.]
April 17, 1936

My dear Debbie:

Tomorrow morning I shall faithfully buy a lb. of Walter Raleigh. I shall use it when perusing some philosophically intriguing aspect of Florida-tanned pulchritude, or ambling mellowly through laughter-freighted pages of G. K. Chesterton, or strolling hop-scotch-like with Wordsworth along fish-less ponds of hinterland, or gamboling along with Shelley and a meadowlark in the air-lanes of birddom.

I'm really having a rather delightful time here in Washington. I've been pulling all the strings possible for a job. I hope one will be forth-coming soon. In the event that I'm successful I shall send an invitation to you to spend a week or two here. My Aunt [Hammock] will be glad to house my friends. She has taken to and taken in Eddie Meima *Nobly*. Incidentally he went back to Paterson to study his short-hand. He has a chance for a job here also. I need someone like him to exchange ideas and life. Of course, if something opens for you, you're coming. Some of these jobs pay handsomely.

I've written a very sober story about two little kids discovering the how of a birth. They witness the birth of a calf in the barn when the folks are not around. Their conversation, I'm delighted to say, surprises me agreeably. The youngster (boy) is especially adept in answering questions to his sister. He doesn't elucidate any.

Without much ado, I've met some communist friends. Washington is sort of Mecca for them; despite the vigilance of authorities. I was startled to learn that all the mail and telephone wires are tapped here. No one calls by telephone. At their house, I met some of the men who are fighting La Guardia, Ritter et al in New York. They must have left their dress and makeup at home because I didn't notice any whiskers and pocket-bulging bombs.

I wonder if you're right about the Helen problem. There are a number of facts to be considered, though: 1. She and her sisters never intended to get married young. 2. Ray [Vander Meer] is quite penurious himself (with the added attraction of imbecility—at least I can grant him that leeway). 3. *She just doesn't*.

Whoever said, however, that I am not capable of teaching her to love me? Aye—I can do that. So perhaps, if I could offer her a home, I might achieve priority over her half of the bed, the books, and the board—which I in the first place provide. But I am rambling again.

I am quite worried about this persistent cold I have in my frontal bones and my chest. It has bothered me for two years now. And even now, as I pen these lines, my quickening imagination feels the effects of barrage after barrage of germs.

Do you remember Debby when I had so much ambition to do things: study, basketball, read, write—how I could do those with impetuous—hypodermiced speed, albeit not with justice?

To-day, I am constantly tired. I fall to musing; not so much about ideas, as about feelings and actions I should do but don't. The fever of procrastination has delightfully entered my blood. One pipe of calmly inhaled tobacco has as much charm for me as two sonnets by Edna St. Vincent Millay.

The only occasion for fire-philliped folk is the mention of ideal-
ism, love, present social justice, sex technique in theory and practice, and kings. Then, mounting an edgeworn enthusiasm, colored
and accelerated by an ever-moth-balled imagination, deepened by
aimless living, and factualized by much one-sided reading, my
heedless mouth froths with illegal terminology wholly Un-Ameri-
can à la Hearst.

I can imagine quite easily that you are not wholly happy. What
I would call needless frustration you would call service to an ideal.
That which I would call de-privileged existence you would term
a period of self-denying, fruitful waiting.

Don't let the fact that you don't earn as much as Joan [Holtrop]
quell your masculinity. Women are taking part in civilization today.
That is right; but things are not organized properly to take into
account all virtue and ability. You are worth a dozen Joans. She is,
shall I say the customary remark, a "swell" girl. That explains my
rating of the *addressed* of this letter. Moreover, take into account
the cost-of-production of each locality.

The larger hand of man's robot time-device is joining the
smaller hand in a midnight cocktail. Thus I shall have to desist these
perambulations in conjecture-land.

In my white linened bed, a volume of Feuchtwanger and a tome
of Marx shall find eventual company with my cheek after the sand-
man has reported to Sleep, "closed for the night." And my untalk-
ative crony, but therefore all the more appreciated, a brown-
bowled depository of Raleigh's weed shall lie on a table subsiding
its warm cheer in the cold of the night.

And thus while the water drips in the kitchen sink, the radio
castinets a decharmed Jungle-rhythmiced jingle, the glasses of my
spectacles are be-clouded with the incessant spattering of pore-
born atoms, I bid you a fond goodnight; wishing that the return
mail shall reward.

Your comrade,
Fred.

To John Huizenga

Pella, Iowa
June 10, 1936

Dear John:

You have settled in your new habitat by this time and the press
of school work has fallen away. No doubt you have also discovered

if I have earned those two dollars or if you had to rewrite and possibly reread the material for a complete, new draft of that Buchmanism paper. Frankly, I was quite bored by the exhibition of extravaganza, and yesterday I noticed a movie reel release depicting the Buchmanites marching a thousand strong to write a brief chapter in the story of man's eternal struggle with the quest of peace. The people's pick-me-up of this emotional scotch-and-soda must be particularly delightful and advantageous to the men who control the lead wires of the meshings of economic autocracy.

I was quite fortunate in my hitch-hiking on my way home. I caught one ride to Chicago (as I must have informed you on the inadequate card) with an interesting salesman, who was constantly suspicious of me. He would lock the car at every stop and make remarks about the possibility of my running off with the car. Naturally, I assured him that he was quite optimistic of my get-away prowess. I tried to be as polite as the narrow confines of my unsartorial habitue would permit. But to no avail. It seemed that I was making the wrong moves and statements all afternoon and he likewise. We were about as polite as two country dames who, become rich, must not betray their oafish environment.

The reception in Chicago was not particularly gratifying either, as Stuart De Jong expected me to ask him for a free ride but wanted $2.50, and I expected him to offer me a free ride and didn't want to pay (couldn't) the $2.50. There we were; locked in loggerhead politeness. I strolled around the block, bought two bananas and two oranges (dinner à la Grand Rapids), and came back with a solution. The world was grey and the fog of despondency hovered dangerously near an attitude of "Hell with youall." I told him that I could undoubtedly secure some money at home. Later, after that distressing episode was exited, I walked over to Pete's [Kortenhoven] house. He was out to the dentist to have his 'ivories' (that word is half and half trite, thus deserves only a half quotation mark) polished. But the old man, amiable old duffer with a grain of sense concerning the foibles of youth, pinch hit with an admirable spray of humor that kept the minutes filled with untedious trivialities.

Pete was solicitous. He talked about the fulminating "Chicago itchuation" and finally rammed a voluminous and formidable "Orange Book" into my pocket with a solemn warning that on the morrow I should not divulge one iota to the son of that odious Albert Stuart De Jong [a relative], who as you know tried to pluck a modernistic plum from a Special Wezeman pie.

The trip home was uneventful.

Well, Dad is not very well satisfied with his Feikema Service Station.[1] It seems that he is losing a lot of business because he refuses to be a well-rewarded public servant on Sunday. We live quite close to the station, and on Sunday, the travelers, accustomed to the Infinite's Day service, park for a moment and look around. When they drive off, Dad says, in not too translatable Dutch, "Potverdorry,[2] daar gaat an other one dat vill noit came pack."

I have offered him a few valuable suggestions, about 40 hours of work, and a few illuminating signs informing the public of the usual ballyhoo about the needs of their car's bowels.

Last week Tuesday my psychological seismograph informed me that deep in the innards of [brother] Floyd's functional apparatus, two disturbing quivers existed. He wanted to try out as a baseball pitcher with the Sioux City Cowboys Western League Baseball Club. Moreover, he was eager to acquire a taste of night life. We reviewed our resources and I must say that in the monetarial drill march, too many Indian heads peered over the heads of silver-headed Miss Liberties. But we departed.

The manager informed him, after he had pitched to every man on the team in batting practice with what I thought fine skill, that although he had as much stuff if not more than any Western League pitcher, he was too green. He suggested that Floyd should play with semi-pro teams in this neighborhood and that next spring when the season opens, they would be willing to take him on and teach him a few fundamentals of mound maneuvers. He also showed him burnt women whose fires did not scorch him!

Then while he read O. O. McIntyre's column and the final score of a Cub defeat, I approached the managing editors of the *Sioux City Journal* and the *Sioux City Tribune*. In a nattily crypticed talk, the latter informed me that he had already taken on two men last week. He warned me that he started the boys out as office boys and from then on let them develop as fast as their ability and the deaths in the force would permit. The former editor was kind. He knew my father quite well. He informed me that he would certainly give me a position as soon as opening occurred on the staff. That was all very fine. The biggest argument for an applicant seems to be that one must be an Iowa boy with a college education. I suppose that statement will take the place of the old proverb, "Harder to find than a needle in a haystack."

Then this past Monday with a $1.25 pressed into my pocket, I

1. At Perkins Corner, Iowa.

2. Damn.

hiked to Pella, Iowa, forty miles east of Des Moines, in four rides. Tuesday, I walked into the combined offices of the *Tribune* and the *Register* and discovered that I could meet neither city editors until three o'clock. It was ten then. I walked out and walked into a very severe hail, rain and wind storm which you must have heard about on the AP and NEA.

I found shelter in an old First Baptist Church and saved my self from a generous natural baptism. I fell asleep there listening to the droning voice of a pastor discoursing on the homelectic possibilities of Rousseau's *Confessions*. Later, I retired to a theatre where Grace Moore sang while the King [Wayne?] stepped out. Incidentally a woman slipped and fell on the freshly painted sidewalk before the theatre and in the ungracious attempt to prove the now defunct theory of gravity by Newton, she broke her arm.

I was informed after the ecstasy of the Kreisler music that there were three thousand applicants, but that the city editors generally selected a man not from the files but one from their memory. So I swaggered over to each of them and put on some "blow." I suppose integrity and earnestness were woefully absent, but there was plenty of noise. I've sent a letter to both and perhaps they will remember me. I also gave your name for a reference.

Tomorrow I intend to leave the home of Garret De Boer, formerly of Doon, and hike to my aunt and uncle living in Owatonna, Minn.[3] From there I shall hike to Minneapolis and St. Paul and enquire about newspaper jobs there. I expect to be home for a week, next week, so please write me a letter and send that vest and *safeties* in it, so long,

> Ardently and fondly yours,
> Frederick

P.S. The fields and pastures are coolly wantable. I feel like grazing with the cows. I asked for a second-hand "chewer of the cud" but the startled clerk banished himself from my balmy presence.

P.S.S. I'll write you from Owatonna, but I expect a letter in Iowa Sunday.

3. Kathryn Feikema Eder and Clarence Eder.

To Helen Reitsema

Perkins, Iowa
"3 o'clock in
the morning"
June 17, 1936

My dear Helen:

Dad has gone to his linen coverlets, perhaps reviewing the movie he saw tonight, *Showboat,* and resting his limbs that must be weary. Thus I am sitting here in the waiting room of his FEIKEMA SERVICE STATION—ALSO LUNCHES, REFRESH-MENTS, ICECREAM, GOOD COFFEE (of which I just had) TOUR-IST HOMES, TIRES, and GENIAL SMILES. WE HAVE THE BEST GAS SERVED WITH THE GREATEST ALACRITY AND WITH THE KINDEST REGARD FOR YOUR POCKETBOOK. Landon isn't the only man with slogan makers fawning for a ripe simony or sinecure.

When I sent that card this morning, I felt dissatisfied with its miserly dribble of detail. To elaborate on it, then, this letter follows.

There were a number of reasons for writing, these will follow in good time. First, though, I believe I should send some sort of apology for the quality of the story sent to the contest. Personally, I did not like it very well. I wanted to present an economic and a moral problem imbedded in interesting narration. The story was not supposed to have a plot. I do not believe that I got that across adequately. But you can judge for yourself. Did you like the inscription? Isn't it beautiful?

Oh, yes, I read the Bible—perhaps oftener (?) than you do. I am sorry, kid, not in the Calvinistic spirit.

To return to the story. I did not have a story handy in my files. Does a transient have files? I hate that designation, Helen. And I did not want that type of story that preaches and quotes texts and the Church Fathers whose dust is now innervating the crops in Europe. I wanted a simple story, earthy and with good people in it. It was hard to write a good Christian story. But there are such people who are good, and a writer must take cognizance of them. But, should I write a thousand such as that, I believe I should become quite sour on the whole mess. The other day an idea came to me, as to why you wanted me to write that story. You see, you are in my mind often. "Did she want me to write a Christian story, for the possible chance that the act of thinking that way might influence me?". . . . But I know you did not mean that.

I've just gone to turn on a different station. That exotic swing music excites illegal thoughts for this letter that is meant for you. And now they're playing *Tales from the Vienna Woods*. Correct? Or some such composition. Can you see that I am getting sleepy?

I've been typing all night. Guess about twenty pages of application letters. I am sending them to Minneapolis, Mason City, and Des Moines. Newspapers. One paper had 3,000 ahead of me. See, what Johnny [Huizenga] has then? He's gone ahead of me, and he is younger. Am I just an ordinary fellow, or not even that; have I been kidding myself about ability, even in regard to my former aspirations for your heart to company mine?

Oh, I'm not droopy tonight. In fact, if you were to speak to me to-night, you would see me quite cheerful. But the little sourness that is in me will have to be out—as I said once, quite often people express a part of themselves that may be entirely unrepresentative of what they actually are.

As I said on that card, I was surprised at the cultural propensity of my Uncle and Aunt, Mr. Clarence and Kathryn Eder. She tried to curb my smoking, the rooms and the house and the lawn are so neat one instinctively tries to be good and nice and polite, and the radio & the phonograph are constantly intoning good music. She plays the piano well, and has an excellent store of knowledge of the best books, plays, and movies. Minneapolis has great cultural advantages in which they participate since they live but a sixty-mile distance from there. And the Jenny Lind bed I slept in and the pillow case my own mother made, formed the most delightful conditions for sleep. I traced with my finger all the embroidery there and saw her fingers flashing in and out, each seam a memory, each finger connoted with my care and nurture.

Good Dad has just come in (4 o'clock) and he instructed me to go to bed. I shall as soon as I've finished this letter. This typewriter must go back in the morning.

Since I left you, I worked a week around this plant, painting signs and doing night duty to give Father a chance to sleep when it is cool. Johnny [brother] has proved to be a sleepy head, and one night they took nearly $100 worth of goods from here while he snoozed. Floyd and Ed [brothers] are out working on the farm. Floyd had a letter from Ossie Solem, football coach from Iowa City, requesting him to pay a visit there. He may get a scholarship and go to school there. He's getting to be a mighty kid, both mentally and otherwise. During the week, the two of us hiked to Sioux City. Floyd wanted to try out with the Western League Baseball team and I wished to see the managing editors of the *Tribune* and the *Journal*. Floyd made quite an impression on the manager, but was rejected not because he lacked the stuff on the ball but because he lacked experience and skill. The gentlemen of the press were nice to me. After that, we went to a movie, ate a sizable meal and started home. Well, we didn't get back until four in the morning, after we had walked about ten miles. The moon was in full bloom and the dew glistened like your eyes do when you're told something exciting.

I've just about given up asking why I am interested in you. It is a fact. So you'll have to bear that in mind. Everything turns to you, more so than ever before. These quiet farms lying in the last generous smile of warmth the sun gives at sundown, the fragrance of the sweet clover and the purple-veiled alfalfa damp with per-spiration of night trying to lull the restless spirits of men, the tow-ering cottonwoods with their ceaselessly fluttering leaves sparkling in cascading brilliance—all these things remind me of those walks we once enjoyed along the flowered walks of Grand Rapids.

But Helen, be careful not to say that I must not write to you or hear from you at all. I do not aspire or think there is a chance. It is merely that I can only work when I know that we are more than just acquainted.

That last visit with you was the most wonderful of them all. When you said to me, in the movie, "You know, Fred, we're getting old," it was as if we were the most intimate of friends, comrades for life, a natural thing, something I wanted so bad once that I swore that I should be the happiest man alive if I could get that far. Well, it seems, I have, does it not? And for a moment, that night, I hardly knew I lived, so staggeringly did my mind career in its in-tense delirium of ecstasy.

Do you want me to erase from myself that which is afterall I, the person that you made and is inviolately bound to you?

Fondly, your comrade, who wishes you happiness and wants a letter very soon, since, besides the other reason, he may leave soon for Denver (two weeks).

Your,
Fred

P.S. Foolishly, perhaps, I carried your letters (the twins or dupli-cates) around with me to-day.

Frederick

P.S.S. It's because I'm lonely for like people. How would you like to tour the West for all summer? You can, if you'll hitch-hike with me!

P.S.S.S or is it P.P.P.S. — Oh, did you see Johnny [Huizenga]? He lives in Eureka! Tell the bum to write.

To John Huizenga

Perkins, Iowa
Feikema's Cottonwood Park
Sunday — July 5, 1936

Dear John:

Illness is responsible for this sudden response. What? Again? If two of my senses, seeing and feeling, aren't deceiving me, I have a very sore foot — in fact, blood poison.

Last Wednesday evening, I ambled my ponderous, shapeless hulk towards my uncle's [Herman Van Engen] farm near Doon, Iowa, where I was expected to care for his chores while he went to the Lakes Thursday, Friday, Saturday. Thursday morning about 10 o'clock, I decided to drive his cows in a remote pasture. Remembering that dry air, hot sunshine, and hot dry dust were good for my itch between the toes, I decided to walk bare feet. All went well until I started a romp with a clever half bulldog–half scotch terrier canine. Unmindful of my footsteps, one of my feet became entangled in a short piece of barbed wire. I was jerked to the ground. (Hell, I'm going to use a pencil. The air is so hot, 110° in the shade, it dries the ink as I write.)

As you can imagine, the cut was quite deep. However, it didn't become inflamed until Friday night. I fell asleep with my foot tied to the upright of the bed, tied if you please with a tightly rolled sheet and a wet pillow. I hobbled over the yard Saturday morning, walked a 1½ miles to get the cows, and hitch-hiked to the Hull Hospital.

Thus I was told of the blood poison. My foot looks like a black, moldy loaf of bread and the streaks of red on my leg resemble a bloody octopus. I discovered I have a temperature of 101 $\frac{4}{10}$ and that Evelyn Roelofs works as clerk in the hospital.

The Nurse or Doctor (both, actually) committed the foot to a long stay on a bed, and naturally, since I'm quite fond of my feet, although I have a lurking suspicion you think of them as inelegant, I went along. Thus, the poor handwriting. Also, I won't be in a position to develop my immediate Evelynish disposition since the bed is inconveniently located in one of Dad's cabins, fiendishly exposed to the sun and dust in the day, and to honking horns and irrepressible dogs at night.

Time out: Cigarette and a psychological bawling out of my kids trying their damnest to disturb my mental equilibrium.

They, [Brother] Floyd and Irene [Faber], have just shifted me to the hammock. That brings to mind what I intended to start this letter with. I've had some time to ponder over that letter from you— quite ripple producing, to say the least. Especially, that Dekker item. Simply say to him the following: Fred's writing for the markets, not for art sake—since STORY likes 'em mushy and sexy, REALISTIC, he tried fatuously to do the same.

Frankly, I wonder if your influence did not have something to do with *If Only*. Preposterous, but humans behave strangely.

You see, John, whenever I write to you, or speak to you, or speak in your presence, I feel so confoundedly ill-at-ease, as though I am trying too hard at times, or as though I'm afraid I can't measure up according to our mutual friendship. I've always had that. I like you so damn well, that I don't want to fall down on something I consider more valuable than anything I know.

As you've surmised, the John in *If Only* was none other than yourself. Since I visualize my characters intensely, you were quite alive in that theme. Could this be a plausible answer? Or is it an excuse? Or am I just lousy?

As a matter of fact, I'm somewhat pleased that you deride my too detailed realism. I've been accused of the lack of that. Moreover, editors have said my characters were too Horatio Alger-like, or Napoleon-like. From now on, good solid, matter-of-fact fellows.

I just thought of a monstrous lie. It's so dry here in Iowa, that if one spits a gob of saliva on the ground, the ground not only sizzles, but the trees bend over to lap up the major lake (lake—since any bit of water is large in this desiccated vacuum). Poor stuff, poor stuff.

Des Moines and Minneapolis were not my only stops. I went there because I had convenient spots to stay. Particularly, near Minneapolis. My uncle [Clarence Eder] is a High School professor at Owatonna. They have no children. Together they have learned the secret of quiet, contented living. They listen only to the best music, read very intelligent books, visit Minn. for concerts, and both work in a garden. They have a lovely clock bought in Germany that tolls out a replica of the Westminster Chimes. Lovely, quiet, solemn.

The house near the Owatonna mineral springs is conducive to happiness. Ordinarily, one might expect that a letter so pointed and so disarmingly frank as yours concerning my ingénue wish to write would discourage me. However, that is not the case. It *is* my hobby to write short stories, poems, and lengthier efforts—how else? What *vocation* can I command in two years' time? Has there ever been an opportunity? Teaching? Hell, I've seen too many people disappear mentally as teachers—Hearst fodder. Of course, I need not become as they. Imagine a new idea at a Teachers' convention! Why, great Jehoshaphat, you'd be called a god-damned "Red."

I've been looking at a cottonwood intermittently as I wrote the above. It seems to me my faith in my work is like that. It takes ages for it to grow. Some day it shall be able to umbrage as many idea-parched people as your statelier Chinese elm (it grows to maturity very soon). Then I can begin to reciprocate to you the benefits I now receive from you.

This is a note from Earl Hall, Mgn. Ed of *Mason City Globe-Gazette*.

"My dear Feikema:

One who can build up as effective a case for himself as you have in your letter received this morning is certainly entitled to some extra consideration. You shall have it when we have a vacancy.

Sincerely,
Earl Hall."

Jesus! Some of the Nit-wits writing to-day ought to be morticianed into that limbo of inter-cinematic darkness, frequently termed the Christian's self-imposed hell. Such as Lippmann, Sullivan, Mallon, Lawrence, etc. What do they say about the Black Legion? Do you know that the Rep. including the Gov. and Henry Ford back it? Do you ask questions? As for me? I shall stir up every nook and cranny to air it. I shall!

Fondly, and recuperating,
Fred.

[margin] Now for some Whitman and stealthy beer! (Oh! I'm part-time correspondent for the *Sioux City Journal* [illegible]

To Helen Reitsema

Perkins, Iowa
August 30, 1936

Dear Helen:

This letter cannot command for its being the excuse of "vital statistics." I am writing because I enjoy talking with you. Referring to the first sentence, I have your word that "vital statistics" is not just a highbrow synonym for idle woman's gossip or the reflection of a woman's glory as mirrored by man's bland assiduity. Lately, you see, I've sometimes doubted my own motives.

The other day I ran down a prickly aphorism (aphorisms usually pare down a truth so much that it loses its cogency): "Woman is a bundle of pins; man is her pin-cushion. When a woman loves, 'tis not the man she loves, but the man's flattery; woman's love is reflex self-love."—Henry Harland. Remember when I accused you of that [self-love]? I recall also one night (a party at Lenore's house in the summer of '34) when you reached for my hand in the car as we drove to Butler Hall. Ah! If I could but harness the humanity cargoed in that simple, age-old caress. (Now that the ink is dry, I'll turn over. Heck!)

I've been reading Charles A. and Mary R. Beard's book, *The Rise of American Civilization*. Rereading, actually. As I imbibe that sober scrutiny of America, I'm more convinced than ever that these little Dutch villages, Grand Rapids, and other religiously snug communities live back in the eighties or still more remote. It's only when one meets outsiders and reads such books that the concept cosmopolitan has any meaning. Isn't it marvelous for a man and wife to work on a book together, and to add dignity, make it olympic?

Ed, Floyd, and John [brothers] are gone. The latter is working for his board and tomorrow resumes high school. The other two are working on the farm. Floyd would like to go to college but he doesn't have any money. Two of the girls [FM's stepsisters] are gone also; one to high school, the other plans to teach in a country school. The smaller children will resume grade school in a few days. Thus I am home alone with the folks. That is, until I find employment. I work the night shift in Dad's 24-hour service station. It's interesting for a few nights. One becomes dreadfully bored with their detailed, raw narrative of immediate, domestic problems. Truckers are especially loathsome.

It happens that this is the morning of Aug. 31, 1936, about 3:45. It's been quite lonely. No one has stopped here for two hours.

I don't believe I shall acquaint you with any of my plans for the future. I know I can't stay here. Because we are closed on Sunday, we lose trucker trade. Without that, one is lost. As a consequence, the funds of the family that were syruped by the flow of lucre are now dry and rasping. Accusations sparkle the non-public family conferences. The other day, according to computation (not mine) some seven dollars were missing. The circumstantial finger that electrocuted Hauptmann pointed unwaveringly towards me. It was quickly retracted when a bit of Zeus's anger emerged from my full-lipped mouth. That's one incident. I imagine such things happen. It doesn't lead to congeniality. I know that I shall not boss, heckle my wife—and vice versa. I shall step out then.

I have just removed my slipper to give a first hand report on the blood poisoning. The scar is still purple and lumpy—otherwise the tendons (which the doctor feared might stiffen) and the skin apparently are in functioning order.

The air is very fresh outdoors. We've had two heavy nights of rain—one night hail stones fell as large as tea-cups. I noticed the moon just now, which must be trimming its wicks just outside your window and fumbling in and out of the gables.

Conditions, economic and as a consequence moral, are very disheartening. Many farmers will not break even this year. Some may have to re-mortgage their small personal property to feed their cattle. Only 1 out of 10 own farms now. This last rain is negligible and avails nothing. Many people are going on relief. Hundreds of boys with a home-hungry look in their eyes and conscientiously at sea drift by with saddening monotony. Girls, bartering their charms for long rides, appear, eat, and disappear in droves. Lovely, plump, deflowered farm girls!

There is a definite tightening of belts and a closing of relative ranks before the onslaughts of the stork and the wolf. Poor deluded people. Hurling accusations, rasping the baser instincts, gossiping vitriolically! Had they enough money, the domestic treadmill would not squeak; let alone the fact that economic anarchy is basically the rodent undermining their lives.

And, too, then—this country with its press, libraries, radios, etc., communication and transport etc., with its versatility and natural fertility still contains a majority whose pretentions intellectually or purposefully scarcely transcend conversations concerning domestic details, fairs, scandal, murder, Hollywood, sport, jazz, and bizarre nondescript tidbits. I thought for a moment Nero's age had come back for a second run on the stage of the world's play-house when thousands gathered to see a woman sheriff hang a ne-gro. Race Hatred! Race pogroms! Spectacular! Especially when a few fought for relics from the dead man. And that first grade mo-ron who kissed Hitler. Bah! I would rather kick the coccyx of Myrna Loy.

We have the instructions from prescient masters! Yet, we have no collective action to train these otherwise virile, jubilant people.

I have been visiting Bill Frankena and Sadie [Roelofs] this past afternoon. We spent, or I did, four hours in Europe where they have been. They verify my statements of Hitler and Mussolini. Eerdmans[1] must have been blind. *Heraus mit dem Juden!* That, says Bill, is a very prevalent sign. They told very interesting stories. With Don [Stuurman], they got along on $670! Marvelous! Let's go! Really?

I do see something of Evelyn [Roelofs] occasionally. Ah, buxom maid! And some brains, too. We don't seem to affinitize very well. Mainly because she won't face issues, despises common people too much, is basically an opportunist, and has half-formed notions and fourth-molded actions of modernity—the Heming-wayish, Steinish, Matissish type.

Say, I've been glancing with half-blurred eyes at these few pages—I do believe that my script, if not legible, is at least uniform. Nicht wahr?

And oh yes. You can't definitely correspond on *that* condition? Why? Shall I presume to enumerate the reasons and Don Quix-otically vanquish them—as I have always done—and I am still here!

1. The family! Ah, yes, that is a point in practicality. Head-cocked, half-sidewise, askance I see it—but is that any of their busi-ness? You weren't asked when Mildred [Reitsema] had about as many duplicated triangles as Cleopatra had, were you? Don [Stuur-man], John, Hank [Zylstra], etc?

2. Ray? Well, you are not married yet. Until then, every mäd-chen is a wise dove on the wing above the snares of masculine at-tention. And if you were Xed by the hierophants of mystery or witchcraft wenders of sterile law (Justice-of-peace), cannot two inter-ested people help each other patch the quilt of unrolling events?

More importantly—I want you to write on the condition as I have outlined to you. I shall be very much provoked if you don't. And if the lightning strikes—well, we shall see if there was more than sulphur in the composition of one Frederick Feikema. As for miracles—you know I don't believe there are such "things", don't you.

I am sending you one or three of my recent poems.[2] Do you remember—

> A book of verses beneath the bough,
> A jug of wine, a loaf of bread—and thou
> Beside me singing in the wilderness—
> Ah—Wilderness were paradise enow!

Affectionately

How about stern criticism?
And—likewise—contributions of your own.

Frederick

2. The three poems—"Reliefer," "Farmer Gossip," and "Rationale"—all relate to Manfred's concern with the hazards of life during the depression.

1937

All but two letters in the extant correspondence for this year are addressed to John Huizenga. They detail Manfred's attendance at Nettleton Commercial College in Sioux Falls, his basketball playing there, and, by May, his job as sports editor at the Minneapolis Journal. *His reading this year is largely political and includes Lenin, John Reed, and Robert Briffault, the Marxist scientist and author of* Europa *(which Manfred calls "the best novel in the Twentieth Century"): The Marxist focus manifests itself in an important event in Manfred's life: the writing out of the story that will become his first novel,* The Golden Bowl. *By late August of 1937 he has written thirty-five thousand words and has gotten encouragement from writer Meridel Le Sueur.*

To John Huizenga

Box 366
Sioux Falls, S. Dak.
Sunday, at noon
[February 17, 1937]

Dear John,

What the hell? Have you lost speech? Has that sector of your brain medecinically described as the seat of writing ability been impaired by some castrophe? Or, does your reluctance in reciprocity reside in fact of my last riotous blast? If so, then forgive.

I cannot help but feel a definite vacancy of meaningfulness since your lack of correspondence. Your picture on my bookcase is a sorry substitute. But it reminds me that something is askew without your bi-annual missive. So this is to eluct a reply.

By the very nature of circumstances this letter will have to be brief. In a few hours I'm off to see my librarian on some important deal relating to my physical development. She is quite a woman. Probably the most interesting I've met because I cannot get serious about her in the old conventional manner. She excites me when I'm with her; when I'm separated from her, I find that I have suave thoughts of her mental quickness and her typical rubbery mind.

Since I wrote you of my good fortune to acquire a job, that job has again fallen apart. Two months ago, I was faced with starvation. Well, not that bad, since I *could* go home—which I certainly did not intend. Finally, the Managing Editor of the local daily arranged a scholarship for me at Nettleton's Commercial College where at present I'm taking shorthand, typing, penmanship, and vocabulary-spelling. It is quite easy. As a result, I've found much time on my hands to read and to investigate women—truly a neglect on my part heretofore. I'm beginning to realize your smile at my adolescence formerly, if not now. I see that I certainly was quite ignorant of their ways and means. That was mainly due to my blinded infatuation for Helen. Thank God, or so, that that is past.

I'm not sure if you heard of one exploit concerning which I must tell you. I know that the story was sent along to the headquarters of the AP located in Chicago. One night, two weeks after I started school, we played Freeman Junior College. For some reason this young man never felt as perfect physically as he did that night. One of those things—yes, it was that, and as a result I dumped in 57 points. I shall never forget the reactions of the opposing center. He tried to stop me, but after each point or two, he would come back to his post and say, "Goddamit, 47," "Goddamit, 49," etc.

I sent a few poems along to a new magazine called the *Midwest,* a Review—published by the Federated Artists and Writers Union of the middle west, a branch of the larger national federation. I understand that they have tentatively accepted them—payment on publication. As soon as I get word, I shall send you a copy. It is primarily left.

You wrote of your admiration for Norman Thomas. I too have admiration for many of the things that he does and thinks. But most of his mental thrusts are askew, to my way of thinking.

Especially does he dub on the question of a People's Front, or Farmer Union Party. He cannot understand the Communist position on that question. He actually believed that the Communists supported Roosevelt—which was a well-hatched lie of the capitalist press. I have investigated that matter, since you brought up that question, and nowhere in the Communist literature or speeches have I found a direct statement to that effect, or even the least hint. I did discover that the influence they brought to bear on Landon and the collection of the reactionaries rallying behind the latter's banner was of such a nature that many people shifted their vote to F.D.R.

Thomas has taken a peculiar stand on Trotsky and the executions in Russia. Before I read the letter I'm sending herewith, the arguments contained therein were quite clear and familiar to me. I suspect that you share, if you are interested at all, the sentiments of Thomas, since I gather from your former line of reasoning that you believe the trial to be a hoax, or least have some sentiment adverse to it. If you do not, it is a tribute that your reasoning is similar to Mauritz Hallgren, a former member of the Committee for the Defense of Leon Trotsky.

There are a number of interesting developments for my immediate future, the nature of which I'm not at liberty to divulge just now. I can tell you this. Last week, I hadn't had spending money for tobacco for a number of days. It happened that I had taken a voice test at the local radio station, and except for my tendency to orate, I was told that I had great possibilities to become a full-fledged announcer. Promptly I went to the owner.[1] I presented my case—also my present impecunity. I was on my way to the elevator when he called me back. He gave me ten dollars, requesting me that I must not reveal this to any one. Supplementary to that benefice he said, "When the new station opens next month, I'm sure that I'll have a job for you. I still have faith in humanity. That's the why of the ten."

That was very encouraging. Peculiarly, he is acquainted with left ideas—has in fact given time on the air to the Communist Ford and Browder. That set-up may have its possibilities.

I do hope that the clipping from *The New Masses* will not offend you, or my letter.

I do believe however, that you pass judgements on the Communists without thoroughly investigating their recent position on major questions. They have become awake—truly the vanguard of the proletariat as Marx said they should be, and as they were not during the early twenties.

1. Joseph Henkin. Three years later, while at Glen Lake Sanatorium, FM received a letter from Henkin telling him that he had the job.

And now, John, do write,
as ever with my fond regards,
frederick.

P.S. I have a new residence—628 W. 13th

To Helen Reitsema

[Minneapolis, Minnesota]
Tuesday Evening
[May 5, 1937]

Dear Helen,

I need not write that your letter was, to say the least, most welcome. Naturally, I should be lonesome, what with a strange city et al. I was too, so I was glad to grasp your outstretched hand. My brother Floyd is here. He is a sport prospect for the U. of Minn. in consequence of which they have given him a lucrative job whereby he can save money prefacing entrance to the U. next fall.

It is a strange sensation, this observing of Floyd now passing through those dubious and devious phases of being tall in the company of "just out-of-college-high-school students." Impulse suggests a too-helping hand, but I learned to wait for his queries— with the other equally responsible result that he is beginning to trust me too implicitly. He takes away much brusque ill-ease.

Then too. I've four boys or men in this house who are fairly intelligent fellows—although they are slightly too avid for bridge and should-be-brides.

No doubt you're all eyes and ears about this job of mine. You should be. Your Frederick has probably landed a position that shrugs responsibility as no other Calvinite could shiver. I'm a sports editor for one of the finest dailies in America—although it is Republican and carapacially conservative. (You should have heard the choice bit of conversation I heard this afternoon.)

My day begins at 8:00 o'clock. I do leg-work until lunch. From then until 2:30 I'm supposed to absorb atmosphere. At 2:30 I type out a dictated (from the ball field) play-by-play account of the Minneapolis *Millers* baseball team for the front page of the nite "Wuxtra."[1] I'm finished at 4:30. Five days a week—vacation (2 wks) with pay. Incidentally the American Newspaper Guild has a unit here. It is a newsman union.

How did I get the job? PULL, PERSONALITY, *ability*, *LUCK!*

I owe you an explanation! When I wrote that last confessional, it was the final bleating of a death-bed (not literal, now, Helen) yearn and a citadel of pride. It's all over now—evinced by my fe-

1. Extra.

male relationships during the winter. I regret to say, however, that if a lady is not my friend, she better use a gross dozen fans (you know those flattery fans of 1915) to protect her vicarious heart. Perhaps it (male-female magnet) is, was, will be always thus. The only reason I'll ever marry now—well, I might be a bit too explicit for our now-proximate and ideological friendship.

Is it all right now Helen?

Yes, I'm still writing—and well. I've been editing a book of poems which I'll send away a ½ year hence. I've thrown away most others. Then I've written countless stories and sketches for my novel (for 1939) besides a weekly column for the 4th estaters.

Jots——What wouldn't I give to hear either you or John [Huizenga] say, "Hell". . . . . Stob say, "Calvin College stands for". . . . . . Unctuosity is frothy . . . . Houseman say, "Let's go!" . . . . . . Jim Kos say, "Ah, there's an interesting evening!". . . . . . . Quick thoughts—Graveyard is a death-depot. . . . . Marion Dekker, the little girl who outrains Ivory Soap.

I'll send you a poem later—if you'll write me.

It's definitely understood? No more words?

May I PERTINENTLY suggest: Robert Briffault's EUROPA, *The Mothers,* REASONS FOR ANGER (A masterpiece of humor, wit, satire, and knowledge) and Dreiser in general?

> Yours,
> to the quick,
> Frederick

P.S. What do you say of my handwriting?

P.S.S. Incidentally, I set a world basketball record last winter— 57 points in one game!

To John Huizenga

[*The Minneapolis Journal* letterhead]
Home address:
628 14th Ave., S.E.
June 16, 1937

My dear John,

Your letter came to the office this morning, and now since the boys have gone out for lunch leaving me to answer telephones until they come back, I think I shall answer your letter immediately. I have much to tell you. We'll get down to the business of journalism first.

Frankly, I like it. I'm a bit of a muddlehead when it comes to correcting AP, UP, NEA, INT news stories. . . . somedays I remember the kinds of marks and instructions to typographers and on other days I don't. My greatest trouble is adaptation to this locality. I have so many names to learn, outside and inside, that once in a while everything is in a whorl. But tracks of good newspapering are being gradually beaten in those motor areas of my brain that form habits, and as Dick Cullum, Sports editor, told me, I have nothing to worry about as long as I continue to learn. He is a silent man, very seldom makes a comment;—in fact that was his only comment to me thus far. Halsey Hall, whom rival sports writers refer to as one of the greatest and most misplaced writers in the journalism game today, is the opposite. He talks, gesticulates, wisecracks, talks philosophy, mythology, culture, books, etc., drinks. . . . . in other words, I have two types before me after which I can formulate the type of action I may use later.

Coming back, I am not exactly satisfied in the sports department, if one remembers my other interests. I like it to the extent that I have no regrets or misgivings. I'd like to do leg work in the city room,—and without a doubt I may get my chance there after a year, when I have come to know this city better. As it is, perhaps this is the field where my writings would or can not fight with my beliefs. For that, I'm glad.

And oh, I feel that I've learned much. Of an evening after work, I sometimes spend two or three hours reclining on my bed, thinking, reviewing, wondering, analyzing, comparing, probing my mind for posts, faults, possible corrections,—in other words I have come to that stage of mental development where I'm taking stock of myself. And God (?) knows how late that arrived. There's a meaningful difference, I've come to learn, between musing and pondering.

A number of interesting angles came up during the past two weeks in connection with American Newspaper Guild which has a unit located in the *Journal*. Your reference to the CIO men in the letter reminded me of that fact.

Naturally, as soon as I heard about a union of newsmen, I was quite interested. I've followed Heywood Broun and his men of the Guild for months. However, I was afraid of making any open moves here until I got the lay of the land. I knew that if my immediate Sport head desired me to go against it, I have to, since he was extremely "put out" to get me this job. However, the Guild continued signing men, until they met and decided to lay specified demands before the publishers. The publishers shillyshallied until the

Guild decided to strike. A deadline was set. The boys in the office woke up. All of the sports writers had been members, but were behind in dues. The plan was then originated to pay up back dues, force a meeting of the *Journal* unit of the Guild, muster as many votes as possible and sabotage the Guild activity (a mutiny within ranks). Moreover, since the *Journal* unit [in conjunction with the *Star* and *Tribune* units with the tacit help of the St. Paul units (three)]¹ was the weakest in Guild strength, but the more dangerous since that action would throw the rest into confusion as they were dealing with their publishers also;—that act was highly traitorous according to the more politically and economically educated city room men. The air was tense—so were my nerves. I was in a devil of a pickle. The Guild was strong—very—yet I was almost obliged by intimation to go with the boys. But I knew that it was a movement (the act of these strike-breakers) that originated with the very highest paid men and who were instigated with the Managing editor by the publishers. Merle Potter, movie critic, declared that if we went on strike the labor unions would help us. Later, he declared, we'd have to picket with them, and by god (not in so many or unelegant words) he was not going to do that and he was "too big" a man for that. I had a number of men here as friends who knew about things and who trusted me. I said in a whisper, "Doesn't he realize in the first place that he is a wage-earner as well as the gravedigger? Secondly, can't he think outside that halo around his head? Hasn't he any human sympathy?" The friend mentioned that to Potter's discomfort. Later, when they proposed to send a new committee with new demands, Potter and my immediate boss mentioned that most of us didn't know the demands the guild was making. Weren't we damn fools to strike without knowing why we struck? (The premise or background is: very few ever attended Guild meetings.) Thus the "old minority or few" argument was thrown out. We, the loyal, we being dictated to by the few! I mentioned publicly (it took a lot of guts and maybe I was foolish at that), "What the hell is this? We're going to ask new demands when we don't know the others? Perhaps we like them. We can't protest, even, against them." That set the boys back a bit too. The thing fizzled out finally. Only, I'm quite a guy in the eyes of the Guild men, and since it is strong now, I'm not worrying. There have been no repercussions in my office. . . . everybody treats me okay.

Finally the publishers came to an agreement. They admitted

they were licked with a strong union town to remember as an important item in the background in case a strike had been called. Among the things achieved are: exclusive bargaining rights as agents for employees, 5% increase in salaries if the new minimum established is below one's wages. Otherwise, the minimum goes into effect. I benefitted by the latter. I get a $100 a month now. The 5% would not have raised the $78 a month to that figure. Again, because the Guild recognizes (at least here) any form of newspapering, I may get credit for a year's work with the *Prospector* since it was located in a town larger than 25,000 people. A technical point!

If that happens to be the case, I'll get $110 a month. Marvelous! Then, there is the 40-hour week, the onus of breaking contract fixed legally upon the publishers since the Guild merely voted to rescind the strike vote and going on record as not having approved or disapproved the new settlement.

About that visit. Most of the fellows are having vacation. I doubt if I can get away just now. I'll speak to my boss about changing Saturday's work to a Thursday of before or after, thus giving me three days. Friday and Sunday are my days off! However, because of the new agreements, I get a week's vacation with pay after six months. That means that this young man can take a week off in November with pay. Perhaps we could arrange for a Thanksgiving weekend. I shall let you know. You must correspond more regularly, at least for the sake of some gadding that we might have.

Love life? Well, not much. I'm not interested in women as I have been. Perhaps because I don't know suitable people. Besides, it takes money. Oh yes, I've had a few dates, one wild party in which I got a bit inebriated with the result that I had a marvelous evening dancing with every available woman on the floor. I bought a radio and after seeing *Maytime, Forever Yours,* and other movies of like nature, my nerves or mind has a tendency (damnit) to romanticize again. I'm now looking for a woman of charm and musical talent. My old girl friend of Sioux Falls is now visiting in Chicago, not here as she promised. Tch. Tch.

Flash: Wally and Windsor celebrated their night of the wedding by drinking. She pulled out her 40-year port and Windsor indulged in cider.

I've been working like hell on my poems again. I took the ideas of the old poems, that is, the better ideas, revised, rewrote, criticized (I'd ask, what the hell is that word here for, or that idea, or that sentiment, or emotion)—all this—until I believe I've done some fairly good work.

Meanwhile, this work here is teaching me technique, care, speed, choice of words (unfortunately, you must allow leeway in this letter, because I notice upon rereading that some passages are obscure) and it gives me invaluable association with some brilliant men in and outside this department.

I suppose that school will be a fine thing for you. You can always step back into the harness. Yes, you should have been working at your new job long before. . . . . . . Well, as for me, I can learn enough facts from my extensive reading. What I need is accuracy. I'd never get that in school. There is no deadline or other demands. Here there are. I need them badly. And as you say, this is a suitable outlet for temperaments of our sort. . . . and a respectable outlet.

I've been purchasing new clothes. I believe that I'm adequately and comfortably clothed now. I must get some of my debts paid soon. And I'll send my $5.00 debt to you some time in the fall. . . . when you'll need it most. And John, my sincere greetings on your 23rd birthday (23rd?).

I have an insatiable longing for mountains lately . . . Which was swelled into a great hunger since I saw *Lost Horizon*.

And, can there be anything wrong with a world that witnesses constantly the growing of sprouts in the field, their unfurling in the wet dampness of the morning and the heat of the day, the crack-ing of corn in the night in its eager haste to stretch out great arms of green towards the sun the next dawn?

> I miss you immensely, just now,
> and constantly.
> fondly,
> frederick

P.S. I'm sending a feature I wrote. I've had five accepted!

To John Huizenga

[Minneapolis, Minnesota]
Tuesday Afternoon
Aug 27, 37

My dear John,

This letter will be written in installments. The immediate receipt of it started off a chain of reflections that I'm eager to get down on paper.

Isn't it strange that as soon as I get a letter from someone, I im-mediately imagine just what I'm to write them?

Just let me in the same ring with you and I'll repay you for those barren two months. Just wait.

Those same two months constituted my summer. And it has
been my best. The first month of the 1934 summer was somewhat
similar. Although I used most of my money to pay off old debts
and to purchase new clothes, I've always had a safe margin for enjoyment. There have been evenings of night baseball (the Minneapolis Millers), concerts (pop symphonies where one could relax,
talk, drink high-balls, dream, loaf), long drives with my house-
mate's car (Ralph Craft, an amiable graduate student of the U.
whose mind is slow but accurate, whose humor is deep and tips
over spilling into others, whose big-heartedness is as large as ideal-
ists want it to be), lovely summer evenings on the foot-bridge over
the Mississippi, books to read, radio programs, a soft bed, long
hours of sleep, long hours of discussion with half-cracked artists,
dancers, poets, aesthetes, radicals, psychologists, assistant profs
that float in and out of this town, dates with good and bad women,
dates with a tall girl by the name of Lucie Lawson who is the state
secretary of the International League for Peace and who is being
considered for the position as regent of the local U., who is a pian-
ist and reader and who is fairly good-looking and well-shaped and
sensitive and radical.

All very interesting. One just drifts through it all. Upon examination, one finds that the mind has been tempered and solaced,
but not exactly improved as to sharpness.

And then, the book. The book.[1]

Well, John, I don't know just how to write about that. Perhaps
I should wait another month before I describe it to you. I can, however, comment on my reactions.

And those of others.

I started writing it about June 15. I told myself that it was for
the fun. And the practice. There was nothing to be said about its
future. Just write on it whenever I felt like it.

You see, I had the idea in mind for three years, ever since I
jaunted to Yellowstone in the late summer of 1934. I met two people
on that trip that impressed me. Man and woman. They said they
were married and that they were hitch-hiking for their honeymoon.

Later, there came the idea to use the man and the woman as the
structure of a story that essentially described the mental makeup
of bums, hoboes, hitch-hikers and the like. Again later, I decided
that there were many boys and girls traveling and drifting from
place to place who were not exactly at fault for the position they

1. This venture later became
The Golden Bowl, published
in 1944.

were in, but that if one knew of circumstances, the whole story would be altered.

Gradually, I got around to taking notes in odd moments; rides on streetcars, walks, talks with people, overheard conversations, etc. About June 15, I decided that I was ready.

Well, there are about 35,000 words. I rehashed it many times. Toyed with it. Played with it. Fondled it. Rewrote whole passages. Then, I submitted it to Meridel Le Sueur, left-wing critic of note. (I had met her on one of these parties and subsequently had dinner dates with her—35 years old).

She met me later. She said, as I came to her table in the Stockholm cafe, "May I go along with you to Europe next summer?"

"Whaaat?"

"Yes. You can go, you know."

I sat down. I tried to keep the table still.

"Yes, Frederick." She pointed to the MS. "It's powerful. It should outrank and outsell John Steinbeck's *Of Mice and Men*. Of course, that's my idea. The prospective public is fickle and they may not do just that."

My face was very red. Altogether in one guey lump I remembered my farm days, college days, basketball days, my days with you, my fumblings with writing before, my awkward handling of ideas and facts . . . . . no . . . . . no . . . . . she was just kidding.

"Well, afterall, Meridel, I haven't had dinner. I may be just a bit light-headed. That's why I'm not laughing at your . . . your joke."

She looked at me gravely. Such a young, embarrassed kid, she thought, I betcha.

Then she proceeded to enumerate faults, corrections, agents, all these without a charge.

And I proceeded to find out later, "What kind of critic could she be?" They tell me that she never gives favorable criticisms unless they are meant. She has been in jail for her honesty.

Others were of the same opinion, about her. About the book.

Then I gave it to an old died-in-the-wool conservative, newspaper book critic and reviewer. She shook her head at the structure, but admitted that since it was a running narrative describing four days, it had its virtues in that respect. She revolted against the sex scenes and the Farrellistic language. She praised the conversation highly. She liked the character of the boy immensely, but the girl was weak (??????). She said I had much work left with it. She wondered about the idea behind it but thought the last few pages of the boy's philosophizing the very best. So she was careful.

Frankly, I'm in a muddle. I don't know how to take it. It's too immense. I get so much advice: leave this out, leave it in; alter that, rearrange this, etc. I have argued about that damn thing for six hours straight with a married woman, Lucie [Lawson], Meridel, an assistant professor, a biologist, and old mother, [Ralph] Craft, a cynic, an aesthete, and a sloppy Red—all in one session. And the discussion was furious.

I have laid it aside for a week and intend to grab it in my big hands again sometime this week. I'll fix it finally just the way I want it—with the aid of the help, of course.

I do know this. I shall not be disappointed if it is lousy afterall. I've had too many knocks in the past. Too many of my dreams have remained dreams. I remember too, your very likable and stable calm in the midst of all such matters.

That has been my greatest benefit from you. Although I know that you've got the same failings and virtues in the field of emotion.

I'm glad to hear that you've finally found a purpose in journalism. That's swell. Apparently you have had the rare opportunity to get the real job that does exist in that field. I can see, moreover, that going to school will be great also. And that trip to Europe? Outside the other consideration above, I've been planning to go next year too. I have wondered a few times in the past if I shouldn't write to you about it, but I considered it too fanciful for my letter!

Friday.

Now that I've reread my first five pages and your letter, I feel that I should make some comment on your description of newspapering. Every day I'm becoming more aware of the ramifications in the machinery that produces newspapers. I'm beginning to feel that I want a chance later on—into the city room, and later on, state jobs.

I'm learning the technique of desk work and make-up problems and the importance of accuracy while under pressure. Each day, my boss gives me more responsibilities; to which no reference is made except in the case of a gross error. There is the immediate feel of pride—which later dribbles off into dreary routine. The point is, the material I'm handling has no significance for me. I want to be in the spot where really vital news is brewing. And there is a lot of it here.

You hear of the Farmer-Labor party in this state, of course. Well, John, this is no heaven for liberals. On the contrary, the gains of the F-L are temporary. They have won despite. . . . despite this and that. And I feel that if I were in a reportorial position to witness the basic moves, I'd find out just what means the conservatives are using to circumvent the liberal gains.

Take for instance. In the recent mayoralty election, Leach, an army general and a rabid conservative, won by a wide majority over Kennie Haycraft, who is F-L, liberal, educated and was an All-American in football. He had everything, one would say. Well, the Communists came out with two special editions of *The Daily Worker* (by the way, that is a new technique of the Reds, to throw in local news with the regular news in a special locally printed edition), came out strongly for Haycraft. They published photographs of Haycraft, Stalin, and Browder side by side. [Missing material].

1938

Early in 1938 Manfred experiences at firsthand the problems of trying to get published. Although Modern Age, Inc., "publishers of books with a radical tinge," tentatively accept the early version of The Golden Bowl, *they shortly announce their intention to publish no more fiction. By May, Manfred is deep into research on Iowa government and politics in order to do a fuller revision. The year's work at the* Journal *he calls "one of the most educational years of my life."*

To John Huizenga

[Minneapolis, Minnesota]
January 4, 1938

Dear John,

You're probably busy preparing for examinations by this time. Hence, I'll shall exercise some leniency. Working on the strength of your request that I should let you know any news about the book, here's the latest dope.

I have an offer.

But, I don't think I'll take it. . . . . just yet. It's from Modern Age Inc., publishers of books with a radical tinge—e.g., *The Labor Spy Racket* by Leo Huberman, some Russian stories by Duranty, a book by the leftist Bruce Minton, etc. They intend to sell their cheap $.35 editions to the working man, or the farmer, or the depressed, or oppressed, howeverwhichway you want it.

Remembering the above for background, here then is what he said, to quote a few phrases: "Your book shows promise. Your characters are good. You handle the stream of consciousness effect very ably. Your writing flows swiftly. And you have content. But, you shouldn't hold back your punches. You should write more convincingly and more strongly. Make your statement stronger. As a result, you show a bit of immaturity. I suggest that you rewrite it with that in view (He means the conclusion) and we'll go to town on it." It was signed by Editor Kirk, the big chief of Modern Age Inc. The letter was rather long and windy, evidently typed by himself, since the steno's earmarks weren't on it and it had five grammatical mistakes.

Now the point is, just what precisely does he mean? I gather from the above-mentioned background that he wants a closed-fist solution at the end to present to his particular audience black and white effects. If that is the case, just now, I can't quite see where that is art . . . . if one still has any feeling of pride about his work. I don't like didacticism. I merely let the characters through their acting and stumbling thinking suggest the idea that they can't be the rugged Frederic's of *Farewell to Arms* but that they must work with people in groups or what not to realize their individuality to the fullest extent. The individual and the group would be retroactive.

Bess Wilson, *Journal* book critic, suggests that I send it to a few more, before thinking of the change in conclusion.

However, if the whole point isn't the conclusion, but is just a general feeling that I'm immature, well, that sort of cancels any encouragements I may have derived from the letter.

Because, for one thing, I can't figure out just where I'm immature. His letter suggested certain spots as being that. People here, with fairly discerning minds, haven't mentioned any such leopardic characteristics. Neither can Bess Wilson.

Well, I'm out for dinner. I thought you might be interested.

sincerely,
frederick

P.S. Also, in order to preserve the framework (four-days running story) I can't very well have a six-months addition which tells the story of his new belief and practice of it. Otherwise, his conversion would be greatly nigh unto religion.

To John Huizenga

[Minneapolis, Minnesota]
Thursday, waiting for
3rd run
March 23, 1938

Dear John:

In a few moments, I'll be outdoors again where the sun is. I've never hungered so much for anything in a long spell. My body craves it just like one's saliva can crave shrimp cocktail.

There's just two of us in the office just now. I decided to start a letter and finish it later in the evening. Or tomorrow, since it is my day off.

This week end I intend to accomplish much reading. As if I haven't always been reading. My eyes are getting very sore again, so I suppose I'll have to go back to the rim and ribbon days. God, how I hate those extra appurtenances. They're a nuisance.

Your letter comes to mind.

There are two notes and tones in it that I believe I should elaborate on. Just to give you an indication of my mental state.

You mention, "By God, kid, here you are faced with a good chance to get published and you can't because the stuff isn't pink enough." Or some such words to that effect.

There is some truth to their criticism, however. Afterall, I'm just a beginner. And I was a bit stubborn. Two or three people here, eminently Jim Shields,[1] an elderly man with the NLRB [National Labor Relations Board], thought it damn good but the end inconclusive. I didn't need any flag waving, he said, but at least don't let the guy and the girl stay in the vacuum of the hobo world. Put them into the world of the so-called decent people who have jobs. And show what happens to them when they get there.

Well, hell, I did protest a little. Afterall, I did the work and I should know the intrinsic unity of the thing. I had a notion that it should remain an indictment of the system that permits bums, and as such it should describe only their life, even though it is only about just two people in the main.

But there was an argument in their criticism, as well as the company's. And afterall, their public is the type that demands some sort of solution, even though it isn't exactly told. And a writer is not a good writer if it doesn't reflect the kind of life that people know and then recognize when they read stuff.

Hence, I did change it.

I entered Maury and Jo into the Gold Mine life of the Black Hills. Just three days. Events move fast. And the only and possible criticism (that is worthwhile criticism) can be that the story was

1. Author of *Just Plain Larnin'*.

mainly functional, psychological in the main at first. . . . . now, it has a great deal of action in the last 40 pages. Which is a sort of a mixture. However, I tried to keep as much of the action in the person of Maury, the boy.

He gets a swell welcome.

I remembered a scene from my childhood. I used it. I saw a man tarred and feathered one day because he had been a bit too wilful in his attentions to women outside of his immediate harem. That was a gruesome sight, and a memory. And I used it here. And, actually, they do treat workers that rough over in the Black Hills where good old bitchy willie hearst has a hand in most of the activity and life and policies.

Thus, it still remains a story of just two hitch-hikers.

The story has been sent off a week now. If they don't take it, well, I'll just concentrate on something else for awhile. Shields and Le Sueur said not to worry if it didn't get published for ten years. It has that much worth. It isn't tied down to a certain year or two. (Well, time to go. See you in a few hours.)

Monday evening prior to a Guild meeting.

Well, the few hours have swollen to a few days. But, it doesn't matter.

Latest flash on the book situation: quote from Louis P. Kirk's letter, president of the Modern Age Inc., Publishers of Seal Books—"Sometime ago we received from you a revised edition of your manuscript entitled, *Of These It Is Said*. We have read this new version with considerable interest, and it is quite apparent that you have made a decided improvement. Some of the taint of immaturity has been removed."

"I am afraid the situation here is a little different now. We have recently set up a full program for the next twelve months, and it appears that we shall be in no position to take on new manuscripts unless they are of extremely unusual character, preferably non-fiction. Naturally this has modified our approach to many competent pieces of work like your own, and we are obliged to discourage consideration of the book this year. I do believe you have done a good job and would suggest that you give serious thought to resubmitting it to some of the publishers here in town. . . . . ." Unquote.

Two days before this letter arrived, I received an ominous warning that the next correspondence from them would be negative.

A local book dealer had heard from them that the company had had poor success with new authors. They have switched to non-fiction of the [missing material].

To Helen Reitsema

[Minneapolis, Minnesota]
1119 6th Street
(new address after
September 1.)
24 Aug 38

Dear Helen,

I too wish to see you again, if only to get your views on the world and its inhabitants.

No, I changed my plans for my vacation this summer. I used a cabin in the north woods, near the Canadian line, north of Duluth. It was near a brook which cascaded toward the Superior Lake from the bluffs north of the cabin. There were pools to swim in and to fish in. I didn't see a soul for five days and during that time, except when it was cold in the morning, I didn't wear any clothes. That was marvelous. I did quite a lot of writing, some reading, but more. . . . I slept as long as I wished. I've never enjoyed life as full as I did then.

Now that I've come back, I've begun to realize how damn futile it is to work for the concern like the *Journal*. One's initiative becomes corroded with falsity. The place reeks with gluttony. Newspapering is a racket and the managing editor and all the boys with their hands in the money know it and play the game accordingly. But then, we must have "the freedom of the press."

I gag, sometimes at the idyllic bliss people, even yourself, live in without ever knowing what the score is. You protest and strut in your narrow way. . . . to be sure, millions of others and also myself. . . . that you are so important and that the things you fight for are so worthwhile. And then, when one can witness a Bishop and a highly regarded minister dip their fingers in the blood and the flesh and the souls of people and relish it with blood dripping from their cavernous mouths. . . . . ah, woman, it is sickening. And an intellectual becomes a raving beast of revenge and justice.

I read and reread that letter of yours to find the unwritten things about yourself. Little phrases have long wind and they tell me that that fine little mind of yours has not got the fire it once had.

You say I write brutally. Helen, you know how much I love to think and feel and live in fine things. Give me a world where such things are possible, where there isn't discrimination just for the satisfaction of the rich (which the Bible says will always be), where a soul can swim forever (life's span) in healthy fulsome living. I can write thus. But there is much to be done. And I, for one, am not going to sit idly by until the whole world and my bursting spirit is smothered beneath the sword of profit and the feather bed of smugness.

Do you suppose that with my love for music, for poetry, for excellent wit, good food, fine people, for brooks, green pine and the smell of alsike fields I would deliberately write of such "sour facts?" Without a reason?

Today, I spoke to a fine old man [Morrison], 37 years in the newspaper trade, once managing editor with *The Cleveland Plain Dealer, The Detroit Free Press,* on the editorial staff of *The N.Y. Times*. Today, he has quit. He said he would not work in a swamp of miasma, in the everglades of foul life. He was through. He asked me, "Why do newsboys drink? And drink the way they do, getting out of sight, living alone until the binge is finished? There's a reason, son. Because they know they live a life of falsity."

Well, it didn't take me long to find out. I know what they do to a certain Governor Benson. No, I'm not speaking of sex immorality, or high living. . . . no, I speak of robbing the people . . . robbing them of bread and shelter . . . but more importantly, years of their life and thousands of years, immeasurable years of meaningful existence.

Oh God. And then you listen to those religious detectives searching for lost souls. . . . when there are no souls to find because our present society will not allow souls to develop or exist. Ridiculous. Oh my God. Listening to pompous fools who go around encouraging God in their long prayers. I choke with human mortification.

But then, we are a democratic people, loving life, liberty, and property (debt receipts and silly back payment notices). We live here for God. . . . . and the rich.

The rich. Poor fools. They aren't so bad. It's the system that does the evil. And then they presume to tell us about Russia. I know about that news. I see it come in. . . . already emasculated and further emasculated. . . . and sometimes mislaid if favorable. Why? Because the monopolists (advertising) won't let it out. Yeah, it's a swell world, and we should not get hasty, because afterall, haste makes waste, and besides, how do we know if we are doing right? Let's make of doubt and hesitation a principle and meanwhile we can have our lovely hours of soft and non-sexual meditation and our beautiful, scarlet moments of ponderings on this world. . . . . we don't know what the score is, so let us muse about our lovely moods and the why of it all and the charming festivity of the abstract Blaue Henein. Sure.

Bah.

Today, some kids swiped my wallet with a half month's salary in it out of my car. I was angry for a moment. . . . and at the kind of living that absolutely produces such characters. And after a while, I cried. Yes, poor souls. I felt sorry for them. They must live. Who knows? Perhaps they thought they were robbing a rich bastard. They were; only, not the kind of richness they sought. And if they would have waited, they would have got, not a curse, a policeman, a cell, a life of misery, or a good solid punch, no. . . . not these, but a long ride in my car and a long talk and then something constructive to help them.

But enough.

The publishers tell me that my stuff is not publishable. (They know that my book is a bold crack on their necks in the long run.) The political thing is just finished. It is to be out sometime in the latter part of September, unless something happens. Modern Age will do the trick. I had a devil of an argument with the collaborators, who refused to use my stuff as I had written it. It was too stylistic and too tough. Well, I let them emasculate it, because in the long run I must get started.

I have found a very lovely girl. . . a Jean Danielson. Young, unbelievably well formed, smart, tall, blond, seventeen, radical, daughter of conservatives who don't know what to think of me, and she writes. . . . even in *The Atlantic Monthly* (won high school poem contest) . . . or has. Probably won't now, what with her radical ideas. Had 'em before I found her. Quite a story how I met her. I don't know about love, little skeptical of that. But we like the same things and she can play a piano. I'm convinced if one is to give the "permanent thing" a chance, one should "comrade" with a similar soul. I like her. And she—for once—me.

My fire?

It shall never die. You ought to see my farm novel. It has tons of dynamite. When it explodes over the literary horizons, I shall be hated with terrific venom and loved—as well,

Yours,
Fred
Write!!!!

1939

Job frustration continues to be a problem for Manfred in 1939. In January, he is fired from the Journal *because of his activities with the Newspaper Guild. He is hired by Governor Harold Stassen to check relief rolls in the Duluth area, finds no evidence of cheating, and is fired when he returns to the Twin Cities. His romance with Jean Danielson is brought to an end by her parents, who forbid her to see him because of his liberal politics, his journalistic background, and his size. The long period of unemployment provides Manfred with the opportunity to work in earnest on what will become his first and third novels,* The Golden Bowl *and* This Is the Year.

To Jean Danielson

[April 19, 1939]

Dear Jean,

Today I saw the famous ghost town of the range. The name is North Hibbing. The geologists discovered that a great lode of iron lay beneath the city and for the past four or five years they have been confiscating the homes above it and now have issued a mandate that all houses for the space of four blocks long and about ten wide should be vacated and moved before two months are past.

Of course, not much will be lost from a housing standpoint inasmuch as most of these homes are in terrible condition. But, they were homes for the poor unemployed people. Now they must move and there is no place to find in the more swankier districts of Hibbing.

There is only one occupation here. That is mining. And since that is very seasonal, and sometimes not that, they have nothing else to do. Hundreds of young people are literally going to the dogs here, morally and physically. And the old people, desperate and lost, tell their children, whom they really love, to get out and shift for themselves. Now, the youngsters have learned that if they get married they can get on WPA. And thus they marry. Which they should . . . . but think of the unwholesomeness.

1. Civilian Conservation Corps.

Today, they were taking in many CCC[1] boys because the army is taking in hundreds of men. And since the war is near, these CCC boys will automatically be considered good material for some fascist bomb.

The relief problem here is much different than it is down south: in the cities, in mid-Minnesota, and in south-Minnesota.

On the other hand, this country is picturesque and so are the people, despite in the first case that lumbering beetles have chewed off the best lumber and in the second case that the mining interests have restricted educational opportunities.

On the basis of sheer guts I got the Oliver Mining Company to let me down in one of their great open pits. They did this very reluctantly. They buzzed and whispered and telephoned and inter-office-memoed each other to death but finally, the big smiling relief guy[2] got an engineer and a geologist to go down with him. They were almost stupefied when I asked to be let down in the great underground mines. That was the last straw. They hemmed and hawwed until I thought they would saw their tongue through their collars.

Finally I said, "Well, you know there are a lot of crackpots coming through here and you must be careful of them. I can understand." They nodded hurriedly, embarrassedly, and relievedly.

Someday, I shall get down in there.

And there is a great book to be written from this territory. A great book. When we get established, we shall spend some time here. Or, if not you, at least me. I should disguise myself and work in the mines for two or four months.

This whole territory seems to be speaking in whispers: so much so that I've gotten the habit of looking over my shoulder every few minutes.

And Aubrey [McEachern], who has been through here three years, is finding new things and is amazed at the questions I ask people.

I understand that the Reorganization Bill has passed. I just wonder what'll happen to me then. They did one good thing though. They passed a new marriage bill and it has the governor's signature. You know, 21 and 18. Of course, we're not interested.

And can I have a letter in Duluth this weekend?

Always and always, the same as ever,
love,
frederick

2. Manfred had a temporary job with the state relief agency.

To Floyd Feikema

[Cleveland, Ohio]
Wednesday night
July 2, 39

1. Robert E. Grant, Paul
Rochette, and Thomas
Duncan. Written in John
W. Huizenga's rooms
on FM's return from New
York, where he tried to
place *Of These It Is Said*
[FM's note].

Dear folks (Bob, Paul, Tom, Floyd):[1]

Let me briefize the letter by making a number of observations:

1. I'll be home Sunday night between 10 to 12 p.m.

2. I'll be flat broke with the chance that my unemployment insurance will be delayed for four weeks. Thus, the commissariat of ways and beans should make proper altercations with neighbors who own gardens.

3. I understand that R.E. "Sherman" Grant cut an 80-mile swath across my divan during my absence. There is no objection except that I will tolerate no carpet bags in lieu of clean sheets and a spick and span contour unless I'm Boothed elsewhere! In other words, I expect a clean evacuation thus enabling me to get a good night's rest since Monday morning I've about three appointments, the 1st at 8 a.m.

4. I have obtained no advance!

5. I expect to hold two quick conferences: with Paul and with Floyd.

1940

Although there are but four letters available from 1940, three of them are very important in exploring Manfred's artistic consciousness in the early years: a lengthy letter to Louis Dwight Cole of the Macmillan Company protests the publisher's rejection of an early version of This Is the Year. *A letter to Ray and Helen (Reitsema) Vander Meer also focuses on Manfred's writing, explaining the rejection of his novels as "too much farm tragedy." A third important letter is written in December to* Poetry *editor Peter DeVries. It is sent from Glen Lake Sanatorium in Oak Terrace, Minnesota, where Manfred had been admitted in April with a severe case of tuberculosis.*

To Lois Dwight Cole

507 Oak Street, S.E.
Minneapolis, Minn.
Feb. 3, 1940

My dear Lois:

As you may guess, the rejection distressed me considerably. I was confident that this time I had hit the mark. I still am. And this

1. The Macmillan Company.

letter is an attempt to answer the charges which your company's[1] reviewer leveled against me.

The charges are quite serious. Thus, I'm going to spend some time answering them. I haven't worked at my writing all these years to permit someone living in New York, far away from the scene of my writing and my living, to condemn it to the ash heap or my files with a mere flip of a brain.

But, before we begin in a paragraph-by-paragraph analysis, I must asseverate that I thoroughly appreciate your kindness, your attempt to understand me and to help me. I also appreciate your confidence in me to pass on the remarks of the reviewer or the critic. Your intentions are clean. You wish to help. And later in the letter, I shall explain just how they've helped.

The critic mentions in the first paragraph that this is not the "first-class" novel I'm capable of producing. Well, I know that *This Is The Year*[2] is not my best novel. I know that better than anyone else. Ten years from now, maybe, we'll have one out. But, this guy will never admit that it is a first-class novel because his criteria are subjective. It'll be great for different reasons than he wants. It'll be great because it will record the happens of people more real than I have depicted thus far, or for that matter Steinbeck, or anyone, including Shakespeare or Tolstoi, or who have you. But the kind of book he wants will have to depict people that live in a vacuum.

2. First draft.

In the second paragraph we can skip all observations except the remark that Laura never becomes alive. Yet the critic has the guts to say in paragraph four that Laura would not, of all people, have found herself in the difficulty described in the "crash" ending. That statement means she is alive. And if I have described her as having that quality, then she has become real. And as to the other remark in paragraph two that my characters are not fully developed, I can only say that is a matter of opinion. Random House, who saw the second copy and who rejected the book for the exactly the qualities your critic praises, made the remark that the only good thing about the book were the memorable characters. And they never breathed Steinbeck. Nor for that matter, did the critic of yours who read the first hundred pages.

In paragraph three, we come to the most serious charge, that I am like Steinbeck in the handling of the sex lives of the people. Now, I resent that. Christ, Steinbeck, for all his good points, is inaccurate there. In fact, he does a lousy job. Take for example his major characters. Tom, Ma and Pa, and in the book, Casey (who was a hound before the book opens) never seem to look at the opposite sex. Except for the time Tom raped a whore when he left jail, he never thinks of or looks at sex. He runs through the danged book like a Christ. Ma never has silly moments. Neither does Pa, who has obviously reached the age where he should be childish and a bit foolish with women. Casey, after the book starts, never fusses with women either. And never in God's green earth can anyone ever prove that these people never are silly and giddy with respect to sex. Besides the self-preservation drive in us, sex is the next most potent and most important. Acts that seem to us most unsexed, are in actuality therefore most sexed, in an abreacted form. Now, every dang one of my characters, Pa with his widows, Hank with Laura and Bertha, Hank with Bertha's sister, Granpap with his granddaughters, every one, has a foolish moment at one time or other. . . . . and that is far more realistic and accurate than Steinbeck portrayed. As a matter of fact, these last five years, I have cut whole acres of sex out of my writing because I felt I had to conciliate a bit to the ignorant intellectuals and to the self-opinionated commoners who might read the book. Now your critic says that copying is all right in itself, but it is not integrated with the rest of the story. Apparently he does not want to believe that people are that way. I merely set it down, distilled a bit for the sake of the prudish, as I saw it. Not as Steinbeck related his story, or for that matter, anyone else's. He says further, that I gritted my teeth and loosened my trousers, so to speak, and gave them a whiff of pubic aroma. Hell, that is false. I have a feeling that Steinbeck is a dodo with respect to his sex. Study his books, if you please, Mr. Critic. He says further that Ol' Granpap is straight out of Steinbeck. Now, in the name of heaven, may I die if mine is like his. Steinbeck's Granpa is a jumpy, bumptious, rebellious old fool, wonderfully portrayed to be sure, but he isn't Dutch, as mine is, and he doesn't have a meagre philosophy of life, like mine has. The fact that I gave Ol' Granpa the job of epitomizing the plight of his kin and neighbors is because he has the experience and the emotional background and the brains and the dignity to do it properly. And, furthermore, it just happens that Laura is almost exactly my own mother who died in 1929 and Old Granpap is exactly my own grandfather, the man who, to give you an example of his funniness, offered me a nickel when I was a kid to sneak up on my mother and pinch her backsides. And my grandfather was a marvelous old father, who had left religion, who was against all forms of law, from an experience-philosophic standpoint. Hank, of all people, is partly myself and my uncle. Pa Bramstedt is my own father, bless his soul.

Now what are the facts of my knowledge of Steinbeck? Three years ago, I read *Of Mice and Men*. Last April, I bought a copy of *Grapes of Wrath,* and read it, and since then I haven't seen the book because my wide circle of friends are reading it. Now I have always fought with those smug bastards in town here who derail his book. He is marvelously accurate in a good many things. I have purposely refrained from attacking his weak points because they were rather forcedly shoved at me in the first place. Why, when I read that book, I gnashed my teeth because he had used so many things that I had intended to use. He recites innumerable stories and wisecracks in it that I had used when I was still on the farm. And last fall, August and September, I was constantly on the alert for anything that would resemble him, and still remain accurate to the people I knew. I had a devil of a time. The point is that both he and I have been damn good reporters . . . and if the critic with a good many others does not believe that such people exist in the middle west, a territory that has never had the justice it should have had in literature, I should like to inform that critic that these hands of mine, these scars of mine have come because conditions like that do exist. And I lived merely in the land of Iowa where things aren't as bad as the dust bowl. I should also like to tell him that the misfortunes of a farmer are damned important things, because I'm not dealing with a minority, but a majority. The average level of farm tenantry in the entire country wavers slightly below 45%, taking the average of the most conservative and radical estimates. And this percentage does not include the great group of farmers who have a nominal title to the farms they live on but whose mortgages make them live more meagrely than the tenant. Actually, the number of farmers who own their own land free of mortgages and who make a good living amounts to less than 20% of the total number of farmers. AND THE ACTUAL acreage of rented farms exceeds fifty percent in the entire country. In other words, this story wasn't intended to be a silly little parlor story of horror and melodrama. It was intended in some respects to be the story of real people living in real conditions . . . . . . What the critic tried to say was that I borrowed Steinbeck's characters. Hell, as a matter of fact, Steinbeck doesn't do as good a job of reporting as I did. Nor, does he know them as well as I did. For example, he never did handle the religious angle of farming communities accurately. He never described how the old order of living, with its highly intensified bigotry and religious zealotry, is slowly breaking up under the growing indifference of the younger generation who have been influenced on the one hand by the new and rapid communicating systems, radio, car, newspaper, and on the other, have been able to see the falsity of borrowed gods of religion. . . . who now, as Hank was attempting to do, and as Li'l Hen and his aunts, Jessie, Jennie and Hattie, and also Herm, are building their own faiths and beliefs that will be indigenous to the soil and to their lives. The critic, as well as Steinbeck, missed that. Thus, the points where Steinbeck and I happen to touch are points so unmistakably universal that if either one of us didn't write them down, we would and could be classified as literary liars. Why, the critic is trying to say that Steinbeck's people are figments of a dour imagination.

Now, it is true that Steinbeck has influenced me. But for none of the reasons that the critic said he did. I have been afraid that it would have come to my attention before. I will tell you. Before, I was highly introspective in my writing and very flowery. Steinbeck taught me to be direct and to be simple. As yet, I haven't mastered that art. When I do, then I'll have a good chance to produce, to my mind, the great novel. Implication? Well, most novels nowdays are lousy. But mine is probably least lousy. Someday it won't be. And if I'm accused of copying Steinbeck's majestic simplicity, I accept it with feelings of pride and justification. Further, look through the whole history of literature and you will find innumerable instances of one author's influence on another. . . . and it was never a handicap in the long run. Thus, suppose I was influenced as he says I was. There's nothing condemnatory in it. . . . unless I have not absorbed it well. And I eliminated that charge above when I said that my sex was an understatement and John's an inaccuracy.

Now as to the "crash" ending of Steinbeck and mine mentioned in paragraph four. I have talked to many people about *Grapes of Wrath*. And the one thing that struck me most was the fact they remembered the story of the book because they could never erase the picture it ended with. And if the "crash" ending accomplishes that purpose, John was right, whatever faults (and it has) it may have. It does the job. Otherwise, why should anyone write, if he didn't intend to influence people? And, I don't think you will ever forget the picture of Laura cutting up the calf to save the baby's life. (Further, from a publisher's point of view, that ending of mine should cause such a furore that it would be its own sales agent, and from a publisher's point of view, that wouldn't exactly be reprehensible, would it?) The errors of John's ending have never been mentioned, that is, the real errors. There have been many off-hand opinions of John's ending, but they have remained opinions, puffs of smoke. The only time opinions become truths is when they are either buttressed by undeniable facts or they become so overwhelmingly universal, they form reality itself. Now, John should never have permitted Rosasharn to take the final spotlight. That is a structural error. She was a minor character and a weak person all through the book. Suddenly at the end, she performs the real job and the heroic job. Tom and Ma should have been in the ending, CRASH or no crash.

Further, concerning the crash ending, he says the incident I describe is incredible. It is not. Two of my relatives saved their lives in a two-day snow storm when they got caught on the prairie by disemboweling their horses. There are many such stories on the plains. I have heard them over and over. There are stories more incredible than that. I had intended to use that ending ten years before Steinbeck's book came out. So, I can't be accused of borrowing. I'm merely using actual material while Steinbeck, in a certain sense, is the real borrower, because his is out of context of life itself. And then the critic's statement that Laura would never have found herself in that predicament is silly. How was she to know the day the baby pains came that the sheriff was coming to get Hank? The sheriff happened to come just when they started. And by the time she had Hank sent off with some semblance of faith, she was practically crazy with fear because she had been holding herself back. Once they left the yard, she was incapable of thinking logically. She only acted on a combination of motherly-animalness. She had to protect. However, if the ending such as I have it, is so braw that it does not leave the reader an emotional effect, if, if the ending is so strong it knocks the reader flat, sure, then the ending is a mistake, because one cannot teach a dead person new principles and new truths.

In the next paragraph, he claims that my five-and-dime hasn't sufficient preparation. Why, fer chrissakes, does he want me to kill 'em off before the farmers explode? The thing was spontaneous. Farmers don't act in a logical groove. They plod along, taking beating after beating, until suddenly, no one knows why or how, they explode. And no one knows when because no one can accurately determine how deeply and how corrosively successive defeats carve out the teachings of society, law, order, dignity, decency. He says further that the actual uprising of farmers was not spontaneous. It was. I was living there at the time. I was a participant. I lived near Le Mars. And the real truth of that incident was never told. The newspapers seized on that incident because it had ingredients favorable to vested interests and to mortgage companies and to New York insurance companies. Why, the damn country swarmed with life insurance investigators like the pantry sugar bowl swarms with ants in the summer. And my story was not necessarily based on the Judge Bradley incident.[3] It was based on many such incidents that never had attention in newspapers. Newspapers were afraid of reporting any and all for fear of further encouraging the populace to violence. Now I'm not concerned at the moment whether or not the newspapers were right in their attitude. I'm merely pointing out that the critic does not know the facts, nor do many other people. And further, the Farm Holiday Association was not organized in the summer of '32. It started in late summer and early fall. And, it was loosely organized by the Farmer's Union who saw that all the spontaneous spirits as expressed in the five-and-dime sales could be utilized to stop produce from going into the cities. The FHA was organized not to hold 5 & 10 sales, but to string cordons of pickets around cities to prevent the egress and the entrance of farm products. Members of the FHA did hold five-and-dimes, but it was not ordered or permitted by the FHA officially. I know, because I was in it, and I know, because I happen to be a close friend of the main leader. There was no one shot in the Bradley affair, but men were shot at, however, in other outbursts against authority, in So. Dak., Neb., Minn., Iowa, N. Dak., but these seldom saw the light of print because newspapers feared that it would encourage more shooting. And there was not a wholesale imprisonment of farmers. The papers said so, but that was done for effect. I happen to know that very few ringleaders were caught. And two of the most important ringleaders escaped to Minnesota where they lived under the protection of Gov. Floyd B. Olson until Gov. Herring and he arranged that their indictments were quashed after tempers had died down. I know that because I know the man who handled their cases here in St. Paul. In my treatment, I kept the most bizarre and the rougher elements out of it, to hit the average case of that sort. I tried to centralize all cases with mine. I bor-

3. At Le Mars, Iowa, Judge Charles Bradley had refused to promise a mob that he would not sign any more mortages; he was threatened with lynching.

rowed aspects from many actual incidents, trying at all times to hit the happy medium. . . . since truth, the thing we seek, doesn't like the exposure at the extreme poles of any given question. Haven't I shown the implications far more accurately than anyone? Including Steinbeck? What I wanted to show was that, from a historical-anthropological point of view, mankind, and all living things, explode under pressure. . . . that lives always represent growth, like the perennial grasses of the prairies. And as for the shooting of Ol Granpap. . . . . well, suppose it was dramatic? Is that a derogatory accusation? I had him shot off to elicit reader sympathy on the one hand and on the other, since somebody had to be shot according to the law of averages of all the incidents, he was the most likely prospect.

To sum it up, I am grateful for his observation that I have potentialities, but I'm a bit of afraid of his demands. I may not be a real artist if I fulfill them. Also, any critic who rejects a book on subjective, narrow bases, should be fired. He is doing his publishing house bosses a grave injustice. He should know facts before he attacks facts such as I had in the book. He gives me a distinct pain in the neck and lower portions of the anatomy on the same side of the body with his New York cave-in-the-wall knowledge of real life. And, luckily for him, I'll never know him personally, because if I did, I would give him such an intellectual roasting that after two hours of it he'd have to learn to think all over again like a person has to learn to walk again after being bedridden four years. And I regret, really, that I'm capable of intellectual discourse of a high order, because when I operate that way, I feel most falsé and most unrepresentative of those major forces of life. I'm sorry that like Locke's *tabula rasa* I can reflect life. That is a sin.

Now, Lois, I want you to understand that I have withheld four-fifths of the actual blast I have in mind, and one of the reasons for withholding it is that the full blast would burn out the neurons and the nerve fuses of any one reading it. The charge would be too heavy. And further, it would be clearer and more coherent if at the moment I wasn't suffering from a malignant sinus infection, so malignant that my groans in my sleep, my friends say, are the most eerie things they have heard or could ever conjecture. In other words, after I have taken a beating for a long period of time, I explode a bit too strongly. And how can I help that? I am much like my father, like Pa Bramstedt when he nearly killed Jessie in the book. I have to fight that temper every day of my life. And certainly, that fact in itself is proof enough that I do not write in Steinbeckian terms, nor do I borrow characters from him.

Right now, I'm in the middle of a new novel describing those people who didn't migrate from South Dakota. They hung on. And I'm afraid if incidents in *This Is The Year* were incredible, most of this book will be considered so, even if I personally knew that I am taming the shrew of truth in it.

However, supposing that I am free of option when it is finished, I am sending it along to you again. I like the way you people handle me. I learned from your goodness in sending the criticism many things. . . . .I have learned things that were necessary and vital. For that, I cannot continue to thank you effusively and sincerely enough.

And, really, I kinda like the critic, though he or she be a muddle-head. I like all people, all life, but that doesn't prohibit my right to have wraths against ideas that people have. Or their attitudes. The poor suckers, they can't help it.

I intend, ten, twenty years from now, to describe in a cycle of from six to ten books my life and those of my relatives. That will be a great monument in American literary history, the greatest, perhaps, because by that time I shall have mastered various techniques of writing, such as adept introspection and "majestic" objectivity. And I will, unless the forces that have been beating on me, my soul, my body, my brain, my training, have finally stilled me. But, like the prostitute without her virginity or intention of virginity, I am ready for them. Let them assail me. I am ready. Always. I just can't be stopped.

And again, really, I am profoundly thankful for the attention. And please let the critic read this. It will do the critic good. And show it to a few others. I intend to send a copy of his letter or criticism and my answer to an agent that I contacted recently so that they will know what they are handling. There can be no harm in that, as I intend that they shall keep it confidential.

Sincerely, gratefully,
Frederick Feikema

To Helen and Ray Vander Meer

Tuesday Morning
507 Oak Street, S.E.
Minneapolis, Minn.
Feb. 15, 1940

My dear Helen and Ray,

I see Doug and Marion [Hall] frequently—they invite me over to tame their sorrel Irish setter, to eat Marion's novitiate magic at the table and to wash the dishes with Doug afterwards. Very often, too, we become mellow and warm with the exchange of memories. And so, after many times berating myself for having missed this Xmas sending you & Ray my yearly greetings, I've come around to the point of writing a short letter.

There were extenuating circumstances, however, Helen and Ray, which circumscribed my writing. Yes, I could have spared a stamp, possibly! Bah, I was so immersed in a personal fiasco at the time I did not have the heart to write anyone. And so, pretty much of a mess inside, I grasped at any straw around—and that was to write.

Now the book is finished and I have a few days to relax, to catch up on my correspondence.

I have often wondered about you two; what you look like now, what you think about, what you are reading, if you (both) have kept the flame burning on ambition's wick.

There isn't much news you'd be interested in from here, except to say what's happened to Doug and Marion. Doug is rapidly inducting his sensitive and his untainted nature into the labor law business.—He comes to me quite often with personal ethics problems, wondering just how he must conciliate an ideal to a given set of facts, believing (God bless him) that I have done so and yet maintained an unshattered integrity. I am to see him tomorrow about an unfortunate case. The man is obviously guilty before the law, and Doug ponders whether he should defend him as "not guilty."

Living is a problem. Any problem is fairly easy to solve until we are involved in part or in whole. Abstractions are the easiest and most fluent of our contributions to life. And so Doug ponders. He doesn't make much money. But so clean and earnest a "spirit" must be allowed to live and to practice. I believe that Marion, who is much wiser and much more profound than he, feels as I do. She is working and apparently is forging ahead in her advertising work with Donaldson's (a huge store) and does most of the supporting. She is becoming quite liberal and democratic in speech. The other day a pleasant, bell-like "hell" rolled off her tongue without her being aware of it. Doug and I had to labor to restrain a proud grin.

Remember the book you read of mine, Helen? Well, I've ripped it up and now, like a cell dividing into two parts, it has become three, two novels, and a play. The play will stay in my files, one of the novels is yet to be written and one has been written and it is titled, *The Golden Bowl is Broken*. I finished it yesterday. I must still prune it for a few months.

In the meantime my longer, 115,000-word *This Is The Year* or *Sorrow From Your Heart* has had two reluctant rejections from Random House and Macmillan, and now is in the conference room at Viking Press. There is really no objection to the book this time, except that I'm unknown and it describes too much *farm* tragedy. Both R. H. and Mac's repeatedly said it was well written and the characters were "memorable." They compare my severity and directness and cleanly knit prose to Steinbeck! My agent feels confident that some lesser known publisher will take it if Viking does not.

Now, if time permits and I don't get work (which I hope I do) I'm preparing a large book of stories and tales and the other novel I mentioned. I have two others in thought process—and a huge seven- or nine-cycle project planned which I will begin about ten years hence. Peter De Vries and I correspond frequently on my poetry.[1] He likes it but raves at my tendency to include too many details in too small a confine. The correspondence is stimulating.

1. FM enclosed four poems—"A Portrait Eschewn," "Homage," "A Mighty Fate Hammers Out," and one untitled piece—all of them about unrequited love. At this time De Vries was editor of *Poetry* magazine.

Personally, I feel that I've pretty well worked out a satisfactory style. My problem from now on is one of organization. But you know my disgust at artificiality of plot and construction. I like to write as life itself flows.

Writing, as D. C. DeJong often said, is one of laborious labor. Knowing that, I've averaged about 12,000 words a week for two years. The novel *This Is The Year,* for example, was written in 29 days; that is, the final draft.

A year ago, I lost my job with the *Journal*. I've had but three months of regular pay since then. But I've always been busy. And I could amaze you with many and sundry stories of social and political issues and people here and even in Wash., D.C. But, I shall save all that for a personal call sometime in the next year.

I had a long letter from Dr. Jellema the other day. I intend to write him today.

My emotional life?

That has gone to pot. Jean's folks raised hell long enough for her to suddenly, inexplicably, love another. They are married and happy. He is an excellent chap, though no match for her intellectually. But life is so rich and strange, I would not begrudge them happiness by constraining either them or myself by my importunate demands. And someday, you'll hear of her as a fine writer in her own regard. Well, come now, write me, my good friends.

Ever,
Frederick

P.S. Having reread this letter, I suddenly feel old. Is this the restraint that I have learned? But, do not worry about my irrepressibility! It is still there, burning, unconquerable!

P.S. *The Golden Bowl is Broken* refers to the Dust Bowl which once was rich with golden oats, golden corn, golden grain, golden pumpkins, golden fruits.

My sincere and warm greetings to Henry [Zylstra] and Mil [Reitsema], Lenore [Stuart] and Ed [Rupke], Ed [Hekman] and Florence [Stuart], your sister Marion [Reitsema] and brother Bob [Reitsema], DeBie and Jo [Holtrop], Pete DeVisser, and others from whom you may feel I deserve interest.

F.F.

To Peter De Vries

[Glen Lake Sanatorium]
[Oak Terrace, Minnesota]
[Summer, 1940]

My dear Peter:

I'm glad to hear that you and Tip [Youngsma] are still the irrepressible and mentally curious men you were in college. I've always regretted the fact that I wasn't awakened enough from my Calvinistic, farmyardish torpor to have joined you then. You Chicago boys were awakened before you started school. Despite the I.Q. faddists (and in affirmation of the recent Iowa studies in mental growth) I'm convinced it takes years to unearth a brain if the selfsame brain has been buried beneath prejudice, religion and has been deprived of words, ideas, theories, books and vital experiences in its early years. Say hello to Tip, please.

I believe this is fresher, in a way. You see, poetry isn't my main interest, though I read a lot of it. I always feel constrained when I try to write it. I need room—just as I hate form-fitting clothes. I'm still too much a primitive. As a matter of fact, I've been told

I'm a curious mixture of child and sage—and as you know, the average of these two extremes makes one comfortably mediocre.

Oh, yes, John W. Huizenga[1] is also alive—and how! And here's a tip. He may do something very original and monumental in history. He and I have been arguing (by letter) about the narrowness of history and he has come to see that a good historian must also know his anthropology, sociology, geology, psychoanalysis,etc.

Oh, life is good! There are so many fields to investigate!

Yours,

Frederick F ———

1. Huizenga was studying under Carl Becker at Western Reserve in Cleveland (now Case Western Reserve University).

To Peter De Vries

[Glen Lake Sanatorium]
[Oak Terrace, Minnesota]
Dec. 9, 1940

[Note to Maryanna Shorba:]
I sent this[1] through my agents in N.Y., though I haven't heard from my friend Pete or them. Save this and send it back.
Fred

1. Rough draft from which a clean copy was made [FM's note].

2. Later *The Golden Bowl*.

My dear Peter:

I never did manage to improve those returned poems of mine for a number of reasons including: first, that life was so utterly absorbing when they came back I had no taste for the work; and, second, that I have the reprehensible habit of regarding returned work with much the same attitude a father regards a child that cannot make passing grades in school.

Since I last wrote you, a number of things have happened. There was the sharp, tendon-cutting, almost eviscerative breakup between myself and The One. There was some intensive novel writing (of which, more later). There was the matter of discovering that both of my lungs were hard hit by active tuberculosis. I have been lying here for eight months now on a "strict bed" routine. And though one lung has cleared up, the state of the other is so indefinite the doctors have told me I should expect to remain strict bed for another year. . . . barring a miracle. The most dismaying item is the "no writing" edict my doctor has issued. He is right—but, sometimes I cannot restrain myself. And so here's another poem.

While *Talk of The Hungry*[2] was slowly forming itself on paper (by the way, the first draft was a four-page section of an unpublished novel of mine) a number of comments on the making of poetry occurred to me.

Other people's poetry has more often than not baffled me. Sometimes I've had a feeling of inferiority because many of my poetry-reading friends could scan the lines glibly, as if they understood them. But the same verses remained stiff, heavy, vague, crumbly to me. And because poems had the official blessing of pub-

lication, I had no other choice but to admit my own deficiency.
And yet, I could not explain why it was that the rhythms I heard
in my mind, the colors I saw, the utter, burning hurts that seemed
so complete and so living to me, could not be poetry.

These "foreign" poems were either too obtuse (for example,
as parts of E.E. Cummings, Ezra Pound, T. S. Eliot, Kenneth Fearing are) or too glib (Tennyson, Longfellow, most hymns) for me.
None of them ever struck me as either moving or directly written. I
could understand Elizabeth Barrett Browning's *Sonnets From The
Portuguese* and, to mention a poem of recent date, Stephen Spender's
first poem in *Poetry*'s November issue. I explained that exception
to my general thesis on the ground that I had had intense experiences similar enough to E. B. Browning and Spender so that my
mind had categories and surrounding webs of feelings ready for
their evocative words. That led to the next problem: for whom was
poetry written? The answer seemed simple to me: for other people,
of course. But a glance at these poems predicated one of two
things: either I was obviously not in the class of "people" or these
poems were written for the poets themselves or others equally as
"touched." And one can readily understand, especially if one wants
to *be a poet,* that such an indictment was not exactly entertaining.

In the act of looking around for answer I discovered a process
in writing I had not always been aware of: namely, that we quite
often examine our own mental workings to understand another's.
We've always done this consciously as a child but the conscious part
has faded as we've grown older. We assume other minds are like
our own. Words are shortcuts and the continual use of words sets
up a type of mental operation that isn't too representative of what
actually is. And at best, words themselves are quixotic. They become extensions of a person's needs or desires—but, because they
only partly represent, they are also binding in the sense that any
set of ideas or words built on previous half-representative ideas or
words must always be increasing the distance between that which is
and that which is being represented.

Thus, in examining my own mental workings while I wrote poetry, I was completely amazed by two things: the tremendous
amount of personal, intimate feelings that were compressed into a
single word and the tremendous jumps between the elliptical words.

Browning, if I remember correctly, was of the first major poets
to floor me with his terse and elliptical writings. Most of the poetry
written since his time has become unintelligible to me. A good

share of *Poetry*'s lines are so foreign to me I often have to reassure myself I speak and read American by picking up a sports page.

Returning to my own inner workings when I write, I believe I can point out what has happened. In our endeavour to be original we are faced with a number of conditions. There is the vast hulking bulk of centuries of poetry. So many forms and styles and expressions have been used, a young poet has the empty feeling there isn't anything left to coin, there isn't a new phrase, or idea, or rhythm left to invent. There are the critics with their cold, slitted eyes ready to identify a past master's echo in the new efforts. There is the tremendous emphasis on the machines and their products. There is the dulling effect of hymns endlessly, droningly repeated each week in churches as popular tunes and lyrics are repeated hour after hour on the radio. Why, the whole field has been so pre-empted by a combination of the past, banality, preachers, singers, machines that the poor poet is driven into muttering unrecognizable stutterings to himself.

Well, what to do, what to do?

If poetry is to be written for other people, I believe there are certain considerations that will have to remain fairly constant. The first of these will be that the poet should remember his reader can be expected to understand ordinary experiences, and as such, simple, direct and connected lines will be fairly well understood. But if the poet intends to put across a *complex* idea, he had better give the reader ample time to adjust himself to the idiosyncrazy or the newness of the coming idea. Jesse Stuart not only has the roots of his living in his poetry, not only has the complexity of his nature delineated in his simple, direct lines—but he creates an atmosphere that is as clear as the blue sky above his Kentucky hills.

It isn't necessary to force one's feelings into "ideograms" or Chinese symbols to write poetry. If what a poet feels can't be written simply and clearly, and thereby be poetry, such a poet, or rather person, had better stop writing. Certainly, concentrated, elliptical writing won't make it poetry.

You have probably heard these things said before—though to read the *gibberish* that some of the *Poetry* articles contain, one would not think so.

Last month's issue had an article entitled *The Poet and Pedant Symposium* by Margedan Peters which contained the information that a Mr. Tate had written in *The Southern Review* "that it is the 'scientism' of our civilization which is responsible for the suppression of the critical spirit . . . . that positivism has reduced the area of spiritual values to the vanishing point and has left us ripe for fascism." Mr. Tate's use of the word "spirit" is the clue to his defeatist disposition. He still believes in spirits and things spiritual, when the modern world, at least as far as its actual living habits are concerned, doesn't believe in them. Science has rescued so many everyday unknowns from the limbo of the spirit that the spirit doesn't exist anymore. The fascinatingly near approach to the answer of the problem, "when does the organic become the inorganic, or vice versa," is indication of the fact that the day when petticoats hid knees like the spirit hid the nervous system is going. The words we frightened ourselves with all these years are words after all—the noise in the bush wasn't the voice of God, or the Great spirit, or the Unknown, but a chicken dusting her feathers.

And the unimaginative, the man who can find no song in a world emptied of spirits or souls or gnomes or fairies, who does not understand that man will (or may) someday calm down enough to help the birthing of the neotechnic child from the rough, foul-mouthed, paleotechnic mother will always be lost and whimperingly defeatist.

For such, one can only have pity and simple ditties.

And, maybe, that includes me.

Sincerely,
Frederick Feikema

1941

Manfred's stay in Glen Lake Sanatorium gives him time to reflect on his life and his literary aims. The letters of 1941 concern three primary areas: his health, his literary projects, and his growing love for Mary- anna Shorba, the sanatorium patient he will marry. Other letters to John Huizenga and to his literary agent, Betty Etter, discuss in detail the regimen of the sanatorium and his improving health, chiefly in- creased mobility and weight gain. In September he learns he must re- main in the hospital until the following May or June.

To John Huizenga

[Glen Lake Sanatorium]
[Oak Terrace, Minnesota]
January 19, 1941

"—it is folly to ask mankind to live givingly (or sentimentally) all year long because of the very nature of our structure and our evolvement.

"We need another mind to construct a key as powerful as the one Marx gave us—and after that another, because none of them comprise but only serve as wedges with which to separate or split a bit of reality and through which to express our immediate concept of what living is."[1] I am becoming more and more convinced that the struggle for ideas and defense of them is futile if one wants to be saved in the sense of feeling on the side of *what actually is,* though they seem very efficacious to them that glow. It is very hard for me to be both "historically" minded and living in the sense of doing what I'm immersed in without question of its fundamental reality. When I am the latter, I am the enthusiastic writer; when I'm the former, I'm the gracious cynic or stoic—taking such things as interminable stays in sanitoria as terminable. Dream of things I want not of the past: I did a lot of that when I came in here about possible sexual congress and the publishing of books.

Visualized characters, not plots, since they insist on their own ends or destinies because of the very nature of the characters, their interactions with others and their environment.

The day starts for us at seven when the sputum cup collector comes into the room with a tray and a barely suppressed flashlight. A few minutes later nurses barge in with emesis basins, wash basins, hot water, and a lot of pleasant cackling. We rinse our mouths (or brush teeth), our hands and face, comb our hair; exchange crude pleasantries about certain emotive powers and the lack of them and about reputed love affairs, pending or past; and generally wake up enough to be ready for breakfast at about 7:40. I usually cover one ear with a radio earphone to listen to music and leave the other uncovered to listen to the running comments. (I'm in a three-bed ward.) Presently, the trays are hauled out and the perfidious bedpan appears. Down go the curtains to prevent the faeceologically curious to achieve satisfaction—and an interminable and a profoundly loathing episode ensues in which all the aesthetic and moral sensibilities one has are horribly outraged unless one suspends cerebration for a term—an easy habit, it seems. Presently, the air and the mind clears of the aroma and the work of curetaking

1. Quote from Huizenga's letter [FM's note].

begins. The beds are made a little later and from then until dinner, nothing happens except the slow working out of the process of stagnation. On certain days, other impedimenta interrupt the morning. We get new linen on Monday and Thursday, baths on Friday, and a trip on a rolling litter to be fluoroscoped on Saturday. There is usually a movie on Wednesday to which we strict bed patients can go on the litters. That and church services in an auditorium with an asthmatic floor provide the only social activity. Can you determine any chink in this arrangement which will allow for a bit of legitimate love-making, and possible copulation?

Dinner is served at twelve with maid service. At one, the floor quiets down and we are supposed to sleep until three as part of the rest hour ritual. Then, basins are brought in for palm-dampening and hair smoothing and at 3:30 one prepares to be invaded by those extremely strange and curious things called visitors who are to leave (relievedly) at five when supper is served. There's a rest hour from six to seven, visiting hours from 7:15 to 8:15 again, and then we get ready for bed. Lights are out at nine in the room—they aren't, however, in the head.

Well, John, that's just about it. There are compensations for men. There are great stories here and with some patience I may be able to get them out of these people. And then, too, I've met quite a fine young lady here,[2] with great similarity to Emily Mark's ability (have you met her yet? I've told her about you). This *local young* lady had added inducements to which I'm more than favorably inclined.

2. Maryanna Shorba.

To Betty Etter[1]

[rough draft]
[Glen Lake Sanatorium]
[Oak Terrace, Minnesota]
Jan. 30, 1941

1. Agent at Lyons & Etter.

Dear Betty:

By this time Peter De Vries has returned *Talk of the Hungry* to you. In case he didn't give any details, this letter I received from him will take care of that deficiency. I'd like it if you'd send it back whenever convenient.

With this lengthy letter I'm sending another poem, *Two Laments,* which in my eyes is much better than the aforementioned. There's another note to Pete [De Vries], but that does not mean you need send this poem to *Poetry* again—if it should be sent out anywhere at all. Those things are in your hands. I trust you to know the market far, far better than I do. A goodly share of my stuff won't be accepted until I've arrived on the merits of the other work.

In the meantime, these things will keep—as will some of those short stories I sent last year.

Let's inject a health bulletin at this point. I haven't had a temperature or a high pulse since July. I've gained 68½ pounds in all for a total of 242½—and I'm still not lumpily fat. The healing in my left lung is slow work and if it is not sufficiently healed by this summer and if my good right lung remains stationary, I may have some surgery next fall; in which case, I won't be ready to leave this place until the winter of '42–'43, although I'll be up and writing by the spring of '42. If, however, I do heal without any more help, I'll be up and writing before then—come hell or high water. I may leave this institution much healthier than I've ever been, though I may not be able to jump over brooks and wrestle with my girl cousins in the strawpile. My health generally will be better, though my lungs will always be weak in the sense that I won't be able to breathe too deeply or rapidly as, say, after a long run. Also, I'll have learned to pace myself which I didn't before. And if food and shelter are available I'll become a fine old gentleman, all things remaining equal.

They tell me now that if I had run around another three months, I would have cashed in—I was so badly undernourished and nervously run down. So, we have the matter of my day-to-day eating to think of when I get out. It would be good if I had a book out by that time with a little cash rolled up for a reserve to buy food with; and, too, shelter.

In many respects, this stay is just what my "guardian angel" ordered. They have a good library here of magazines and books of every sort, and this, along with presents and the services of a rental library, enables me to read widely and intensively. You may be interested to know that I've prowled with my curious nose in anthropology, geology, sociology, evolution, political science, philosophy, modern psychoanalysis, and, of course, general literature—all with the intention, and I believe the partial result, of understanding how complex this animal we call man is. If I were to comment on myself coolly, I'd say I've matured considerably.

The main purpose of this letter was to give you a sort of brief sweep of my projects for the next five years, and perhaps, a longer period than that. An agent should have some conception towards what direction the author she represents seems to be tending—or wants to tend.

You know about *This is The Year* and *The Golden Bowl is Broken*.

2. Later *Sons of Adam.*

The latter, of course, is in the first draft stage and needs considerable clipping and embellishing.

The Hog-Killer, or *The Dude and the Duke (Son of Man),*[2] of
which I had about a 100 pages written when they ambulanced me
in here, is the story of Benepe Martosi, who as a sensitive lad from
a Chicago suburban family of some fineness and discrimination,
went to a middle west slaughter house to earn his living. The terrific impact of living in a loud, clanging packing plant where hogs
are screaming through their gashed and blood-spilling throats temporarily disjoints his normal living pattern so much that first he
hurriedly falls in love and then one night stabs his wife like he stabs
the hogs. From then on he is in flight and the problem becomes
one of alternate flights and attempts to reach normalcy. On his
travels he meets a man in whom he recognizes a dignity he wants.
Curiously this man is a descendant of a crested family, but the very
characteristics Benepe Martosi recognizes as good are those which
caused this man to leave the comforts of the aristocratic family.
Benepe, on his flight, changes his name to Ben Mart.

After this novel, I wanted to write a shorter piece about a young
Jewish girl who madly loved a cheat. The cheat was very clever and
psychically chaotic. Her struggle to straighten him out and his
struggle to make her like himself comprise the themes of the book.

Then, there was the really good book—a story of a (Frisian)
(Dutch) family (though it could be of any family), of a father and
a mother, and their ten children, five boys, five girls. I wanted to
write twelve chapters or parts, each member of the family having
a turn in being the one through which the story is written, from
the father, mother, oldest child, and son on, through to the youn-
gest, who would emerge as the dominant character, though the
book would really tell the history of one family's struggles, pover-
ties, triumphs, sorrows in the last forty years, beginning in Chicago
and ending in the middle west. There is actually such a family I
know with whom I've spent a good share of my youth and my pres-
ent-day vacations. As a religious, economic, social and anthro-
pological unit
[missing material]
Perhaps others may think I'm diffusing my energies too much. I
believe I am not. I have a slow nature and cannot do really profound things off hand—even though I can grab A's in graduate
work without really stirring a finger. These stories of people must
live with me for years and years—and the longer the better—on

a relative scale, of course—since, if one waited too long, death would be the publisher.

Anent my slow, but glacierishly accumulative writing habits, I'd like to add that *This Is The Year*[3] shows such indicative evidence. Hank and Laura, Li'l Hen, Ol' Granpa, and Pa are fairly real and actual characters—but many of the others remain comparative shadows. I had visualized the good ones—but not the others. They were tossed in whenever needed. This is perhaps due to the fact that I hate detailed plots. Before I begin I run these main characters through a series of situations. They become living to me. When the writing starts in, the very interaction of the characters with themselves and with their environment sometimes demands a new course or movement—and when I need a few faces, I grab a handful. That is a weakness, I know, but also a strength—since by allowing the characters to live as they seem to want to live, they and their country do not seem carpentered. My next problem seems to lie in the area where I am weakest—the accessory characters. And, I'll work that out too—someday.

Well there it is. I'm afraid you really got something on your hands when you found me—for better or worse—or worse still. And even if my health would leave me, I'd get the hell out of here, pour out the stories in some room or cabin on the last few beats of energy—and call in the watching cats in the sky for their feast.

Betty, do I frighten you?

Anyway, I'm on your side.

Very sincerely,
Frederick

P.S. Incidentally, a few Professors at the University who dote on me want me to get my Masters degree in sociology so I can qualify for social work. The state will pay for my tuition and books, and if I can earn a few shekels from my writing, or elsewhere, for maintenance, I can probably prepare myself to make a living for a family (?) that way since my work doesn't look like best seller stuff. Maybe we ought to work out a best seller plot just to get started—though I'd hate it. Well?

F.F.

3. Part of the original became the story "Footsteps in the Alfalfa."

To Maryanna Shorba

[Glen Lake Sanatorium]
[Oak Terrace, Minnesota]
10:31 AM
May 18, 1941, Sunday

Maryanna, my good one, my wife,

You wrote, "It (the future) will be good and full, if I have you to share it. But it is necessary that you have all that you want, that you be happy. That's all I worry about."

I have only one regret— that I did not say those saving, soaring words, those noble and wifely ideas first as your husband.

My darling, do you know it is the first time I've heard those words? You want me to have all I want. Love is the word to describe my great Maryanna. All I want. All I want. Those are the finest words I've ever heard, my lovely Maryanna.

Honey, you shouldn't worry so much about me. It is you who has not had a full measure of affection, who needs to be happy, who needs all she wants. I want you to have that. That's all *I* worry about—how I can make you happy. (Even if it includes your joyous angers once in a while.)

Honey, if you are needy, ask and it shall be given you if I have it.

How lovely and warm and close and dear and wonderful your slow kisses and caresses were last Wednesday night. I've been full of dreams about them since.

Maya Maryanka, can you come Monday to kiss wildly and to hold fiercely your

own
Frederick?

[margin] I placed some of your violets in my Bible for preserving for our first night of love!

To Maryanna Shorba

[Glen Lake Sanatorium]
[Oak Terrace, Minnesota]
7:30 AM
Sept. 15, 1941

Maryanna, dear one,

If I get a good report on my X-ray next week, I can get my first half hour walk the 6th of October—if I'd press him a little. And I really am tempted to do so because I'd like to take long walks in the glory of the fall weather with its great golds and heliotropes and scarlets—and if I wait too long into October, I'll find that the color will have gone. I guess I'll just wait to see how fast fall will come upon us.

Thomas Wolfe's *You Can't Go Home Again* strikes me as more

of a narrative than any of his other books—but there are really some very inept passages. You can tell where Wolfe had terrific hangovers but insisted upon writing anyway. (Drinking is foolish if one wants to use the brain, isn't it?) Or, when he just couldn't get started some day but angrily typed or wrote on.

And then he tosses such vague terms as Time and Space and Evil around with too much abandon, as if these things existed as eine Ding-an-zich, a Thing.

His conversations, too, are bad. They are not alive. They do not sparkle. You can't see his people gesticulating even when he gives copious directions for you to think so.

I've read nearly half of his latest book and he has portrayed one character very well: gum-chewing, complacent Myrtle.

It looks as if we will have a good day—the sun is shining and the few clouds I see are innocent of rainy intentions.

No doubt my two brothers will show up this afternoon. And I will again steep myself in some more family lore.

Well, honey, I must hurry now to get ready to leave for town and you. How I wish I could be with you this winter. Who will take my place at symphonies? I feel like a robber by not yet being free to take you there. You better get some tickets with some of the women at the club.[1]

So then, my dear one, we have come so far.

We will go on.

I love thee, Maryanna.

Your own Frederick

1. Sara Hurst House, a half-way house for former patients.

1942

This year is important to Manfred, for he leaves Glen Lake Sanatorium in March. His increasing good health and energy enable him to go to work for Modern Medicine *in September, and he marries Maryanna Shorba on 31 October. His March letter to Dr. Sumner Cohen, a sanatorium physician, expresses his goal: "My life is in the chance that I can become a really fine writer. . . . I'm not living just to live."*

To Sumner Cohen, M.D.[1]

[Glen Lake Sanatorium]
[Oak Terrace, Minnesota]
[March, 1942]

1. This letter was written because of a mix-up in x-rays. For a few days we thought I had a new spot in my left lung, plus fluid [FM's note 23 December 1957].

2. Sara Hurst House.

Dear Doctor:

I am tired this morning because the possibility of my staying here and my losing a place to live in for a while after I leave makes me sleepless and jumpy. I must get out of here.

People have been preaching to me about using will power, and by people I mean a few social workers, friends and doctors, as if, first, a thing such as will power existed as an entity, and second, as if I didn't have any. It isn't as simple as all that. Not very many people possess as erratic, as tempestuous, a nature as I have, and I think I have done pretty well—not so much because of will power as by the fact that I want to write. Everything revolves around that cardinal fact.

If what I have now is not going to prevent me from leaving at my regular discharge date then there is no point in my staying longer now when I've got a chance to get a place to live for a number of months before I go to work. I know of five men who are eligible for that club in town[2] and all five can go within just about a month, and all five have been recommended by Filter. And right now, there is but one opening for which I have been approved already. If you wait until May 15 or whatever to discharge me you're sending me out without a home. I'll have to work immediately. I'll not stay at Maryanna's because I don't think it's right to stay a while with the one to whom one is engaged; further, I haven't earned my right to stay there, and still further, there is a chance that I won't even be asked because of the possibilities of changes in the family setup there. No, that's out. And where else? No where else but to work.

Now you may not understand that if I do get work it's only to keep my body and soul alive so that I can write. If I leave in May I'm going to keep up my studies at the University so I can qualify for that teaching license as a sort of job insurance, and I'm going to continue writing. I live for that as I said. I don't give a damn about a career in such mundane fields as jobs offer. My life is in the chance that I can become a really fine writer. And I mean that. I came in here not caring to live except that I had a faint hope that maybe I could write in here. And they promised me at Lymenhurst I could. And I haven't been able to until last December. I'm not living just to live. Hell, anybody can do that. An animal does that.

So if I go now to the club I'll have my eats taken care of for a number of months while I finish my studies and get a long running jump into my new book. I've fought for twenty-five years to be a writer despite jobs, poverty, ill health, narrow provincialism and religiosity of my Calvinistic folks at home and personal defeats and a hanging, forboding sense of inferiority, and I'll be damned if I give it up now.

What do you think I came to you for last February? Because it was a lark to ask to go early? Hell, no. I was ready to leap out of the window and to go, hitting the roads again, or find a hole somewhere where I could write, unmolested by nurses, patients, fools, nincompoops, janitors, and telephone calls, roommates and a host of other desiderata. I don't need rules and signing out sheets and a nurse to tell me what to do now. Those things are for children and the other members of what Swift calls the most miserable creatures on earth. (Sure, they're wonderful, but there's no reason to be full of illusions about them.) I'm not one of these who keeps on smoking two packs and a pipe and cigars a day, or continues drinking, or excessive fornication because he's got his glands full of ambitious sperm, or who doesn't take his walks every single day. The sense of those things were explained to me and then the next step was simple. Health results from such and such conditions.

In reality, it has not been simple. I know I'll never smoke or drink again, and I will always walk now. Those are ascertainable facts. But I do know that this place will drive me to them again. This is a hell-hole, though it is a wonderful place too. I know what it has done to me, but it is getting on my nerves. It has been for months. And I came down to you in February to get a date and then to fix my mind on it or else I would have gone then. I didn't tell you that because you have far too many worries of your own. And I thought it was part of being a member of society, to set an example, to work out one's own problems as much as one is able to work them out here with a pair of eyes directed at one from every imaginable angle.

If it had not been for Maryanna, I would have gone long ago. But she, the dear, noble woman, so kind, so gentle, so smart in the way she handles me, she has kept me here. And at what cost? The cost has been heavy for her too. Money, time and patience. . . . and the fact that she has to come back here after she has left this place. She shouldn't be coming here. It's a crime for her to be coming here. She should forget this hole, or jail. . . . even though we've got our lives to thank to it. It is an unnatural place for one who is healthy and ambitious. People are jammed down one's throat all day long. And I haven't yet found one single person here with whom I can really talk. I haven't been able to talk to my friends with whom I can talk because there is a constraint in trying to make moods and minds meet in the narrow, dictated visiting hours. I've been dying for music and intellectual companionship ever since I've come here. No one, after a bit of an acquaintance, has been able to supply that; except Maryanna. And what chance do we get to talk? By the time we warm to each other, the whistle blows. And there's the constant chance that someone may come butting in, and so one rushes to get it said, which spoils it. And when we do get a ten hour, we've been planning on it so long, with such feverish preparation, that when it comes the whole day is as tight as a whiplash. . . . and it cuts us for days. It's hell to have to get a bit of life by telephone every day where both of us have to wait a half hour to get our calls through. It's hell to have to get a bit of life by vicarious means such as letters and messages. It's a miracle that we've been able to last as long as we have. If I go to the club, we'll see each other every day and our relationship can become natural, can grow. And weekends, we can go home to Mother.

And I've got to have her, Doctor. I've not had a woman friend since I was seventeen when great Mother died. I had no sisters.

If I can't go next Friday, or at the latest, Monday, then I might as well leave now and begin working now. . . . because then I'll be away from this dungeon (it's really wonderful, but not for me anymore) and I can see her and I can write in a private room. Afterall, one lives for happiness, and each one of us has his or her terms of definition for that word. One doesn't live to make a chart look good, or to fulfill rules.

Right now, I'm healthier than any of those kids staying at the club. I know about them. I've heard too much about them already in that respect for me to consider staying here.

And I think I've done pretty well taking the cure here too. It's been a tough job. And I think I'm done. I can't convince myself any other way. I couldn't all last night.

Perhaps if I had shown a reaction in my temperature last night, or pulse, or in nauseam, why then the argument might have gone different. There is no soreness, no ache, no nothing. It's all the same.

And I wish I could eat a good hearty meal once instead of this dieting, dieting, dieting to keep down my weight. I ate a full meal three weeks ago at a friend's house and I gained five pounds. It took me a whole three weeks to get down again. I had to skip a meal, and half of three meals to get down. And after that had to starve to keep it at 256, the last two weeks of that three-week period.

I'll wait until Wednesday noon to see what results we've got from that test, though even if that is a bit cloudy, what difference if I can go in May anyway? Now, I'll get a place to live and to get some work clear away that I'll surely do too if I have to work.

Don't misunderstand me. You're a great, noble doctor. I'm not railing at you. I'm just getting all this off my chest to see if I can't think a little clearer to see my way along. But I'm almost positive that staying here will wreck more than it will do good.

You doctors don't know it, but you had two strikes on you when I met you. A careless, pill-injecting, nurse-chasing, operation-hungry, country doctor let my mother go. But I've been able to see in here that that isn't true of most of you. It's been hard to overcome that powerful initial impression, but it's been done. I used to get along without you, bloodpoisons, bad cuts, colds, broken fingers and toes. This time I was too sick to argue.

But you've been a great doctor. A great one. I should really say, instead of what I wrote above, it's been you and Maryanna that have kept me here.

But I've had enough now. And I want to insure myself some sleep and eats and a roof by going now.

Besides, I want to take advantage of the kid's vacation to make up for all those feverish and nervous and unhealthy hours we've had to spend in here.

And now for a walk.

Fred.

1943

The letters in 1943 reflect Manfred's very important decision to write full time. After a frustrating disagreement with the staff of Modern Medicine, *he quits work there. In the spring he assists for two months in Hubert Humphrey's unsuccessful mayoral race. Several letters detail his negotiations with two different publishers—Reynal and Hitchcock in New York and Webb in Saint Paul—for the printing of his first novels. During 1943 Manfred also makes important literary contacts* *with Joseph Warren Beach and Robert Penn Warren, with whom he discusses a political novel Warren is writing (*All the King's Men).

To Frank Taylor

1076 18th Ave., S.E.
Minneapolis, Minn.
July 26, 1943

Dear Frank,

I am glad that you are sending back the manuscripts. For some time I've had in the back of my head the vague feeling that I was not doing justice to the themes in them as I felt they should be treated. What I had written was paltry compared to the concepts I had in my mind. And if I am on the "move" as a writer, it's because the concepts are great, or good, and I am moving toward them.

By the end of this week I hope I shall have sent the first quarter of the new book.[1] Strictly speaking the fifty or so pages I'm sending you are not a quarter of the book, for the first draft of the second quarter is already a hundred pages long. But it happens that these first pages are of a certain unity.

The first quarter shall describe his first days in the sanatorium while he is still quite ill. In the second quarter, he'll begin to feel much better and begin to wonder if he shall live, and if so, is living worthwhile . . . and in thinking this over, he exhumes his past, thereby revealing to the reader how it came about that his "love" left him, that his "dream" had become bitter to him and that his body had disintegrated because of tuberculosis. In the third quarter, he shall begin the buildup, or the bolero-like working up exercises which shall not disturb the carefully balanced metabolism of his body. Then too he'll explore the San a little, discovering odd people, discovering its secluded nature. And this period ends with him receiving an ecstatic week's leave to his new girl's farm near a lake. The fourth quarter shall deal with his preparation to meet life on the outside again with his rebuilt body and his new self, much stronger than it had ever been. Parenthetically, I shall suggest that the San strengthens or weakens people. But in no cases do patients come out exactly as they were when they fell ill.

I feel you shall be surprised by the title of the book. I'll keep that until you see the first pages. It has many meanings and is "catchy." I sometimes use it as a mild cuss-word.

I am working 12 hours a week for the *Argus* (weekly paper I told you about) for $15.00. They're still interested in a column for $25.00 a week, and when that comes through I'll be earning enough

1. *Boy Almighty.*

in two days to call it a handsome salary. That should free me for writing. I must be free to do that. Maryanna may go back to the campus this fall to teach, or to instruct a little and finish her Master's. That too shall help a little. The only thing we're worrying about now is moving . . . though the OPA [Office of Price Administration] is friendly.

Yes, I must be free. It's been miraculous, life's been, these last weeks. Yes, it's been hot, but I've been soaring here in my den, writing and dreaming and composing and loving it. The stuff comes easy if I have time and can work it every day. My mind feels as light and swift and high as a bird ghost. Just wait till you see the writing.

2. Editor at *New Republic*.

Bruce Bliven[2] wrote me he liked an article I sent and if I won't mind a little cutting, he'll use it. Great! That's the start!

3. Taylor had suggested *Boy Almighty*.

Frank, man, I send you a handshake![3]

Yours,

Fond greetings to Nan [Scanlon].

To Paul Hillestad

1076 18th Ave., S.E.
[Minneapolis, Minnesota]
[August 5, 1943]

My dear Paul:

After our telephonic talk yesterday, I decided that I had better make up my mind about some things. Some one book publisher had better take precedence over the other in my mind.

As you once remarked most things in life depend on two things: economics and personal impressions. In my mind, it's a toss up between you and Frank Taylor as persons. Either one of you makes an author *feel* that he is a person, that he is a friend. Both of you seem mature, considerate, far-reaching in your precepts. But, it's the economics that's beginning to tell. Reynal & Hitchcock, if they want, can do more for me in a selling way than you can because they can afford to put more time and money into a venture. I have no desire for riches, or for more money than my family needs. But as long as I'm in a spot where I've still got to earn my money from efforts that are not connected with my serious writing, I've got to be realistic until I can live as I want.

I've been checking the people Taylor has seen. I've checked their impressions of what his impressions of me were. In every case, he was more enthusiastic about me to them than he revealed to me. (Except, of course, this telegram now.) I like a man who operates that way. He saves you from hurt. You know he is sincere when he does talk. Part of me was a little reluctant to learn that, because I'd had a strong prejudice in your favor. You'd smiled at me, and that in a world that hadn't given me many smiles. And I'm one of those queer bugs that feels he must do something for people that smile at him.

Now this is what I'd like to do. I feel that Frank doesn't care much for *The Golden Bowl Is Broken*. I think he'll never publish it even if all my other books are abounding successes. He just doesn't care for it. That's the way he operates. For myself, I do know that I do not intend to rewrite that book, except for little parts, maybe, and that it will never be published if it's assumed that I'm to work with Reynal. So, again, assuming that I'm to work with Reynal, you can have it. I shall write Frank and ask him if he is willing that you shall have it, if he wants to be the first to publish me, if he is willing to let you have it after the others come out. Like every writer, I'd like to see that book published too. As a job it is the nearest to being a whole of all my books.

Frank hasn't offered me a contract yet. I don't like to rush him. I want to see what happens in the next few months. I think I owe it to myself to make an attempt to land a contract with them. I hope you do not blame me. If, however, they agree to the above proposition, good. Then maybe I can repay you for what you've done for me so far. You have done a lot. Inspiration. If you're still interested after this delineation of my feelings, let me know. Call me, or write me. Then I'll come with the book, and the new stuff. Then, too, I'll write Frank to get his opinion. So, think it over. (Steinbeck did the same thing with his *Pastures of Heaven*.) Moreover, I don't think I ought to interrupt my present work on this new one, called *Boy Almighty*, to work on another, unless it's of a minor nature. There, I think I've got most things down on paper.

Yours,

To Frank Taylor

[Minneapolis, Minnesota]
[Middle of August, 1943]

Dear Frank:

I'm sort of in a dilemma tonight. After the receipt of your telegram I went down to see Hillestad today. He told me definitely that he wants to start me off, wants the "Bowl," but, wants a contract covering "the works." It has taken him all this time, since last

February, to make up his mind. I said, "No, I'd like to try Frank's outfit first. I'd like to wait to see if I can land a contract with them . . . if I can't, is it all right to come back to you?" He said, "Sure. It's okay. But what's Frank got that I haven't got?" "Nothing, except that I think Frank can do as much for me, as an editor, and more as a member of a company that has a better sales organization." "What is it you want?" "Well," I said, "Paul, I want to get as rapidly as I can to the time when I don't have to work at a job. . . . I know that I can't write as long as I have to work. I freeze up. Just look at this stuff, now that I've had all day time to warm up my writing motors and unloosen the hold my prejudices and my fears have on me. Jobs have a tendency, even, to tighten their hold. And so, Paul, I think Frank can get me there quicker. And, I like Frank a lot, Paul." "Well, I haven't thought much about an advance, but I might consider it." With that, except for his favorable comment on an oil I'd done on an illustration board, we parted today.

Well, I came home to think it over. Here we are, Maryanna and I, with but sixty dollars income a month. She isn't sure she'll get the journalism assistantship because it's not customary for Journalism Dept. to hand them out to the same person two years in a row. They told her they'd let her know in a few weeks. Moreover, I don't want her to work full time at a job, certainly not an overtime war job. You see, damn it, she and I must both watch our resistance. We both've got tb walled off inside our chests and we've got to keep those walls thick and strong. Besides, I don't ever want her to say that a full-time job kept her from writing, as I firmly believe that if she ever gets the urge she'll show me a trick or two about writing.

Now, the last few weeks, to give me a lift, she's filled in for me at my job at the *Argus,* just so I could devote more time to *Boy Almighty.* (The telegram hit the women like a heavy fist, man! Women are shoppers, you know.) And I know that on the days when I did work, the stuff the next few days was thin again, and awkward, and not at all like the stuff you've got now. God damn it, Frank, I wish I was one of these cusses who could relax in his spare time, but, God, Frank, I just can't do it. Just can't. I'm sorry, but I can't. I wouldn't bother about this letter if the past years hadn't proved it.

With these ideas grumbling around in my mind, I called Miss Clapesattle. I asked her what chance I had to get a small grant from the Rockefeller Foundation which would permit Maryanna to take my parttime job (since parttime jobs are very scarce) and together make ends meet. She said that the applications for grants close the

1st of September, and remain closed until February of next year. She said that I would need, in addition to a letter of application, a letter from some publisher, you, Hillestad, and maybe also Gray,[1] in which there would be favorable remarks about my writing. The book, *Boy Almighty,* would have to be shown as dealing with some kind of Minnesota life, etc. I suppose that a letter from Paul with his offer, and a letter from you, would do it. But, Helen and I both questioned the wisdom of applying now. First, the book is strictly not a regional thing, at least, would not be as much as the theme of *This Is the Year*.

Second, I probably could get a much larger grant, covering a full year, next February if, in the meantime, I push *Boy Almighty* towards publication . . . and could get it in any case should you decide against me and I take Paul instead. Third, if, as I plan, I aim to spend three or four months down through the Missouri valley, studying, listening, absorbing. (I wrote the book *This Is The Year* after I left and I've never been back and so I've never really looked at the community close at hand for the purpose of writing about it.) I should do it next spring, say in March, April, May, June, and with money from the Rockefeller to pay my traveling expenses. If I take a grant now, the one next spring will be gone.

Thus, boiling it down, the problem is to beg, borrow, steal, or be advanced money now until next February so that I can finish BA unhampered by worry and be free of projects and go to Nebraska, Iowa, the Dakotas, and Montana.

I feel I should start *This Is The Year* next, and next year. I think about it a lot in spare moments. In fact, I've had some other big ideas pop up and am most anxious to get a share of them done as soon as possible. They ache.

Gosh, you don't know how I feel about begging like this, but you know what I've done since you've smiled at me. Paring needs to an absolute low for these times, I think $300 with M. working a little too would take care of my needs until February 1st. Then the big grant could start. . . . unless, by that time, you have other ideas. But, remember, I'm most anxious to spend a lot of time going back to the Big Valley of Columbia[2] where men are always optimistic, refreshing myself, listening to their talk, sketching and painting like mad so that the book would literally smell of the country. I might add that the $60.00 a month job at the *Argus* is tenuous because my boss and the owner of the plant don't get along and I'm expecting a blowup. And, I know that the owner, a Republican state repre-

1. St. Paul book reviewer James Gray.

2. FM believed America should have been called Columbia.

sentative, will not like my article in the N.R. [*New Republic*] when that comes out. And he says he will not take a "column" from me. I'm too liberal, he told the boss.

I am writing. I've got a good start into the third quarter . . . that is, of first draft. The first draft comes easily . . . it's the work after that takes time.

In any case, I'm waiting for you until you signify otherwise.

Yours,
F.F.
Feike Feikema

To John Huizenga

1814 4th Street Southeast
Minneapolis, Minnesota
September 15, 1943

My dear John,

I think I shall just sit here and write you some lines. Just to talk to you. I get damned lonesome for you sometimes. Except for moments with my wife, you are the only person in the world with whom I can bare my deepest feelings. I wrote your mother the other day, asked her for your address in case you'd moved since I last heard from you, received from her a photo of you taken in your navy uniform. (Do not protest. It did not do you justice, as I very carefully explained to Maryanna.) She tells me that you're beginning to adjust yourself to the place. In a way, I'm a little glad that you're being exposed to the rigors of training (I can safely say that after you're in!) (and behind the safety of my tubercular walls) since I've always felt that you needed a little sanding by hard life, or rather, since you've had impecunious days, by coarse, rough life.

Let's start this all off with a little gossip. Mayhap an item may lead to an idea. First, we've moved to a new place. It's a flat and near the U. and much more comfortable than our old house. We seem, so far, to have a congenial landlady who is willing to fix a leaky faucet, or a rickety toilet seat, and to wait a few days for the rent in case my bones ache too much to climb the stairs (she lives up, we on the first). This flat is convenient for Maryanna who expects to work on her thesis for a Master's this year and to work with a special group from the U., journalism, medicine, science, sociology, anthropology, etc., who are going to study the impact of the war on a small community near Minneapolis. And it's convenient for me for I can trot over to the library or to any of the experts near here as I need them for my work. I've spent a lot of time the past week waxing, mopping, washing windows, hanging curtains, cleaning and painting furniture and so on. I helped pack and carry and move the furniture and after it was all over took an X-ray to find that I'm in as good a health as I'd ever want. Of course, I sleep a good eight hours a night, always, and too, my daily afternoon nap, and my hour's rigorous walk per diem. And my milk and greens and raws and proteins. I'm beginning to enjoy the regimen I follow. I fancy, sometimes, that I know pretty concretely the sort of thing you fellows in the service must undergo, except that having yourself for a top sergeant is not as easy as having a stranger for that post. One hates to hold too basic a dislike for one's own person. My weight has settled a little, to 240, where it's supposed to be, says my Doc, and I do not appear so hideously and gargantuanly huge as I did here a while back, and as I did on my wedding picture. My kids will have an odd picture to look back to, if we have any. (Not any in sight yet . . . unless something began last night!) [matter deleted]

Tuesday, Sept. 21.

Well, John, back again. I have an idea that this letter will be long, written over many days. Tonight a little politics. Concerning the '44 election next year, my own reaction on how to vote for President would go something like this: Roosevelt if Wallace runs with him; if not with Wallace, then for Willkie if he runs on the Republican platform. Though, I must add, that I shall be mightily tempted to cast a vote for myself if I'm forced to consider Willkie. I have been considerably surprised by Willkie. His change-about is most puzzling. I'm never quite sure if he's putting on an act of liberalism because that wins the most votes, or if he really and sincerely has come, because of pressures not political only, to think elastically and considerately of the mass of people. His book, *One World*, is rather naïve, I thought, but it did reveal a wide sympathy for many diverse sorts of creatures, and that is more than one can say for most Republicans. I would like to meet him. However, I feel that even if he were a thorough liberal now and elected to the White House he would be helpless in the presence of the wolves in his party, helpless and entangled in the great power politics of the monopolists, just as Roosevelt now is rather acquiescent to the importunate and reactionary South.

It is Wallace that I admire. The more I hear of him, the more I like him. And this is significant. I've attended a number of labor banquets where all the speakers work on this idea that next year labor will heal its wounds and close its breaches and vote in "good" men. Whenever Roosevelt's name is mentioned, there's but mild applause, but when Wallace's name is mentioned, the laborers shout hoarsely and stamp on the floor and whistle like men after hot ass.

Roosevelt is a rubber band, a politician. I do not believe he is a sincere liberal. I never have. Had not the pressure of events pushed him to use drastic measures, had he presided in the peaceful days of the 20's, he would have been as conservative as Hoover. He reflects his times. That is probably a virtue, considered some ways, as Laski wrote in another book. But, it does not make him a Lincoln, or a Jackson, a man with resolve who by sheer power and a great heart hews a new path for the ignorant and, sometimes, stupid masses to follow. I feel Wallace would be like that. I feel he has dipped deeply into this problem called life, in the problem of what it means to be a neighbor, to be hungry, to have dreams. He has studied life. And he has come up or come through with a few convictions, though he is not stiff and unyielding in the face of new facts, new ideas.

I think he is nearer to truth than most men when he says that this world, that is, the economic world, is being run by power, just as you wrote a few years ago, and in this case, the power of the cartels, and international financial houses. The powder and shell boys are pikers compared to these. I feel too that the basic motivations in the minds of these power boys is not that Hitler is a menace to civilization but a menace to their structures. They had hired him to lead an army against what they *thought* (and maybe is) was a threat to themselves, namely Russia, and they were fooled when Hitler turned on them and became a power himself. That's why Chamberlain said so vehemently (and he so weak a trembling man!) "He is completely untrustworthy!" Chamberlain had a considerable personal fortune invested in German property.

Yes, sometimes I'm afraid this is too a foolish war. Sometimes.

Saturday, September 25.

We've just finished cleaning the house for the week, a two-hour job, and I've taken a walk past the stadium where 37,000 howling jacks and jennys are hoarse over the fact that the gophers beat the tigers from Missouri where mules are raised. The sun has been very bright these days, and was so today. When the sun does shine in this moody, cloudy state, it is a noble wonder, with an enormous blue bowl of a sky, with an occasional plume of silver clouds.

We saw the movie, *Bataan,* last night. It was brutal, and terrible. It was a well-done movie. But what rags people are. They can take those movies in stride without a quiver these days. Me, the things hit with the force of a first menstruation. (In this connection, booksellers tell me that good novels sell best in the Armed forces, sell poorly in the civilian areas. For two months, one rental library here could not rent out a novel to anyone. All they'd take were detectives and mysteries.) I thought, as I watched that picture, that we human beings, Japs and Germans included, are still pretty much animals. We're still growling and fighting over goods and meat and produce just as the animals fight in their worlds. There was a short in the theatre depicting mountain cats fighting over a deer. The movements, scowls, threats, strategems, gentle purrs was about as similar to the movements, scowls, threats, strategems, and purrs in *Bataan.* There was very little sympathy for the foe. There wasn't a Gandhi in the crew. Not even on *our* side. I thought too that if it happens one of my brothers, or you, dies in this war, or anyone else dear to me, I'm liable to be a very bitter man when it develops, later, this war has not been fought so much for freedom, or a better way, or for the common man, but for the huge interests. Christ, how terribly bitter I'll be. After the picture, I had a half notion to go down town to Freddie's Cafe, where the fat cats of the Northwest hang out, to ask them, as they stand at the bar, drinking and fingering their dried-up peckers through their pocket walls, "You know, sir, my brother's liable to die in Sicily, Italy, France. . . . . how much are you salting away now? I don't mean bonds, I mean profits?" And go from one to the other. There aren't ten guys big enough to toss me out, and I can out-talk and out-argue any cockroach there, illiterate plutocrats! Christ it gets me mad . . . any one making more money than he needs for average living requirements is, as Romain Rolland says, a monster. (Howard Hoving wrote me a disappointing letter. Stilted, ignorant, prejudiced, narrow. Christ, doesn't he think? read? I'm so disappointed I hardly feel like writing him anymore. I think that if he were exposed to a chance to make a million, he'd be fool enough to do it. Christ.)

Monday, Oct. 18:

Good morning, fellow. I've just turned off the radio. In the morning there's a program of semi-classical music I listen to to start off the day. A constant exposure to good music has made of me a note-mad fool. There are times when I feel I can't write a letter without a little music about. By this time you've gotten the mags. I hope I did not get you into trouble. I wasn't sure if they inspected the mail of their constituency or not. I have very little conception of your world. You must tell me. Give me a description of a day. I was quite pleased to get a check from *N. Republic.* And surprised. I sent in a fast runoff piece and to my amazement they wrote back, saying the piece was entirely printable but that I should make it statewide. I had confined it too much to the city elections. In the letter they sent me, there was a slip from a reader at the N.R. to the editor on which he wrote I had a good profile style. The word profile was "quoted" and later I discovered that this reader also worked for *The New Yorker.* I understand some of the editors work for both mags.

'Tany rate, I dug around for some facts from the Farmer's Union "idea" man, from the Farm Bureau, from a few senators, from a few traveling government men, etc., and whipped it out. It was a little long, they wrote back, but they would try to use it. Then came the check, two months before they printed the thing. They took out some of my editorials, some of my choice adjectives, but in the main, left it exactly as I wrote it. I've been asked to keep an eye open for other materials for a "Report."

Of course, Veenstra read it, and sent me a letter flowing with "revolution" and so on, with some affection. I'm proud of fellows like Norm. They may go way off the tangent (if he did?), but they're alive. He hasn't slid back into the comfortable routine of a job and a wife and the Republican party. Meima wrote me in his customary testy, bitter, ironic manner. What mighty frustrations the lad has! As I wrote him, he needs a little intercoursing. The hell of it is he's too damned shy. The Army hasn't helped him either. Typical of Meim is this story. He and Fortch [Fortuin] and Dave Weinbeek were out wolfing. They found two women; or rather a woman and a cow. Fortch, of course, got the woman in the front seat with him, while Dave and Meim apportioned the cow between them. Afterwards, I asked Meim what sort of female he had gamboled with. "Well," he drawled slowly, "well, from the territory assigned me. . . . I gathered she was a human being."

More dynamic, John, has been another writing experience. Last winter, I ran into a local publisher of farm mags who published his first book, a best seller, *The Mountains Wait,* by Theodor Broch. It was a non-fiction book, illustrated by Rockwell Kent. The book sold well, was very well done up. This fellow, Hillestad, wanted to look at my novels because he also wanted a start in the fiction field. And he wanted to be very careful of the books he started on his list. He read everything I had and then couldn't make up his mind. He was reading materials sent in by a host of other American writers, and for a while I thought he was just stringing me, though he spent a lot of money lunching me. I'd made a few pen-and-ink illustrations, charcoals, pencils, and a painting for the cover, and he liked them so much that he said he'd let me illustrate my own book if he took one. He had Rockwell scheduled. I was astounded. For you see, taken all together, I've not spent much more than about 80 hours working on my drawing or sketching. I haven't touched it now for two months, though I'm beginning again today for a couple weeks' work of a few hours a day.

In the meantime, the chairman of the local Rockefeller Institute for grants to authors became interested in me. She read a book of mine and then steered a man, Frank Taylor, from Reynal & Hitchcock onto me. Frank, I believe, had something to do with *Wind, Sand, and Stars,* with Kazin's book, *On Native Grounds*, a lit review and interpretation. Frank looked me up, checked into my stuff for a month, then spent hours going over it with me, spent hours digging into me. He was most gentle, yet firm. He acted less enthusiastic about me in my presence than he did in others'. We discovered that I was apparently troubled with inhibitions, prejudices, and fears. There were times, he said, when I wrote as brilliantly as any man in America today. But, there were spots when I was a dud. He made the remark that my gentle, smiling nature hid a repressed nature, hid a tortured and, as a result, inarticulate nature. But, it was there. So then we checked back. For I know—though everyone likes to hear such guff—that I have it in me, but I just can't get it out. . . . I'd always thought it was because I had learned Dutch first as a kid and then had to learn American when I started the primary grade[1] to discover that when I was not worried about food, or time, or a job, felt free and musical, I had written the good stuff. The bad stuff looked like tired writing. This whole probing was a wonderful experience. It reminded me of some of the mind studies we used to make on each other in warm, keen friendship. He suggested that I should do nothing but write for a few months. No work, just write. Well, it happened he had come along just after

1. FM heard Dutch and Frisian but always spoke English [FM's note].

the Humphrey campaign this spring. I had spent two whole
months of 16-hour days in it and had enjoyed the great burst of information I'd picked up. I was one of four fellows that was in on
all the good and the corruption. (You should hear the tales I can tell
you now of corruption, of advances made by sinister forces to
probe a new man, of the squeeze they put on, of corruption and
gangsterism in labor, of a night when we had to escape with some
campaign stuff right in the middle of a blackout, wonderful.) (By
the way, I was glad to know too that I could take such grueling
work without getting tired. I gained weight during the work. So
now I know I'm really in pretty good shape, John.) And, I was
broke. The little money I had saved up from the enormous good
salary at *Modern Medicine* had been poured into the campaign. But,
my lovely and good wife came through. She decided to work those
two months to give me the break. So, I began, keeping an eye on all
the signposts that Frank and I had unearthed.

I sent him, after a month, the first quarter of a new venture.
(Frank had decided, meanwhile, that I had hold of two tremendous
ideas in my old stuff. One of the tragic optimism of farmers in the
dustbowl, the other of frustrated women. Doctors claim that nearly
¾ of American women are frustrated by sloppy husbands. As a nation we have more frustrations than any other race, even savages.
We got all the frustrated of Europe over here, it seems. And have
carried on the traditions of frustration veiled, of course, in religion,
etc. Savages have orgiastic rites which work off their women. But,
says Frank, the writing of those two themes is spotty. Why can't
you lay them aside for a year, or two, and then swing into them
again. When your mind is free, and elastic. They can be epic and
we don't want to spoil them. No one else has tried them, or talked
of them. They'll probably be your masterworks, so let's make them
good. In the meantime, what else have you in mind?) This new venture was a story of my life in the San. It was to be very personal (it
has deviated from that by now) and very introspective. It was to describe the spiritual, mental and physical breakdown of a man, of
his near death, of his eventual recovery . . . and more important,
and this last came out as I worked along, of his discovery of himself
and of his realization of his relation to life. It was to be called *Boy
Almighty*. It was to describe a boyish nature, willing and naïve, believing in the essential goodness of life. The tragedies of his life he
believed to be unreasonable. Life was actually good, and the hurts
and pains mere aberrations. Well, he gets hit so hard he almost

falters, and wonders. He almost comes to hate, but he feels that this isn't much of an intellectual improvement on his old loving of life. He realizes the tragic essence of life. As Yeats once said, "Until you learn life is tragic, you do not live." Now, he accepts people as they are. The acceptance is muted. If he had not come to see this, he might have slunk down into being a cynic, or a recluse, or a fool. That is not to say, he becomes an U. Sinclair, who loves blindly. No, it is a sort of philosophical resignation to the way things are. All through the book a symbol is used, the flame. The mind is a flame, a candle, a wick, a fire. To the extent that it is lighted, it reflects intelligence. But it never is bright enough to erase the circumambient darkness. As you will see, the Boy part is this gentle willingness to love. The Almighty part is his ability to see himself, to see the world, to be the curious prober. He is a sort of scientist. Scientists are boy almightys. They are naïve, yet they can leap great distances, can light up huge areas of the circumambient dark about us.

It was an immense task. Yet, I had thought about it so often in the San I thought I could do it. Well, after I sent in that quarter, I was shaken. I sent it in on a Saturday, and by Thunder, the next Tuesday I get a telegram from Frank to this effect: "Your transition is staggering. You are most decidedly off to a wonderful start. I am terribly happy for both of us. Things in the office are terribly jammed up. Don't be upset if you don't hear from me immediately in detail. Keep writing. By next week you will have a detailed critique."

Two weeks later I got another: "Relax and keep writing. Check for one hundred dollars on its way to you with letter of explanation. In the faith."

Well, the critique hasn't come yet, but the money did, and more letters. The main reason the critique hasn't come is because I have sent him the second quarter and no doubt he is busy with that.

And, still another "well." I finished the first draft last Friday. John, it was a revolution to me. It was, in addition to the excitement of spending all my time writing, it was an experience in introspection. I discovered concretely what it means to have inhibitions. I caught myself wanting to lie, too often! Then I'd probe the impulse. And discover it was something I had wanted to hide, even from myself, as if Myself could not stand the shock of exposure. It was a deadly business. And, in the process, I discovered to, or rather, I convinced myself, as to what I'd gotten out of the San.

Before I had only known vaguely. Now I have a fair idea.

Now comes the job of rewriting, polishing. It seems that is my next great job. The first one was of cracking my inward reticence. The second, my sloppy writing habits. I wasn't self-critical enough. It is most difficult. If one is too critical, the style suffers in spontaneity. If one is not critical, it is full of solecisms, incongruities, jumps, etc.

In the meantime, my wife and I were going through an interesting period. She knew I was writing truth, and was as anxious, and as filled with anxieties, as I was. We had some little spfffts now and then. But, we seemed to be big enough to get above them each time and laugh at them. We have learned to probe each other. Naturally, I'm not a great prober, nor a greatly honest man. I hide, deviate, slink, as much as the next man. But, women, I'm sure, are less inclined to enter a talk with an open mind and heart in the search for understanding, than men are. Women think there's a purpose behind a talk. There usually is, but there are times when certain men like to talk to discover and to explore. And they, being aware of what prejudices, and hates, and secret, unconscious drives may do to a thinking, try to circumvent them, or expose them, or trap them, anything, just so that the conversation may bring something. I told her one day that since the last talk I had with you in Cleveland, and that one wasn't too good because we were rushed, I'd been lonesome for companionship. And I have been. To me it has been a daily tragedy that I must live apart from the one man, the one person with whom I felt impulses, only half-realized, to talk freely, to explore, to be companionable. You are the only man I have ever loved. (And I hate the touch of men on my skin!) Why, John? Why? To me, what the hell are fame and glory and successful writing and all that junk . . .? Immortality is only the holding for a little while of the flame. There is an eternity for me, but it lasts for me up to and into the moment of death. And so I want to have my fun, my enjoyment, my feeling of absorption of life here, now. I think it is so god damned foolish to be separated from a man I know and respect and admire and to whom I feel free to talk . . . just because we must work out a career. Sure, careers, yes, we must have them. But I wonder if they are as important (to me) as your friendship is? Friendship by mail is like intercourse by mail. Can't we manage to live in the same town after the war?

And I think you'll love Maryanna too. She is much like you. She needs a lot of exposure to people like us. She can be one of us. She's not a very good cook, nor a great housekeeper; in fact I'm better at these than she, but she's a great companion. I'm damned lucky. But, that's not enough. I want a man friend too. You.

Well, to come back to the thread I dropped a moment ago, this Hillestad fellow suddenly made up his mind. He wanted to sign a contract for four novels, (*Boy Almighty,* the other two themes, and a fourth one that Taylor thought lousy. The fourth one Hillestad wanted *first*. Odd!) And he offered a check, a fat advance. Naturally, I'm interested in starting publishing houses out here. I don't like the N.Y. crowd because I feel they're provincial. We "provincials" know the currents of our own locale plus those of New York. They only know theirs, which is not America, but a province apart from U.S.A. But, at the same time, I realized that not only was Frank (and he's from the West) a better, a deeper editor (he likes Parrington, Smith, Cuci, Beard, Brooks, and many another historian) but his company could take me out of fear of want . . . and perhaps permit me to choose a city near where you'll settle after the war. (By the way, how do you like Denver? And the towering mountains?) And so, I'm hanging on with Frank until he can give me a contract and a fat advance. Otherwise, I'm going with Hillestad.

And now the chairman of the Rockefeller outfit suggests that I can get a grant from them as one of those "ideas" is of a regional nature. (Hell, it is, but I don't intend that it shall remain regional. It's going to be universal by the time I get through with it!) That'll come through in March . . . with a little luck.

Winter has come. The brilliant gold-rusts of fall have fallen and crumbled and rotted to brown and gray. The furnace is on again. And it seems tragedy is all about. I love life, I love people. I love the streets and the farms and the bars, snake-armed trees, but it is a terrible thought to me that all this struggling and composition of matter into active forms is futile, that a thousand years from now it will be a thin, quarter-inch thick layer of rubble over the earth. It is tragic that I can't be with you, or that we can't be with you. It is tragic that I'm gettin' older, nearer death. It is tragic that Maryanna's family, with the exception of her mother, has been wiped out, relative, son and father, wiped out. It is terrible to see my lovely, blond brothers in the services, grown up from their babble of seven and five and four, from the day when I'd lift their little pink fingers over their toes. I was home two days to see them, and all day long a refrain ran through my head, "Strange, strange. Yet, it is the truth. Strange."

John, I am not afraid of death, per se. I fear it, but I can face it. But it is such a terrible thing that I want the moment before I die to be so full of exultation that I will feel some compensation for the next moment, death.

My little brother, Henry Herman, 16, was here this summer with me. He worked in the U. Library. It was wonderful to watch him. Just like I was when I started Calvin. He'd hear of a strange mag, *New Republic, Nation,* etc. He'd hear my liberal friends rant and rave, he'd get that young curious-eyed, smiling look on his tender, pink face, and his blue eyes would nod and the next day he'd look it up in the library. Or of a book. Before the summer ended, he almost spent his last two weeks' earnings buying books to take with him to the "desert," as he called it. He's back in Iowa, now, getting his last year in high school.

"Strange, strange. Yet it is the truth." John, John, my love.

To Frank Taylor

Feike Frederick Feikema
1814 4th Street Southeast
Minneapolis, Minnesota
October 7, 1943

My dear Frank:

Was over at the Beach's yesterday; became involved in a long talk on great men in literature. He made the observation that our nation wasn't ripe yet for a Tolstoi. (That was after I observed I thought most intellectuals very childish and immature in their thinking and in their attitudes.) I agreed with Beach. Neither our most intelligent readers, nor our most distinguished publishers are ready for a Tolstoi. They would not recognize one. I did, however, differ with Beach on the time that a Tolstoi, or a great man, would arrive. I thought it possible he might arrive in our midst, within the next twenty-five years. I pointed out that Shakespeare must have been quite a sudden surprise in his time.

So then we began to probe into what constituted a Tolstoi. Beach thought, first, it took a man who could write well, that is, had some competence as a stylist. Tolstoi's style isn't obvious, or exceptional, or flamboyant, at least not as obvious as was *How Green Was My Valley*'s curious whine. A man, said Beach, who is poetic in style and nothing more is but a Swinburne the musician. Further, the great writer must have lived in an age where people are able to understand him, or he'll be lost. Some men are lost. It was an accident that Maugham's *Of Human Bondage* was caught up by the English. (Though Somerset isn't really my idea of the great man. He goes through the motions, yes. He has a neat style. He is precise. He has sympathy. But, he is not deep enough.) Then Beach became silent.

"What more?"

"What do you think?"

I answered, "He must have depth. That is, he must be Olympian so he can see far, and deeply. He must be a philosopher. More, a scientist. He must be able to draw so far away from people he can see them as they are, animals with a little whitewash. And yet, too, he must be able to live; that is, be sympathetic, and be as close to the people as he is to himself, have pity for people's failings, and emotion for their hopes, and be involved enough in the problems of living to join movements and to offer to help his fellow man."

Beach nodded. "Where is there such now?" I hesitated. "Steinbeck is the nearest to being such. When you read him you hear echoes of his sympathy, and you feel, through his chance phrases, through the very direction with which he strikes people with his light, that he is sitting high in judgement. But, I think his perch is not lofty enough."

Beach nodded.

I left Beach then.

Frank, I've never enjoyed life as much as I have these last two months. I'm married, got a home, a radio with noble music, books, and I'm writing, the thing I love most. I've got time for walks and long probings and musings and broodings, and. . . . Christ, man, for the first time in my life I'm really happy. Weeks fly past like giddy thoughts at youth. And it's because I'm having so much enjoyment out of life I'm sending you these paragraphs. They're signposts. They should tell you more of what I'm like. Perhaps the opinions are boring, but what's important is that they did go through the head of a man who's writing a book. And for that reason you should hear of 'em.

P.S. Reading the new October *Common Sense* "Quotes and Un-Quotes" reminds me that I think New York people are very provincial. They know only N.Y. We know N.Y. plus our own provinces. We, out here, are the cosmopolitans.

To Frank and Nan Taylor

Feike Feikema
1814 4th Street S.E.
Minneapolis, Minnesota
January 4, 1944

Dear Frank, and Nan:

I've just heard from Robert Penn Warren (who heard from someone in the English department) that Nan has been seriously ill and that she's had a serious operation of an osteomylitic nature. And I must write immediately to express my sympathy. Are you sure you have a good doctor, a good surgeon? I discovered from my San friends and *Modern Medicine* friends that many bone specialists are not too well acquainted with the bacterial agent in this disease. I do not mean to frighten, only to suggest that you make sure of your physician. That and your attitude are the two most important aspects of any successful convalescence. Actually one can do very little to help another 1500 miles away, or even one immediately near, but I do remember that letters and sincere words were wonderful things to get. So I'm sending you a 265-pound, 6′8″ handshake, Nan.

And Frank, the news also explained why you hadn't written lately. Well, we managed to meet the rent and most of the current bills this past week. (Though a relative had to make a fuss, which I ended abruptly with quick, effective command.)

Sitting here, day after day writing away, hearing the neighbor ladies wonder what the hell I'm doing, "not workin' in a factory," I conceive of my work as a holy task to keep one light alive in this terrible disease of war that's hit this earth. I know it is argued as necessary, but it is still an evil.

It was fun getting to know Warren better. The more often I meet fellows like him, the more sure I feel of myself, the more at home I feel in this narrow, cramped world. Down where I was, I felt very lonesome. No one was near to know what I knew, or what I wanted to do. I am more at home in an hour with a man like Warren, or Beach, than I am in a lifetime of living with my old friends who have no notion of what I want to do, or am doing.

Warren has a keen, rangy and luminous mind. We caught on to each other quickly. There is no job, in the "job" sense, but he has something for me to do. He wants to pick my brains, as he put it, to help him with *a political novel*[1] he's writing. Then, when he's done with the provisional draft, he wants me to read it. I feel honored. Apparently Beach and the *N. Republic* article did it. No money was discussed. But I think I'll get a lot out of it. We talked manuscripts and publishers. He likes your Erskine. And can

1. *All the King's Men.*

that sonofabuck walk! He says there are few to keep up with him, who ask for "no quarter." He was glad to know that I liked walking "nine miles in a couple of hours!" My God, man, he uses a stride as long as mine! And go, my God! he roars along, a half step ahead of me, all the while pouring out a perpetual stream of very literate talk. He must have thought me a dolt until we got home to his house to drink. And he catches at things about him. He is keenly sentient. A fine man. I hope he'll let me know him better. Met his ailing wife too. We talked of a dinner for later, and many walks for the two of us. In our talk we discovered something possibly sinister between Maestri of New Orleans and Stassen of Minnesota. Both used the same man in their first campaigns.

Warren liked you. And Nan. And again, my hearty wishes for your good health, Nan.

Yours, a bro.,
Fred

1944

The letters of 1944 record the birth of Manfred's first child and the publication of his first novel, The Golden Bowl. *In these letters, Manfred explores his Frisian background and its connection to Anglo-Saxon writings, and he corresponds with writers such as Henry Miller, David Cornel DeJong, and Wallace Stegner. In letters related to politics, Manfred modifies his earlier left-wing views. As to his literary pursuits, he chooses Paul Hillestad of Webb Publishing Company over Frank Taylor of Reynal and Hitchcock and continues to defend his independent literary stance. The awarding in March of an eighteen-hundred-dollar grant from the Rockefeller Foundation, University of Minnesota, motivates Manfred to do local research of flora and fauna for* This Is the Year.

To Paul Hillestad

[Minneapolis, Minnesota]
Jan. 2, [1944]

Paul—

I'm not interested in painting a story, or in painting a theory per se. I'm more interested in reporting, or reflecting reality; and, incidentally, in offering a comment or two on the passing of experience through myself.

In this book, I'm not interested in a "good" ending, or a "sad" ending.

I'm trying to reflect here this situation:

Here is a piece of earth.
On it grew grass and
animals of various sorts.

a. tyrannus rex
b. goats and tigers
c. buffaloes
d. Indians
e. white men.

This bit of earth sometimes
proves to be a tough place to
exist in. There is the drouth,
in this instance.
Some of the white people leave.
Some don't.
I report on what causes these people
to stay.

Too, I see that when they can't get what they want, they resort to dreams.

That last "poem" is the dream they comfort themselves on, and it is over this that Maury shakes his head.

All through the book, there have been hints that the family supports itself by the dream they have of the land—and that Maury sees that the dream is not enough. He stays with them not because they finally have this dream fulfilled but because he needs the warm companionship of people. And it is only this kind of people who are his. (Just watch the N. R.[1] and E. W.[2] make comments of this nature about the book.)

In its way, the book is a profound study of simple people trying to survive under duress.

Fred

1. *New Republic.*
2. Edmund Wilson.

To Henry Miller

Feike Feikema
1814 4th Street S.E.
Minneapolis, Minnesota
January 4, 1944

Dear Henry:

First, to answer some of your questions, or remarks. There are no bookstores in the Twin Cities as you describe. One of those like unto the Argus, or the Gotham, is the Bookhunters, 15th and 4th S.E. But he is a left-winger, and tries to keep the books he sells within the dollar range. He was acquainted with Ben Abramson. Immediately, I asked him why he didn't carry your books. He looked a little oddly at me, asked did I know how much they cost?

There's another bookstore that might be interested in carrying your books. He's Ray Van Der Hof, Minnesota Book Store, 14th and University (these are all near the U., the only place where there is some semblance of human decency . . . though not much) and he carries many high-priced and unusual books. (Not that I have you pegged as esoteric, myself, but that these birds think you are.) Just as soon as I can afford it, I intend to order your books through Ray, or at least one, so that he gets the habit of looking for your titles and will put some on the shelves for people to look at. (I've been preaching Miller now for three weeks, high and low, and now the two copies that were in the library are out, and there is a call for them, I hear.)

In the meantime, I should tell you, I found two copies, above-mentioned, in the University Library. A liberal head of the department of English (Dr. Beach . . . he also was responsible for getting Robert Penn Warren to teach up here despite the fact that these prigs up here are afraid of the man and his analytic pen and his strange revelations about sex) saw that some of your work was bought. They were: *The Colossus of Maroussi* and *The Cosmological Eye*. I started the latter first.

If you don't mind, I'd like to offer you my reactions. When I get through, you'll probably remark, "Well, so! The bastard! Lot a guts he has!"

I liked Max. I liked the way you presented the haunting problem of the Jew. It has bothered me. There is so much pressure on this question, that I find my needle flying in every direction but a steady one. I liked that Dieppe story very much. Here you are at your very best. Everything was clear, precise. A person knew he was in a real land, a real world, at every turn of the paragraph. The world was roomy, and right here in my den. Your tactile touch was at its height here. And your sense of humor wonderful. I laughed and rolled in bed. My wife took up the book then and then she laughed and rolled. Then we both had a wonderful talk about it. I liked Hamlet and the Tailor Shop too. The last was a fine gallery of characterization. Rather, I met some fine joes and sure want to thank you for bringing them to me.

The Colossus is what the title suggests. Great. I've read many books on Greece. Right now I'm in the midst of two concerning it: Plato's works and Durant's *Life of Greece*. So, you were exposed to a mind that was in the way of being refreshed. And you came off with flying colors. It rang true every step of the way. And I may say, aside from the literature in it, that I learned more about the Greeks from you than from the two aforementioned macs. No matter that sometimes you flew, or took off from reality, and wrote your own. The point was that you brought me the wonderful story of the magic unfolding of man on the surface of this globe, of the tragedy that, though this life flowers, it must die . . . or rather, will die. And someday, if this earth cracks, or the sun cools, it'll be as if it had never been.

Katsimbalis sounds like a great guy. Have any of his works ever been published in the American language?

There is another feeling I have about your writing. That you sense keenly the fearsome truth that just working and breeding and eating are pretty flat things, not much different from animal existence, except that "we" happen to be doing them. That the truly interesting and significant thing, though it too is doomed to death in time, is the struggling or the spirit or the vital energy or the pulse in the body to reach out through the universe and capture for itself some identity, some permanence. You and I and Beethoven create to cut our notch on the handle of the universe. Are you intrigued in astronomy? In anthropology? In paleontology? In philosophy? In any study that unbares the plot of our lives? I am. I hunger for it. I crave it. I love it better than sex (and God, how I love that!) or port wine or good food or praise. I'd rather sit one hour with the wide horizon of a friend's mind than with anything I can think of. But, there are so damned few of them. In fact, I've always felt very lonesome wherever I went, and there was once a time that I thought I was very stupid because I just could not talk to average people. And now I know why.

Another thing. You say you paint. By God, man, I discovered when I was laid up in the San that I had some talent at lines. They gave me one of those I.Q. things. I finished and had all correct before the time was up in an exercise on forms, or lines. So, I thought,

Christ, I'll bet I can paint. Or draw. Started out, and now I got some things here, which, though feeble, are as good as some over in the gallery. Some of the profs there want me to start taking classes. I won't. The point of this drawing thing is, that I feel I could do anything I wanted to, if I had the time. I feel, too, that you think the same thing about yourself. I feel that men who are near-geniuses, or actually geniuses, are men who think they could do anything if they took the time to do it. And, often do. History is full of their biographies.

Back to you. I'm very curious to know just the texture of your argument with American publishers. Just what do they tell you? Just what do you tell them? Your letter sounds very reasonable, so I can not imagine you arguing over one word, when writers know that a word or two, with writing being such a subtle and a flexible science, would not stand between you and publication. It must be the general air, or tone, or your materials, that they resent. Or, has it been that you were burned too sharply by life, and by the few publishers you met, and that as a result you condemned the whole lot as a bunch a bloody bastards? I am asking this because my publisher, Paul Hillestad of the Webb Book Publishing Company, St. Paul, Minnesota, is very curious about you, has read the two books I mentioned, and might be approached. He has a bunch of bastards on the board of directors there, but he himself is a fine edi-tor. Not once has he tried to change a word in my manuscript. He just says, "Well, Fred, this didn't seem to ring the bell. You can leave it, if you want. That's up to you." Of course, I go home, and wonder if it *did* ring the bell. And find, often, that I can ring it more clearly. He doesn't mind a rough word either, particularly if it's part of the scheme of the man. (There is the board, though, and they are something to contend with.) Can you tell me a little just what has been going on in your mind about the publishers?

Doughty wrote, *Travels In Deserta Arabia*. Also *Mansoul, Dawn In Britain, The Clouds, Adam Cast Forth, The Titans* (all long, un-rhymed pentameter verses.) He is much like you, in a way. He fought like hell for the exact way he punctuated his sentences, for the English he used, etc. He felt that the English Language had become bitched, that Spenser and Chaucer, not Shakespeare, were the titans, the natural fathers of our literature. He said they wrote and spoke the richer language because they kept close to the origi-nal roots of the Angles, Saxons and Frisians. Well, anyway, after you catch onto his charming uses of odd words, and his peculiar rhythms, he is a titan himself. There are descriptions in *Arabia* that are the most powerful I've ever read. He was the first white man to ever have traveled in inner Arabia, back in the '70's. His firm manner of sticking to his notion of the truth evoked grudging respect among the deadly Moslem Arabs. And he came out alive because of this uncompromising regard for truth. He was suave, of course. He did not pick fights. But, when it came to an issue, he always spoke out. He became a legend among the Arabs. They swore by him in time. And he, a *nasrany*! Doughty, who died at 85 in the '20's, says he wrote the book as a long poem. And it is that. I have the feeling of traveling with your great Greeks when I read him.

By the way, I find in both you and Doughty and Whitman a curious and wonderful rhythm. Not alike, but every word has an exact duty to fulfil in the weft of your rhythms. Reading you three men has finally got me to a point where if a word is off in my MS, I must go back twenty pages to make sure that its replacement fits. And if I alter it very much, I practically have to start reading from the first word of the MS.

More later.

Next day: Doughty was reviewed in a last summer issue of the *Time* magazine.

Webb's publish textbooks and books on agriculture for the middle west. Last year, they came out with their first professional publication, *The Mountains Wait,* by the former mayor of Narvik, Theodore Broch, who was imprisoned for a while by the Nazis. He is a brilliant man, very democratic and sympathetic to great art. He is not, however, a great writer . . . though his book is of interest. My novel, *The Golden Bowl,* will be Webb's first novel, as well as mine. You may not like it as well as the next one scheduled, *Boy Almighty,* which is somewhat in the order of your *Colossus,* except that I had to make my own Greece in the San.

While I was in the San, a roommate of mine and I got to talking about Swen Hedin's travel books, of India, Tibet and yak dung. We started to make up a fine Chinese dialect, swore in it that the other spoke a great accent, etc., just like you and the Greek did on the island of Corfu. God, I laughed when I read that part. We went on pleasantly deluding each other for days in just that vein.

January 14, 1944. Well, yesterday Webb's gave me a contract to have the *Bowl* done this spring. I got a good advance on it.

Yours,
Feike Feikema

To Frank Feikema

[Minneapolis, Minnesota]
Feb. 5, 1944

Dear Pa,

Well, it will be sometime in late spring, or summer (August), when my book will finally come out. There may be a delay because there is a paper shortage, but I think the authorities will let it be printed because it is a story that should be told about you farmers, and the tough time you people had to struggle to live out there in the burnt and gray prairies. Some people are not going to like some of the language I used, or the ideas, but as Old Feike, your father, used to say, "Bullshit, it's the truth, ain't it?" So, it has to be told as I did it. And that's the way I feel about it. In fact, some of the relatives may be mad, but they can go jump in a lake. I want you to know that I wrote the story that was as true as it was without naming names. And if I am a little rough in spots, it's because I'm a chip off the old block, Pa himself.

I've told Andy Feikema[1] about it, and he's excited. And so too Olde Romke Feikema[2] of Hawarden, and now he's braggin' and blowin' all over Iowa that that Feikema boy he sure can do it can't he? And he was very pleased to hear that I had signed it with my name, Feikema. He was afraid that I might have Americanized it.

Unless I'm lucky, I won't make millions on it, but I will make a fair living, as good as I'd make at a job. Only, I like this better than a job. This way I'm my own boss and nobody can tell me what to do.

Just as soon as it is out, I'll send you one with my signature. And if Johnnie is still there, you can have him read it to you. I'm sorry that I am not there to read it to you. As I surely would. And I am sorry now that when I was 18 or 17, I didn't read to you more often back there on that farm. After our mother died, I guess all of us were a little uncivil for a time, and I as much as anybody else.

But I want you to hear it read to you, every blessed or cursed word.

Be good to yourself, Pa, you're the only father I got. And I want to keep you for many years to come.

Love,
Frederick

1. Cousin of Frank Feikema.
2. Uncle of Frank Feikema.

To John Huizenga

Minneapolis, Minnesota
March 4, 1944

Dear John,

Finally your letter. I dropped all work to read it and read it. And study it.

You must promise me now that just as soon as you arrive in New York you will drop me a note telling me of your address. It need not be a letter. A card is all right. I realize, vaguely, how difficult it is to write letters. But if you will just drop me a card, I'll send you a longer letter than this will be; and I'll probably have some choice bits of news that you will like to hear, I'm sure. And there is also a possibility that I may go to New York for a week this spring when the book is ready. So, be sure to drop me a card.

Yes, the book is in the works. I think the publisher wants it to come out in August or September, to catch the rising fall book market. The first one is to be called *The Golden Bowl Is Broken*. It is a story of the Black Blizzard of 1934. It depicts simple people battling the elements. It is dramatic in form, with very little reflection. It has a deep meaning. It shows how people live by dreams when they can't get what they want from reality. It's either that or insanity.

Boy Almighty is still not done. Like bread dough, it is still rising. And we felt that, as a cook is foolish to put still rising dough in the oven, *B.A.* should be held out for a while yet.

I wrote you last fall that Taylor of Reynal & Hitchcock seemed a very good editor, possibly better than Hillestad of Webb in St. Paul, Minnesota. Well, I had only what these men "told me" to go on, but after I got to know Paul better, I discovered that the bigger of the two men was right here in St. Paul. When I saw some of Frank's later editing, I discovered that he was going to have me fit a notion of what he wanted writing to be, and not what I wanted. It is foolish to ask a man to write like another. I could never write like you: complex, sometimes prolix, sometimes involved. I work best with three-word sentences. And three-word sentences are most effective in novels. For if the words are held up in the brain where the meaning must be threshed out of the abstract phrasing, the sense of it will not stimulate the emotion or soul very readily. Best way is simple chords which the brain can instantly understand and will pass on into the emotional setup.

So Taylor seemed unsatisfactory. Besides, with Webb, I would be his first novelist. And I would be helping western publishing along. And I would be in an enviable position ten years from now should Webb become topnotch.

And Hillestad proves to be a fine, learned man, with keen tastes. [matter deleted]

Love, from both of us,
Maryanna and Frederick

To Henry Miller

1814 4th Street S.E.
Minneapolis, Minnesota
March 11, 1944

1. Published in *New Republic*.

Dear Henry:

I'm going to punch the next man in the nose that gets ugly about you. I've been having all sorts of arguments about you, with people who read your "open letter,"[1] but nothing else, and who think that you shouldn't have "cried." And most of these people who react this way are persons who wanted to write, but, in the face of poverty, were forced to work instead. And so here they are now, 40, and still no book. And they look with rancour upon any man who chose the other course, writing and starving. And so when this starving writer, you, has the guts to complain, well, he's a crybaby, because he asked for it. Jealousy, my man. Jealousy.

But there was one unexpected ally. A woman, Meridel Le Sueur, a communist, who came to your defense. She does not blame you for raving against the Americans for having ignored one of their finest writers.

Well, I hope my arm-waving about you stirs up enough interest for them to buy your books.

Your generous offer floors me. I want to read you, should buy your books rather than get them free. But since I can not buy them *yet,* and do not want to rob you of your royalties too much, I'm only going to ask for *Hamlet II* so I can finish that argument and for the *Tropic of Cancer.* I've told Ben to send me damaged copies, or demonstrators, not the best. Later, this spring, when I come to some more money, I'll buy your new *Tropic* and your *Black Spring.*

Hillestad has not finished the Hamlet book yet. He has been out of town for a while, has been buried in a flood of work. But he will read it, he says, and will do it when he can really give it close attention. He too, by the way, falls in behind my argument on most counts.

I'll have him write you when he's finished with the two Hamlet books.

I must tell you that I've just finished Art Machen's *Hieroglyphics,* and that it has helped me understand your particular contribution to literature. He spends most of his time expounding the meaning of ecstasy. And it is ecstasy, wonder, otherworldliness, the feeling of man's strangeness in this Universe, that are exactly your attributes. You have so unlearned the prejudices, the habits, customs (both good and bad) that make most people civilized that you have become a free-wheeling soul, independent of all rules. You are above them. You are of the future races. The children of the year 2010 will read you as if you were a next-door neighbor.

And they will go back to you for another reason. Your style. It is no accident that your style is so accurate and so lucid. That took workmanship of the highest order.

The N.R. says it will consider me as a possible book reviewer. I hope (as I asked) they will let me review your new *Tropic*. I may give you a sock or two on the chin, for as a reviewer one must put down honestly what one feels, but I'm sure that you will know that you are being tagged by a friendly boxer who enjoys a good session of mental play. (That is, assuming I can hit you.)

My father, retired farmer, now lives in Bellflower, Calif., and if I go see him, someday, I'll visit you too.

F.F.

To Wallace Stegner

[Minneapolis, Minnesota]
May 7, 1944

Mr. Stegner:

About two months ago I finished reading your *Big Rock Candy Mountain* and I have been unable to get it out of my mind since. I feel I know something about the northwest, about Minnesota, Iowa (where I was born), S.D., N.D., Montana, Idaho; and from this knowledge may I say that you have caught the true spirit and feeling and meaning of this country?

The idea of "We'll make it next year" has intrigued me for ten years (I've just won a Rockefeller grant on Regional Writing on this theme), and it was wonderful to find it done so well in your book.

I can not forget your description of the boy's ride across Minnesota towards the west, of the man's ride in the night with the very car becoming a sort of cat's whiskers to feel out the danger in the night, of the man's death and the powerful arch of his chest in the coffin. It seemed to me that in that last scene you had caught up the whole meaning of the book. Some of my critical friends tell me the book was too long, but I could not get enough of it; enough of the poetry, of the blue skies, of the long unrolling plains, of the abrupt mountains, of the people who ran over this land like ants and did not know what it was (and still don't), of the sense of doom and of death that dogs all of us at all times.

Wallace, I do not know if you are wearing the mantle of greatness that Lewis speaks of in *The Sat. Review of Lit.* (April 15, 1944), but I do know that you are the greatest in the Northwest. I had hoped to do something for this territory, but I'll have a long way to go before I get anywhere near you.

My first book is coming out in August, by the Webb Book Publishing Company in St. Paul (a new firm) (to push a western publisher, I decided in favor of them over Reynal & Hitchcock) under the title, *The Golden Bowl*. It is about the dust bowl in S.D. in 1934.

Again, Salute!

Yours, a brother,
Feike Feikema

To Paul Hillestad

[Minneapolis, Minnesota]
May 9, 1944

Dear Paul,

May I suggest that you may be making a mistake not to read the "black night" chapters carefully? It is on them that the book takes its leap upward at the end. These chapters depict his situation before his entry into the San. (Of course, if they do not attract attention, something may have to be done about them. Mann has many such passages in *Magic Mountain*. And so has Warren in his *At Heaven's Gate*. Both of these two books are very difficult to understand. But once a reader catches on what's up, they are very good.)

If this was just to be a San story, I'd chuck it. The book has to be rooted somewhere, in clay or muck or sand or whatever; and in this it happens to go through a San. For me, the real thrust of the story is elsewhere. He was a defeated man, in ambition (his Roots In The Soil), in love (Martha 1), and in providing himself with enough food to be earning his way in society (job). One of the reasons for using the device in the first eighty pages of allowing the reader very little flame on the hero's wick was to also give the feeling that the hero has very little ambition to live. However, once his body starts to get its regular food again and begins to heal, he has to face the problem of Martha and of the ambition. That's why the Black Nights start. And, they also serve to explain him.

As he goes along, his blood and marrow and physical energy improve. Willynilly, the powerful animal of him thrusts him ahead. Presently he begins to do mental things a little. The animal curiosity in all of us leads him on. A routine settles into his bones. A wonderful mind (Fawkes) and a wonderful "father" (Dr. Abraham) work their subtle influences on him. He meets another woman who begins to replace Martha in him. Slowly the powerful tug and pull of the physical world draw him on. And he is strong enough (though terribly bewildered for a time) to ride the storm of Fawkes' loss. He is strong enough, too, to ride the storm of seeing that Mary is not an angel, that she is like Martha, or rather, like all women, or, again rather, like an animal (heifers a-search for a bull). He learns to adjust himself to reality as it is. B.A., by the way, is a novel that pictures modern man in the modern world; that is, it is man in relation to the universe. In the old days, it was man in relation to God. Now it is Man in relation to the real world as the scientific feelers of the human race find it to be. I have yet to read any novel that has pictured that problem. . . . of modern man in relation to the world as the modern man conceives it. It is a new problem. (That is, in fiction. It has been all around us. But no novelist has as yet gone to work on the problem. Steinbeck, Hemingway, all of them, have been at work with the problem of man in relation to his disillusionment that God is not in his heaven.)

This is a novel of a troubled man in relation to a troubled world which he conceives to be, in the light of the best findings of science, a clod accidentally alive with growth. (See Schopenhauer chapter. See Fawkes-Frederick colloquy chapter.)

Now what relation has Martha and hunger and pricked ambition got to do with this? Because in the analysis of these problems, the true nature of life, of the world, of the universe, is partially unbared, that this is all but a little fuss in the evolutionistic unraveling of a skein (which, in turn, is but a little fuss again). There is no meaning in anything if it is related to something outside ourself. There is a little meaning if we learn to live with this knowledge and learn to get out of life what we can and then let it chuck us out.

What is Martha? She is a pretty little girl. If you believe we are all God-creatures, she is a pretty girl gone astray. If you believe we are all animals with a little gift of light thrown in, she is a normal young heifer behaving in a normal way. She is attracted by the big bull that passed her way. But why should she stick by him? No reason. To think she should is to think that marriage is eternal or good or normal. Marriage is not. It is an unnatural relationship. Men are supposed to (granted that nature made them) impregnate females. That is their job. A woman is "supposed to" pick the most eligible bull so that her children have some protection and so that they will be "good" children. If she isn't interested in having children right away, what's the harm in her running around a little, peddling her tail?

Maybe you don't like all this talk, but that is the way I see it. And to me it is beautiful, not dour. I believe we are much more animal than we think we are, and also much more "lighted" than we think we are. And this belief or hypothesis (for that is what it is since Reality is always eluding me or eluding the scientists, though the more we find out about it, the more impersonal we discover it to be) has given me less headache and less heartache than any other, and has given me more fun, has given me the outlines of a greater challenge to do something. In fact, the greater the universe and the more insignificant I become in it, the greater is my urge to cut my mark on the stone of eternity (which in time will also wear away). I've had more ambition to do things since I've discovered this hypothesis than ever before. It has given me enough dignity to understand Jean (the original of Martha 1), to accept my wife's true nature and to want to live with her, to forgive or to live with my mother-in-law, to keep my eyes relatively free of wild patriotic fervor about this War (for I still think that wanton killing is terrible in the sense that we are robbing ourself of a little victory).

Motivation in Martha? She needs none. There are some there, however. Her mother didn't want Frederick.[1] Martha was encouraged to cheat. She really didn't love him. (See first night he saw her. See the Housman poem. See what Frederick's friends thought of her. See her "doll play.") Motivation for him beating her? Calling her "whore"? What bull likes to see another bull actually impregnating a heifer he has had his eye on? And given Frederick's childhood, protected, idealistism-fostered, reared in a God-run-world . . . surely the problem just leaps higher than ever. It will be fun too if you find a single paragraph in this book for which I

1. Later called Eric Frey. *Eric Frey* is an anagram of *Frederick*.

have not intended a jab in relation to the overall philosophic scheme.

Love,
Fred

P.S. About my remark that I like to please first of all such minds as Wilson, Burke, Cowley, Warren, Crowe, I. A. Richards, Beach, Muller, before I please the average or the upper class or the professional intelligence. . . .

I do not write with their standards, or with their ideas, or precisely as they would write a book. But I want to write a book good enough to earn the respect and the attention of these men. I reach as high as I can and hope that the reach is near the top.

Just as you love book form and type, have come to understand Updyke,[2] etc., which no average professional intelligence understands, so too I like to work with the best minds in my field. There is greater pleasure in knowing that one is a companion, a working buddy, of the minds who work on the outer edges of progress or knowledge or science or literature, clearing away the first reaches of darkness that everywhere surrounds us than it is to satisfy the frustrated, the smug, the satisfied, the unimaginative, the non-profound, citizen. It means more to me to get a quiet nod of the head from Warren, or for that matter, from yourself!, than it is from the giddy teacher or stenog or friend or Woman's Club president. I think a writer must always lead his public a ways; work near them and with their inhibitions and taboos and religions and beliefs and foolhardies and at the same time strike ahead for the personal truths one sees . . . the first to be legible, the second to be listened to.

I'm no slavish follower of Burke or Wilson. I'd probably argue like hell with them should I see them. But I do know they're the best around.

And, as you said, the man you should please most is yourself. But what Yourself wants varies with each individual. The Yourself that runs me is one that wants to compare himself with the best in sight.

F.F.

2. Typographer.

To Dr. and Mrs. Garrett Heyns

[Minneapolis, Minnesota]
June 7, 1944

My dear Prof. & Mrs. Heyns:

Last night my wife and I saw a movie short about the Michigan penal institutions, and in it, I saw you. Just before you came on the screen, I leaned over to say to my wife, "If I remember right, one of my old teachers[1] runs that shebang." And then, there you were!

1. At Western Academy in Hull, Iowa.

I have often thought of writing you. But it wasn't until this spring that I had an excuse. You see, I wanted to write, bearing gifts when I did. Teachers like to know what happens to their former pupils. I taught three months[2] and it is a great thrill to have some of those kids write me that they are making progress as writers.

2. Practice teaching.

The excuse? Well, this spring I signed a contract with the Webb Book Publishing Company of St. Paul to have my first novel, *The Golden Bowl,* published this fall. I have already seen the dummy and have corrected the galleys. Furthermore, I was also fortunate to win a Rockefeller-sponsored Regional Writing Fellowship ($1800.00) which will help me finish my third novel, *This Is The Year.* My second novel, *Boy Almighty,* is finished, too, and is scheduled for late spring sale. Briefly, the *Bowl* describes the dust bowl of '34 in South Dakota. It is slim, a little harsh, at times poetic. *Boy Almighty* is somewhat on the order of Thomas Mann's *Magic Mountain,* as it describes modern man's relation to his universe with a sanatorium as a background. *This Is The Year* is going to be a farmer (illiterate, inarticulate) battling the impersonal elements like a blinded Cyclops. He will be Fris, though that is to be incidental.

I bring you these little notes of success because of a remark you made one day to Garritt Roelofs. (I write to him, too, once in a while; usually after his father and mother tell me I should.) There had been some sort of uproar amongst the wild students and you and he were standing in the doorway of the office. I was standing near, just inside of the assembly room. You shook your head, and muttered to Garritt, "You know, I sometimes wonder if all our work is worth it. Look at those wild Irishmen, those wild goats from the farm." "Yes, I sometimes wonder myself." "Still," you said, "still, it will not be in vain if sometime, somewhere, out of all this mass of ignorance we start off a genius who will contribute something to the world." "That's it, that's it!" exclaimed Roelofs. Now, the words may not be accurate, but that was the sense of it. I remember that I stepped back and went to the window and looked out over the rolling country, thinking about those words. And that night when I started my weekend, seven-mile walk toward home, I swore to myself, to the blue-green waving grass along the road, to the wild sparrows, to the skies, to my secret ego, that I would be that one person who would vindicate my two Garrett teachers. I do not know if I can qualify as a genius. Of course not. It is difficult to measure oneself. But I do know that, as I approach the outer city limits of Art, what I said that day was only a child's babble on an open prairie beneath an armless sky. Because to get here, with some little short victories gained, has cost me much.

I would like to tell you a little of what has happened to me since you ushered me into the world in 1928. I went back to the farm for two years, forgetting nearly all my learning except my lust for reading. My mother died in 1929, leaving six boys, no sisters, and a wild-eyed father who took out his grief on his oldest son, myself. (But I never struck him.) In '30, I left for Calvin. Played some basketball there, learned to write a bit, won some honors, also a bad reputation as a rebel. Chucked my teacher's certificate, and started roaming the country for three years that took me from coast to coast, led me into all kinds of dinky jobs and all sorts of situations. I never dropped my dream of becoming a writer. Wrote poems as I went, smiled at people, read Whitman and the Bible, kept up a correspondence with three friends. Finally, ill, a little bitter, and radical, I got a job with the *Minneapolis Journal* as a sports reporter. Resented sports. Wanted to get into political writing. Did, only it was on the side. I helped dig up a lot of stuff for the Farmer-Labor Party of Olson and Benson. Became acquainted with them. Of course, I was fired. Bluffed my way into Gov. Stassen's office, got a temporary job but lost it when I refused to give information about the CIO's activities in the north woods. Broke down in health in '40. Spent two years in a San. Entered as a far-advanced case of tuberculosis, complicated with pneumonia and pleurisy. Once I got around to thinking perhaps there was something to live for, gained 104 pounds and did not need surgery or medical aid to cure it. Took some courses at the U. of M. here, but found the Lit. Dept. boring, so took on a job as editor for a medical magazine, *Modern Medicine*. Wasn't allowed to put a little style into it, and quit after a year. Meantime married a lady I met at the San. She is an assistant in the U. of Minnesota Dept. of Journalism. Humphrey was running for Mayor on a reform ticket and I went to help him. We lost by 4000 votes. (I wrote up part of this episode in an article on Minnesota politics for *The New Republic,* Oct. 11, 1943.) About that time Frank Taylor of Reynal & Hitchcock, N.Y. publishers, made a swing of the country and looked me up. On that same trip he found Lillian Smith who wrote *Strange Fruit.* He looked over all my stuff, suggested that I was making the same mistakes over and over and then tried to get me to drop some of my grandiose schemes of building my books on intellectual foundations. "Streamline 'em. You want to make some money, don't you?" Meantime, the Webb people here had come out with a finely bound and edited book by Theodor Broch, mayor of Narvik, *The Mountains Wait.* He was looking around for a novelist as he wanted to become a first-class publisher in the west. I thought, why not? Those N.Y. birds shouldn't have everything to say about the publishing world. Besides, this will be in the way of a new adventure. (And I think it is going to work because the advertising firm handling his account are trying to tell him and myself that *The Golden Bowl* is better than *Grapes of Wrath.*) (It probably isn't true, but I don't think I'll bother to relieve them of that idea.) (*Boy Almighty* is by far the better and more profound book.)

And now for a series of "do you remembers": 1) I never walk up or walk down a flight of stairs but what I recall the day you saw me grasshoppering up the steps three at a time and you made me walk up one step at a time and walk down one step at a time. 2) Everytime some drunk sidles up to me and asks, "You know, mister, I don't wantcha to get mad or anything, but I'd like to know how tall you are. Me and my buddy had a little bet and we'd just like to know. Huh?" I remember the time in the W. A. library when you commented, "Sometimes nature stresses brawn, sometimes brains." And even before Strootman, Jacobs, et all, birds who always laughed at me, could get their faces together for a snicker, I said, "And sometimes stresses both." And you blinked, smiled, and said, "Atty old comeback, Feikie."

3) One night I came home to my folks with Hardy's *Tess of the D'Urbervilles.* It was fascinating, though I didn't understand the seduction scene. My mother, however, did, and the next week she made representations to you to keep an eye on my reading. I still can't decide if she was right or wrong. You were very patient, however, in explaining this "evil" to me, and beneath it I caught a vague hint you believed it was a sin to keep masterpieces from me. 4) I also recall the time some bird stole money in the girls' room and

you gave the whole school lie-detection question-and-answer tests. Nobody was supposed to know what was up. I did, however, because I had heard of the stealing, and had also been digging around in some detective books. And I remember that every time you mentioned a word that would fall in the "stealing field" I had to fight an impulse to put down a completely innocent word. In fact, a couple of years ago, when the FBI dropped in on me to question me about some friends of mine, I was afraid that I might answer wrong because I could see that the answers could have been the other way, too. 5) Another time, right after you finished your prayer in chapel exercises, I blurted out the first phrases of "Heere, zegen deze, etc." The philistines around me chuckled, and when I came home that night I made strong representations to my mother that I wasn't going to offer that little prayer anymore after father finished his. I knew how full of vagary my mind was and how little I listened to the heavy Calvinistic intonations.

I would also like to tell you that from local state officers of the penal system I have heard many favorable things of your work there. I glory in it. Because I know what a corrective and a stimulant you were to me in Iowa.

What has happened to Bobby [Heyns]? And your little daughter? And were there others? And Mrs. Heyns, I remember your charming smiles and how friendly and warm you were when my tall earnest mother used to talk to you. My mother longed for the life you lived. She hated the drudgery of the farm. She longed for the world of ideas. That's how it happened she read *Tess*. And just before she died, we were becoming "idea" pals. Looking back, I can see there was a brain in her, and a finely-tuned soul; and many of her expressions, some bitter, some exuberant, had the ring of poetry. I can remember them today. My mother was strict, but she was capable of enormous tolerance. When she died, she said to me, "Freddie, I don't know what's to become of you, and your ideas. You sound so funny to me. You are not very religious, are you?" "No, I guess not." "Well, son, only one thing I ask of you. Act out what you believe. If you are heathen at heart, be it in life, too. Don't be a hypocrite."

Only one of my five brothers lives in Iowa today. He is on the farm [Edward]. One [Abben] is a Chief Petty Officer in the Navy, and has been, among other places, at Guadalcanal, Tarawa. Another [Henry] is just going into the limited ASTP. Another [John] is a corporal in the Army. Another [Floyd] is an accountant with

General Mills, and an assistant manager at that. You wrote in my
1928 annual, "At Feike's request I am writing 'something' in his
book." Could you write 'something' in a letter to me, sometime?

Your,
Feike Feikema

To John Huizenga

[Minneapolis, Minnesota]
August 4, 1944

Dear John,

Perhaps if I had been a bit more energetic in paging you in the
hotel called America, I might have been able to arrange for a meeting in Chicago. Actually, the Chicago trip burst upon me like a
summer shower at 4:11 in the afternoon. A friend of mine, who
edits magazines for the Farmer's Union, and the political gang I
knew, were responsible for getting me to go along. And I was fortunate enough to be able to live in with others in Chicago. I rode
in a Zephyr compartment up and back, and that was a piece of luck
too. These friends very kindly made room for me in one they had
ordered months before. So, I went as a lobbyist.

Naturally I was bitter about the Wallace frame-up. I saw it coming. And, actually, the liberals have no complaint coming. They
have never organized very thoroughly. Every time Roosevelt was
accused of defection from the liberal way of life, liberals talked of
organizing. But by the time they started to do something, Roosevelt would perform some liberal trapeze act and they'd settle into
their nests again. It has only been recently that such an organization has started, Hillman's Action Committee, and now the Citizen's Action Committee. And they have been partly responsible
for the defeat, or the cracking down, of Dies, Caraway, Smith,
Kleberg, Costello, Starnes, Holman, Reynolds, and perhaps even
Mr. Fish. (And that terrible Clare Luce who, in histrionic cantos,
wept for the Jims she didn't get a chance to screw.) (Douglas' wife
wasn't much better.) This movement was also astounding in its
push behind Wallace. It is a genuine sign of power. In the meantime, one must hold the nose and vote for Roosevelt. (Voting for
Dewey would be even worse.)

The convention was a riot of humanity. I got many things from
it. First, I caught many accents of speech. I have been trying to train
my ear to catch folk expressions and metaphors, to catch speech
accents, etc. And the convention was a bedlam of them. Second,

I saw how hysteria can sweep a crowd, and make bosses (Hague, Kelley) cower momentarily. Third, I saw how excitement can erase inhibitions (married men out crack-hunting) and expose the bedrock of the well-brought-up.

When we got off the train, we were met by a merchant named Harold Huchberger who is a friend of Kelley and Alderman Touhy and Deputy Commissioner of Police, Elwin Rowe. Rowe was there also, dressed slouchily so that at first I confused him with a Teamster's Union gangster. But presently I was made aware of his power when he pointed out to me, after a call from the cop night-desk, Jimmy Petrillo and his hoods (armed!). Outside stood a huge new car, door open and facing the street with a man sitting behind a sub-machine gun in the back seat. Petrillo took instant resentment to me. I was too big for him. I was a hulk that, in his eyes, could not be easily terrorized or intimidated.

The next day, I went to the convention in the morning through the offices of this Huchberger. Police lines vanished like magic when we approached them. People disappeared from seats when we approached them. I felt like a heel. I hate to accept privileges others don't get. My conscience still bothers me about this. That's why I'd hate to become an officer. Couldn't stand it. I may have a better brain than most people, but I don't think I'm any "better." And the having of a better brain should preclude any notion of superiority. Brains, real brains, usually detect a common humility amongst us all. I saw Ickes argue before the Illinois delegation in the Touhy headquarters. Saw the delegates revolt against Kelley. Saw Kelley cleverly switch them behind Lucas and keep them from Wallace.

In the afternoon I called your mother. There wasn't much doing that day at the convention. I made a few business calls relative to the book's coming out (now set for September 14) and then headed for your home on the I.C. Your mother and father met me on the sidewalk, welcoming me just as my own mother would have if she were alive today. Many things she says irritate me just as my mother would irritate me, but her prevailing mood and attitude is essentially just like my mother's. Your father is a fine man who has never found his level . . . some few notches above where he is now. He has the motions of a good practical mind: it keeps boring down to the bedrock of facts. They fixed up a highball for me. Told me that you liked to fix one for yourself and your father. They showed me pictures of you and your lovely sister Kathryn, gave me a picture of you standing in blue near the house and smiling as I remember you smiling when we were at the height of some exuberant moment. Then we had a rich supper despite her promise to me over the phone that "it must be simple." We talked until ten to eleven. It was hard to tear away. It has always been difficult for me to break away from them. Always. It would be very easy for me to adopt them for my parents.

The next day the maelstrom was in earnest. Huchberger took me to the Cook County jail where we met Warden Frank Sain. He and I took an instant liking to each other. We went through the whole jail, inspected (and I cried inwardly all the time, slowly tearing my heart with my outward sang-froid) the electric chair, heard how they use the four-button system so no one cop knows who throws the switch (because pals of the condemned have heard coppers confess in the after-brawls), heard how once a fuse blew out and the poor bastard sat there waiting and the doctors kept watching for the steam from the sponge-contacts, had my picture taken in a nervous, hilarious moment à la convict, saw the German spy Haupt and tried to talk to him. John, there is very little difference between that jail and the San I was in. The food comes up to the floors the same way, there are trustees, disciplines, and bars (the one visible, the other invisible). Altogether I spent a nostalgic day there. Warden Sain was interesting. He had come there an untutored jailer, with no training in sociological or psychological thought. But after some ten years of contact with the unfortunates, he had come to the conclusion that, though it was not safe to turn loose men who had few safe inhibitions anymore, they were fundamentally not at fault. It was the fault of early training and impoverishment, if such be faults. (These things "are.") "A stricter and an understanding father, and two-bits now and then. . . ." he murmured to me.

Then back to the convention Thursday to see the Roosevelt demonstration, the Wallace speech (heroic!) in which he said that the Democrats can not successfully play the role of the Republicans, nor can the R's. play the role of liberals, a meeting with Wallace (whom I met thrice earlier in the year), and a general milling around through hotels.

The next day some more of that, and then home. And on the train, the tragic news.

Monday: I have a bit of news for you. We are expecting a young heir this fall, sometime in the early part of December. It was a surprise to us, particularly to me as I had supposed that anyone with as much tubercular history as I had would never become fertile again. There might be plenty of arrows, but no striking power, was the concept I had about it. (Of course, we always took precautions.) But we are glad. Maryanna is a little worried about her health, though she feels fine, has lost no meals as yet, looks better than she ever has. She always had a vague cast of pallor about her, but this has disappeared. The hot weather is uneasy for her. I have felt the little feller stirring under my hand already. He usually raises a rumpus when we're settling down for the night. This whole business is not strange to me. I am astonished that I behave as if my being had expected this and knew just what to do and to think. The stream of my conscious thought is almost the same as it always has been, except that here and there a small eddy, a whirlpool, appears in a different place. Maryanna has quit her job at the University. We are living on my grant money now, but I don't want her to become a housewife. I imagine that we shall have to share more of the house-work. She still writes a weekly script for the radio, and now and then fills in editing jobs around town. Perhaps all this stuff bores you, but I am telling you these things to give you a feel of our life.

Your letter was one of the best you've written. Not that writing "good" letters is an aim in itself. It was casual, and relaxed. I like the letters you put time into, because they give me the feel of your mind. But the casual letters are the best, because they give me the feel of you. When you give me what you feel at that moment, you are giving me a better picture of what the long view of you is than when you reach in yourself and try to give me the long view.

I have a brother in the South Pacific, Abben Clarence Feikema. He is a petty officer aboard a flattop. Last we heard from him was that he was in New Guinea. He is tall, blond, blue-eyed, (a little nervous now) and looks and acts a lot like I did when you met me in Iowa back in 1929.[1] He has finished high school and is just beginning to feel his way into the idea world. He has asked us to send him *A Tree Grows in Brooklyn, For Whom the Bell Tolls.* I think he has potentialities. He has been in the invasion of Africa, at Guadalcanal, Tarawa, and now at Hollandia. Maybe at the Marianas, etc. by this time.

You know, we have an interesting English Department at the University of Minnesota. There's Robert Penn Warren who has written *Night Riders, At Heaven's Gate,* and a volume of Poetry. He has not hit the best seller lists, but he is a serious artist, and a very

1. Actually it was 1930.

good one, and has just been given a Poet-in-Residence position with the Library of Congress for a year, a high honor. Then there is Dr. Joseph Beach who is being quoted in the serious critical works of Burke, Wilson, Muller, Crowe, Tate, and others. Beach's novel and poetry stinks. He knows it. But his critical writings, *American Fiction,* and the *Twentieth Century Novel,* are excellent and far in advance of the time. These two men along with Tremaine McDowell, an anthologist, are tops in America. Usually English departments are filled with old-fashioned scholars and dodoes.

It has been most pleasant to get acquainted with these men, to test my knowledges against theirs (and to be found wanting in some respects), and through them, to become acquainted with the best in the fiction (serious) world. A long time ago I remember that you told me I should study the masters, and study the techniques of fiction. I eschewed the idea then. And with good reason, I think. I needed more experience, more knowledge of what life was than I did technique. Technique can be learned by anybody with half a brain. But the business of learning what life is, what you yourself are, of penetrating the mysteries of your mind's relation to reality, are things that take wholesome brains and a lifetime of sweaty work. You must have a passion for living, a passion for honesty, a mad hunger for truth. So, instead of following your advice, I drank lustily of life and of books outside of literature: anthropology, the theories of chemistry and physics, sociology, psychology, everything that might help me open the reluctant windows of my mind and smell the world outside me. I find now that I have so much to say that it will take me sixty years to get it said. There is hardly a fact now, a thought, a feeling, a nuance, which is not related to information a hundred, nay, a thousand times its size and worth. I have so much to write about that my biggest job is not to get it down with accuracy, but to get it down so that it has meaning and relation and interest. Thus, finally, at last, I am returning (as you said I should, and would) to the business of techniques. And they are rather easy to understand. They are easy to understand because art is the business of selecting the best fact out of a hundred similar facts on the same subject. The more you know and the more you have to say, the more the word "technique" means.

Writing is not necessarily the result of inspiration. If one is going to wait for a mood, or inspiration, to write a book, he will never get it written. It is labor. It is first of all training, training yourself into such a routine, a habit, that when you sit down to a typewriter, you begin pouring out related materials without really knowing how it is done. And some mornings you have a fever in your veins and then the stuff lifts. And some other morning you are angry, and again the stuff crackles. And some morning you are low, and the stuff has a melancholy, turtledove-song accent. Writing is learning to concentrate and unify your personality into becoming a working tool, ready to work at a signal. And even when you are not up to it at promptly eight o'clock in the morning, you write anyway, and usually much better than you think. The writer in you is a personality all by itself and it bosses you and runs you and makes you a strong character. Short quatrains may be the result of sudden inspirational bursts, but epics are not. They come from sustained effort, from sweat and headache and growling guts and colds and carbuncles and broken fingernails.

These things, these facts, I find corroborated in Edmund Wilson, in Kenneth Burke, in Herbert Muller, I. A. Richards, Taine, Emerson, etc.

And believe it or not, I have been reading the Fowler boys (grammarians in England) and find that I enjoy them. And other books on construction. I find too that the American language is much richer and more beautiful and more apt than the English. One has to be careful in choosing the American idioms, because many are fleeting in worth. But some are magnificent, and I intend to develop a real American flavor and style in my writing. I use the grammars as something to go by, or from, as something that will give me a historical feeling for the worth of today's textures. Shakespeare picked up the language of the street, whorehouse, alleys, provinces. If he had used the language of the Elizabethan intellectual, or the court, the stuff would have been insufferably dry and boring. Well, John, write me. Soon.

Love,
fred

Maryanna sends her fondest greetings.
[margin] I went to the Democratic convention in Chicago. F.

To Robert Penn Warren

[Minneapolis, Minnesota]
September 25, 1944

Dear Red:

I've been down to the Webb plant to autograph a book I am sending you. Your wife has probably been telling you about it, and that, along with Beach's and Gray's interest in it, may make it interesting enough for you to look into it too. Please remember that the book does not touch (in my mind at least) the second novel that we hope to publish next year, and certainly not the third that I'm writing here for the Regional Writing Committee.

We understand that the reception to the book will be good. A week ago the Chicago *Sun* broke an early review on it (Sept. 10) that was very pleasing.

Note to Cinina: Have you gotten your money from your maid? When I learned that the Armstrongs and others were not coming until late afternoon, I decided to go home. The truckers were very careful with the fragile things, and I made a point of carrying most of them. If you don't get that money item cleared up, I'll be glad to look into it for you. And any time you want an errand run, I'm at your service.

Red, I just simply can't get to like Hardy. Years ago I read his *Tess of the D'Urbervilles,* and read it for the seduction in it. Felt it was boring then. And now, reading his *The Return of the Native,* I am astounded that critics can talk about him so soberly as one of the great. Some of the ideas he has, and his prevailing mood, may cause serious comment, but the writing is pretty corny. He keeps telling me things I already know. He repeats the obvious. His metaphors are stretched. His conversation stilted. (Fellows like Fielding, Tolstoi, Turgy, have conversation that, though not real, is readable and plausible.) His women have ridiculous sentiments, his men act like castrated gentlemen. Reading him I wonder how in the name of heaven the English have offspring. Too, his book is full of construction material, which, standing all around the structure, blots out the beauties that are there. The chapter, "Journey Across the Heath," for example, is superb, and is the only place in the book where he really moves and sparkles, where he illuminates your mind.

I have been unable to get into Conrad either, but for other reasons. There I find wonderful style; and the conversations, though never spoken by human beings, are at least very readable and not offensive to the sense of progress in the book. It is something else there. Perhaps the mood. Or the thick involved style. Or perhaps I'm not ready for him.

I find Tolstoi wonderful on third reading. I've just finished reading his *War and Peace, Anna Karenina, Master and Man, Kreutzer Sonata.* His attempts at intellectual penetration usually clog the works, but he is readable even in these spots, mainly because you're wondering what his querulous old mind is going to rumble about next. Tolstoi is very aware of change, of movements, of the evanescence of ideas. He knows that as long as truth thunders behind the words they'll have some meaning, but that truth or reality or stuff sometimes retreats or vanishes and then the words are fluff. I do not find him very dramatic, or exciting, (no faults, of course) and he does not dig very deeply into people, though he knows a lot about them.

Finished reading Muller's *Science and Criticism,* and haven't made up my mind if he's written something there or not. Main difficulty is I don't know my science well enough to know if he knows his. Hence, his conclusions will have to await a few years for vindication.

I find that Burke's *Attitudes Towards History* is very good. Most important idea I've got from that book is his notion of succeeding syntheses, each one including the one before it and adding a new light, much like Einstein includes Newton. He develops this by tracing the courses of Jewish, Greek, Roman, Renaissance cultures. A man can profitably examine that structure for novel-writing. Doesn't each movement in a good novel do the same?

You have missed some wonderful fall weather. There has been no frost yet. And many days of wonderful glass-clear skies. There is a ripe smell about, of tomatoes cooking, and apples rotting in the twisting green-grey grass, of weeds spraying their seeds to the winds. I spent some more time in Iowa and South Dakota, talking to farmers, and walking over the countryside. Walked twenty miles one day. Cut innumerable slips of weeds, bushes, trees, vines, flowers, stuffed them into wax sacks, and had them identified here at the U. Also rocks, soil, clays, etc. I have been reading weather reports, etc., until my head resembles Venus with its perpetual envelope of clouds and fog.

Say, that Pennell guy in *Rome-Hanks* hit all his bells with the same clanging sledge-hammer.

Let's hear from you, fellow.

Best,
F.F.

To Henry H. Feikema

[Minneapolis, Minnesota]
November 2, 1944

Dear Henry,

How I laughed when I read your letter! And had tears, too! It was so like you. And like myself. I feel very sorry for you. I had almost the same feeling when I was in college. In fact, when I came back from a Xmas trip home in 1930, and had seen all you saucy fat kids and had become thoroughly lonesome, I was ready to leave [college]. The climax came when I saw my marks in English. F! Which was a failure, of course. I started to cry and began packing. Two friends heard about it and they came upstairs and asked me if I wanted to go to a doughnut shop for a cruller and a cup of coffee. I had heard of this place and the idea of a fat cruller appealed to me. We took our walk. All the way from the dorm to the place and back again, they said nothing about my leaving. And then, at the door, they said, "Look, Feike, you're just as good as any hobo in here. Better than most. Don't be a coward now. Don't let us westerners down now." (There had been quite a bit of talk that the eastern American Hollanders were better than the western.) "Besides," said one of the two, "you're a Fris, an' they never give up."

Well, I sucked up my tears and my hurts, and gritted my teeth and swore that the bastards would pass me in English. Well, they did, but I had to suffer a lot of boring hours. College is often very boring. Sometimes I wonder if it is worth it. But usually there is one professor who makes up for it, and he opens a door that will never close. That door is freedom, mental freedom. Just think, had I gone back home, I would never have written *The Golden Bowl*.

Your letter sounds, too, as if you are afraid you are about to flunk a course. A student, a smart one, can often feel a flunk coming. Is that your case?

Well, maybe a layoff for a week, an I-don't-care-attitude, won't hurt none. It'll free your mind and give it a rest.

As for giving you permission, it isn't for me to give. You are far enough along to make your own decisions. You are more mature and grown than some eighty-year-old people I know. So why should I be asked to give you permission? I may have an opinion or two on what you do, but I'll back to the hilt whatever you decide, fellow.

Just think, here is Maryanna. For seven or eight months now, she has had to look forward to a date which can be, for a time, nothing but terrible pain for her. She has a month left. Each day she has to think about that day of pain to come. Each day is clouded by it. True, it is glorious to have the son, but, still, there is that unknown pain to come, and perhaps worse. Now, don't you think you can stand nine months of educational drilling? True, the pain is terrible, but there is some little reward, too, isn't there?

Come, hit it hard until at least Christmas, and keep after that transfer. We are looking forward to your coming.

Or is there some trouble you are in? Can I help?

Now, for a bit of good news. We heard that the Navy is going to buy a slug of 650 of my books. (Maybe the Army will, too!) That sells out the first edition, or nearly so.

And I was mad, too, the past week. That's why I didn't write you. That bastardly *New Republic* wrote that I was imitating, or was being influenced by, both Steinbeck and Wolfe. Those guys are good, but I don't want that comparison. It was a lousy trick.

Love,
Ff

To Clayton Hoagland

[Minneapolis, Minnesota]
December 12, 1944

Dear Mr. Hoagland,

It was most heartening to get your letter. To get one like yours is reward enough for having struggled for what seems eternities. It has been a long haul from the family on an Iowa farm, where father was illiterate but passionate and where mother though brilliant was turned to an enclosing Christianity, to a point where I can not only read but write a "good" book. And, I feel I've only just begun to climb. I feel sometimes like a vast Siberia, still mostly inert, frozen, still only partially awakened. And each time a new province awakens, I find treasures I never knew I had.

I am beginning to understand, concretely, the expression of the old Church Fathers that the Lord Our God had directed their hands in the writing of the Bible; and therefore that it was the Lord's testimony, and as such the truth. I feel that same way every day I work here in my den. I am always surprised at what comes out. It all seems a miracle.

Of course, I am a conscious artist, as much as one can be such. But I am about as conscious an owner of myself as a miner is of the gold in the soil. It really all belongs to Mankind. I only happen, as a mind, to be squatting here.

1. *The Golden Bowl.*

I too was disappointed in the reception my book[1] got in the east. I had expected good reviews from the *Times, Sun, Herald Tribune, Post* (and got them, I see), but also from Wilson in the *New Yorker,* from the *Saturday Review of Literature,* from Cowley or Mayberry, from Margaret Marshall, from Weeks at the *Atlantic,* from Chamberlain at *Harper's,* from DeVoto. But they have been silent. And most surprising, I hear of good reviews from the Coast, from Chicago, from Omaha and Milwaukee. I felt that my book would be too serious for most run-of-the-mill reviewers.

The sale has been good. The first edition is sold out (3200) copies and the second is now running. The sale has been steady. It is fun to see where they come from. Boston, little stores around Harvard; and (Prescott?) Los Angeles, Chicago, and heavily in the Twin Cities here. Many individual orders come from young and still rebellious English instructors and associates. Isolated writers send for single copies. A few critics. The kind letters they write is heartening. But of all of them, I welcome yours most. For I felt in your review, which was sober, restrained, that you had pierced through to where I sat and felt me and knew me and with lighted eyes had put out your hand to me.

You will be interested, no doubt, in the immediate future books I have planned. (I have ten warm plots at work now and each day I add a phrase, an idea, a reflection to them. I get them at all times, and I take rapid notes and each morning, before I begin the work, I throw them in the proper files.)

The next book has been tentatively titled *Boy Almighty.* It started out being a diary of my experience in a tb sanatorium, and ended up by becoming a sort of novel. And the main character changed, left my person and grew up and became himself, one Eric Frey. He entered the San a broken person, broken in health, broken in love, broken in ambition. In the story I trace the slow evolution of his recovery, and, most important, for the other is only really a background for the following idea, he seeks to understand his relation as a "modern" to a world whose foundations have been radically altered by science and industry. While the universe is beginning to mean more to us, our very life is beginning to mean less to us. At first, because he had to find a scapegoat, he accuses his father for having brought him low. Then that concept is penetrated and exposed. But the mechanism or hunger for a scapegoat fastens on certain friends, then on his environment, then on the old Jehovah of his youth, and then, at last, he sees that what really runs the show is an impersonal reality, an impersonal universe, that can be chaos as well as cosmos. Each of these scapegoats he names The Whipper. It is the wrestle, then, between the Whipper and Eric Frey. And most of the book, strangely enough, takes place in a single room in the San. The book is surprisingly lively, and moves faster and more intensely, and more poetically, than the first one. *Boy Almighty* will come out in '45.

I am now at work on number three, and am half through with the first draft. I write very rapidly in my first draft, spend years polishing. (I rewrote *The Golden Bowl* seven times.) This is my third shot at this present idea, and this time I've got the range and the pace. It will be a very long book. I feel like a fly sitting on a pan of rising bread dough. No matter where I press down to keep it within reasonable length, it bubbles up elsewhere. So I am just letting it go. This book is again the farm, and man's relation to an impersonal universe.

By the way, there is a chance that I may go to the European theatre for a time. I want to know concretely what my generation is going through. I want to write of the war someday, too. I think I can. What I have seen so far has been slush. (Though Brown's *A Walk In the Sun* wasn't bad.) I already have the basic idea and plot for the war novel. And will spend ten to twenty years building it.

Your remark about Steinbeck was interesting to me. I have read Steinbeck. All of him. But I have read others too. I have looked into almost all important writers, including Shakespeare, the Bible, Charles Montagu Doughty, Chaucer, Dickens, Thackeray, Fielding, Hugo, Hauptmann, Mann, Homer, Plato, Aristotle, St. Augustine, Hegel, Marx, Lenin, Dreiser, Hemingway, Caldwell, Dos Passos, Freud, Melville, Whitman, Tolstoi, Rolland (Romain,) Burke (Kenneth), Henry Miller, Hooten, John Strachey, etc. Of them all, I have read Shakespeare, the Bible, Steinbeck, Doughty, Tolstoi, Whitman, the Frisian Bible, Melville most completely. I think Doughty and the Bible and Whitman are the Titans of them all. I think Steinbeck is sincere, and honest, and poetic in a "tight" sense. But I do not think he sees very widely, and is at times uneasily self-conscious, particularly where he wants to keep from us that he has been feeling sorry for his characters. I recognize Wolfe as a great artist but can not read him consistently. Joyce is next on my list. I hope I have not been too presumptuous to put this all down, but I felt talkative after getting your heartening letter. I just started reading your wife's[2] novel when my wife grabbed it.

2. Kathleen Hoaglund.

What I saw was rich with Irish dialogue and childhood scenes. I am looking forward to meeting you, and shall next year.

F.F.

1945

In 1945, Manfred enjoys a generally favorable reception of The Golden Bowl, *which goes into its second printing this year. He wrestles with Hillestad over the publication of* Boy Almighty *and progresses in researching and writing* This Is the Year. *A one-thousand-dollar grant from the American Academy of Arts and Letters in March allows him to continue work on* This Is the Year *after the Rockefeller grant runs out. Literary contacts continue with Robert Penn Warren, Van Wyck Brooks, William Carlos Williams, H. L. Mencken, and others on the East Coast. He, Maryanna, and Freya move to their new home (later called "Wrâlda") in Bloomington.*

To John Huizenga

[Minneapolis, Minnesota]
February 26, 1945

Dear John,

I intend to take it easy this week. For a period of about twenty days I've been pounding this typewriter in an attempt to get out the manuscript of the second novel, *Boy Almighty*. I hadn't looked at it for ten months and during that time the publisher had gone through it four times hunting for boopers. When I got hold of it again I found a few things to iron out, also to rewrite or repolish. So for twenty days I've been sweating in here while Maryanna has been trying to keep the baby hushed in the house.

But this morning I decided that I would lay off for a week. I was getting so screwy that, like last fall, I was walking into the kitchen when I wanted to go to the bathroom, etc. And she has gone off to the Historical Society to finish gathering materials for her Master's thesis. So, the baby is in the other room, quietly sleeping, and building up a big hunger for the ten o'clock feeding. The baby, I find, is fascinating. I never dreamed I could be fond of the danged little thing. And we are half sure that she'll be a smart little codger. Already she is aware of tricks to elicit our attention, and we have to steel ourselves against her agonized calls. We don't want to spoil her. And the name Freya (after the goddess Freya, goddess of plenty and music and joy; also the root for the word *Frisian*) fits her. I usually help Maryanna with one or more of the feedings, have learned to change diapers, sometimes even wash her. But my hands aren't very adept at most of those matters.

The book, *Boy Almighty*, is, strictly speaking, not a novel. It is really a "scripture," a recording of suffering. I found some lines from Whitman that express it perfectly, and they will very likely be the frontispiece:

"A man, yet by these tears a little boy again,
Throwing myself on the sand, confronting the waves,
I, chanter of pains and joys . . .
A reminiscence sing."

I have tried to record my experience in the San. It is not about myself so much as it is about an Eric and a Fawkes, and a certain group of women who revolve in and out of the mother-complex constellation. Eric was broken when he reentered the "womb" and was whole when he was cast forth. My wife has read it and thought it a "strange" book. A bookseller read it and screamed that it was too pretentious, thought I should have stuck to my "farm writin', because I knew that best." I don't know. I think I knew the San (the womb) much better than any of them. That damned place made me as a person. Anyway, it was fun writing and wrestling it out of myself, it was great sport fashioning the poetry in it, and it was even more fun trying to work out an idea that I had in mind. (A modern youth cut adrift from the old universe where God came to his office at eight in the morning, and thrown into a universe where all is chaos. And then, his attempt to find some sort of salvation, or happiness in it, a brief victory.) My second hunch is that only a handful of people will understand what the hell I was up to. You will be one of them because it expresses many of the things we used to dream and talk about.

Now for some news. Maryanna and I have taken a desperate gamble. We have borrowed an enormous sum of money and have bought a house overlooking the Minnesota river, just south of town. It is on a high bluff and through the huge ¼ inch glass window (about ten feet long and four feet high) we can see twenty miles up the river valley. It is country there, though we do have a telephone, electricity, mail, laundry, newspaper, indoor toilets, etc. We also have ten acres to go with it. The view is magnificent, and

1. Northrop Beach, M.D.

we were very lucky to get it. The rich have all bought out the bluffs along there so an ordinary mortal doesn't have a chance to get in. That is why we were lucky. We had a doctor friend[1] who knew the owners. The owners' son lived out there, wanted a young neighbor, liked us, liked what I did, and decided to let us buy a part of their property with this five-year old house on it. We really have something there. The place is not yet outfitted for winter, and we may have to keep moving back to town each winter until the war is over. But it can be winterized after the war. It has a huge graystone fireplace in it, big porches, and a good-sized living room. Some of the other rooms are small, but they can be enlarged by including parts of the porch. These rich folk built the place for themselves so they put in the best. Both Maryanna and I feel a little guilty that we are buying this when the nation is at war, but on the other hand, if we didn't, we'd never get out there. Besides, I feel that I have fought one good war already, and one is one too much for any life-time.

Also for the writing. Since the book has been published, I am a target for too much attention. I don't like it. I like my music, my books, my walks, my countryside, my thoughts. I like people but I want to meet them at my own convenience. And I like to live with my family. Maryanna, I think (one can never be sure what a mate is thinking), likes the same thing. If it develops she wants more action, well, there's nothing hindering her from driving in those fifteen miles to a job or a position. The University wants her to resume work for them someday. And she'll probably do that, or wind up in a publishing house. In some ways she has odd careless ways, but in others she is extremely painstaking. It is about the right combination for me, because the care she expends is upon ideas and thought. The other just sort of drifts along. I'd go nuts around a fuzzy female; though I do like things fairly neat around.

The problem of money is always there, though. The first of May, the Rockefeller thing runs out and then we're thrown upon the mercy of the public. The book is steadily eating its way through the second edition, nearly 4000, and there is a steady demand for it. We are still getting reviews, now from the solider organs such as *Esquire, American Mercury, Saturday Review of Literature*. We understand from an announcement in the March *Esquire* that Sinclair Lewis is going to do books for them, and that he is going to discover tomorrow's big shots amongst today's youngsters. Two he mentions for a starter: Stegner (*Big Rock Candy Mountain*—a very

good book and a wonderful young talent, also born in Iowa, also
a writer who loves his Midwest America, etc.) and Feike Feikema.
We were properly astounded. If his first article in June or July does
give us a boost, maybe the money angle will right itself.

Many of my friends think I am nuts for staying with a western
publisher. Particularly now since Alfred E. Knopf telegrammed
me last week asking if I would care to join his stable of stars. I
turned it down. This Webb outfit has plenty of money, they have
been in the textbook business for many years, they have a skeleton
organization in the sales field, and they have a great young editor.[2]
He is shy, self-effacing, brilliant, deep, and extremely well-read.
He is a lover of books. As my first will show, he knows what makes
a book look stylish. He is an artist to his fingertips. And he knows
how to handle me. I have a field day every time I see him, watching
him use the right technique to control my bullish nature. Also my
ever-present boasting ego. He understands that unless I roar a
little, that is, feel confident, I can do nothing. I have to have a
warm-up. He has had offers from the east, but, likes it out here, has
a dream of setting up a house of literary taste out here. And just
as Knopf publishes Borzoi books, he intends, this year for the first
time, to publish what he calls Itasca Press books. Itasca comes from
the two Latin words, Veritas Caput, meaning, True Source, a reference to the source of the Father of Waters, the Mississippi in this
state. The Itasca Press will be the true source of the midwest (and
universal) literature. You see, I just couldn't leave him. We have too
much fun together, plotting our little writing and publishing bark
through the rough waters of capitalist system, and fighting the big
monsters that live in New York. (New York has been very slow to
buy our books, to give reviews. They are now beginning to get on
the boat. But the book has sold surpassingly well everywhere else.
Very heavy in Boston. Many young college profs are buying it for
contemp.) Just the same it was an honor to have Knopf come after
my contract. *The New Republic* listed the most notable books of
1944, and a little over half of them were Knopf's.

The first draft of number three is also finished, twenty days ago.
Now begins the long haul straightening it out, polishing, checking,
rebuilding, etc. That will take at least a year. I wish it wouldn't take
so long, for I have three plots or ideas demanding attention. One of
them is yelling very loudly for me to get at it. And then there are
seven other ideas that are already warming up. Christ, I wish I were
three guys for a while, because right now I feel I am hitting the ball,
too.

2. Paul Hillestad.

About this thing to Europe. Your remarks are considered and worth some thought. I did not, however, expect to come out of Europe with any real knowledge of battle conditions. The book I have in mind is something like you suggested, the refitting of this vast army into the body of society again. But I did want to see where they had been, to see what they did, to look at the same mountains, the same valleys, the same peoples, to see rotting things (I hate them, but I must see them too), and if possible, to smell and see one bit of action, just to get an inkling. As you know, I only saw the Badlands once, but I wrote such a vivid piece about it that I get letters and reviews from all over saying that is the best part of the book. And I know that I have a strange power of seeing the past exactly as it was. I can go out for a walk, look at a tree or a river, and come back to the house and reproduce it exactly in an oil or a sketch. Isn't that called an eidetic memory, or something? 'T any rate, there it is; I should utilize it.

I hear, however, that my TB history will keep me out of Europe. We are going ahead with plans to live out in the country, and when you come to town next winter on your leave, we shall be expecting you to come out there to live with us for a few days. Or, if we have come to town, we will be right here, because Maryanna's mother is going to keep up this apartment. (Mrs. Mary Shorba) I think our telephone will be listed as Minneapolis, so you'll be able to find it. Otherwise, just call the newspaper, they'll know.

It has been very amusing to notice how some of the critics, suddenly realizing that the *Bowl* is somewhat serious, became overly critical and tried to find a weakness. They usually wind up by saying that the plot is feeble but the mood and the action vivid. They suggest that I write best under inspiration, or accidentally. Fools. Asses. Christ, before I write any chapter, I have a half dozen pages of words listed which slant in the same direction, that is, toward the end of the chapter. I also list the sequence of action that the thread shall take, I make sure that it furthers the main theme of the book, I deliberately try to figure out how to get the reader involved. For example, that last chapter, they say, is a piece of sustained outburst writing. Hell, if ever I worked like a machine on a piece before I started it, that is one. I knew that by the time you got to the last chapter, you, the reader were thoroughly the character, Maury. So all I had to do was to get a piece of sand inside Maury's eye and some dust in his throat and some in his ears, and in his hair, and in his toes, and then you, the reader, would have them too. From that point on, I kept opening up the width of the

sand-storm, and finally, the whole damn universe was in an uproar.
And just before I opened the quiet piece where he wakes up with
the bit of sand scratching in his eye like a blood-seeking weasel,
I gave you a fanfare of thunderous notes, the great down-riding
of the prairie windstorms. The book appears simple, but the fact
that it is interesting has its reasons. Now, I do not say it is a
profound story, but I do know that it has more in it than they
think. This next one is even more calculating, and subtle, and the
third, still more so. These fools who ask, "Have you had an inspiration today? No? Come over and look at this lovely thing, etc." get
me enraged. They don't understand that writing is hard labor, that
it is a constant struggle. I work out these outlines and lists of words
and so on for a very deliberate purpose. There are mornings when
my blood soars. When such a morning arrives, then the materials
for the outburst are ready to hand, and they are the *right* ones, and
so then a wonderful passage. When it does not, I write anyway,
and then I have a quiet passage with the *right* things in it. Writing
is a constant effort to catch those mornings. And you do it by laying
out a solid program in advance with the hope that out of twenty-
five sessions, you land one big fish. (Say, if you haven't got the book
by this time, please send me a hurry-up letter in return. I'll send
you one by post. What if you do have two? There are only a half
dozen first edition copies left at the office. Please let me know about
this, John. There is more than one reason why you should get a
"first.")[3]

Well, and now the baby is percolating in the bedroom, so I had
better get it fed and changed. It is a wonder to watch it. I am learning a lot about the human mind from it. It sees me grin. It tries and
tries. For days it tries. Then, one morning, out of a thousand shots
at it, the lips wrinkle just right. And you let out a burst of joy, and it
hears it, and it tries again, just like the last effort, and it does it
again, and presently, it has learned something. I am reading Edmund Wilson, Doughty, the Bible, *Mankind So Far, The Book of
Naturalists,* Stegner.

Love,
Fred

P.S. We so want to see you soon, John. Soon

3. *The Golden Bowl* was dedicated to Huizenga.

To Paul Hillestad

[Minneapolis, Minnesota]
February 28, 1945

Dear Paul,

I am very upset. Right at this minute I don't give a damn if I write another word or not. Why? Because it is disheartening to think that after all the work I have put into the *Boy*, cutting, polishing, honing, pruning, and rewriting (each sentence at least a half dozen times; more than I put into the best parts of the *Bowl*) I have to consider the idea that a little over a third of the sentences are still of such a bad nature that they need tampering with. Because as I see it, if a sentence is good, or even not half-bad, it should stand if it is the author's preference. I can take any sentence you ever wrote and improve it to my mind. That does not mean that I improve it for others, but to my mind; just as you think you are improving mine according to *your* mind. Further, I feel that either I have arrived at a point where I am 51–49 an artist or 49 to 51 a hack. I think I am an artist; certainly if some of the hoboes who sign their names to books claim themselves to be. After a certain point of excellence has been achieved, a sentence or an idea can be written as many different ways as there are competent people. And if it is to be mine at all, let it be truly mine, and not part yours too.

In that connection, I still cringe everytime somebody praises the *Bowl*. There are parts in it that are not mine, that are yours. The second chapter was boiled down from some 30 pages to 26, at least some pages were cut out, and the last part of the book was altered a little. Now I know that it improved the book, but it was not me, and I don't want credit for it. But at that time I was so anxious to break through, and I was so impressed by the improvement that I swallowed and took it. But now I know that if some critic were to go grubbing around in it he would find things that were not sparks caught from my forge, but from yours. Most would be, but some not. And his picture of me would not be accurate, nor honest. I am interested in that integrity, that honesty.[1]

It would be another story if I had an average mind, with average interests, and average tastes. And with these, would suddenly decide to write. Whatever I'd write would undoubtedly be bad, and amateurish. And you would have the right to grind it down finely and even insert words, etc., beyond the mere business of correcting boopers. But I am more than that now. I have dreamed and read and created poetry all my life. I have tasted the good poets too. I have come to a point now where I enjoy a sentence that does not

1. In the margin, beside this paragraph, FM later wrote: "This is exaggeration."

have a comma in a certain place where I'd put it in. I enjoy a phrase for its elegance, its variance, its oddity because it is not mine but some fellow man talking naturally to me. How disappointed I'd be were I to discover that the very word or phrase or use of a comma was inserted by an editor and not by the master I loved! Now the *Boy* has passed through that sensitive mind. It has been polished and tested with an eye to how it looks to me and to how it will look to another as I want him to look at it. (Not as he wants to look at it! But the way I want him to look at it.)

Moreover, there is a point beyond which an author can not go. If he does, he begins to strain. If I have to put much more work on it, I won't sign it as mine. Because I know and I feel, and with all the sincerity in my heart I say this, that more will strain it. And I don't want to take credit for any basic improvement coming from you, or Hemingway, Lewis, Etc. I want this to be Feikema with some of the colloquialism thrown in it (and I use them consciously most times: when I do not I readily admit it to you), I have always striven first for what I think is my truth.

Further, if *Boy* lacks a "key," well, then it does. But I can't see what it is. And if you supply it, or Doughty, or Hemingway, I'd agree that it was good, and would improve my work, but I wouldn't take it. I might let you have the book so that I could pay back your investment in me and my book. But never would I agree to call it mine. I would feel terrible if I did. I do not think, more-over, that the "key" lies in altering sentences that have passed my eye a half dozen times. (That is really true, Paul. I swear it.) If my tastes (as I outlined them above), solidified and purged by the con-stant reading of masters, and penetrated with what creative and critical brains I've got, don't make it publishable, then, well, throw it away; or take it, and publish it anonymously. You see, what you have done goes beyond the mere questioning of an occasional word *to see if I knew what I was doing.* It goes beyond catching boopers. It goes beyond proving the book. It is creation in its own right. And I can't agree that it goes in my book.

(Let me throw in this remark: it really belongs above; my mind is in such a whirl I have to catch as catch can;—but that article in the *Sun,* though it was good, and very good, was not really mine. I am not sure that I feel right about that either. In fact, I find that I don't want to think about it. But, you see, I don't like to hurt any-body, to the point of not even letting them think that I am hurt, and so I try to hide. I know I should blurt out, but then, again, I am afraid that they'll think I'm cocky, because a man who has lifted himself a little becomes an easy target. It's like the Knopf thing. Sometimes my "better judgement" or calculative mind or something tells me I should go with him. But, deep down, I've set my bull of a soul into staying with you and no Reynal & Hitchcock or Knopf sweet talk can alter the course I've determined on. And it is exactly the same sort of feeling I have about this book, and about altering. Maybe it is wiser to change something to improve it, but something tells me that outside of the honesty and possessive arguments, it is not *right*. That "right" I can not explain to you, any more than I can explain why, really, my person or my bull of a nature has decided that you are my man in the publishing field.)

And then I get so irked, so tired, so sick of doing a thing over more than a dozen times. I don't mean the labor of working a sentence. I mean something vaster than that. I mean, I don't like to have to consider changing my mind about the rightness of the *Boy after* I have laboriously, tediously, honestly, painstakingly gone over every phrase, idea, plot, etc., and finally, at last, after grave reluctance, say, "well, except for boobers, this is it." And *believe* it! And then, to find, afterall, that I was wrong. To go through this process will destroy me. It is saying that all the pain and labor and honesty that I have put into it have been in vain, have been thrown away; that once more I must fall in love with it and start all over going through the old love phrases and notions and fears and anxieties. Well, I can't do that more than twice. It is like having four orgasms with your consort within the hour.

Who must I believe? I respect Maryanna's judgement. But she differs on points with you. *I* can see both so well I can agree. But where does that leave me? It leaves me mixed-up, uncertain, unsure. And it leaves me this when I really am sure, and certain, but I only want to make certain that I hurt nobody, or that I haven't been cocky, or overbearing, because I know those weaknesses are within me. Who am I to believe, when I *feel* that my judgement is as good as the next man? Besides, when what is concerned is my *own* mental blood?

Besides, remember how we got excited when Mary [Shipley] jumped the word *Long* and others like it? How Spier thought it pretentious (if referring to *Bowl*) and archaic? That those passages we thought poetry should be taken out? And how it has been the serious reviews who have caught exactly at those things where I stick out? Who am I to believe?

I have to say at last, this is me. I have done an honest job. I have
worked hard. Here is my heart and my work. If it is not great, so be it.
If it is, so be it. It is at least me, not a tinkered tampered me. It is truly
FF and that's it.

Now you know that I am not sympathetic right now to the obscurity of Stein, to Joyce. Yet, if all their stuff had been edited to
plausibility, might they not have lost the precise thing that caught
the eye of the thousands of young writers, including Hemingway,
who learned from her, and who were influenced by her? Hemingway says she is his greatest influence. Certainly my work is not as
obscure, or as hard to read. And my ideas are clear, if simple, and
they usually say what they mean. As for the colloquialisms? Well,
are not most of the straightaway narrative sections of Hemingway
colloquial in the eyes of the old time purists? I have a right to use
many of them if I have *honestly* and with an *open mind* or an aware
mind decided to use them?

(This letter sound mixed up? It should. It reflects a mixed up
world. Besides, the telephone has rung four times since I started it.)

I remember what happened to Doughty. When I first started
to read him, without any knowledge of him save what appeared in
Time, I felt he was awkward, odd, ungrammatical, etc. But I got
about half way through, and, suddenly, I got used to him, and I
liked it, and pretty soon I saw that, in his own right (and what a
right!) he was correct and beautiful. He had something that not a
single man writing in England since the time of Shakespeare had.
Granting him his premises, and his canons for his own books, he
is consistent, he knows why he does something. In fact, I can't
agree with him to the point where I've gone through my own book
of his and put in many punctuation marks. I do so that I can read
him easier. But I would never, never say I am right. I am doing it so
that he won't spoil something in me I want to keep if I am to keep
liking him.

I think we made a mistake letting Lyman see it. We are good
enough to know what we are, and how good it is. And I would
never trade my sensibilities for his. Has he ever said a certain poem
over and over, for the sheer texture of it, its sound, as I have? Does
he read as broadly as I? Can his mind, on a straightaway IQ test
(providing both of us do the best we can) stack up to mine? And
even if it did, why should I listen to him when it will be *my name*
that will be signed to the book?

No, I must say that I can't go along with you here. If you feel that it cannot go as it is now with just a few little boopers caught, well, too bad. We'll junk it. I know I can not permit it to go with what another puts in, or cuts out. I know I am superior to Lillian Smith, and even if I were not, I could not live with myself if it was changed beyond my own conception of it.

Throw it away, or let me have it, and we'll let posterity monkey with it, if they want.

Because I respect you, because I want to be absolutely sure, I am going against my feeling and judgement and deliberately make myself read this thing once more to see if I was honest and close and tight and hard about what should go in and what should go out. And I'll type out the thing. And have it neat. And if then, beyond boopers and errors in grammar, it needs more, to hell with it all.

Damn it, Paul, how can anyone know how much work I put into a book in two years' time? two years of supremely intense concentration and love? How can anyone understand in three nights (as Lyman tried to do) what I, a mind at least as good as his, worked at for hundreds of days? I would never presume to say it of anybody living with me.

I hope you feel that while at times, in this letter, I've roared, I've also been full of humility, that I have tried to be as honest as I know how, and truthful, and tactful yet forthright.

I want to do what is right, and I am inclined to feel that my right (a considered one, an honest one) is the right right for me.

Please do not feel hurt about this, my opened hand. And before I start reediting this letter, before I start putting in knavish, designing phrases, I am going to mail it.

Please understand too that you are my wonderful friend, but at the same time, I must get this out of me, this expression of how I feel about this book. Good lord, man, look at the feeble second books of Steinbeck, etc. and then compare this one with theirs.

Yours, a brother,
Fred

P.S. I shall tell you something I haven't mentioned. I really feel that the book has been tampered with too much already. That is, a little bit too much. When I can change, upon advice, a dozen sentences in the book back and forth, back and forth, I've gone too far.

Now, please, don't think that I think that every word I utter is perfect, divine, unchangeable. But I do question the right of an-

other to substitute words that are no better than mine, agreeing
that mine are passable; and I question words that are not mine. It
must be all mine, or none of it. (I wonder if Hemingway or Steinbeck would be caught [missing material].

To John DeBie

[Minneapolis, Minnesota]
March 20, 1945
1. Maryanna's mother.

Dear Debbie, Jo, Jim,

First, some news. We have borrowed some money from a friend[1]
and bought a place south of town. It is in the country, there are
farms all around us, and we are situated on a high bluff overlooking
the Minnesota River. Out of the huge plate glass window we can
see twenty miles up the river valley. It is fairly new (six years old)
and needs to be winterized. It is made of natural shingle outside, all
on one floor, and pine walls. It has a huge graystone fireplace,
modern conveniences, and some furnishings. We bought ten acres
with it which includes a woods down in the bottom. We have a
garage, an extra cabin, a toolshop, a woodshed, and an extra privy
in case the inside toilet works goes haywire. We were extremely
fortunate. One of our friends knew the people. They were rich and
wanted a neighbor for their son and wife who live there. And they
went about selecting and chose us . . . probably because I bragged a
little that I had once fixed fence and could milk cows. I'll probably
wind up being a serf. We are moving there after April 16, though
our address may remain the same for a while since Maryanna's
mother is going to take over this apartment until next fall when
we'll find out for sure if we can get winterizing materials from the
WPB.

I have been sitting here for an hour trying to figure out a way
to explain my position to you, but have been unable. Each time
I hit on a device it either does me an injustice, or it insults you, or
it makes a sneak out of me. I guess the only thing to be said is that
you and I have grown apart. We have worked out different emotional values and each time we touch each other's taboos, we let out
a yell, without really knowing why, nor even being able to explain
why in emotional terms.

I can't for the life of me see why I should become contaminated
when I use a device to portray the reprehensible. How else can one
portray a truth? Besides, why not portray the reprehensible?
What's wrong with that? You wonder if I should use the exact
words to portray the way a farmer lives. I think I should. Provided,

that some selection is used. You can't put down *every* word, though you can put down *any* word. A novel, a poem, is always a concentrate, a synopsis. To portray a scene you need to kick out a lot of repetitious material or else you bore the reader. You need to select the most typical of each series of parts or movements. I love farmers, but they bore me to death after two days. If I were to give in great detail all the things that happen (*all the things!*), the reader would be bored too. But if I give him an organized sampling, related to an idea or a plot or a bit of action that I have in the back of my mind, I can get anybody to read about the farm with great interest. That is what is meant by "writing genius." As for showing Maury having calls to nature, well, frankly, it didn't seem necessary. I did have one scene, but I threw it out because it did not drive the story home. However, I have one such scene in *Boy Almighty* (Number Two) and perhaps will have in the others . . . if they seem fit and proper to the story. I can't be too concerned about touchy readers when I am busily pursuing what I think I have seen in life— truth. You have to have a bit of an eye on the public, yes, but not too much either. If thinkers did have, they'd never create anything new. If this is truly God's world, He shouldn't have any objection to my talking about any part of it. You mention Hardy, Rawlings, Douglas, Rölvaag, Dickens. In the first place, those men were working in times that were fastidious, and it never was pointed out to them that perhaps there was more to life than what their narrowed eyes were seeing. But did Shakespeare shut his eyes? (I don't mean those emasculated editions we saw, but the real Shakespeare? Have you ever looked up those seemingly innocent little words in even our effeminate editions? Looked up their source? Man, they're full of rich earthy meanings, which our backhouse talkers employ today.) What about Villon? Rabelais? Proust? Zola? Tolstoi (the real edition.) What about Chaucer? I have the original and with my knowledge of Frisian, which is very similar to Old Saxon and Old English, I have many a chuckle and think how much our culture has backslipped since we've become so blasted prudish. Debbie, our nation, religiously or morally, has had the deep misfortune of having inhuman molds (established by the New England Mathers and Cottons) set for us to live in. Our women, over seventy per cent of whom are frustrated, have taken over our moral code. Our aunts, our mothers, our prissy sisters, have made weak-backed eels out of the men, simply because they have grabbed up and perpetuated the first moral codes laid down by the early pilgrims. And all incoming people since have had to live in this code or move on. (As did the Mormons.) For example, in France, the men urinate in public, in little stalls along the street. Women can see them. Think nothing of it. And the real Rölvaag, I understand, was full of words that the translators eliminated. As for Douglas? My God, man, he is obviously and admittedly corny. He couldn't write a line of literature even if God were guiding his hand. And he admits it. Have you read his letter to the *Saturday Review of Literature*? He says he knows he is writing trash, that he is out to make money, that it is easy to sell rehashed biblical materials to an uncritical public. Anything with Jesus in it sells. Even intellectual, religious get taken in on that. And what about the original Aristophanes? the real Homer? the real Euripides? the real Horace? the real Petrarch? Boccaccio? Petronius? Ovid? Burns? Have you ever read *Poetica Erotica*? You should raise whoopee with your librarians in that town. It is my considered opinion that some unmarried, or unbedded, females control the culture of that town, and that is worse than (or at least as bad as) the methods of the Hitler book-burners. If my little daughter closes her eyes to some aspects of nature, or shivers like some of my silly old giddy aunts, I'm going to be very disappointed.

Please, Debbie, don't think that I explode like this when people write me about my book. I have gotten letters from nearly all of my literate relatives about it, and I have taken great pains to be kind and tolerant to them, to explain, explain, explain, and to do it with the greatest warmth. I do not like to hurt anybody . . . up to the point where they restrict my sense of right and then I frankly tell them to go to hell. You should have heard me handle a certain reverend who came to invade my home and berail me. I waited for four hours for him to assume some human form but finally it got too thick for me. He prayed at lunch, which my ailing wife fixed up for him, and his prayer was not directed at God, but he was using it as an excuse to bawl me out. He called me every name he could think of in polite terms, using the prayer as a shield. I waited until it was time for me to give thanks (which I never do audibly anymore at the table) and then I gave him a dose of his own medicine. The man left here considerably shaken. It was brief and it contained a reference to the poor sinner who merely prayed for forgiveness and who was glad he was not the long-winded pharisee that was glad he was not the sinner.

I had some relatives who wrote to say that I had disgraced the name of Feikema. (Who ever heard of it until I got under it?) I had some holler, "What would your mother say?" (See what I mean about women-control?) What if my mother did not agree with me? What I would do would be my business. I do not tell her how to live (supposing she were alive). I have others tell me that I should never set foot on their yard again. I will, however. They aren't big enough to throw me off. And no bullet will stop me. Debbie, it took courage to publish that book, a courage that transcends, possibly, the outright action of battle. My relatives, at their wits' end, send ministers to me, thinking that since they can't argue with me, he certainly can. Which is ridiculous, because I have yet to meet a minister who is my equal in argument or knowledge. Ministers are usually the most boring people I know. When I was in the San, what kind of letters did I get from my religious friends? (DeBies, Van Der Meers, Jellema excepted?) Nothing but tirades. "Good for you. At last God is getting even with you. You had it coming." Etc. From Wally De Jong who married my cousin, from ministers, oh, from all the miserable excuses parading as human beings. Not one word of kindness to a man who was dying the first four months in the San. And who were the kind writers, the inspiring ones? The atheists like Te Velde, Veenstra, Huizenga & strangers I never heard of before. Not that I need kind words. But what I mean to get at is: Christianity is supposed to offer a haven and a comfort for the weak & weary in the struggle of life. To offer love. And yet, despite all those things, I still bother to write kindly and frankly to my relatives. To explain. My wife thinks I am a fool for doing it. But, I cannot forget that once I too was ignorant and humble (and still am) and that, if you listen closely to my footsteps on the walk, you can still hear the footfall of the farmer.

I think I shall quote you from a letter I wrote to my aunt who married a high school teacher. She is intelligent, fairly so anyway, and she was shocked by the book. She thought she was going to get a doxology, I guess. Furthermore, she was the one who read me fairy tales when I was young, who opened my mind. And in a magazine interview, I told about it. And she was pleased until she got the book. So I wrote:

"And now about profanity. I have given those remarks very serious thought, as I did before the book was published. Uncle Hank, his wife, the whole family, the Dutch ministers in Iowa and Baldwin, Wisconsin, and others I know, object to that violently. I have pointed out to them that Ma Thor and Kirsten do not swear, that they are typical farm women, that they read religious magazines (see p. 131) and that it is only the men who swear. This is the truth. How can one present a man who swears without showing the swearwords? (I don't write "blanks" for I don't trust the reader's ability to supply the right filling. Besides, he might use worse than I intended!) How can you taste salt without the salt having saltiness? The idea is ridiculous. The minister said it was not God's truth. Well, my response to that is that it is the truth that I have seen. If I were to present a bum who was a goody-goody, a sort of cute Sunday school rascal, do you think that serious literary critics of art and literature would look at my book? They'd laugh at it. I'm not interested in rendering Sunday School tales. That's for those who like that sort of thing. I like life, and the truth of real life. And since the earth is the Lord's, and all that therein live, I feel that my truth is as much the Lord's as is any minister's or Ladies Ebenezer Society's truth. The only people who even as much as mention the swearing are the religious Dutch. When I tell people who know real art and literature what my Dutch friends think, they are astounded. You see, my theory is that all things under heaven can be beautiful. It all depends on how you look at it. As long as I have tried to be sincere, and honest, and humble, those who object to my books are only digging intellectual graves for themselves."

Debbie, how do you manage to buy groceries, clothes, books, magazines, etc., without contaminating yourself? "You people" came to this country to either get religious freedom or economic freedom. But today "you people" are so blasted intolerant that you do not even tolerate the notion that other people besides yourselves may get to heaven their own way. You send the most reactionary, hide-bound, turtleshelled people to Congress, who, in every move they make, betray the very freedom your forefathers sought in coming here. (I don't mean you directly. You are the yeast in the Dutch that saves them a little in my eyes. I mean the Dutch group as a whole. You and Van Vliet and others are wonderful children of God.)

About the book. The second edition is selling. The sale is approaching the four thousand mark. We are still getting reviews, and now they are getting to be hysterically favorable. They throw adjectives around just like I do when I lose my sense of proportion. The second book is having some trouble. Some of the boys looked at it and didn't like it. They didn't like the poetry and the philosophy in it, didn't want anything but the farm stuff. Once the cook fries the potatoes a certain way, it must always be fried that way, it seems. Well, they can go jump. I'm going to try to be original every time I write one, and make each one different. I have seen what has happened to Lewis. (Even though he is paying me a compliment on page six of the March *Esquire*.)

If you want, you can read this letter to the gang.

And thank you again for the lovely gift from Jimmy.

Maryanna has written you?

Our love to Jo and Jimmy.

Affectionately,

FF

Maryanna, Freya, Fred

P.S. Helen Reitsema and Van Til wrote for autographed copies. (Sent me checks.) But I haven't heard since. I suppose they were insulted. I can understand that "delicate" Helen and Ray might be, but tobacco-spitting Hank? And you know, in his letter he had the guts to say that I was "insincere," had always been. To heck with keeping my mouth shut out of respect for their feelings!

[margin] Have you read Parrington's *Main Currents In American Thought*?

To John Huizenga

[Minneapolis, Minnesota]
June 23, 1945

Dear John,

The first of the summer hot days have come at last. We've had a particularly weird spring: long stretches of cold weather, of torrents of rain, and very late frosts. Many of the oaks and elms outside our cottage are stubbed and frost-frizzled.

But we love our little place. Ten acres, it has a cottage (built just before the war with a wide, high window fronting a long twenty-mile valley, and set up on a very high bluff) and a garage and a cabin (where I am sitting now, listening to Tschaikovsky's music). Our friends and relatives are as excited about it as we are, and they constantly come over to get another look. So we have had some busy weekends. The place is in the middle of a game refuge, so we have a host of rather tame animals: rabbit, jackrabbits, some deer, snakes, salamanders, milk snakes, frogs, and neighbor's sheep and cows and horses. Also birds: the flaming tanager, the gold oriole, the goldfinch, the yellow warbler, red-wing, thrasher, martins (they share a house with sparrows and starlings! an almost unbelievable fact!) hummingbirds, cowbirds, jays, robins, crane, etc. Our huge bluff is a mass of purple and pink spiderwort, and penstemon, and peonies and iris. The wind blows up the hill, throwing your hair in your eyes, and the oak leaves turn over and show their pale green underclothes, and the birds, the hawks and martins and swallows, dip and rise and play in the air currents.

Our cottage is lined with knotted pine, all wood, with cedar shingles all around, and it is fit into the hill as if it belonged here ever since the middle Wisconsin glacier, tiring of its long haul from the north, dropped the massive load of till, now a countryside.

And the place teems with old ghosts, of olden days, long before even the Indians came. Just outside a lane lies a huge bulging worship or burial mound left by the mysteriously disappeared Moundbuilders. Our house is built on a hut-mound, and there are others scattered around. An ancient trail traverses the side of the hill, angling slowly up it, coming up from a twirling spring, green with water-cress. The trail crosses the country, and even today, men can trace it by plane, for vegetation does not grow well in it. It is like a farmer's dead furrow. I have read about them. One theory is that they lived here 10,000 years ago, and may have been a lost tribe of Ainu. (Now in Japan, and probably the only truly uncontaminated whites in existence.) But whatever, and whenever, they have left an indelible mark here, perhaps far more lasting than anything I, or my descendants, shall make.

The baby is growing, and she is a delight. She is quick, and still has red hair and green-blue eyes, and she is long-legged and large-headed. We think she is smart, and well-behaved. Her mother is wonderfully sensible about raising her. Maryanna is quiet and self-contained, and the child seems to be absorbing it from her. She has begun a self-wiggling motion in the jumper or romper. And she is fascinated by fruit and newspapers. There are times when we are positive that she responds like a grown human being.

A local storekeeper just stopped in to bring me a snath (handle for a scythe) which are hard to get nowadays. I need it to cut the grass that the lawn-mower doesn't get. Someday I'm going to run a dozen sheep over the place. They'll keep it down, and keep it neat, besides pay the yearly taxes on the place. I'll get them as lamblings in the spring and sell in the fall. I really haven't got the shelter for them in the winter.

I've been fixing fence between ourselves and the neighbors from whom we bought the plot. And I get a particularly keen delight out of setting absolutely straight fences, and well-anchored corner-posts. They are banking people and are constantly amazed by exploits that I think are quite ordinary. The old farming knowledge comes in mighty handy out here.

But it isn't as isolated as it sounds. We have electricity, and later will have a phone (there was one in here), connected with Minneapolis. Cleaners, mailman, school-bus, milkman come past the house. Ordinarily a woman would object to such isolation, but for us, it is swell. We were getting, and will get, too much attention as it was from casuals.

By this time Kathryn [Huizenga] will have told you about our brief meeting. She has grown up, and is a complete and organized female. She is on top of the talk, has a grasp of conversational complexities, and is very charming and pretty. The young navy Ensign I was with, married, was quite entranced by her, and told me of it. A fine sister, John.

Also met Howard [Hoving]. Met his wife. He has suddenly hardened. He felt like a stranger at first. And his wife is cautious, almost unsure of herself. Howard has taught her to like music, and some books, and she is developing an attitude toward culture and art generally. We were just getting acquainted when we left.

The award was stunning. We discovered that it was William Rose Benét who reached down into the pile of books published last year, and who pushed the committee in to taking my book.[1] The other fiction award was *Boston Adventure* by Jean Stafford. Where were *A Bell for Adano,* and others? It seems unbelievable. Most of the grantees, in music, sculpture, were much older than I, and also a damned sight more cocky. Some had the notion that the old fogies of the American Academy of Arts & Letters were a couple thousand years behind the times. For myself I felt that I was willing to keep a respectful silence while one thousand dollars was being handed me. And as a matter of fact, the whole damned thing was thrilling to me. Kenneth Fearing, one of the poetry grantees, had a bun on, and was contemptuous of the old boys. He also paid out some cheap remarks about my height, etc., and after awhile I slyly laid a trap for the twerp and let him have it. I said that it never fails. I go into some bar somewhere and some nixwit comes along and wants to know how tall I am, etc. He later came around and asked to take me out to dinner. But we were busy.

I liked Van Wyck Brooks, who presented the awards. He is old-

1. Sinclair Lewis had a hand in it, too. He told me that in January, 1946 [FM's note].

ish, but with young eyes and mind, and he wished he could live another fifty years to witness the coming renaissance in American letters, which, he said, is coming. We spent a fine half hour over tea, along with Benét and his wife.

We also met Jean Stafford. Liked her. She has a wonderful face, full of ache and bewilderment. Her writing strikes me as having hit its full blossom. It is pressured. She has taken an ordinary talent and dressed it to its full possibilities, almost to a point where it groans with carpentering.

Marguerite Young, who is being hailed as a sort of modern female John Donne, I met too. She has a flat exterior, evasive brown dog eyes, a shaggy mass of hair (William Carlos Williams says all she needs is a whiskey barrel and she could pass for a St. Bernard.) and slovenly clothes. She affects. However, she has a brilliant mind and is at times very far ahead of us with it. But she writes this unintelligible garbage. It is just impossible. I know their argument: tired of the usual, the normal, they are trying to make each sentence, each phrase, as meaningful as possible by injecting into it as many points of reference to culture, coming, going, gone, as is possible. But my argument is that no human mind can take in, at the same time, eight philosophies, or meanings, at a crack. In fact, it is moods that readers take in, and to get moods across, you need word-time, or just plain lucid writing. Why waste what little mental energy we have on the method of presentation? Why not use all of it on the idea itself? Hence, present it so clearly the reader is hardly aware of style or presentation. So it goes.

William Carlos Williams charmed both of us. He has had a slow following, but it is growing, and there is no doubt in my mind that he will go down as one our real poets, at least one of our better minor poets. He has a medical practice in Rutherford, and for years has been writing about his patients, and about his lonely walks. He wished that we could have stayed longer. We can't talk after death, I said, and he agreed. He is about as honest a person as I have met, and yet incredibly shrewd and penetrating, with a fine sense of humor.

God damn it, it's hot. I just pulled forward in my chair, and I'm sure that about six acres of old varnish are now firmly affixed to my back.

We met many others, mostly fakes, or pretenders, and some queers. And we managed to get around New York so that Maryanna could see the sights.

Your remarks that you are uneasy about my second book are
well taken. All I can say is, wait until you see it. Afterall, if I had told
you about the *Bowl*, its plot, you would have wondered how in hell
I could have written a complete book on so slim a thread, or so thin
a characterization. It's all in how it's done. The *Bowl* is a prose-
poem of a dying earth. The earth is the main character, the others
are only in there to get it said.

My own feeling is that the second one has more poetry in it,
it is at times more restrained, at times wilder, and it carries such a
wallop of realistic recording that it can't fail to hit across there. I
have no idea if I have a best-seller or not and if so, it wouldn't be because of the ideas I have in it. It'll be because of a half dozen scenes
in it. Yes, art comes first, but if money will come with it, sure. So
that little remark about my artistic integrity, I think, misses. Besides
I feel that no one can deliberately write a best seller; at least I could
not. I'm not good at fabrication. And I write best when I write
what I know. And there is every likelihood that I'll write a best
seller quicker that way than the other. Steinbeck's agent has already
sought me out, and has my things. Eventually they'll buy them just
as they bought Hemingway, Steinbeck, etc., she says. And last
week Mr. Wilk of Warner Bros. called all the way from New York,
asking, would I like to write scenarios in Hollywood? I said, no.
No, I liked it here. Was getting along. Wasn't interested in a lot of
money . . . now. Suggested that he buy the *Bowl*, and he said, hell,
there ain't no dust bowl now. I said, it'll come, though. He said,
aw, hell no. I said, it will, and you bastards will pay through the
nose for the book then. They like that kind of talk, it seems. The
sums they pay for scenario-writing are fabulous, but I notice that
most writers who go there never are heard from again. They might
not ruin me, but they would sour me. I'd get bitter and disgusted
with that crowd. If I do go, it'll be just for a few months so that we
can winterize our house. And I'll tell 'em off every second of the
time I'm there, refuse to do nothing but what I'm interested in, because, hell, I have nothing to lose doing it. A man's got to have a
sense of pride around cocksuckers.

Your remarks about psychology or refined freudianisms is well
taken, too. I don't read it except to see what they're doing. My only
feeling is they they often make a fuss where there isn't trouble, and
don't understand the human animal very well for all the books they
write. They should read a little geology, anthropology, biology,
to get a bit of a perspective about where the animal came from in

the first place. I'm coming to the conclusion that antagonism between humans is unavoidable. It just happens we are here, and it
just happens we joust. The moment a bit of sun-energized matter
gets itself organized into the personality of a weed, sheep, or Pete,
it can't help but live off a neighbor. It must feed to survive.
Something's gonna be eaten. And so living together in a purely arbitrary affair, and a practical one. Russia is the only nation that acts
as it believes in that matter, while the others put out guff and act
in reverse. Jews are being persecuted in town here, John. And I've
had just enough training and momentum in co-operative living
with people to be furious about it. And to see moody days ahead.
When are you coming home? I won't be going away. TB is the
block. Write soon. Very soon. And I'll send you book number two
in the fall. If you like this one, I shall be very happy. Yes, you did
help me. You were something to please. You had high standards,
and, because I liked you, I kept trying to get above them. And then
the fact that you were interested in hearing from me all these years
. . . well, I just never thought of not having you in there.

Our very best, man,
FF

To L. F. Utecht[1]

[Minneapolis, Minnesota]
July 14, 1945

1. Warden at Minnesota
State Penitentiary.

Dear Mr. Utecht:
I am hearing strange rumours about the treatment Earl Guy
is getting there. I understand that he must work in the hemp mill
and cannot write when he feels so inclined, that to write his first
book he had to promise to go back to work afterwards—a sort of
promise-under-duress affair. If it is a state law that he must work
in it, you are absolved, of course, but the law is not. I also hear that
you called him a "crackpot." That is unforgiveable. For you are condemning thereby some of the very great names of all time: Francis
Bacon, Poe, O. Henry, Cellini, John Bunyan, etc. These men too
were considered odd by the average and smug of their time. I
would like to have a statement from you on this.
Further, to take up the matter of Earl's writing, I consider him
one of the better young writers of our era. I am not alone in the
opinion either. Harry Hansen mentioned him in 1943 as having
written one of the ten best books of that year. And he has had acclaim from other eminent critics. I think you (or the state law sys-

tem) are robbing us, the public, of cultural reading matter by keeping him from writing. We can use him. Yes, I know he "owes" society something according to your set of morals, but I feel he can give it more than he owes. And he can give it more than any other man you have behind the bars there. And he can give it more in the form of books than in the form of twine string. Any moron can wind twine, but few can write notable books.

And, again, to use your terms, if he must do something "hard" to pay off this debt, surely no more arduous task can be found than writing. It is an anxiety, and a turmoil.

And last, I'd like to know what the policy is in Minnestoa: do we punish or rehabilitate? If the latter, what in the name of common decency is Earl Guy the genius doing behind a machine? Except in so far as he wants to and needs it for his writing, a matter he must determine for himself? I'd like an answer to that.

I am enclosing a clipping to identify myself. And I would like it returned. Please.

Respectfully,
Feike Feikema

To John DeBie

[Minneapolis, Minnesota]
August 22, 1945

Dear folks,

Maryanna and Freya have gone to town for a few days to spend some time with Gramma Shorba, and to do some fall buying, and some visiting with friends. This leaves me a widower out here in the country. I miss both very much, and yet I am having a fine time of it too. For once I can read and read, and work and work. I've just now awakened from a nap on the hard-cot. My eyes are still sticky with sleep. But here, on the typewriter was a memo: "Write Debby." So, here it is.

The day is as clear as glass out. The valley lies far below, peaceful, alive with the wriggling river and the pollen-heavy corn. A train is pounding down the far side of it, and the box-cars and engine and coal-tender look like toys, unreal, two-dimensional, as if they had only wheels on one side. This morning when I awakened I found the valley full of a silver mist, tufted at the top like a silver-blond boy's hair. I stood for a long while, watching it, thinking that I should get busy and write, and yet, thinking too, "What the heck, this is real and that word-factory, that's fake." But afterall, it's the words that keep me alive, and keep me awake to the beauties. I write in a little cabin off to one side of our cottage. It is small, but I can roar in it all day long, and no one to hear or to bother. Behind me is a toolshop, woodshed, and garage. Of course, I'll have to go into the house this winter.

Our cottage is made of pine and is cedar-shingled. There is a lot of work yet to be done on it, and it seems we can get the materials, now that the war is over. We are going to have radiant heating.[1] Most of the house is paneled in raw pine. We intend only to surface it with an oil to keep the natural color. Maryanna doesn't like the sharp glinting surface of varnish. Any day now the well-driller (we were getting our water from a neighbor through shallow-laid pipes) will be here, and then the carpenter and cement-man. I expect to help.

I've been quite surprised with my strength. I hope I haven't overdone it, as one never knows that fact in TB until long after. I've dug up a garden from virgin soil, built a long fence with still more to do, cut down some trees, rearranged some of the landscape, cut down acres of sumach (horrible pest that grows like the Canadian thistle), grown a garden, and swum. The neighbors have a wonderful pool, and when the hot weather came at last, we helped them use it. We've gone swimming in the moonlight a few times.

The next novel is in the proof stage, and will soon be bound. I think it will hit the market somewhere around October. It's been titled *Boy Almighty*. The first book is somewhere between the 4000 to 5000 figure. A few are still selling. You might take a look at the cover of the September *Esquire,* by the way.

I still hear from John Huizenga. He is somewhere in the Philippines and says that he may have to stay a long while after the war. There's one bright young man who's had a huge chunk cut out of his life.

The horrible war is over, thank God. And now we have the atom bomb on our hands. I wonder what our Reformed Celestes are thinking and saying these days about it. Their little worlds of heaven and earth are getting a shaking by it. Earth will vanish if we don't control the atom-smashing properly. And heaven too, since it was, according to my idea, a mental creation. The theologues must be in quite a pickle these days, too. If they claim that God knew all along how the atom works, that he can even reconstruct for judgement day purposes all the thousands of bodies that disintegrated and became atmospheric dust in Hiroshima, then they

1. Never installed; instead, an oil furnace was.

have to admit that he was mighty niggardly with his news in the Bible's Revelation. Maybe our Church fathers didn't have the inside track afterall.

The program you people have outlined for your club sounds wonderful. And your idea that maybe your neglect of ideas has made the modern novel seem unsatisfying is a good point there. I am wondering what novels you read. If someone were to ask me what modern writers I liked my list would include: Steinbeck, Hemingway, Dos Passos, Otto Storm, Jake Falstaff, Stegner (he wrote a wonderful novel of the northwest called *The Big Rock Candy Mountain*), Robert Penn Warren (*Night Riders*), Dreiser (poor style but a mighty heart), Wolfe (over wordy), Thomas Mann, Sholokov (?) *The Don Flows Down To The Sea* (a great book, great!), and *Capricornia* by Xavier Herbert.

But it is best to read the masters. Afterall, it is folly to think we can have as many in the last twenty years as mankind has had in three thousand or more. I like Charles Montagu Doughty, who wrote *Arabia Deserta, The Dawn In Britain,* etc., best of all, better than Shakespeare, yessir, better than any. He has made me feel lonesome for Arabia. There are times as I work that I'll look up and long for Arabia. When a man can make a country so real that one gets lonesome for it without having seen it, that is writing!! And I'll wager that no one you know has ever heard of him. In fact, see if your library has him. If they do, it'll amaze you. Should you begin him, make yourself understand that he may be very dull at first. That is because he used so many old English words, and Arabian. He knew nothing of the literature of his times because he was too busy travelling. But he had steeped himself in Chaucer and Spenser, and he thought he would redirect the "polluted" English of his day with one mighty Titanic effort of his own.

Well, time to get outdoors and work.

Yours, fondly, fred
FF

To John Huizenga

[Minneapolis, Minnesota]
November 10, 1945

Dear John,

At last I have a free Saturday morning to write you a letter. My correspondence has piled up to discouraging heights. But people had to wait until I got some work cleared away.

First, a little description of setting. Right now, behind me, a little four dollar stove is chortling up the chimney, and keeping my back warm. The little cabin is not yet completely cozy. I am waiting for the throw-aways from the main house, which the contractor is now working on. As soon as enough loose lumber and wall-boarding piles up, in this cabin it goes. But the little thing is snug, however, once the fire is going. And it is certainly better than working in the house where there are all sorts of interesting distractions such as a well-proportioned wife and a lively child. And a puppy whose voice is changing.

The contractor has been slow getting at the house. First, it's help. To find a good neat carpenter is practically impossible. Then, to find a good cement man is even harder. And last, the materials. They just ain't. But somehow, I've done the impossible, and I think I have the three items coming together at last. In the meantime our unfinished house is bitter cold some nights. Two nights ago, in the snowstorm, I put coverings over the air-vents of the basement (I invented a device for it, with the contractor's approval). My fingers became so cold I was afraid to put them in my mouth for fear they would stick to my tongue like chilled steel.

And (Just now The Boss stepped in to ask me to start the car. We can't find a good garage man to find out what's shorting the motor. I cranked the car, and now's she's off.) then I've cut an additional swath alongside the lane to widen it. Cut down an elm and two oaks, all huge and mighty. Then we blasted the stumps, and when we ran out of dynamite, got down on our hands and knees and grubbed. A lot of physical work, and I often wonder where my strength comes from. It amazes me, but, though I am becoming leaner than I was two years ago, I now weigh 275, and feel very powerful. In fact, I think I am healthier now, knowing how to keep the rules, than I ever was. One day I even worked a bucking scraper behind a tractor, eight hours, a man's work if there ever was. And the next day didn't feel the worse for it.

I love the work. I think that in a way I've returned to youthful ways and scenes. The idea of a few chores each night appeals to something deep, almost primitive in me, something put there when I was a boy on the Iowa farm. It seems right. I come in to supper with a ravenous want for food. Sometimes I take a bottle of beer, or a glass of flaming-red port, and sit by the fireplace before sitting down to sup. Those two hours in the afternoon are the peak of the day. (As long as I can keep writing and reading the other hours!)

Another reason for my business goes to my writing of the third book. It is a massive book, almost as long as *Anna Karenina*. It is without any question one of *the* books I shall write. Structurally, I've built as carefully as an architect fashioning a Gothic cathedral. I've spent hours and days and weeks on research, just to make sure the minor details such as fact, names of flowers, grass, trees, etc., are right, not guessed at. Did I tell you that I walked miles over the terrain described two years ago? Clipping weeds and plants and flowers and trees, collecting bits of mud and stone, and taking them back for experts to name and place for me? Also that I have read meteorological reports until I buzzed with massive air masses moving down from the refrigerator that is Canada? Some artists laugh at me. Let them. I know what I am doing. I know that the facts in themselves aren't art. It's the weaving of them. And since something is to be weaved, why not the truth, or real things, as they are? And incidentally, one finds such a mountain of wonderful names and ideas and experiences in the classifications of these things. (For example, I've often wondered why the name Abben, my brother's, came as it did, spelled with two b's. It's a family tradition. Well, I now discovered why. Reading Fris history [there's a Fris immigrant in the book], I discovered such names as Tabbo, Abbo, Ubbo, Ebben, etc., all of them ancient princes, warriors, heroes of Fris legend. You see, people named their children after them like people today name children after Roosevelt or Joe Louis.) One has to be careful, to be sure, with such masses of detail. The book should never show notebooking. But that is the challenge I accept. It is the challenge all writers who try to be great artists accept.

Now this third book had to be ready by the 15th of December so that the editor could read it, prove it, and then we could start putting it into type next spring, and have it ready for fall. He wants to send it around to various Clubs, Book, Literary Guild, etc., because it has such possibilities (despite its art!). Hence, I've been rushing.

Boy Almighty lies on my desk now. And on Nov. 27, it will be officially sent out as published. We are already getting reactions, and those that read my first, are considerably, and apparently, pleasurably surprised at its contents. It is different, bigger, and, as one guy put it, it is fascinating in the true sense of the word. Like a pair of snake eyes.

Some are offended by the egotism of the main character. But they miss the whole point of the book. It is only the strong who survive the ordeal he is placed into. Oddly enough, some think it is me, and that they are surprised to think, I guess. (Because I appear "shy and modest to strangers"?) Well, as a matter of fact, though I did borrow heavily from my life, I utilized the cantankerous, egotistic stuff from friends and from momentary fits I had myself. They, the surprised readers, forget that each man is many people. And, if the real truth is told, if a real entering into a character is made, no matter how feeble, or weak, or willy-nilly, egotism is the core.

That leads me to another point. I feel that there have been, since about the time man became a two-footed creature, two powerful characteristics in man: the one egotistic, the other cooperative. He has survived the jungle ordeal because he has had a measure of both. I think those that have stressed the co-oping have failed to accept the deeply moving power that is self. And those who yell about freedom and competition between individuals fail to see the other. The first thing is ego, the second co-oping.

Some think this kind of approach is gloomy. I disagree. When you approach the idea of building a house, don't you make a point of knowing stresses and strains, terrain, etc., exactly so that you can build a good house? And the more you know about the details, the more you make a point of truth, the better the house?

About the Atom Bomb. Funny thing is, the afternoon it was announced, I was having a talk with a professor of English[1] about the proofs of my book. He tried to tell me that certain scientific words couldn't be used as literary words. I agreed that not all could, because of sound difficulties, etc., but that he was way off the beam, that all the words we have today, every last one, has come from humble origins, from seemingly unpoetic origins, that in Elizabethan times, Shakespeare was considered a "poplar" author because he loaded his book with the "artistically selected" idioms of his day. Most idioms, figures of speech, are passing, but that's exactly the business of a really great artist, to stick his neck out and make choices. If you miss, well, hell, then you just don't happen to be great. Or even good. So what. Each tries, however. And then I went on to tell him that this war has made a profounder change in the peoples of the earth than the first World War did. I told him about the tremendous scientific knowledges that have been pumped into young minds, millions of young minds, who will be the reading core of the postwar world. They will be the core of the rising intelligentsia of America. They will truly inaugurate the new age coming in. (By the way, I think society mutates, jumps, and

1. Joseph Warren Beach.

doesn't evolve as some think, and I'm sure we are in the middle of a mutation, a jump, a transition period right now. We are part of a popoff period.) And those boys, and girls, I said, will like my book, will like its odd air of glittering steels and space-spanning thoughts, the poetry of all these things, will like the idea that all of life has a right to be considered worthy of entering literature's pages. He asked me if I thought I knew enough about this "New age of steel thinking?" I said, I didn't know, we'd have to see. But, I added, just to give a hint of how much I might possibly know about it, I'd predict that in a few weeks, maybe even today, this afternoon, they'll loose the atom bomb on some city. He pahed the idea. I crossed my brows, went into great detail on just how it worked, and, bless me, if at the moment I didn't seem to understand nuclear fission even. And blast me, when I left the house, the evening paper, tossed just then up on his porch, announced the first atomic bombing! (Probably "accidental," but just the same, I did have a "feel" for it, as I suggested in the book.)

John, when are you coming? Rush me your address on a card so I can send you the book. Please. I don't want this one to circle the globe before it gets to you.

And, if you are coming in January, do let us know in advance so that we won't miss each other. There is a chance, an outside one, of us going with another couple to Arizona. I need a writing rest. For a month.

The baby is growing up, is standing already, is about ready to walk. She circles the play-pen in a flash. She has learned to clap her hands, to wave, to greet us with "Hi," to say, "What's that," "Hot," "Whhooooo" to something that seems terrific to her, to drop her hands in her lap to my words "All done all gone no more to eat," to shake hands, to play with two or three objects (that is, put them in each other, say a spoon in a bowl, or a small ball into a jar, etc.), and to expect her dad to play with her on the couch every evening after supper. She sounds pathetically lonesome when I don't do it. She even goes to the pooper in the bathroom occasionally, and when she does right, you should see her dear mother praise her. We are trying to soft pedal our scoldings and to accelerate the praise. At least at this stage of the game. She is fascinated by books and magazines. She has hypersensitive eyes, can spot a dot the size of a flyspeck across the room, confuses flies for raisins and goes into ecstasy when she sees one circling her golden-red head. She exclaims at the falling snow, and sometimes, I think, reflects, in her sudden sobering of eyes, her upraised hand held stilly for a moment, the very profound meaning of the gentle whistling flakes as they fall from the skies. Slowly the little mind is beginning to raise out of the bog of body, slowly (like trying to build a roadbed across a swamp) a bottom is coming in, and soon, in two years, she will have piled in enough experiences to have the roadbed emerge on top in the form of memory. What a tedious, what a glorious, what a daring thing the mind is. How much it has to take in before there is an outgo. How much we owe to those who have gone before. How much vanishes forever that no one ever remembers, or guesses might have been. To have a child, and to have it truly, is to learn self, is to discover that beneath the sea of passing time lie thousands of buried, swallowed up, cities and cultures. And terrible, lonely, wrenching tragedies.

John, do you know, I have a wonderful wife. I would say so even if her and my ways should part. I shouldn't say this, because it is embarrassing, no doubt, even to you, my friend. But then, I consider you such a great friend I dare to tell you. In my household there is very little pretence, very little frittering away of maintaining pride, etc. In my household there is freedom, a closeness to what is real and alive, an awareness of passing life and its forever vanished richness, an awareness of coming life and its eagerly anticipated wine-red tang. Yes, I lost many freedoms when I married. But I gained back many more! I would never trade it back. And if I should ever lose the married state, I know I'd never get it again in this life. We are both very impressionable. But we are both egotists too.

John, come soon, I think of you often. Every time I hear music.

I like it here. I don't realize I'm a writer out here. It's only when I go to a bookstore where the females flutter that it suddenly dawns on me I'm an author. That's the way I want to keep it till I die.

Love,
Fred

To Henry L. Mencken[1]

[Minneapolis, Minnesota]
December 19, 1945

1. Manfred learned later that Mencken was of East Frisian descent [FM's note].

Dear Mr. Mencken:

I bought your *American Language* in April of 1944. I was in between writing books, and so promptly plunged in. I read until my eyes stung. You see, I had found in your book 769 pages of argument in support of my own feelings about language and about usage. Again and once more I'd send my manuscript east, only to have it come back either rejected or with suggestions that I clean up certain sections, particularly the conversations. Anxious to get on, not sure of myself, with my eyes full of reverence for the eastern literary gods, I sometimes tried to follow their advice. It was like trying to teach a man from Mars to pitch low and outside to Jimmy Foxx. Once an editor got excited about my book and sent me a check and told me he would begin work on it. When I saw the hundred pages he mutilated I almost killed myself. He did correct an error or two, but he killed my metaphors, metaphors I had spent months polishing and sharpening, he killed all the conversational brightness and aliveness, conversations I had spent years collecting while hiking through the country. I felt he was killing everything I had lived for. I searched my heart, of course, to see if I wasn't a prima donna, something I didn't want to be. Thank God, I found your book. From there I promptly went into Berrey and Van den Bark's book, bought Skeat's *Etymological Dictionary of the Eng. Lang.,* Botkin's *American Folklore,* began reading magazines on American Speech. From these I learned that my notebooks are indeed valuable. About that time I found a young editor working for a publishing house in St. Paul, Minnesota. The plant he worked for had been publishing farming magazines and textbooks, but was interested in entering the book trade field. They took on my first novel, *The Golden Bowl* (This was an actual phrase used by farmers in the dust bowl; and I didn't mean to move in on Henry James), and published it in September of '44. The book is jammed with phrases and words from the Midwest, even has some songs in it never printed elsewhere. The book got small but good reviews, and to my satisfaction, the more "intelligent" reviewers mentioned some of my pet metaphors, and most of the midwest boys mentioned the soundness of the casual talk between the bindlestiff and the farmer.

But I'm rambling from the point a bit. Some time ago I bought your *Supplement* and am working through that. And again I find powerful argument in my support. There are some things I want to talk about, both in it and the first book. You mentioned "You Know Me Al," said that Lardner scorned writers who put "feller" in the mouths of hicks. I disagree with Lardner. (Witherspoon lists *fellar,* I see.) It all depends where you live. In my *Bowl* I have the bindlestiff who comes up from Oklahoma say "fella," but the S.D. native says "feller." The S.D. bird also uses "winder" for "window," "swaller" for "swallow," and in general shows a tendency to crash his "r's." I have not determined to my own satisfaction whether it is the nationality (Scandys, Dutch, or Fris, or Scots, etc., from Northern Europe), or if it's our own northern climate that makes people roar their "r's." In any case, my notes show that as you move from north to south, the tendency to slur and to blur the words increases. Well, there were other such things in your book. Matters of opinion mostly.

You made the comment in your first book that farmers do not create slang because as a class they are stupid. I do not find that so. I find that they are very ignorant, of course, and I find that there are millions of sleeping brains among them. Here and there you find an awakened one, and he is usually very good. He is direct, he is unabashed by city slickers, he penetrates, he is elemental, he is alive. I am a farm boy, didn't leave until I was eighteen. I also worked in factories (New Jersey, Minneapolis, Michigan) and I find about the same proportion of sleeping minds among them. The city worker is, in the main, a little more articulate, moves quicker, has his light a little higher pitched. My own father couldn't read or write, yet he spoke an excellent American. He was devilish quick. He took one look at the first car to come to our countryside and got in and drove it off. He adjusted rapidly to radio, to airplane travel . . . all he needed was a chance. He had been too busy breaking sod and raising six boys to get himself literacy.[2]

2. It later was determined he had dyslexia [FM's note].

When I look through American writing, I find only a few who use American with accuracy. Dos Passos, Steinbeck, Hemingway, Stegner, Hammett, Caldwell, Lewis. Of the lot, Lewis has the best conversations. Dos Passos is good too. Steinbeck is often phoney; is often inventive. His Okies do not represent the real ones. (I realize this doesn't necessarily mean his art is poor.) Hemingway reflects European bars. Caldwell gets the South, I feel, though at the same time I often find phoney rings in his too. Stegner doesn't reflect his northwest too well in conversations and idiom, but he does get the feel of the physical landscape and the nature of the people. In those respects he is the best in the lot. But as you suggest, Lardner is the greatest of them all. I read his stuff with delight; in fact so much so that I mustn't read him a week before I begin working on my own stuff.

Has it ever occurred to you that Mid-America, for better or for worse, is going to put the final stamp on American speechways and idioms? West in *Plainville, U.S.A.* talks about the size of the families out here, and how over half of the kids run off to the big cities. He is right. And these kids take with them their idioms, manners, morals, habits, and infect (or influence, as you will) the coast cities, both Atlantic and Pacific. The basic habits you learn before sixteen stick with you for life. And for the New Yorkers, and New Englanders, to issue manifestoes, dictionaries (that Webster outfit is years behind us out here), rejections, is sheer futility. We would have overwhelmed them long ago if many of our fugitives hadn't turned traitor on us. (The most vehement New Yorker I met was born not fifteen miles from my home. The fool! He's cut himself off from a most vital spring of life.) (And yet, all unconsciously, he still lives out patterns that he acquired as a youth in northwest Iowa.)

I am enclosing a clipping or review on my second novel. At first, when I read it, I thought "Wow, this guy is intelligent. He understands me." But when I got to the last paragraph, I changed my mind completely. The fact that he didn't understand that I was more interested in "living American" than in what is expected of a college graduate completely destroyed him in my eyes as an "intelligent reviewer."

If you are interested in looking at my books, that is, for the idioms and phrases that I've collected, I'd be delighted to send them on to you. *Bowl* is full of the stuff; certain characters in *Boy* are alive with it—notably Pa and Minnie. My next book, *This Is The Year,* ready next fall, is going to be the best of the three.

By the way, being a Frisian has also been an incentive to studying words. Frisians are ancient cousins of the Angles and Saxons, and I find to my amazement that I can read Old English with ease. My father speaks Frisian and American with great ease, though he stumbles in Dutch, even though he goes to a Dutch church.

Yours,
Feike Feikema

To Van Wyck Brooks

[Minneapolis, Minnesota]
December 20, 1945

Dear Mr. Brooks:

Many, many thanks for your most kind letter of last summer, which I did not expect; and especially many thanks for your writings. I have been meaning to write you all summer, but each day I got further and further into your work, and each time I persuaded

myself to wait until I read more. I must tell you how I hated literature in college. My professor didn't particularly care for American
Literature, bragged so hard about European, particularly the God-
fearing Milton, that I came to hate the courses with him. (Curiously enough, I was always fond of him; he was a nervous, crabby,
brown-eyed man who had had a bleak life and you felt sorry for
him.) So you see I really had only the vaguest notion about my literary forbears until I read your books. I like instantly what I found
in *On Literature Today,* immediately went down the street with a
few bucks in hand and bought *Opinions of Oliver Allston.* What I
found there was even better. Every page was an argument favoring
my own feelings about what I should write. Threshing my way out
of the jungles alone was tough, especially when I met at every turn
at the universities the modern Eliots and Crowes and Tates and
Techniques. Somehow, in my bloody, bruising way, I had managed
to hang onto the belief that I should present life as I found it, to
communicate my own intoxication in it, my love of life, of the natural functions of man, of my bewilderment but yet interest in life.
Truth was most important. All the other stuff about building complicated plots, etc., was really only incidental. If one knew these
things, good; but it was only adding an extra tool to your work-
kit. I liked too the stress on the fact: "Allons, the road is before us."

(I am sitting here in the sunlight right now, looking through
an enormous plate glass window, facing our valley—the Minnesota River—and looking down it for twenty miles. All afternoon
the shadows have been changing. The valley varies from minute
to minute. The windmills on the horizon seem to walk across the
hills. The farms, below, and above on the hills, spread out like vast
sheets of linen white. And I am eating a red apple, snapping the
bites into my mouth, tasting the running juices, suckling it and
thoroughly enjoying it, exciting my taste bulbs, and enjoying the
moment to the full. For I am writing a friend, someone who knows
exactly what I mean when I write about the wind brushing back
the green grass from the forehead of the hills.)

In Allston I found many things I liked. "Children always have
secret words for their infantile concerns, and the Symbolists played
at literature in little groups like children." "Personal hieroglyphics."
"There is such a thing as dying from over-stimulation. Whatever
is worth discovering in my own mind only comes to the surface
among quiet conditions, in which one thought grows beside another and I have time to compare and reflect." "As for country liv-

ing and country habits, they suited his nervous temperament, for he could not stand late hours or exciting parties, and he found the bourgeois regimen the best for work." (That's exactly how I feel. I get up early in the morning, write until one, lunch lightly on greens, milk, and eggs, nap, work some more until three or four, knock off and putter about on the yard fixing fence or taking a long walk along the bluffs or riding a cultivator with a farmer nearby. I love our little ten-acre place, like the enormous bluff we live on, like the neighbors, like the slowness of the mail, all of it. I am sure that in some degree I am reverting to boyhood days when I had chores to do in the evening for my father. And I remember him so fondly now. Every time I tackle a fence, I recall some admonition about how to set the pole or to crib up the wire that he gave me when I was an undemonstrative lad. When I'm boarding up a wall in the garage, or toolshed, I can hear his clear voice instructing me. And when I've finished poorly, I can see the scorn in his eyes, hear his cutting words, "My God, boy, you must a done that in the dark!" My father lives in Artesia, California, now. He still hasn't bothered to learn to read and to write. And now he holds my books in his hands and sits there, wondering what's in it, and gets my step-mother to read to him, or one of the neighbors. He comes home from his little job in the evening, and shouts into the door, "Well, an' what happened (in Fred's book) today?" And it is he who has inspired me to tackle my third novel. It was his nature, his fire, that evoked the character Pier in it. The title is to be *This Is The Year,* and it'll be out next fall. I'm writing the last pages now.)

"It is said to be courageous to be frank about oneself. On the contrary, it only requires talent, but it requires talent of a high or-der." "I wished to be an underling . . . my major responsibilities all lay elsewhere . . . I saw this clearly because I wished to be a writer." "If my letters were ever published—which heaven for-bid—it would be seen that I have always been a most inju-dicious letter-writer." "He rejoiced in the long obscurity that favored his growth." "Tell me how a writer feels at the dentist's, and I will tell you how he writes." "It is the tough-minded who achieve the hopes and aims of the tender in heart." And so on and on.

From the *World of W.I., The Flowering of New England,* and *New England: Indian Summer* I got wonderful pictures of Thoreau, Amy Lowell, Emerson, Henry James, and Hawthorne. And Mar-garet Fuller. I would never have met them if it had not been for you. You gave me the very feel of their clothes, the very smells that made their nostrils tremble. It was an education. Of the three books I like *Indian Summer* best. I think your *Washington Irving,* however, has the richest phrasing and texture of interesting fact. Cooper comes up as a very distinct personality in your hands, and I *felt* his shortcomings so vividly that I worried I had them. (Which reminds me: I spent about a year reading Doughty's *Travels in Arabia Deserta.* He made his life in Arabia so real to me that often, as I walk around the yard, or wake in the night, I feel profoundly lonesome for Arabia, I feel I want to go back there. When a man can so write about an experience that you, the reader, feel lonesome for his life, like a grownup longing for the good old days of youth, that, sir, is writing. And, I found that same element in your books. I now often think of America, of Lowell, Whitman, Cooper, Emerson. Especially of Thoreau.) I have taken courage from what they have done, from what you have done, and I am going to go up the road I always felt I should take. My mind bristles with plans, with plots. I have two powerful ideas brewing now for books four and five. And in the background I already feel two more, nay three, and all of them alive. I have taken voluminous notes on all five, get ideas about them every day and carefully note them down and drop them in the file. When I came to the file of *This Is The Year* some time ago, I was astounded to find the mass of relevant material I already had on hand. Yes, it is irritating sometimes to stop in the midst of an experience and note it down. But when it comes time to write, there they are: notes not even God could inspire you to write.

I hope you like *Boy Almighty.* To me it is chockful of feeling, of poetry. I know too I should have spent ten years on it, but I have other books to write. And I wanted to spend that ten years on *World's Wanderer,* No. 5. *Boy Almighty* was most full of "wonder," but *World's Wanderer* will have even more of it. And music. And pain. And hope. The title of No. 4 is to be: *A Child is Born.*[1] Here there is to be wonder at the fact that human preoccupations with morality etc. mean little to the powerful workings of nature. A young girl is to have a fatherless war-baby which neither she nor society wants . . . but it comes on anyway and is born. (By the way, did you get a letter from the Guggenheim people? I put your name down as one of the people who had read my book, and who might be interested in what I was doing. I need that grant . . . . I was hesitant about putting your name down, but, at the last moment,

1. Later to be called *The Rape of Carla Simmons.*

couldn't resist it. I felt that we were friends after our meeting in New York. I know too that one has to be careful about making new friends, but yet, I still wanted you down there even if you were reluctant.)

There was only one thing that at first disturbed me about your literary histories. You shifted subjects rather rapidly; though, to be sure, the connecting link was there. You see, I am very sharply aware of moods in a book, and when I'm in one I don't want to be disturbed out of it until I hit either the end of a paragraph or chapter. I want the signal first. However, after a hundred pages, I got used to it; and at last, began to use it myself, I noticed. In fact, I had to be careful not to read too much of you at one sitting for fear that you would be writing through my typing fingers the next morning. Very carefully I fitted you in between Parrington's *Main Currents,* Beard's *Rise of Am. Civ.,* Doughty's *The Dawn In Britain* (an overpowering work), Stegner's *Big Rock Candy Mountain,* and an occasional modern novel. Reading you with Parrington and Beard was an experience! Three keen minds playing their lights on about the same periods of history. It gave me an acute feeling for the passing of time on this continent.

I do have a few good contacts here. There's Meridel Le Sueur, James Gray, Joseph Beach (*The Twentieth Century Novel*), Robert Penn Warren (who has a keen mind but whose likes and mine don't often jibe), Ann Chidester, Eric Russell Bentley, etc. I see them often enough to get into a good argument, but not often enough to let them influence me.

Well, the evening's chores beckon. The house is becoming cold. I am here alone and drive into Gramma's where Maryanna and little Freya are staying. Our house is still unfinished, and it is really too cold for them. But I stayed on because I can work here, and then too my good dog Debs is here and needs food and attention.

Affectionately, and knowing that
I owe you a great debt,
Feike Frederick Feikema
Fred

1946

In this productive writing year, Manfred completes This Is the Year, *which Doubleday publishes; he compiles several short stories into his fourth book,* The Chokecherry Tree; *and he begins to develop his concept of the "rume," the autobiographical genre that he will define and illustrate in the* World's Wanderer *trilogy. Manfred visits Sinclair Lewis and decides, at Lewis's suggestion, to deposit his papers with the University of Minnesota.*

To Alan Collins

[Minneapolis, Minnesota]
February 7, 1946

Dear Mr. Collins:

The letter from Lewis immediately tells what is up. Webb and I are breaking up.

If I could have made a living for my family I think I would have stuck to Paul. For Paul was a very good friend and a very good editor. Paul opened the door for me when most editors in the East wouldn't give me a look-in, and when they did they so wanted to distort and rearrange what I was doing that I was almost ready to call it quits forever. It was Paul who helped me find myself.

I've had much pressure to go to an eastern house, as the appended telegrams and letters from eastern houses will attest.[1] But always I was able to resist it as long as I saw my way clear to make a living and to feel that a sensitive, understanding editor was necessary.

And then Red [Sinclair Lewis] came along, and he raised so many pertinent problems that I once more reconsidered my connections with Webb. There was no assurance, I felt, that within five years they could do a job of distribution that say a Random House or a Knopf could do, by which time I might have passed a sort of peak as a writer, particularly if my writing was attended by no success (the two often go together). So, though I did not show the letter to Paul, I did tell him its nature and asked him what he thought. Both he and Reuel Harmon decided that maybe I could better myself in the east. And both felt too that if I were to ask you to take me on, you should feel free to shop where you wanted. They are giving me a full release. You should get a letter from them with this mail. (There is a clause in the second contract which mentions an option on *This Is The Year*. They may make reference to it.)

1. Knopf, Doubleday, Dutton, Rinehart, Random House.

Well, now that I've gotten this far, where to now? First off, of course, I must ask you if you're interested in handling my account. (Paul made arrangements with Annie Laurie for movie rights on *Boy Almighty* and *Golden Bowl*. No doubt you want that on the new book. What about the first two? Let me know and I'll immediately send her a letter explaining the situation and asking for a release.)

Assuming you take me, then where? Well, four houses appeal to me: Random House, Knopf, Doubleday, Viking. Random House because they have a good editor (Saxe Cummins), Knopf because he sent those telegrams and he does handle a select group of authors, Doubleday because they are anxiously looking for a "literary author" to make up for the Du Maurier type of book they publish (an author of theirs told me they feel the literary authors are avoiding them—this might be a good reason to join them because they'd go out of their way to handle me sympathetically), and Viking because they have Pat Covici. I stress the editors because that is important to me. It was the very core of my feeling for Webb's. (And western publishing.) I don't want to give you the impression that I am dictating to you; only that both you and I will be happier if we can get the right man first and then the company. From all I hear Saxe Cummins is wonderful. Knopf may have a very fine man. Doubleday has Ken McCormick, whom I've met and like. Pat handles Steinbeck and my stuff is in his direction. In this connection, I'd like to mention that Webb's have sold the *Golden Bowl* reprint rights to Grosset & Dunlap and it's to appear this summer. (Don't you get a commission out of that? I always meant to ask Paul.) This might work in with Random House since they have connections there and would know about my work. Well, what do you think? (I am sure that Red will be very glad to have Saxe or Cerf call him at Duluth about me.)

I am enclosing the contracts for both *Boy Almighty* and *The Golden Bowl*. I signed those two under the name of Frederick Feikema. Since then I have begun signing all documents under the name of Feike Frederick Feikema as that includes both my family name and my legal name.

I am having *This Is The Year* retyped and should have that along to you in a couple of weeks.

In Knopf's telegram of last year it seemed he wanted to buy *Bowl* immediately and do something about it in his own right. *Bowl* is gone to Grosset & Dunlap now, but perhaps somebody (Random House) may want to buy *Boy Almighty* and publish it under their imprint. Paul published 5,000 [*Golden Bowl*s] and just about 3,000 have been sold. Grosset & Dunlap have already asked for reprint rights on it, but it would make both you and I more money if republished first. If so, remember, there are some corrections to be made for the next edition.

I want you to enroll me in the Author's League. I can't say why I never joined before.

Would you want more clippings besides the few excerpts I'm sending you with this letter? Maryanna, my wife, is keeping them in a folder.

Should I come to New York to talk things over? When?

Paul tells me that he thought my new novel *This Is The Year* (he finished reading it while I was gone to Red's house) much superior to my first two books. He did say it had a few weaknesses, and it will be interesting to see what you say. My own feeling is that it is a tremendous step forward, that a couple more steps like it, and I'll be somewhere near where I want to be as a writer. I have plans for four more books and I hope to write them in the next six or seven years. Three have been named: *A Child Is Born, World's Wanderer, The Frustrates*.[2] I will begin *A Child* sometime next winter after I've outlined it and finished collecting notes. (By the way, the Guggenheim people have asked me to apply on the first two. I should hear from them any day now.)

Do you want more copies of *Boy Almighty* and *Golden Bowl* for some prospective editor to read?

Waiting, ever your,
Feike Frederick Feikema

P.S. Maybe you can start dealing for *Boy Almighty* right away as it's only a little more than two months old. Pub. Nov. 27. My telephone number, in case it is needed, is:
Minneapolis: Bloomington Exchange 170W.

P.s.s. Ed Ketcham and Donald Grosset made the deal for *Golden Bowl*.

2. Later titled *Sons of Adam* (1980).

To Sinclair Lewis

[Minneapolis, Minnesota]
February 10, 1946

Dear Sinclair,

I thought you might like to know that I sent your name in as reference to Henry Allen Moe of the Guggenheim Foundation.

Also that I have sent on your letter to Alan Collins. With it I sent my own letter, the contracts, and copies of telegrams, letters, from Knopf, Dutton, and others. The letter left last Thursday, and on the same day Webb's sent him a note which released me from further connections with them.

I didn't quite follow your advice all the way. Instead of writing for my MS, I went in to get it. I felt that it would be unfair to grab it without some explanation. Afterall, I thought, if one is married and takes a week off and meets a better gal, he owes the one he left some sort of kind word. Paul himself was very fine about it. He agreed that I had better take my things east. His bosses weren't as eager, however. I shall miss Paul. Not so much as an editor now, since I have pretty well made up my mind how and where I want to go. I'll miss him as a friend or a brain against which I threw ideas.

Your arguments were overpowering, especially since I had already half-decided there was something wrong with a guy who went around expecting people to give him awards, etc., instead of taking a firm grip on his financial contact with society. Furthermore, as you say, I couldn't afford to be a double-martyr: a writer trying to arrive and a publisher trying to arrive.

I told Alan I wanted Random House to get first crack because of what I heard about Saxe Cummins. Then Knopf. Then Doubleday because of editor Ken McCormick. Then Viking because of Pat Covici. I think Random the best bet, mainly because a branch of theirs, Grosset and Dunlap, are already doing *The Golden Bowl* in reprint next summer.

Since I had but one copy of *This Is The Year,* I had to have it retyped. This will take another ten days or so.

Red, I don't think I could ever get enough of you. You are a flame, a living enemy of enveloping Chaos around. (Don't write. Save the energy for a paragraph.)

Ever, your
Fred

To David Cornel DeJong

[Minneapolis, Minnesota]
March 10, 1946

Dear Dave,

A week ago last Friday I bundled up the damned thing (*This Is The Year*) and sent it east to my agent. I was exhausted. And since then have had to fight one mad night of flu and vomiting, and a lot of silly people who want me to come to parties (they've heard I was through with another book). I worked so hard I feel guilty of having wasted nine days of reading novels. (*The Great Gatsby, Nightshift* and *Whistlestop* by Maritta Wolf, *Focus, Boston Adventure,* etc.)

I'm also in the process of changing publishers and don't know quite which I should take. I loved my editor out here, but I wasn't making money. In fact, we're losing rapidly even and despite fellowships, etc., and since I had had five publishers all the way from Knopf, Doubleday, to Dutton, and Rinehart after me, I decided that maybe the agent could do a little auctioneering. (Alan Collins of Curtis Brown, Ltd., handles my stuff.) Knopf chased me for quite a while but I resisted because I wanted to set up a western house along with setting myself up as a sort of writer. A weekend at Sinclair Lewis' convinced me that being two martyrs is foolish. (Sinclair, by the way, mentioned your work without any prompting on my part and was I pleased. He was surprised when I told him that I knew you, went to the same dungeon, etc.)

Sinclair is still a furious yellow flame. But I'm afraid he works too much from irritation rather than genuine love for anything. He has love, but the other is the strongest. He has been very kind to me, is unusually wise. He refrains utterly from telling me what to write, raves about the stuff, and then, quietly, goes about helping me get fellowships, etc.

I liked your *Somewhat Angels,* and was surprised by its contents. After reading the reviews I was again struck by an old theory of mine that book noticers should learn not only to give the outline of a story, but its smell and feel. (Of course, if they could do that, they'd write themselves.)

Mrs. Brain was wonderful. I've met her many times. She is a deep type, actually, and that's the kind I go for. The little southern gal I've met too, and I think you got something there about southern womanhood. In fact, the whole book struck me as an understatement of a great truth: namely, that mankind is not meant for marriage, that it is completely and thoroughly a thing of convenience, that a marriage of passion can become a marriage of companionship, that "love" can become "profound friendship." And what more fun is there than to have as your best, your most intimate friend, someone of the opposite sex? Representatives from two worlds talking over their findings in life?

(It happens I'm crazy about my wife, and on that basis should believe in ideal love, etc., but my brain tells me different, and It I must believe.)

The poetry: well, without doubt that is where you shine. However, for some damned strange reason or other, there are types of poets and poetries that do not stir me. I think it goes back to Jakie. I think he killed in me a natural love for it. And only if some motivation is kindled in me, can I get into it. Funny thing is, I'm nuts about Doughty's obscure things, and, of course, I like Whitman and Wordsworth and Chaucer and Spenser. But there were reasons for me getting into them. Modern poetry I've been unable to get into.

I did spend a lot of time with your *Across the Board,* because *you* wrote them, and I must say that I got more out of yours than most poetry written today. I particularly liked *Outside the Town* with its phrases: "chasing the hoops of spring" and "recross your iron ricrac bridge," all of *In Due Season,* especially "fenceless summer seasons"; *When In Autumn,* "In his eyes I saw autumn cupped like ale around August's candle already happily snuffed"; *Question*; *Lama Sabachtani,* "is this my soul or is it June?" *Home Again*; *Ours Is An Honest Generation,* "and the mind revolving its old stones upon a detriment we should no longer grind"; *Ritual And Penance,* "and her heart wept sympathy like a ravished bride lying agape on a rock-of-ages-rock," "High piano of clouds"; *Trial And Error,* "the bock-beard wagging"; *How The Watchers Have Soured,* "Let us go home and part our cold knees to the fire"; and last, the fine and moving *In Memoriam.*

I can not give you analyses: I can only tell you what I like. I have never been very capable of telling anyone why any book is a work of art, though I *know* why deep inside me, often better than the best critics. It is that inner "knower" of me that dictates the rules for my writing, and it has been he who has gotten my books published, not the advice of friends and "editors."

Well, friend, write again. I won't greet you in Fries this time. Curiously enough, I can now read Fries pretty well but not speak it. (I can hear it in my mind, though.)

Best,
fred
F.F.

To William Carlos Williams

[Minneapolis, Minnesota]
4-27-46

Dear Williams:

I am not sure either which will win out, the artist or the person.
If the person, I will die, because it will die. I am hoping that the
artist will win out. That's why I'm turning my whole soul, my mind
and my heart, on the problem of what I shall write in the future.
For two years now I've been able to live (and my family too) on the
few fellowships I've been able to win. And in that time I've taken
a tremendous step forward from the almost inept, bumbling, well-
meaning, fearfully frustrated, passionate, hot-and-cold boy I once
was.

But it now looks like I'll have to go back to work somewhere
to keep us going as animals. And my writing will stop because I
simply do not have the energy after that damned TB siege.

I get wonderful letters, Brooks, Lewis, Warren, DeJong, yours,
others, but they don't bring food. Peculiarly enough, I work best
when well-fed, when I have no immediate financial worries. I don't
need the goad of poverty to drive me ahead. I'm so damned full
of writing energy, ideas, dreams, visions, I could live in a vacuum
for the next forty years and yet turn out twelve to fifteen rich books.

My next novel is ready, *This Is The Year,* and in many ways it
is a better job. There are passages in it that *Boy* don't touch. I spent
a lot of time, since 1938, on the idea, and I hope I've really constructed something this time. (There are parts too that are not as

1. *The Chokecherry Tree.*

good as *Boy.*) I'm starting number four, called *Hero,*[1] and am hoping that I'll be allowed to write *A Child Is Born* and *World's Wanderer* before the door closes. I'm ready to write them now. And
then there are three other projects that I could start within three
months. But each of these should have time. After the first draft, a
lot of time. Hard work. Discrimination. Constant retesting and
evaluation and careful honing.

I have a beautiful little girl, Freya, seventeen months old, who
babbles and walks and hangs onto my knee. She already has the
gesture that to me typifies inspiration, that typifies the way my
mind feels. She raises on her toes, throws wide her hand, palm up,
and looks up, and cries, ecstatically, "What's that?" and "Ohhh!"
whether there is anything to look at or not.

You hit exactly right when you wrote, "You're a good deal pre-
historic in your approaches to the relationship between individuals." It has always been my theory that you start from there before

you begin evolving or creating or noting the modern psychiatric fluff-fuss. It's (the modern notions) all very nice today, but a hundred years from now psychiatry will have matured a bit, and all these novels based on today's findings will be old. What will live will be the basic things. That's why I feel highly complimented when someone writes that I have "poetic understanding of character."

I shall try, I promise you, to make all these yet to come unique creations.

We both, Maryanna and I, want to tell you too that we were entranced with your volume of poetry. A lot of it I didn't quite understand, the references weren't warm for me, but the total effect was powerful. I got to know a brooding, very kind, at times very wrathy, poet. I noticed particularly the love for particular people, for particular things, for singleness of things. Flowers, horse-dung on the streets, the cheated woman, the river, after the rain, the spirit rustling behind windows and always looking out. In fact, though I don't know the particulars of your life, have seen you but once, I could still write you down, that is, your essence. (What is essence? I don't know. I know, however, how you seem to me.)

Greet Hoagland and Kathleen for me. I am going to write them a long letter soon.

Ever,

To Van Wyck Brooks

[Minneapolis, Minnesota]
May 6, 1946

Dear Mr. Brooks,

It is probably a good thing you didn't come up in March. The house was open to the winds on one end, and it would have been most uncomfortable for you and your wife. We hope that by fall our place will be habitable, for both us and our company. In many ways it has been both a bad and a good winter for me. My family, Maryanna and little Freya, had to go to town and stay with Gramma. That was all right. But what was bad was my having to stay out here and to drive in twice a week to see them. It was too cold on the floors for the little child, and Maryanna doesn't like cold feet either. I managed to get by the first part of the winter wearing my boots. I also closed up the house except for one room, moving my typewriter and a few books into it from my working-cabin, and held hard. There wouldn't have been any point in going to town myself since I would not have been able to find a decent room for work. Furthermore, I had the dog Debs out here, and occasional workmen, and so we thought it best to break up. I didn't like it at all.

The child is a wonder. I mean in the sense that she teaches me so much about my existence. She is a constant reminder that the bands of culture and society are thin ones, that talk, and books, and ideas, and music, are all miracles, that we have wars because the preying animal in us is an uncomfortable prisoner. And what is most miraculous is that deep in the animal, a liking for love and comradeship and play exists. Maryanna is very carefully recording everything, and maybe she will at last find something that she can get her mental teeth into. My wife is a very brilliant woman, but somehow there has never been a push, an effervescence, a bubbling over of energy. She is retiring, moody, shy, with occasional periods of sharp wit and gay excitement, of deep emotional "religious exaltation." Somehow, she seems just right for me. There are only one or two people (of all those I've met so far) that I can get along with on a day-to-day basis. Almost everything she does is non-irritating. Her habits, talk, mental speed, all seem right. And I know that I would long ago have sickened of many another woman. We sometimes wonder if this is a good thing because when we see relatives from the farm country, or even some of our idea friends, we seem to have trouble making them understand us. We talk a strange tongue to them. Our neighbors are farmers, and retired town folk, and I know from their strange looks we are regarded as squirrelly. Our days are full of music, talk, reading, work (writing, that is; at least in my case) and we just don't seem to have time for gossip. Or plugging work. We have to be very careful not to offend them. (I hope this doesn't sound snobbish; I'm sure it don't because some of the snobs we know think we're squirrelly too.)

The "good" part of the winter outweighed the "bad" (three sieges of flu, three colds, loss of weight, etc). My mind was exactly as you described Mark Twain's. "His mental Niagara was always pouring away." It was almost terrifying. I hardly dared write a short story, or even think of one, for fear it'd grow into a novel. My doctor had asked me, once *This Is The Year* was done, not to do anything requiring long range emotional excitement. And so I thought I'd turn out a few short stories (for income, and to use up some ideas that strayed out of the reach of the novels). First thing I knew I had a character who insisted on more work. His name is Elof

Lofblom. He is a college graduate who has no specific training and so can't get the job that fits his notion of what a hero should have. He bums around, and finally returns home where his father greets

1. Bracket and line by FM.

him roughly. He carries with him [*Moby Dick*] [1] *Peregrine Pickle,* which all through the book to be, he is trying to finish, and also carries a few lessons in Accounting by Correspondence which he thinks will get him into a well-paying job. *P.P.* is the dream side of him; accounting is the labor side. But he never gets away from his boyhood community again. Gradually, despite struggles, and protests, he sinks slowly away into the common mass of people. And becomes the village queer duck. The title is to be *The Choke-Cherry Tree.* In other words, it is a novel. I must write it before I start on *A Child Is Born,* and *World's Wanderer.* The other day I started another little story about Grampa Fedde, and he threatens to use up more literary room. What am I to do? I intend to close the door to these people and write what is on the board first. *Hero,* then *A Child,* then *W.W.,* then *Pilgrims,* [2] then *A Son of the Road,* [3] then *Idyll of the Old Faithful.* [4] Another thing I noticed: that most of these people come from a territory called Siouxland. (I drew a map of this area for *This Is The Year.* I am sure that over half of my work will tie back to my "boyhood heaven and hell." It is land adjoining the Sioux River running between Sioux Falls, S.D., and Sioux City, Iowa. Already I've peopled it with many towns, mostly fictions (though real) and people, and situations, and tragedies.) O God, if only my health holds and we get an income. (This last bit we lived on less than a $120 a month, and if we don't get sales soon, I'll have to go back to work and quit writing. A terrible thing. I think I'd rather go to jail or commit suicide than do that. Imagine working for some practical executive on a newspaper, or even for a University department! Like Elof, I have a good mind but can't turn it to anything that will give me a living!) (That reminds: Guggenheim said *NO.* I guess Carson McCullers got a renewal and that stopped me. She is a good writer, however, and needs help as badly as I perhaps.)

2. *Sons of Adam.*

3. An early title of *The Golden Bowl.*

4. *The Wind Blows Free.*

It was the "money" question that drove me to leave the Webb Pub. Co., in St. Paul. Paul Hillestad and I are still friends, but after many a talk, he agreed that he simply could not get the distribution that an eastern house could offer, that I could not be both a martyr as a writer and as a fellow publisher. I am trying to make a living writing, and so must somehow be practical about it. It is not a gamble for me, as there were seven different inquiries from publishing

houses in the east asking if I were satisfied, and they didn't know
I was contemplating leaving. Right now we are awaiting word
from Alfred Knopf, who wired me twice last year for the rights to
Golden Bowl.

I should tell you too that Sinclair Lewis had much to do with
the change. First of all, he gave his agent Alan Collins a pep talk
about my work, and then gave me one for being a fool to not think
of a livelihood. So Alan is going to handle all my stuff.

May 27. I have word now from Mr. Knopf and he isn't too wild
about my thesis. He claims that I have done too much violence to
the language, that I have based too many of my metaphors on physiological processes. (And what else could I base them on when it
is Pier's book, the man of the wild?) I have sent back my reply, and
am now waiting again. Meanwhile Doubleday is going to look at
it too.

You cannot imagine my joy in discovering your article "Tradition of Rootlessness in Sketches in Criticism." It seems to me you
have caught up exactly what I tried to do in this new book of mine.
It *is* "a sombre epic," as Knopf and the movies say it is. And it deals
exactly with the tragedy of what happens when man tries to love
the soil in a wild, chaotic, unreasoning way. Pier did have some elements in him that might have led to a wise love of the land, but he
was handicapped by what he had been handed from his father.
Knopf thought there was too much horror in it. Exactly. That is
the terrible consequence of what happens when the soil and man
do not become loving and working partners. (As a matter of fact,
I am rather shocked to think that I wrote a "shocking" book. To
me it was a passionate avowal of *my* love for the land, it was a stirring, eloquent book, full of exalted poetry. That is, to me.) You may
be sure that I promptly quoted the entire passage to both my agent
and to Knopf.

He quibbled about my use of language on other scores too. I
had to write back that I wrote American, not English, that I did
intend to use very heavily the idiom of the midwest (as highly selec-
tive as possible, of course) because I thought that it was rich with
poetry and American meaning. (It is my theory that the midwest
idiom and speechway will dominate American Literature in time to
come. Families are large out here, but the farms no longer require
large families. Therefore, a goodly share of the seventeen year-olds
leave for the cities, for the west and east coasts. They leave, however, after their ways of thinking, talking, living are pretty well set.
And this constant flood will vitally affect all the large cultural cen-

ters. And thus it can very well be that just as a certain dialect became the official English of England, so too the midwest idiom may become in time the official American.)

Well, I shall persist in my ideas on what I shall write. I shall make very sure not to miss anything in their criticisms, but at the same time they shall not keep me from the sweet fruits of creation. My way. Your warnings in *The Ordeal of Mark Twain* are a constant and a powerful reminder not to let anyone water me down. I do not want to be bitter in my old age for having allowed a Howells or a Livy to take liberties with my "forceful" language.

The week Maryanna and I spent at Sinclair Lewis' house was electrifying. Seeing him is like grabbing hold of a live wire and not being able to let go. He is a flame. He is old now, but still the old mane can fly in the wind, the eyes bristle with sarcasm and fire.

One moment he is quiet, says nothing, smiles outwardly at all the talk buzzing around him. Suddenly, a flying spark from the conversation will light on a memory of his. He warms up, his eyes open, his lips begin to quiver, to prepare the forceful dramatic emergence of a mighty expostulation. He waves thin long yellow hawk arms. He directs and drives a long finger directly at you, and a book explodes in your face.

One moment he is kind and loving, gives his entire heart away. The next moment he becomes crafty, shrewd. When he plays chess, or Monopoly, he plays for blood. It was infinitely revealing to see how he chuckled over another player's bankruptcy. In fact, in real life, something happppened that told me something about his coming forth out of America. That he was born to a middle class family, that that is what he delights in even though he constantly lampoons it. He was selling his house. A banker and his agent came in to buy furniture, to buy the building. They argued over tiny pennies and dimes with the greatest of relish. It was a great good game to him. He is aware of what he is doing, but at the same time, he allows the momentums that had once trained him as a boy to once again take him in hand.

He reads well. He has unusually good taste. His reasons for liking certain writings, writers, seem to me the right kind of instincts, intuitions. And he loves music. He had a phonograph-radio playing modernistic music all evening long. The house was alive with wonder, lofty exaltation. Rarely did we talk about ourselves. It was mostly life, art, books, tales, embroidered stories from our early boy days, embroidered accounts of travels.

He is tremendously suspicious of women. He is incredibly ugly;

though after a half hour the males forget about it. The first few days he hardly noticed Maryanna. He talked to me or to his other guest. But I could see he was watching her. Watching her to find his usual complaints about women reconfirmed in her. The third day he suddenly decided she was "just perfect" for me. He kissed her hand. Then said that afterall perhaps she was "just right" because she behaved more like a man than a woman. There was a party one night and a judge's wife challenged some of his comments about marriage, etc. He flared up, wildly, seemingly unreasonable (actually there was a long history of irritation and this was another of many rough brushings). He left the party, roamed through the enormous rooms of his Tudor mansion. He stood looking through a window, watching the steam rising from the ice on Lake Superior lying far below. Presently, cooled, he came back, and he tried to smile, and yet excuse his tantrum by saying to her (by looking at me, as if I were the one he most feared would take it wrong!), "When you know a man has a sore spot, why do you persist in probing it?"

It was an experience to know and to see just how a great (yet frustrated) writer lived if only to compare your own life to his. You learn what you should not become, and you learn what you should stress what he did not.

I should write you too about my discovering Smollett. My Mother-in-law bought a set of his works at an auction sale. They had been edited by Saintsbury, and the print was lovely and open, and the backs were in gold-embossed leather. I have now finished all his novels, and discover, in a very concrete way, that this modern age goes back a good long way, a long way beyond the date of my birth. I am also reading Doughty and Chaucer, and soon expect to read Spenser. (My Frisian really comes in handy, do you see?) I bought a 1788 set of Spencer, the Bell edition, and so with my magnifying glass, I shall set to work. At the same time I plan an exhaustive study of Mark Twain, Emerson, Thoreau, and Poe. But especially Mr. Twain.

How is your work coming? I want to tell you that I think your idea that we are all part of a chain, and working together toward a common American destiny, is exactly how I feel about the matter. May we meet soon.

Yours,
fred

To Alan C. Collins

[Minneapolis, Minnesota]
May 19, 1946

Dear Alan:

I think it is possible for Knopf and I to get together. I am very enthusiastic about him as a publisher, would be even if he turned me down.

I will not say I will not make changes to improve the book. But I will say that the evidences of bad writing he offers do not convince me that it should be rewritten. For example. "Long billowing plumage, etc." does not refer to a blizzard. It refers to a frosted window. Just look at that paragraph again. P 676. The Old Dreamer's sermon is not a horrible mock heroic so much as it is a description of what happens when a man is alone and takes himself too seriously and preaches the sermon he might have preached. Everyone, at one time or other, rants and raves, and waves an arm at "them" when *he is sure he is alone.* I might backtrack on the "And she too etc." sentence, though I must say that I had looked at the sentence often enough, had consulted dictionaries on usage (and Mencken) before I put it in as is. The business about Nertha's tongue, the children snotting, and the raw-skinned face seems perfectly all right to me. No harm at all. It is even a beautiful and wondrous description. That's exactly as it is. Masturbation? Check Hemingway in *To Have and Have Not,* Jackson's *Lost Weekend.* And surely it is more normal for Teo to play with himself sexually than it is for Joyce's hero to play with his anus. And so on.

But the real point is: I want to know what happened to Knopf between pages 200 and 400. At 200 he said "I would have said without hesitation that I was reading a major novelist writing, at last, the American *Growth of the Soil* or the Great American Farm Novel. At 400, what I principally felt was revulsion, etc." And I can only get that by a personal conference with him. His letter does not tell me. (Incidentally, if he will allow me a little bravery here, I'd like to say that "at last Feikema has written the American *This Is The Year* by Feikema." What I mean is, Knut is pretty good, but I'm not so half bad myself.) (That bracketed sentence leads me to something else. I think I made the mistake of writing a note to the editor about what I thought I had put into the book. If I had come in with my horns down, my bugles muted, he might have had a different reaction.)

And certainly there will be no harm in being more specific about trip-wires, farm finance, windmills, fenceposts, fencing, etc. He caught exactly what I was doing. Telling about machinery in *process*. I had been accused of writing Sears Roebuck descriptions before.

I'd suggest that Knopf read it again and mark down on little slips of paper all the things that irked him, or that he didn't get, then have me come to New York by plane (six hours from here) for an accounting. (Don't mark the copy. That drives me into a rage. The slips feel like suggestions.)

I want to make sure I'm not missing good advice before closing the door to him.

I also want to make clear that I just didn't toss off the book. I studied each word, sentence, paragraph, at least a dozen times. For cadence, meaning, graphic quality, rhythm, poetry, tie-in with the major movements. I am a craftsman, an artist, and not a fictioneer. Also, I don't intend to be watered down like Twain was, don't intend to feel ashamed in my old age like he was. I write from my heart, from my experience, from my knowledge or my belief of what the American writing has been, is today, will be tomorrow. You should see the infinite pains I take with one word. The tricks I'll try to knock it out of the text if I don't like it. In fact, so far I am not convinced that the "language" in *This Is The Year* is "horrible." (However, maybe I can be convinced.)

"Such a violent fellow with language!" Well, when I get through using the American Language it will be forever changed. Say like Shakespeare changed it in his day. I am sick of the pallid language we use today. It simpers, even in Hemingway, Steinbeck. It is full of affixes, of vague polite abstractions. Look, let me quote you from Jake Falstaff who wrote "Words" (a poem I might well have written):

I am a lover of stringent words said rightly:
Not of the small words, smiling and hiding,
Not of the honey words, simpered so lightly;
Let me have Cossack words, striking and riding.

I am a lover of unruly words that wrestle:
Words that are hard as a spear or raw as a hole in the
gut;
Words that are bellied like sails, and sentences built
like a vessel;
Ultimate words that, leaving, snap the jaws shut.

"Itches in their crotches." What's wrong with that? A truly Twain-like observation of men going on a stag. Rabelaisian. Feikema.

I am writing this from my experience. My first editor bucked
on many of the things I wanted in *Boy* and *Bowl*. But I talked him
into it. And what happened? The very things he wanted out got
me excited comments from Van Wyck Brooks, William Carlos Williams, W.R. Benét, Sinclair Lewis, *New Republic, St. Louis Post-Dis-
patch,* James Gray, Warren. And not from "overpowered" salesmen
writing in book review sections. Every time I followed someone
else's advice, I stumbled. It was not me. It didn't sound like me.
When I followed my own nose, it was alive, real, sweeping. That
is my experience. If Knopf can convince me that what he wants
changed represents me too, well and good. (Sinclair Lewis tells me,
"Don't listen to people when they tell you to change. Or rewrite.
You're an artist. Better than most of us ever tried to be. It's your
work. Not theirs. And if you should change it, do you think they'll
be happier? And yourself?")

So, let me come to New York. Ask Knopf if he can forward me
money to make the trip (later to be deducted from the advance or
royalty—and if he doesn't take my book, from whatever advance
I get from someone else). I ask this because we are down to ten dollars, our credit is exhausted, and we are really in a hell of a fix. (I
was sick for the fourth time this week since last fall. Not so good
for a lunger. Too much worry, too much work.) (And tell Knopf
that he won't be sorry. I'm sold on him and I'll work myself to the
bone for him. In fact, let him read this letter.) (Airplane, because
I can't get Pullman berths to fit my frame. And I need ten hours
sleep out of twenty-four or my clock will run down.) (I don't have
pneumothorax, so I can take plane.)

Please write me soon, because I'm really in a stew. And I'm so
anxious to do right without compromising myself. Please.

Yours, best,
fred

[margin] P.S. Also make sure they read *Boy* and *Bowl* so that they
will get a glimpse of my direction as a writer. Be sure about these.

To Ken McCormick

[Minneapolis, Minnesota]
June 11, 1946

Dear Ken,

It was good to hear from you, and also to hear from Alan that
you agreed to the terms. It means that I can get a furnace for my
house and insulation, and still have enough left over to live decently

till the first of the year. It is very important because I had a hard time convincing my wife we should live out here in the country, but I felt it was best for both her health and mine, and also for my writing. Here is where I belong. And except for some trips that I'll be making, to Europe and elsewhere, this is where I'll live out my days, right next to the soil I was reared on.

We were very lucky to get this place. Our house is on the very tip-off edge of a bluff and we can look twenty miles down the wide Minnesota River Valley, toward the southwest. We have ten acres, some up on the bluff, some down in the bottom. I have a big garden, and I have built up all the fences around the place, have whiskered the trees, have planted lilac bushes and other flowers, have built a fence around a neglected vineyard. This spot reminds me of the wonderful Sioux River Valley and at the same time leaves me within driving distance of symphonies, libraries, friends, and fellow writers. (We are having a regular renascence out here. I don't know how good they all are but look at the following: Heggen, Shulman, Smith (Ray), Erling Eng, Anneke De Lange, Dan Brennan, Ann Chidester, Harry Reasoner, Sheila Alexander (to be published by Webb this fall—a fine book she has!) Margery Chute, Thelma Jones, Earl Guy, Harrison Salisbury, etc. (And then we've always had Beach, Le Sueur, Gray, Robert Warren, E. Russell Bentley.) When you come out I'd like very much for you to take up our guest room (when it's done) and rest you up some with this bird-song quiet.

I am working away on *Hero*. Also, we found a lost MS! In 1937 I lost a sheaf or book of poems, ready to be published. My wife thinks they're very fine, but I call them "youngish." I have other poems and later on, maybe I can collect them all for a book. But that is later on.

I am proud to be published by you. I spent all Friday afternoon in a book store looking over the type of book you publish, trying (and succeeding) in selling myself on Doubleday! And tell George Shively, "Bless your Heart!"

Yours,
Fred

P.S. That cash will help me and my wife stay ahead of our TB. We're going to load ourselves full of bright red food energies!

To George Shively

August 17, 1946

Dear George:

I am sending the manuscript back to you today via Railway Express. This folder with the letter contains a lot of stuff: material for the publicity department which I thought you'd like to look at too, a clip of stuff about *The Golden Bowl,* a clip about *Boy Almighty,* (to help in promotion), and the two new maps.

About the maps. Could they be used? I feel that it's important for the reader to get a good visual outline of the country, of the farm and its environs, and of Siouxland (my literary territory). If these aren't good enough for reproduction, then we'd better have new ones made. (Maps in Doughty's *Travels in Arabia Deserta* were of great aid.) (Also, I think the maps will pass as an author's scratching. As a professional map-maker, they wouldn't, of course.) I think that when they're reduced to book page size the little tails and so will vanish.

About one of the photos. I've marked one of them as my favorite. It has not been used in any connection; is the proof, not the final doctored photo. (But you people will know best which to use.)

I tried my damnedest to cut the book. If a section looked likely, I'd take down all the things I thought the book couldn't get along without, and each time, got too long a list. Any time one writes a book according to a tight outline, he just doesn't waste motions, it seems. For example. I thought of cutting out the entire section of Cephas' story. Well, first I discovered there was a hint in there that Pier would look for a new woman, there were facts of their poverty, there was a suggestion of relief from agony through the use of humor, etc. The reader had to have some preparation for the first chapter in Book Five when Pier goes to Kaia. I tried like hell to cut it instead. And you can see that I did cut it a little.

I did cut the masturbation scene as you directed. I have saved the original and am putting it into my journal. I thought it a wonderful and poetic description of a little boy discovering his power.

I tried to tone down Red Joe. I did in a couple of places, as you suggested. I tried other places too; could find no replacement for what I wanted to take out, so kept it in. I did fix up the diarrhea business a little. I went back to my notebooks and luckily found the exact expression I'd once heard. At the time of writing, I couldn't find it. I also find it now in *Western Words.* I've heard it often out here.

In the case of the Old Dreamer, you were right. So, I decided to call him straight Pederson, except where Pier thinks of him. That is, I the writer call him Pederson, but Pier sometimes doesn't. I simply could not cut Pederson's sermon, but I did fix the passage up. I found that I had not indicated that he was slowly slipping into mild senility. I also suggested that he was aware he was talking "out-loud." As we all so often do when we are alone. I've rendered many such a sermon, and judging from the gesticulations of others I've seen alone, they do too.

Well, George, I want to make a note of your tact, your enthusiasm. I am looking forward to our meeting someday. After that, we both will know what we *can* write to each other. Also, the words in the letter will have the sound of the voice; and if some are strong in print, they may be mild in speech. I'd like to spend a couple of days with you. Until we really get acquainted. Hope you like the autographed books.

There may still be slips of the typewriter or pencil in the book. Those I give you unqualified permission to correct. If they don't turn out right I can always catch them in proof. E.G. I have a bad habit of using the suffix "ed" for "ing," and vice versa. There are, no doubt, misspellings too. Correct them all.

Also, be sure to send a set of proofs to Bernard Fridsma, 1017 Alto Avenue, S.E., Grand Rapids 7, Michigan. Bernie will be the final Frisian eye to look at the Frisian words and Frisian customs. (He already has been most helpful.) He'll then send the set on to me, and I'll incorporate his suggestions onto mine. I do this because he has a religious bias, and isn't too interested in my detailing that there are "woaste Fries," or wild Frisians. Furthermore, I disagree with him on some of the spellings, etc. Just the same, I want to know where he thinks I'm wrong.

Report on health. Went through the U. of Minn. health clinic, find nothing wrong but a little tumor on the tendon of my little finger (left hand). It is to be cut out soon. It is *not* malignant.

The U. of Minn. library is thinking of collecting Feikemania. (Say, that sounds like a disease. Mental.) Feikeiania. No, that's not it either. Anyway, they want to start collecting letters, notes, personal bits, manuscripts, etc., before they are lost. Sinclair Lewis told them to do so. I haven't made up my mind. I do have some very "hot" correspondence which I want to use later for books, but am not sure that a possible "enemy" should go browsing through them. I'll talk to you about this later.

By the way, I'm spelling "strawhat" together all the way through. But I may have missed it here and there. Well, that does it. If I think of any more, I'll write right away.

Best,
Feike Feikema

P.S. Tell Ken McCormick a very brilliant man by the name of Gordon Roth (newspaperman, radio writer, etc.) has written a book. I read the first half and thought it very absorbing. (From his report I'm not too sure about the last half.) Address: 180 Bedford S.E., Mpls.

Also, that I enjoyed *Mankind So Far*, liked the looks of *Latin America* by Crow (the binding and print were especially wonderful!) and will soon get into the quinine thing. In the meantime, ask him if I can have (be sure I may do this, please!) *The Bitter Box* by Miss Clark, *The Bulwark* by Dreiser, and *The Greek Reader* by Whall (sp?). I am embarking on a Greek adventure. Am reading Homer, Plato, etc. Also, when you send proofs, send list of marking instructions.

Best, ff
F.F.

[margin] P.S. I think the prelude and postlude give the book a frame, give it a force, a philosophic or timeless backdrop which will help the reader accept the "fate of Pier."

To Robert Penn Warren

[Minneapolis, Minnesota]
August 26, 1946

Dear Red:

I took two turns up and down the lane wondering if I should write you right away, and then I decided, what the hell, if I wait until next week compunctions will hobble the idea, and he'll never get it. Because I'll probably feel then that maybe I'm being garrulous, or probably I'll feel that Red'll pull that smoke-cloak around himself if I talk frank—the one he uses when anybody gets personal in his presence.

Red, not ten minutes ago I finished *All The King's Men*. Red, it is a tremendous book. I'd like to write about it, and damn it, I don't know where to begin.

But let us say first that I was moved. Terribly moved. And that to me has always been the final test. Not all the fine little verbal criticisms and observations and finical applications of various tests. To hell with that when you get the other. Being moved, so moved your head sings and you hardly hear the damned crows cawing in the cornfield where they're ruining the crop and you feel dramatic inside as if you could slay a thousand dragons and you feel that if Joe Stalin walked into the den you could lay down the law to him.

This book affected me differently from anything you've written so far. The others felt obscure to me, sometimes tinkered a little, often jerky. I liked them, liked the fluid poetic lines and paragraphs, like the characterizations, etc., and I was moved at times, and certainly, at the end, always felt you had great talent, that you were a master. But none of the other things hit like this one.

Not that you, this time, had more concern for your reader. You did, but you were busier with something else. What happened is that a great idea and a great mind met, and there was an explosion, a black explosion on white.

I hardly talked to my wife, anybody, while I read it. It was like grabbing hold of a wire charged with a powerful current. And like the jabbing series of stings that is the alternating current, the figures of speech came winging along and stung me forward into more and more of the agony. Rarely did I stop to examine the figures of speech. I am doing that now, after. But at the time they got inside and past the eyes and then blew up even while the eyes were busy receiving the new one. It is not unlike the work of a jet plane; while one explosion is lifting another pops up so that the momentum is never lost.

Time said "slick." Slick, hell. This is style. This is craftsmanship. This is poetry spun like the silvery fine wires of a spider's web. Only this is not made of weak stuff. The wires are wires of steel-and-silver alloy. More beautiful than one, more powerful than the other.

And it is not Huey Long's story only. Nor, even, Burden's. It is more. It is the story of man, coming up, dripping from the vast outspread ooze, discovering his power, and his power of Idea. And not knowing what the hell to do with it. And if he does, what for? Your expression, "terrible division of their age," refers not to 1900–1939. It refers to the time since man became man out of savagedom, and it reaches forward into the moondusk of the future. On page 276 you say "he had made some good out of bad." I would say "good out of what is." Because what is, is this friable animal creature we are into which by sheer great accident brain was grown (like cauliflower out of mud). And from it has come the cumulative charge or battery which is History. You got that all in there.

And I liked Jack Burden. I liked him because Jack Burden is just about the only guy who can ride easily in such an "age." He has the caution of Aristotle, the caution of Aurelius, the caution of the scientist, the caution that is yourself. It is sweet-cane to dream of heaven. And to swim in it. But it is not the truth. The truth is that we are animal, and it is a terrible truth. And it is a terrible thing to live with it. But I'd much rather live with Jack knowing about it than I would with somebody who is naïve and unknowing. Because in Jack is the hope that, maybe, afterall, the base is not just casual accident but has meaning in an absolute sense. And if not that, Jack is at least the most likely fellow to grow up into an Olympic-eyed Plato (without the slaves who support him).

It is also the story of Floyd Olson, Roosevelt, Stassen, La Follette. Not one of them is further removed from Willie than a step. They are that close. And Humphrey is now moving into that situation too.

I've marked the book from head to foot (and when you come some day, and you feel you want to, and won't mind my waving arms and wild eyes, I'd like to show you each spot I've marked and try to tell you what exploded in my mind. If you don't mind.) and I'll pick out a few things.

"the old white thunder-mug." "a couple of hogs lounging down there on their sides, like big gray blisters popped up out of the ground." "a pair of eyes would burn at us out of the dark, etc." p 53. "ectoplasmic fingers of the mist reached out of the swamp etc." "But it was her fudge and I let her cook it." (The use of Jack as narrator gives the book a life not unlike *Wuthering Heights*) "bucknaked" "the skin lanked down" "when a woman makes a sandwich out of one of your hands" "saving up one little twitch and try like a one-nut" (and the echoes of sound or of syllable: "*pat*ties *pot*ty-*b*lack"—see Burke on this—"*All The King's Men* by Robert *P*enn Warr*en*" "two *coup*les to give him the stirr*up cup* "*sup*ine and *s*lightly *cup*ped") "tooled" "sulls" "lowdan" (low Dan) "A person with deep inner certitude of self which comes from etc." "the wind blows great chunks of gray sky in off the Atlantic which come dragging in so low their bellies brush the masts and chimney pots, like gravid sows crossing a stubble field." "It is buried under the sad detritus of time, where, no doubt, it belongs." "Thus the fact of his death was absorbed effortlessly into the life of the community, like a single drop of stain dropped into a glass of clear water. It would spread outward and outward from the point of vindictive concentration, raveling and thinning away, drawing away the central fact of the stain until nothing stood at all" (in this connection, see Schrödinger's *What Is Life* where he describes the Brownian movement or chaos) "the incident of the new kiss" "We wrote every day, but the letters began to seem like checks drawn on the summer's capital." "like the ocean chewing its gums." "*ma*ssacred off at the neck and *ma*rcelled etc" "you got the impression that they were like weapons just loosened and riding easy and ready in the scabbards." and so on.

Can I call your attention to the following? P. 99—"bemused"—is that the right word? It is right, but in the context, it throws in a different mood. Who is "bemused,"? P. 116, line 9—isn't there supposed to be a "who" after nigger? Transition, page 128. "When he got back etc." you wonder who *he* is. Of course it's the Judge, you discover, reading on. P. 139—spelling of "whimsey" or "whimsy"? "Delirium for every seismograph" on page 154; isn't that mixed? P. 242—"condon." That's probably the word you "heard." I usually thought of them as "condums." Page 304—we get a lengthy description of Jack's nose . . . which we should have had before, I feel, because at this point, I had to alter my notion of Jack's physical setup. Page 338—A bad *i* in business, line 7. "Unplumbed waters" on page 360? Unplumbed? Also, p. 272,—"want" in paragraph 6 or "went?" P. 162—"spewed smoke?" "Spew" suggests wetness. P.117—"know" or "known" line 3?

How about having the Great Twitch wrestle with the Whipper? But maybe not. Both were outgrown by the end.

I notice an interesting resemblance between Doc Beach and Judge Irwin. And Sadie with Brenda.

The book is like an onion. It is not like a string with a series of notes on it, like in Steinbeck. You go around the story and take off a layer. Then tackle the next layer, all around. And then, on and on, layer by layer, deeper. And each time you learn more and more about each one. In one sense it gives the story an unusual "not-told-yet" quality. I am not sure I would like to do this, but I know I like it here. For example, I wondered if I shouldn't have known about Anne and Jack earlier in the book. Then the meetings they had would have taken on more bite. I knew something was there, but

I didn't know what, and, hastening on with the main story, I forgot it, until I got that business when he was 21 and she 17.

Red, I owe you much. For the example you set. (I am terribly impressionable when people do not *preach* at me.) For introducing me to Burke. For suggesting a way of behaving as a writer. All hail to an older brother. My best to you, "mei Fryske hânslach" (with Frisian handshake or handstroke).

I am,
your Feike

To John Huizenga

[Minneapolis, Minnesota]
October 5, 1946

My dear John,

What you wrote about the man coming before the artist hit a loud and clamorous bell on this hill here. It is something that I decided on a long time ago, and which accounts for my not wanting to see too much of writers and artists and singers and movie heroes generally. Before I had "arrived," as they say, I knew intuitively that pomposity and artifice were not for me. One of the things I got from Lewis last winter was that at least for the most part the man was in charge there. Yes, he chose to get on his high horse once in a while, usually when he was badgered by strangers for autographs, and so on, but when the doors were closed, and you were alone with him, he was a real fellow. He hates fakers, is very very quick to catch them up, and literally bursts into tears when he meets genuine people.

The first time this idea really hit home was at a meeting of writers back in 1939, just before I left for the San. I listened to them talk over tea and over a meal later and then over drinks. The dirty stories were all right, but the crap about their ego and their destiny and their tricks in making a scene move, and so on, was a hot iron in the quick of my soul. So I've always tried to avoid meetings of this sort. I don't mind meeting individual writers, good ones, but I think I like to meet them because I really like human quality more than I do their artist side.

One of the reasons I'm so fond of my wife is that she is not a fawner. She is real (she even gets so excited when a real friend comes over that she doesn't know quite what she's doing; even acts a little dizzy, belovedly so) and she has a hard brain when she puts it to work, and she has an incredibly delicate approach to things, a most remarkable complement to my nature, which could easily be completely brusk and galloping. I am absolutely sure now that I could not have set up a successful marriage with any one else. I was sheer lucky. It just happened to turn out right. (Or as right as such things can be.) I know of dozens of women, nay, all the women I've met I'm sure I would have murdered or divorced by this time, because they would either have tried to boss me outright, or would have tried to exploit me, or would have gone around gushing they were married to a Writer, etc. It hardly seems to make any difference to her. She acts as if she is married to a male who just likes music and books and honest talks, etc. (I have been very careful not to mention these things to other men. I tried to once, and only got a bitter, envious look for my pains. Furthermore, it just isn't wise to awaken sleeping dogs, as my gramma says.)

And then when limited success did come, and I heard all the compliments, and heard venomous remarks, and was dined and wined a little, I saw how easily one can be taken in by such social things. It's all done so suavely, so smoothly, as if it were fundamentally the right thing to do, even, that if it were not done it would be a wrong, that it's hardly a wonder that many an honest and warm-hearted soul is corrupted. If one hears compliments day after day, the impulse to believe them is enormous, is almost undefeatable. In my own case I wasn't too sure I could stand it, so I made quick haste to get the hell out of town and out in a part of the country where I might be relatively inaccessible. I like a few friends, not mobs of lemmings. I like my walks, my family, my garden, my crude workshop. And the mail. To me that is the life, and I hope to God I can pursue this kind of living to the end of my days. I find I am happiest this way, and not the other way where I listen to all the soft and degenerating blandishments of empty souls. I hate all parties and simply cannot understand why people rush to get to them, or hold them. (It's gradually soaking in around here too, and so we get fewer and fewer invitations.) (I might go to parties with some anticipation were I a young man on the make, for there are all sorts of makees around.)

I have given the problem of just where the man leaves off and the artist begins a lot of thought. It is not easy to pin down, probably never will be. There can be no rules about it, it is purely a personal thing. I like my work as a writer, love it, and I think that saves me from being self-conscious about it. And keeps me what I was, a bumbling farm boy. The blandishments are sweet, very sweet, but they are never as good as potatoes and meat and carrots and radishes and onions and raw red snapping apples from the orchard.

The communists really put one on the spot. I find myself for many of the things they are for, far more than I ever was for good measures the fascists were accidentally for. This involves being called a fellow-traveler, and this one resents. It is devilish hard not to get emotional about the dilemma, and to see the issues as they should be looked at. The Wallace thing is a case in point. I am completely for him, soberly so, but what has enraged me is the way the press, all of it, has distorted his words. The relationship between the headline and the body of the story was like the marriage of a pig to Aphrodite. And the editorials . . . why, it seems they read only the headlines and built their cud-chewings around that. My friend Humphrey let off steam about the disservice Wallace had done to democratic ideals, and when I called him, and pinned him down, and forced him to talk, he admitted he had not read the speech or the letter (which was the best of the two, by the way). You can imagine the hell I gave him for that. I called him out of bed early one Sunday and made him listen for a whole hour. He tried to high-hand me a bit, but I would not shut up even if he and his whole police force were to beat me up. Humphrey seemed to think that Wallace was dividing up the world in two halves; which he was not; he was only describing the situation as it was; that while Russia was insinuating herself into all her border countries, we too were involved in all the Latin Americas, that while Russia had kept her Army intact, we had the overwhelmingly powerful Atom bomb and hundreds of bases within a thousand miles of her borders, etc. And neither America, nor Russia, seemed to care about whether the world was to be literally blown up. My argument was, and is, that all considerations stem from one fact: that the next war will kill us all. The problem is to get both Russian and U.S.A. & Britain leaders to see this too.

At last the furnace is being put in. The ducts under the house are set, and now we await the machine itself. It is all in the city office of the manufacturing plant except for an electric motor.

And, we got our windows and doors, so it looks like we may get our house shipshape at last. At last. There may be delays but by next January we should be warm. The storm windows won't come till next year. They are fixing only the regular casements.

The garden produce was simply marvelous this year despite a

dry August. We've had many rains the last month, and despite a few frosts, the pickles and beets and carrots and even a few tomatoes continue to thrive.

One more thing about that artist-man business. I feel that if a man really labors at trying to produce a good work, he, in the process, becomes a man. Just as a man on a farm becomes more a man when he successfully weathers a year of reverses and troubles and sweaty labors. Perhaps that's why some artists are not real artists. Their sickening talk about tricks and plots and turnovers indicates they want to avoid the work. They seek shortcuts, not involvement, not living, not profound seeking. It is so easy to tell yourself that you work, when you don't. A real man is always restless, and a real artist is the same. Well, enough of this. I want to talk to you about this someday.

There hasn't been any news about the book except that they are carefully working out a presentation. They tell me they have statements from Van Wyck Brooks and Sinclair Lewis for the jacket. That they are going to use some maps I drew for the endpapers, that they destroyed one set of plates for the jacket because it wasn't suitable to the spirit of the book. It sounds like understanding in publishers' row.

Book Find Club, 401 Broadway, New York 13, N.Y.

The past three weeks I've been working on a Guggenheim application. Most of the work involves the argument or outline of the work. I feel that I've got hold of something for them, even if it does not yet show through in the outline I'm sending them. Last year I came within an ace of getting a fellowship from them on the same idea. Since then it has become "grown-up" so to speak. I'll know in March.

I must get ready for a trip to town. We are going to a wedding tonight, and before I go, I've been asked to take another look at a letter I wrote for the ICCASP[1] to The President.

Write when you can. Even just a note. We think of you often.

Freya now has bangs. And speaks in full, rounded sentences. But she seems completely stupid in matters related to roosting.

Love, from us all,

1. Independent Citizens Committee of the Arts, Sciences and Professions of America.

To President Harry S Truman
Washington, D.C.

[Minneapolis, Minnesota]
October 6, 1946

Dear Mr. President:

We are writing you in the interest of our lives.

On this Sabbath day, when all the world should be at worship, when all the people should be enjoying the sweet comfort of giving weary arms and backs a rest at last—the country folk idling the day through watching domestic animals nibbling grass in the moist swales, the city folk out riding over the sumac-flaming bluffs behind the city—on this Sabbath day, we find ourselves trembling in fear of our very lives, trembling in fear of what lies directly before us: *total destruction of ourselves, our dear ones, our pastures and our fields, our libraries and our concert halls, our horses and cows and pet dogs, every living thing either in heaven above or in the earth below, or that is in the waters under the earth.*

Up until two weeks ago we had the feeling that, somehow, you had our welfare in mind. We felt that you were our leader in these perilous times, guiding us from a period of war into a period of peace.

But today, this Sabbath day, we are no longer sure. Mr. Henry Agard Wallace has resigned from your cabinet . . . at *your* request.

To us that means you no longer wish to take advice from the most society-minded brains of our time. To us that means you wish instead to take the advice of those who do not seem to realize that a new age, the Atomic Age, has now enwrapped us. To us it means you would rather trust the judgment of people thinking along military lines of 1939 than you would the judgment of those who know that another war is the end of civilization as we know it.

For another war *does* mean the end; and not our victory. Surely you know that in the next war both sides will be using the Atomic bomb. Surely you are aware that one nation has already decided to give its scientists ten times the support our American scientists are getting, that a humble little Japanese scientist with just a few dollars worth of laboratory apparatus, and a walk through destroyed Hiroshima, came within one step of reconstructing the Atomic bomb.

Just what the phrase "the end of civilization as we know it" means is difficult to grasp. The human mind rebels, bucks, at the attempt to understand it.

Nevertheless, if we value dear life itself, we must all try. You, as well as Mr. Wallace. You, as well as all other leaders of the world.

The ball of earth that we have been living on is in reality a flying Persian rug. To us it has always seemed indestructible. It has worn well, it has served our foot most faithfully, it has filled our bellies, it has thrilled our minds. It has even supported us in a void.

We as a people have lived on this rug for an incalculable time, sometimes in happiness, sometimes in contention, most times in the interest of survival. In the unrolling of our life, a few of us, out of curiosity, out of need, have discovered that this rug of ours, like most rugs, has an attribute that is both a strength and a weakness. It has a single strand running through all of it: the atom. While it unifies the whole, it also offers the unraveling of the whole. Pull it, and the whole separates, scatters, vanishes.

This discovery has raised consternation amongst us. Fear, trembling, has entered the lives of us all. Protests have flown. Prayers have ascended.

The discovery in itself is not an evil. With brains, with care, we can use it to give unto all mankind a most wonderful surcease from difficult labors. Not only for the nobility, but for all of us, every one of us. A veritable heaven on earth.

But what are we doing? What are we doing? We are giving it into the hands of masters of destruction, to irresponsibles, to Ares of the idiot brain, to our conscienceless armed force. We are giving it to the quarrelsome, to the Achilles' and Myrmidons. We are allowing those who do not know its true nature to control it, those who do not seem to worry that if the rug parts, scatters, that all of us will be plunged into a void that has neither height nor depth nor width, that has no measurability known to man, that cannot be related to anything touched with the fingertip, seen with the eye, tasted with the tongue, smelled with the nose, heard with the ear, sensed with intuition. Where even heaven with God and all His angels and the saints and all saved souls have vanished. And purgatory and hell. Where all, all is gone.

That is the situation we are in.

Mr. President, let us put this on a personal basis. Should the Atomic War detonate over us, it will mean your death. No longer will you be able to play your piano, and take your brisk walks, and attend family picnics, and play poker with your jokesters.

It will mean the death of your daughter, Margaret. No longer will there be a dear daughter getting a diploma, a dear child with an arch smile, and pictures in the society sections of the nation.

It will mean the death of your wife, and of *our* First Lady of the Land.

It will mean the death of your aged mother.

Mr. President, we have heard a scientist say: "If it wouldn't be that I have a dear wife and children, a few heart-friends, and some books I'd still like to read, and a few vistas yet to see, I'd say, 'To hell with the bloody stupid fools. Let 'em die. They aren't worth my time. They won't listen to what I have to say anyway.' "

We have heard another say, "You know, I stand alone, I feel like a prophet trying to warn the rest of you lemmings, lemmings rushing into the sea and sure destruction."

We have heard still another say, "You know, if it wouldn't be that I feel so guilty, if it wouldn't be that I helped to make the damned thing and then like a fool handed it to quarreling children, I'd tell the whole lot of you to go jump in a lake."

Mr. President, has it ever occurred to you to wonder why it is that for the first time in the history of the world, for the first time since they graduated out of their medicine-men role, scientists are actively getting into politics?

Mr. President, we would like to ask you something. We have heard you, and others in the administration, declare that our technical knowledges of atomic energy should be withheld until the international control and inspection system is working to our satisfaction. Mr. President, isn't that sheer presumption? How can we be trusted when it was we, the United States of America (would that *we* meant the United States of the World) were first to use the globe-killer? Were the first to loose on innocent civilians a bomb whose radioactive product was a death ray, belonging to the poison gas classification outlawed by the Geneva convention, and which we warned other nations to respect many times during the war past?

Mr. President, and we take a deep nervous breath as we contemplate it, you are forcing us to think wild thoughts. We are beginning to feel like trapped animals, and like trapped creatures milling about, we are about to become dangerous. Beware that we do not take it into our own hands to bolt usual good sense and custom, for we, as a people, simply cannot afford to let office-holders drive us straight into disaster. We will tolerate depressions, hard times, even near-starvation, but never our total and final and non-resurrectable death. That would be sheer madness. Even a wild beast would have enough sense not to tolerate that.

Imagine a family taking a ride in the cool of a green evening. Suppose too, by some twist of fate, or accident, that the irresponsible member of the family somehow got behind the wheel, and that the other members, out of a sense of politeness, and even fairness, decided to tolerate the driver for this one ride. Can you, however, imagine the family restraining itself when the driver suddenly heads the car straight for the edge of a precipice?

But enough of such dark melancholy thoughts. We wish to be reasonable. Mr. President, we beg of you to reconsider your present course, to at least reread the letter Mr. Wallace sent you in July.

Mr. President, in the name of God, in the name of humanity, in the name of anything you hold dear, save us from an interstellar calamity!

Believe me, Sir, faithfully yours,

Feike Feikema

for the Board of Directors of the Minnesota Division of the Independent Citizens Committee of the Arts, Sciences and Professions of America.

P.S. Ironically enough, if the unraveling does overtake our flying Persian rug, we won't be able to blame you. Neither of us will be here.

F.F.

1947

Enforced idleness early in the year due to a growth on his hand allows Manfred the opportunity for reading and planning. By February he is writing the second draft of The Chokecherry Tree, *which he forwards to Doubleday, has outlined* The Primitive, *the first book of the trilogy, and has planned books six through nine. In this year Manfred begins to write* The Primitive, *which he projects to a length of eleven hundred pages. Though* This Is the Year *appears on the* New York Times *bestseller list for four weeks and the* New York Herald Tribune *list for two, Doubleday loses money on the book.*

To Van Wyck Brooks

[Minneapolis, Minnesota]
March 7, 1947

Dear Mr. Brooks,

A long difficult winter is almost over. Very soon now I can get out in my garden and my pasture, and can turn off this oil stove beside me. Spring will be an enormous time of happy work.

The winter has been difficult because we were so short of funds. Our income was good, but the expenses we had to meet in connection with the finishing of our cottage were so high that we were always behind; and are still behind. This coming summer I've got to get hold of a few thousand over and above our living expenses. Costs are terrible; and we had done only what was absolutely necessary to make the house warm. We have a furnace now, and the windows and shingles and siding are all there too, so we have a livable unit. Later, when the money is there, we'll put on the trimmings.

The winter was tough too because I had a growth taken out of my hand,[1] and that not only cost money, but took valuable working time away from me; almost three months. Of course, I got in some reading, a lot of it, but it happened that I was just bristling with ideas about both my fourth and fifth books, and was very anxious to get all down on paper before they vanished.

1. Dupuytren's contracture in the left hand

Last fall I personally insulated my little cabin or workshop (it is separate from the cottage), painted it, had the womenfolk put in some curtains and linoleum, and bought a fine Silent Sioux stove. The place is quite snug most times; it is only when the temperature drops to 20° or 30° below that the floor gets chilly. But I wear thick high boots and socks, and thick woolens, so it is quite bearable for even a person who has once had tb. The warm house and the cooking of my wife and her mother have been welcome; I had only one cold all winter.

Reading, of course, really makes up in many ways for worktime lost. In college I made a slight acquaintance with the old masters or classics, Homer, Virgil, etc. This past winter I developed a hunger for them, so bought some translations, and went to work. I was astounded to find that Homer was a fine farmer, his remarks about bees and flies on the milk and the bull standing supreme over the herd and the purple furrows in the valley, were as fresh as if he had only written them yesterday. And it surprises me that scholars should have been so slow in discovering the difference between the *Iliad* and *The Odyssey*. I was instantly aware of the change in mood, the change in the attitude of men toward animals (the dogs,

particularly), the change in attitude toward the weather. At first
I thought maybe the *Iliad* had been written by young Homer and
the *Odyssey* by old Homer, but there were basic things that argued
for two different authors. Virgil pleased me too because of his
immense knowledge of the country (no one pointed such things
out to me in college; that I as a country boy should feel Virgil and
Homer cousins of mine; no doubt the English prof wanted to keep
such mundane things out of his lofty lectures!) but he didn't come
up to expectations. Dante's *Divine Comedy* was also disappointing,
though I imagine that for a religious person he is very rewarding.
Camoëns' *The Lusiad* was truly wonderful. (Probably because I
took a fancy to Fanshawe's translation.) But it was Goethe's *Faust,*
Parts I and II, that really thrilled me; probably because I can read
the German a little. The mood or the mind behind it captured me,
and gave me many hints to use when I begin writing *World's
Wanderer,* the fantasy of the giant. Then too, reading in *Beowulf*
was a surprise; probably because I could hear echoes of the old Frisians, my âldfaers (eldfathers), and could in many cases hear Beowulf talk, hear the exact sound of the spitting and coughing verbs,
just as my grandfather and great uncle used to bray them. I intend
to make a journey to Frisia someday, stay there long enough to
relearn the language (they tell me I spoke it as a baby, along with
the American) and then once more tackle the Anglo-Saxon poems.
(Next on the program is Chaucer and Spenser, a complete and
thorough rereading.) My greatest joy, of course, is still Charles
Montagu Doughty. Now that I've read Homer and Virgil, and
have read Doughty's *Travels In Arabia Deserta* and *The Dawn In
Britain,* I feel that he towers over them all, a mighty literary
titan.

I've done some reading too in modern psychology, but my feeling about that is that too many of us are impressed by the workings
of the intellect. Marx once said that religion is the opium of the
people; I'm not sure but what intellectualization isn't even worse.
I've nothing but contempt for these bright children of restlessness
who leave Toledo or Des Moines and go to New York (it is just as
much a tragedy for midland brains to go to New York as it was a
couple of decades ago for New York brights to go to Paris). I've
met them in New York, and they are just about the most unhappy
people I've seen; and in many cases very provincial and stupid. I
note with some satisfaction how very well all my relatives and their
friends manage to avoid both divorce and the analyst's couch.

Time, Life, Fortune, New Yorker, et al, bristle with these tom and tabby sophisticats.

The renaissance in writing out here continues. In the last year or so, the following youths have had novels published: Dan Brennan (*Never So Young Again*), Ann Chidester (*The Long Year*), Laura Baker (*The Red Mountain*), Eric Sevareid (*Not So Wild A Dream*—personal history), Sheila Alexander (*Walk With A Separate Pride*), Catharine Lindsay (*The Country Of The Young*), Bud Nye (*Home Is If You Find It*). This does not count the published work of Warren (*All The King's Men*), Eric Bentley (*The Playwright as Thinker*), Meridel Le Sueur (*North Star Country*), Herbert Krause (*The Thresher*). In addition Virgil Scott will soon publish his *The Dead Tree Gives No Shelter,* and two other lads have finished fine novels and are just now going after publishers. (No doubt many, many more are writing.) Of them all (the new ones) Alexander and Scott seem the most promising. Alexander is particularly wonderful; she is miles ahead of Welty and M. Young, and somehow reminds me of Cather. She has the clean style of Cather, though, of course, the subject matter is different. Alexander is a woman who is both mother and poet; and she is not a woman poet trying to ape male ways, or trying to have herself a career patterned after the masculine ideal, but as a true woman, a mother having babies. (Women can have careers outside the marriage in a womanly fashion, you know. Women who try to be more male than the male get under my skin; just as males who try to be more woman than a woman do.) I feel too that Scott will raise a little fur when he is published. And we all know how wonderfully Sevareid writes. (He and I were both fired from the *Minneapolis Journal* for the same reason at about the same time.)

Best of all, we are starting up a magazine; to be called *The North Star Review.* We will publish anything from anywhere, as long as it is good; we just happen to be out here instead of, say, New York or Boston; and, if it seems we publish a preponderance of western people, it is because we happen to feel a certain way, rather than that the published work excels anything coming from hinterland.

We hope to get the first issue off in May, and hope to get two off this year. It is to be a quarterly. I won't have much to do with it; I go to editorial meetings twice a month; but will, of course, talk about it everywhere. It is being published by a little publishing house (they have a printing press in the kitchen) The Prometheus Press, St. Paul. (They have published four volumes of poetry, and have managed to sell out every printing! Ray Smith's *No Eclipse,* Leiberman's *I Have Seen Their Faces And Can't Keep Silent,* Erling Eng's ??, and Marie Burns' *Father Elegy.*) (Yes, Webb's is still going: the Alexander and the Baker things, mentioned above, were published there. Alexander's is due March 31, 1947; I had an early copy because I was responsible for her going there. Mr. Hillestad and I are still fast friends.). . . . So you see, there is a tremendous ferment out here. Beach, Warren, Bentley, Scott, myself, Ray Smith, Saul Bellow (*The Dangling Man*) see each other very often.

I must also thank you most heartily for giving permission to use a quote on the jacket of my new novel. I had given strict orders to my editor Shively that your letter and the one from S. Lewis and William Carlos Williams were to be regarded as confidential, as letters to aid them[2] in deciding whether they wanted me or not, and to give them some notion as to where I might go. But they were so delighted with them, had already gotten Lewis's permission for a quote without calling me, that I decided to go ahead. I am tremendously thrilled that you should like me and like my work, would like to shout it from the housetops, but at the same time I would like to enjoy respect from friends all by myself. One doesn't deliberately advertise love. But, it is on the book now; and all I can do is promise you that you shall not be sorry if I can do anything about it.

I am most interested in seeing your next book. How is it coming? I have yet to read *The Pilgrimage of Henry James* (I just got it the other day) but I want to wait until I've read some of James' work. (I don't feel too sympathetic toward him.)

Notes: Novel four will be *The Chokecherry Tree.* Novel five, *World's Wanderer.* I've postponed *A Child Is Born* for a few years. I am also working on a new name or category for some of my books. *Boy Almighty* should not be called a novel. The word "novel" is too inexact; that is, for my purposes. And for Wolfe, Melville, etc. It does fit Lewis, most of Maugham, Dumas, etc. Affectionately, fred (I am sending you a specially inscribed book in a few days.)

2. Doubleday editors.

To Frank Feikema

[Minneapolis, Minnesota]
March 8, 1947

Dear Pa:

In a few weeks, you'll be getting a book from me. (This time I'm only going to give a few books away; and of course, first on the

list, is my dear Pa. For every book I give away, I've got to sell 10
others. I simply can't afford it. I get six free books. Two I save for
my future children. One I give to Maryanna, one to myself, one
to Pa, and one to Maryanna's Ma.) (And if the domeny wants to
read my new book, or anybody else, tell them to get their own
books in downtown Los Angeles. Everybody gets their own washing machine; they can get themselves each a book if they think it
worth reading.)

This book is dedicated to you, Pa, and to a friend. To both of
you. I mentioned the friend's name because he has been after me for
years to keep writing, and to write about Iowa. So, half goes to
him. The other half of the dedication goes to you. For it was from
you that I learned so much about farming, which goes into this
book. Also, I wanted to get it on the record that you have not lived
for nothing, that somewhere it is recorded that all the hard work
you have done in life has meant something to somebody, to me in
particular.

You will notice, if you read the book, that often I have taken
things from your life. The fall from the windmill, the fall off the
barn in the manure-pile, the many things that happen to a man on
the farm. But they are things that could have happened to anybody,
and so, really, the man Pier is not you. Pier is also Uncle Hank
[Van Engen] and his fighting to make a living, also Gorter, also Simon Baron, also all those farmers I knew who fought so hard to
make a go of it. So I made up the character Pier, and made him the
average representative, the common man on the farm. Remember
what that elder said, Ma, about "karacter?" So don't let anybody
ever say to you, "Oh, so it's about you, huh? Or, Ma, huh?" Just say
nothing, and turn the conversation. They don't know any better.
I made up all the characters. Nertha, the wife, I made up out of my
head and from a picture I once saw in a newspaper. Kaia, the bad
woman, from another picture I once saw in a Sioux Falls newspaper. I used Alde Romke's name because I like the name, and because I felt that it would give the story a taste of being real. Alde
Romke is a combination of Robijn De Jong, and Grampa Feike,
and Omke Romke of Hawarden, and a few other old men. In
other words, "character" again.

I use a few swear words because I have to. People do swear in
life, religious or not. And if I am going to give a true picture of people, I've got to put down their sins too. I am not trying to write
uplift stories (that's for others and those stories are all right too,

only I don't like to write them) but stories that will give an exact and a true picture of things as they actually are, and were. If a man gave you directions to go from one city to another, and told you that the road was fine, wonderful, no holes and bumps and no bridges out, when all along bridges were out, what kind of man or reporter or direction-giver would he be? You'd call him a blasted liar!

No doubt I should have put other people's names on the dedication page too. But I have room only for one, at most two, so I had to choose. I chose you and Mr. Jim Shields. I hope you like it. I hope you'll never be sorry.

The baby is fine. She is getting quite tall, and plays with her dolls and her tea party dishes all day. She wears the bathrobe you gave her, and we keep telling her about who gave it to her.

Maryanna has had to work full time again for awhile to help pay for the bills while I get out a new book, number four. I lost a lot of time this winter with that hand operation,[1] almost three months. Besides the money it cost.

1. Removal of growth in hand—Dupuytren's contracture.

[Matter deleted by author]

Well, much love to you. And, please, Pa and Ma, dear Pa and Ma, if my book bothers you, just lay it aside. Just look at it, look at Pa's name once in a while, and let the rest lay in peace. It isn't necessary that you have to look into every last thing I do. I like to know about Pa's work in general, but I wouldn't want to know about every last little detail for every day of his life, either.

Love to all, best from us all,
Freya, Maryanna, and fred

To Herbert Krause

Feike Feikema
Rural Route 4
Minneapolis, Minn.
March 31, 1947

1. *The Thresher.*

Dear Herbert:

I feel ashamed. I bought your book[1] the day after its publication, read it, sent off excited letters to various people—but not to you. What a heel I am. And now your most generous letter.

I think what I was really waiting for was my wife's report on it. She has been working and housekeeping both, and so has not had time to read it yet.

I want to say, however, that I loved the wonderful tragic poetry in it, that I felt the metaphors using farm terms were marvelous, out of this world, that I was terribly moved by the clean open pictures of the farmers doing their threshing chores. I felt sad that there would be many thousands in the east who would never appreciate what you have done with the country idiom. Virgil's work is loaded with such things too, and yet I've never heard him appreciated for his knowledge of people close to the earth. Gray gave you your due on it. Hail!

> Always the best,
> Feike Feikema

To John Huizenga

[Minneapolis, Minnesota]
July 26, 1947

Dear John,

Things are in a state of abeyance here. We are awaiting word on *The Chokecherry Tree* from the publishers, and since we are down to our last few dollars again, we are just a trace uneasy. At least I am, because the book is a slim one, and one not in the tradition of the first three. I don't know what they're going to think. It was too good to lay aside, and I myself enjoyed thinking about it, so I had to send it off. I can't think of anything more to do on it, except a final rereading. This time the subject is a "sheep," in violent contrast with the "bull" that Pier Frixen was. And, the book is as biting as a chokecherry. The bite isn't on the surface, but underneath, after you've bitten into it. All I ask of it is that it will give me a living for a year and a half, long enough for me to get the first draft down on *World's Wanderer*, the first real piece of work to come from my fingertips. *Wanderer* has just about got everything, at least as an idea, and after I get it written, I know that I can begin to think I'm a real artist. I have hinted as to its contents to a few people, and their eyes bug. I've even got a new name for the form, and the one writer I mentioned it to is now eager to use it too. I had to wave a big fist over his head to keep him from grabbing it first. (I let him know I would club him if he took it. It was mentioned only as part of confidential conversation. What I saw in his eye taught me to shut up about it from that point on.) I can say briefly that *Wanderer* concerns a certain Thurs who has what mankind has been vaguely hinting it wants to have too, except that those who know him think he is an enemy. That is, the people he happens to meet. (A few close friends are for him, knowing what he means to civilization.) I am going to try to grab by the balls the problem of genius arising out of the human animal, and how the implications of genius can be inimical to the fundamental nature of the human evolutionary competitive animal. The description of these two phenomena catch all such problems of sexual love and mental love, race hatred and brotherly love, etc. The idea is of such universal nature that it can pick up all the violent problems of our time, including the problem of what the hell to do with atomic fission and its products. The book will concern a musician, but that's just the medium through which I will work. And despite the glory I expect to relate about creation and music, I'm afraid I will have some very gloomy things to say before I am done. I've got the book outlined in detail; I've spent days and months getting material together, have almost burst my head with various learnings, and the more I go into matters, the more I am entranced with the central thrust of it. I've literally stumbled onto something wonderful in my soul or mind or personality, or whatever it is that is *I*; and I know truly now how the Biblical writers felt when they said God was guiding their hand and pen. In fact, the whole thing has such dynamics of its own, I can for once sit back and use understatements and undertones and still get enormous power. It will take me and use me to write itself. You may wonder how I shall describe a musician. Let me mention quickly that four weeks ago I started taking music lessons on the piano. And today I can already play the simpler pieces of Dvořák and Chopin and Beethoven. Not too well, but enough so that I know that in the next half year I can really play for myself some of the better pieces. My piano teacher is in an uproar about it. And she is already laying plans for me to study for many years. I've also started soaking my mind with musical jargon, listen as much as I can to a neighbor wife here (here for the summer) who is a fine player.[1] I've also the advantage of two musical ideas which I think are original and which I shall use in the book. I can't for the life of me understand why no one has written them before. Well, this is enough for you to get an idea of what I'm up to and what the future holds.

I had a long talk with your mother over the phone from my hotel room. I was sorry I couldn't drop around. I was in Chicago for only a few days, and all my time was taken up. The so-called Writer's Conference was a hoax. The writers are ladies in the menopause phase and, by some trickery, they invite successful writers down for lectures. The trainfare and hotel room is paid for; and since a writer is always interested in taking free trips, he goes down.

1. Mary Leren

Usually to meet the other writers who are trapped into coming. It is disgusting to have to talk to a batch of menopause minnies whose interest in you is a result of hot flashes. And not your art. However, as I say, I did get to meet a lot of fine writers who came around to be seen, and sometimes it seems to be a good thing to talk things over with fellow tradesmen. Your mother related to me the state of your health, some of your adventures, etc., and suggested that we drop in to see her and Kathryn in September when I intend to make a visit to Michigan with wife and babe by car. We may do that.

I made one quick visit to the Adler Planetarium. That is tremendous. When it was over (while we gazed at the moving stars, *Largo* was played) I didn't dare get up because of my wet eyes. But all around me, the moment it was over, there was immediate talk of mundane things, like going to the can, eating, fighting, necking. I had actually visited the mighty heavens, and had truly felt the enormity of the unmarkable interstellar spaces; they acted like they had been handed a cookie to eat. It's after such adventures with my mind that I can not, can not, can not, understand human strife, or any strife. (And even when I see strife, I can't help but marvel at and admire the process of strife. Wonderbar.)

Before I forget, I must tell you that a friend of mine, Richard Scammon, is also there in Berlin. He is attached to General Clay's office, and has something to do with the politics there. He's a great big giant, heavier than I, and a very fine mind, and the son of a great scientist. You might keep your eye cocked for him, as he's wonderful company.

The liberal movement is pretty thoroughly split here now. Between the PAC-Wallace group and the ?-Ada group. (Ada equals: Americans for Democratic Action.) I have withdrawn my interest from both, have decided to sit back awhile and watch things. My eye is on the bigger thing. What the hell are we going to do about atomic fission? All problems start with that. Hints thrown out by local scientists here are terribly upsetting. I've gotten so now that I'll consider voting for a man like Stassen instead of for Truman if only because Stassen will be a little tougher resisting military men. I am almost certain that Roosevelt would not have used the Atomic Bomb. Truman was easily talked into it. I know that I for one would never have ordered its use. Had we not used it, for example, the horsetrading now going on between Russia and America would have been on a different basis entirely. I am almost certain that the Russians are now acting tough because of fear. Bully fear. However, it's hard to tell, mainly because I am looking through AP wired glasses. I am hoping that the British will show us something soon. Or else it's the end. And all such interesting little things as Feikema writing *Wanderer* will mean nothing, will vanish like a drop of water into the sea of chaos. And I will say, to give a hint of what I think of present day politics, that both PAC and ADA give me that uneasy feeling I get when I am in the presence of wild-eyed Calvinists. Neither has the answer. And since they haven't, and since my joining them means I haven't either, and also means I'll probably be party to the world's destruction, I've decided to sit back and look at things as calmly as I can. Perhaps that may be the right course to save things. I am terribly sorry to have to report such gloom. And oddly enough, when I contemplate my private life and my creative work, I feel happier than I ever have in my life. Perhaps against the background of world gloom, the otherwise easily noted petty troubles of married life and petty irritations of writing vanish like black-masked men disappear in the black night.

Freya and Maryanna send you their greetings. We'll miss you this coming August. Maryanna is never stirred by my male friends. But she was by you. A most interesting fact. (Am reading Chaucer in the original, the Frisian Bible—Job—, *Jean-Christophe*, and, of course, the greatest of them all, Charles Montagu Doughty. Ask your English friends about him. Also Shaw and Hamsun. And a fat book on anthropology. Besides the music.)

Write me, John. Love,
Fred

To George Shively and Ken McCormick

[Minneapolis, Minnesota]
November 29, 1947

Dear George (and Ken),

I hope you won't mind all this correspondence. In another month, I'll be deep in the writing of the trilogy, and you won't hear much from me until I come out on the other end of the first draft. So now's the time. Especially since I feel that I must clear up, to some extent, whether or not I'm to use the term "rume" in connection with the work. Since I've last written you, I've had misgivings about giving up so soon a term I've harbored these many months and which came to me only after many years of search. I still feel

I must use it. Those "avalanches and mountain-movings" I spoke of, have, now that I have had a look again, only reconvinced me to keep the term "rume" for *World's Wanderer*. That little retreat in the last letter just means that I am highly impressionable and by nature amiable. (We can say on the jacket: "The first of Feike Feikema's long awaited trilogy of rumes is the story of a modern day giant, etc. ("rume" is Feikema's newly coined term for autobiographical novel; see the preface,[1] "Concerning the rume").")

1. Later made a postscript.

I really don't feel I shall be called "precious" for having invented this term. Precious implies someone who thinks daintily and out of line with the onward sweep of literature. Would Fielding have been termed "precious" had he been inventive enough to have called his *Tom Jones* a "novel"—his own crude term being "prose epic"?

The term "novel" is too loose, too inexact for me. I've never liked it too well. At least, for certain of my work it is too inexact: *Boy Almighty*, *World's Wanderer* and *The Bold Have Wings* (once titled, *A Son Of The Road*).[2] I write this sincerely. I feel this. Feel it. "Novel" does, however, somewhat fit *This Is The Year* and *The Golden Bowl*. I never wanted to call *Boy* a novel. I was talked into it by the editor because he had to have some term to sell it with. Just take a look at the curious wording on *Boy*'s jacket. That was directly as a result of our arguments on just this question. And I would have had my way then had I had my term "rume" ready. The terms "auto-biographical novel," "biographical novel," "historical novel," etc., are, compared to such a neat and hitting term as "essay," "sonnet," "epic," "tragedy," "comedy," etc., indeed not very apt. It's time somebody came along and swept them away with the brush of a big hand. The term "rume" fits neatly and poetically in with the last mentioned set. The thing is, had my name already the magic of a Hemingway, I could bull it through right now.

Moreover, let me add, that the way I intend to use "rume" just doesn't mean only an auto-biographical novel. It means more: "Here, I, Fred, am transmuting my life into a work of art. This is my experience. I was here. In this time. And this is what I saw and what I felt. And now, after long *ru*mination, I 'ru' (Aryan root, meaning to sound, cry out, bray, yell) it forth in song among you all!" Wasn't this the profound impulse of Sappho? Wolfe? Goethe in *Sorrows of Young Werther*? Melville? Doughty in *Arabia Deserta*? Wordsworth? Shelley? Byron? Sheila Alexander in *Walk With A Separate Pride*? Maugham in *Of Human Bondage*? They didn't write

2. A portion of *Morning Red*.

novels: they wrote rumes, poems. Personal agonies exalted into works of art. Which is at once auto-biographical and universal. That is the rume. A novel is something entirely different. Writing a rume is the discovery and the capping of an inward gusher. Writing a novel is the discovery and the description of fellow human beings outside one's self. Anyway, I'm going ahead with the essay, and then, when all's done, we can have a talk over ale and roast meat, when I'm most amiable. (Thurs' name now is Wraldson. The third rume is now titled, *The Giant*.)

Always the best,
fred

To Maxwell Geismar

[Minneapolis, Minnesota]
December 16, 1947

Dear Maxwell:

Yes, I've not only heard of *The Last of the Provincials*, I've just finished the Cather section. The local book page gave it to me for review, and so shortly I shall try to return a favor. So far I'm tremendously impressed. So much so, that I've ordered my book store to get me *Writers In Crisis*, and in my mind I've put you right up there with Burke and Brooks and Wilson and Parrington, all of whom I've read (and I even *read all* their work). I've only recently plowed through the critics on the theory that I might learn a little discipline, at least mental, and maybe even a kind of self-critical attitude. I had to do something to bring the gusher under some sort of control. Anent my reviewing, I want to say, don't expect too much. I'm only a "feeler" and merely put down my personal feelings.

I knew I should have told you more about my application. I made my first one in the fall of 1945, at the instigation of Dean T. Blegen (a wonderful man). The Dean wrote Moe and Moe asked me to apply. I did, everything proper (except probably the synopsis), and sent in the following referents: Sinclair Lewis, Dean Blegen, Van Wyck Brooks, Dr. Richard E. Scammon (Dean of medical school, a genius in science, and a man who is writing an enormous work on human measurements, not only physical but otherwise), Mr. James Gray, Mr. William Rose Benét. When I didn't get it, I asked Moe to send me the books I had sent in, plus some of the material, as I said I wanted to try another place, needing the money so badly. He agreed, suggested that I keep some of the material on file, and reapply for next year. I did, and wrote the synopses you read, and sent in the following referents: Dr. Tremaine McDowell, U. of Minn. English Dept., John Sherman, local critic, George Shively, my editor, Paul Jordan-Smith, Los Angeles critic who with Floyd Dell edited that great *Anatomy of Melancholy* edition, and Joseph J. Firebaugh, prof. at Denver U, who wrote a glorious review of *Boy Almighty* in the *St. Louis Post Dispatch*. Again I didn't get it. Again Moe suggested to keep my file up to date. This past fall, before the Oct. 15 deadline I sent in a new outline, this time very cryptic and to the point, and sent in Mr. Virgil Scott's name. And I would have had Mr. Moe get in touch with you the regular way except that he had no more copies there of any of my plans. I had to use my own. I realize now I should have sent him my only copy anyway. You may also like to know that Blegen and Moe are close friends, and that Moe is from Minnesota. Blegen has said that he would have bet his wad each time that I would get a fellowship. I do think that my synopses were too "grandiose" at that—though not to me. One of the reasons it is now a trilogy is that were I to compress it all into 600 pages it would burn people. And this time I want it to ride easy; something like *The Chokecherry Tree*, my next one—although that book is a little too thin to suit me. If you think I should have others write, let me know. I'll do what's correct. in fact, I suggested to Moe in my last letter that perhaps the Foundation did me a favor in making me think about the book an extra two years. Which they did.

Someday I'd like to have a talk with you about *Year*. A lot of people think it is autobiog. It is not. It's only in *Boy* that people have been able to point at people they think they recognize. My relatives, however, just simply can't imagine where I got all the people for *Year* and *Bowl* from their country. Those two are works of almost sheer creation.

Nertha is not my mother because I want to do a rume[1] about my boyhood and her. Kaia never lived. Neither did Blacktail. My father is occasionally like Pier, but actually, is very quiet, sits for hours by the stove with his pipe, looks like a distinguished statesman, straight, white, and very fatherly. He had one bad session once, for about four years, when he was a little wild. But you see what happened was, I got hold of an idea, about man not only raping earth and woman, but also his own life and origins, that he carried ideas for his own salvation around in his own head, like a hammer one can't find which is already in hand, that he carried also

1. *Green Earth*, 1977.

the seeds of his own destruction within, and all this was truly the history of mankind since "mind" first began to emerge. Mankind is on the brink of destroying itself today; and possibly, too, even on the brink of giving itself a heaven on earth. You know, that human body of ours is an uneasy landlord with that new tenant, the mind, up there in the attic. And Starum never existed in northwest Iowa, though there are little Frisian settlements scattered over the midwest (which I've never lived in). Also many individual East Frisian families scattered around in Lyon County. I never saw a five and ten sale, never saw the Holiday strikes, never fell from windmills (those falls mean something, by the way). Teo? Yes, some of the things that happened to him happened to me, but they mostly happened to my brothers (I have five, all almost as tall as I) when I was gone. Especially Floyd. Romke? Well, my own grandfather was an agnostic and a socialist, almost tarred and feathered in World War I (they were afraid of his six-shooter). Romke was his brother who I saw but once or twice. But he was a legend amongst us, and so I made him up. Soil conservation? Didn't know anything about it until recently, and then decided it would serve my literary purpose. Old Dreamer? Never met him as a real man. Just made him. And truth to tell I had a 96-page shorthand outline for the book. The first draft followed it almost exactly, amounted to 776 pages in manuscript. I rewrote it all many times (only one page went into the book as I wrote it), cut out huge chunks, replaced them, wound up with exactly the same number, as I remember. I had tried that idea twice before, thousands of pages, but they didn't jell, were bad, etc., so threw 'em all away except for seven incidents (which I will publish in a volume of shorts someday) and the third time plotted everything out in great detail, all the speech, grasses, flowers, walked over the exact terrain I had plotted for the book, set a town in a bit of still wild country there, and then, let fly. And when I had finally done, sometimes rehoning a passage as much as 49 times (I counted the corrected pages!) I couldn't change a thing. And today when I pick it up, I can't find anything wrong with it. (The other three books, yes, they are bad in spots to me.)

Or else, let's put it this way. I'll write 30 books before I'm through. And every damned one will seem so real people'll swear that they're all autobiographical. Now either I am a tomcat with 30 lives, not nine; or I'm a creator. Take your choice.

Dear Max. I must live. I have sitting here on my desk the almost worked out outlines (with voluminous notes) of four other novels or works: a duology, a trilogy, and two single novels. And I hope to get at all of them after the present trilogy. And besides, and please don't tell me I'm crazy, I also have notes and plots worked out, simple ones, for at least six more. With the titles! By Christ, I wish I did have thirty lives to write them. We must meet; talk; write. You're of my age. And you could help me discipline volcanoes blowing up in my head. And! I have a talented wife. She's writing a volume of poetry. And so good. Tell me what I should do.

Yours,
Fred

To the Reverend Henry De Mots

[Minneapolis, Minnesota]
12-27-47

Dear Henry:

No, my father hasn't written about the incident. But then, I don't think he will. Long ago I warned him that he was probably in for some grief because of me, and I spent some time preparing him for it, just what to say, and to think. I tried to tell him that he no longer lived in an iron-tight religious community such as his fathers had in the Old Country, but America, where all have a right to pursue such interests, religious and / or atheistic, as their consciences may dictate. And be right. It was quite a choice to make for me, but in the end, I just simply could not let his wishes, or anybody's wishes, dictate my life. I had to be responsible for myself. I despise hypocrisy.

"You know better," is often thrown at me. Do I? Because of my early training? Well, here is a fact not too well known by my Calvinistic brethren, that I had a wonderful grandfather who was both a socialist and an atheist.[1] He died when I was a boy, but he left a tremendous imprint on my mind, despite the fact that all the relatives tried to bury him, literally and physically in an obscure place. He was ahead of his time. He came to this country for religious freedom too, you know, only in this case, atheistic religion. And moreover, there was another powerful agent at work in my growing up: my mother's determined wish that we live what we were. She was a glowing Christian, wonderful, but she was so great a Christian that she could say to me, on her deathbed, "Fred, my boy, I can see that your path is going to be different from what mine was. I'd like to see you in heaven with Jesus and me, but don't act the Christian if you don't feel it. If you don't feel it, don't live it.

1. Actually, he said he was an agnostic [FM's note].

Live out your feelings." That from a country woman, and a Christian, is a quality not even found in our present day U.N. councils.

Of course I believe in what I write. Of course. Is there any reason to think, on the face of it, that you should be more honest than I? Of course. And curiously enough, I too think that I have a "call." That I must follow it. And I will follow it into death. And that is, that I am in the service of absolute truth. That is not a pinned down truth such as the term God has become for you, but a living and vital principle which helps me see more and more just exactly "what is." (I write this in no hope of convincing you, but only to give a hint or two that I might be just as intelligent as you.) I write what I hope are artistic truths, historical truths. And the more I do, no matter what anybody else says, the better chance I'll have as a by product, of creating lasting works of art. My stuff is not popular, never will be in my lifetime. (Though already fellow writers are beginning to send me "hail" letters.)

I visited Calvin last September, and also some of the Calvinist communities in New Jersey. I had a fine time, and would have had more, if only I could have found as much humility among them as I find in myself. They simply can't understand a person who might be a trifle different from them. Tolerance in those followers of a man of love just simply isn't there. Odd. You must pardon me if I do not write at length because I have a policy of not expending too much writing in letters while I am in production.

Yours,
fred

2. De Mots was a New York Giants baseball fan.

[margin] The Giants² are on the way and will become a great team. Such talent!

To George Shively

Dear George,

This will be an enclosure with your birthday card.

When my wife and I read Alan's statement that up to Nov. 1, only 7741 had been sold, that 1400 had been returned, we almost fainted. After some silence, my wife says, "Well, anyway, we did get some wonderful letters this year." "What letters," I growled. "Those from other writers." After some thought, it was with some difficulty that I did think, I recalled that every now and then we got some fine letter from a fellow craftsman, which came and I hardly noticed them because I was busy or they were buried in other mail. And now we think that a recounting of them might be interesting to you too, besides a bit of salt to go with that horrible news.

First, we got still another letter from Brooks, a special Xmas card, with an autographed picture (it is now framed and he will watch me do *Wanderer*), much in the same vein. Also, a letter from Maxwell Geismar, enthusiastic, and saying he will endorse me for a Guggenheim, and that he had already intended to do a piece on yours truly for the March "Town & Country," and would I please send him my earlier books (which I did, from Webb, autographed). Then a fine note from Kathleen Hoagland (*Fiddler In The Sky*, for Harper's; she's doing a new novel for Fischer there; and also did 1000 Years of Irish Poetry for Devin-Adair). "Clayton (her husband, editorial writer for N.Y. Sun) and I were disgusted not to see your book listed this fall. What is the matter with America? They list every God damn thing that will be dead in a year and ignore you. And you are the only one hewing epic work out of the great living rock heart of this country. Work that will live and grow in stature." And Herbert Krause (*The Thresher, Wind Without Rain*) "I say right off, 'This Is The Book.' What a vigorous, unbroken bull-creature and a tale it is! It is like nothing I know of in American writing today. As far as I am concerned, the scenes between Teo and his father, the conflict between a man as earthy as his land and a boy dreaming his visions into fulfillment, have never been so poignantly delineated, never so sympathetically portrayed. I'd like to have done them." There was, too, Virgil Scott's comment and letter (He's just finished his second novel for Morrow, *The Hickory Stick*; it sounds great): "Mister, it is terrific, and this has nothing to do with the fact that I am your friend. I have not read a book which was so intricately woven and so tightly knit. There are individual sections, too, which stand out like you do in a crowd. The chapter called Fall in the first book is the best written piece of nature that I've ever read, for not only does it capture the sense impressions of a moment but also is one of the best examples of foreshadowing I've ever read. *Grapes of Wrath* is a very great novel and one which will drive its way out of the mountain of contemporary literature and get read long after we are dead, and I think *Year* is just as great from the point of view of brilliance of individual passages and greater from the point of view of complexity of conception and execution." And Willard Motley's "I admire you and your style of writing." And Jack Conray's cryptic, "Wonderful realism." And Michael Straight's letter and later his comment to Henry Wallace at lunch, "Like Sholokov's *Don* books, only better." And Nolan Miller's (Harper boy; *The Mother of Time*): "You will never be finished, endless as weather and seed and flower. You're 'wonderful.' You are a grown yet questing thing." Well, after those, a man feels better. First stop for Rixey's photog[1] was here, a whole morning. You probably won't be hearing much from me for a while, for *Wanderer* is rolling, the first sentence was "in" there. I am cutting wood to *save* on the fuel. Hello to Ken; he might be interested in this.

1. From *Life* magazine.

> Affectionately,
> Fred

1948

For Manfred, the year is dominated by physical and financial problems. After several grant rejections, he finally gets a Marshall Field Foundation grant for twelve hundred dollars, an advance from Doubleday for one thousand dollars on The Primitive, *and a one-thousand-dollar loan. Literary successes include the warm response to* This Is the Year *and high praise for* The Chokecherry Tree. *On both political and literary issues, Manfred continues to speak his mind, expressing concern about capitalism and atomic power.*

To Dr. Harry Wilmer[1]

[Minneapolis, Minnesota]
January 24, 1948

1. At Mayo Clinic. Wilmer was one of FM's roommates at Glen Lake Sanatorium.

Dear Harry:

I haven't answered you because I have been looking through my things here for quotes and passages. And for some reason can not find that wad of stuff I had as base for *Boy*. I have one place left to look, but I am almost sure it is not there. What I had in mind was to send you pieces of a diary I had. One I kept in a journal, and another I had in a packet of tear-offs. It's the tear-offs that are gone. The stuff in the journal is personal love stuff. And does not reflect what you want. Also lost, and probably at the same time, was the first real draft of *Boy*. I have only the second or readable draft.

I think you should mention, though, two facts that struck me most significant. One was that I could never remember the names of my roommates should I happen to meet them on the street. I would know their faces, but never their names. Even my doctors lost their names. That is unusual in me because I think I have what is considered an unusual memory for even the very smallest details. (As witness in my books.) The other thing was that while still in the San I was given the job of passing out the mail and other such little roving jobs, and that I couldn't take it after a few days. I couldn't eat, or sleep, and all because the horror of seeing dying people churned my guts up. And what really hit was that they weren't noticeably dying, or quickly dying, but dying cell by cell day by day, slow, lingering, with no hope. I shiver today thinking of it.

Moreover, I am convinced I first worked at *Boy* not for the purpose of art (though it became that perhaps later) but for the secondary purpose of getting rid of an obsession. It was a catharsis. A blood-letting. A public confession. An open psychoanalytic purging. It's obvious too when you read it. None of detachment that Thomas Mann got into his *Magic Mountain*. Were I to write it today it would be quite a different story, and in a different mood, let me tell you.

It's perhaps a good thing we didn't come down. That very weekend the proofs of the next book, *The Chokecherry Tree*, came from N.Y. And since they moved up the date to April 8, I had to hurry them back. So I didn't rest one weekend, because right after I piled into *Wanderer*. (I now have 202 pages.) I think too that I had better not plan on coming there for autographing if *Wanderer* is still spouting around that date, but we'll see. Perhaps I should lay off two days. We'll see.

You are indeed complimentary in thinking of quoting *Boy*. You are welcome to quote as much as you want anytime you want.

All our best,
Fred

To John Huizenga

[Minneapolis, Minnesota]
April 27, 1948

Dear John,

Since I last wrote you I've finished the first volume of the trilogy, that is, finished the first draft. And now between the first of

May until January comes the polishing and finishing. The title is still *The Primitive* and I feel that it contains the best writing I've ever done. Nothing matches it. And I am eager to get it published so you can have a look at it, and also get the rest down on paper so that you will see all the nuances and inner meanings come to light. I am now sure that it will come off. Every time I think about it, no matter if it's after a bottle of beer or three in the morning, I like it. I have only one misgiving about it: I may have some lawsuits on my hands. For though the central drive reordered the facts of my experience, there are little side eddies that look pretty literal. Since I feel like Goethe about such matters, that is, use anything and everything, including literal quotes and literal events to suit "my caprice and purposes," I have let the words fall as they wanted to fall. Moreover, you might as well get set for it: A fictionized John Huizenga is in the book parading as Huse Starringa.[1] I can't help it. And in the face of any modest or practical protest from you, he's going to stay in. Should a rumester such as I keep out of his work outpourings one of the most wonderful of his experiences in his life, namely, knowing the real John Huizenga? That were to cheat the concept of my becoming a writer. Either I write what is in my heart, or I write fakery. (The word *rumester,* by the way, will intrigue you. I am going to call my work a "rume." It is a new word, and it means autobiographical writing lifted to the level of art. Remember Wolfe's novels? *Of Human Bondage*? Lawrence's *Sons & Lovers*? Goethe's *Sorrows of Young Werther*? Those are novels which arose out of a novelist's personal life, not out of his general observations on life around him. I am thinking of separating the field of the novel, that which is really a rume, and that which is the novel. The word comes from the Aryan or Indo-European root meaning Rhu, to bray, to speak from the throat. From it such words as ruminate, rumor, rumen, etc., have come. I made it rume so that it would fit in with the literary climate of such words as rime, time, clime, rune, poem, etc. At the end of the trilogy will appear a little postscript about the matter, and other writers and critics can take it from there. It just happens that I feel, as an artist, there is a vast difference in conception, execution, structure between the novels *Bowl, Year, Tree*, and *Boy Almighty* and *World's Wanderer*. I feel it like I feel the difference between woman and man. I write both novels and rumes. Fielding and Richardson embarked on a new type of writing which was later called a novel. And I feel that had Wolfe and Maugham and Lawrence had before them the con-

1. Later changed to Howard Starring in *Wanderlust,* the revised version of the trilogy.

cept of a "rume" as we today have the concept "novel" before us, they would have written better books. As it is now, critics are apt to jump us for writing "autobiographical" novels. And we tend to shy away. And instead of building out of the self or auto, we tend to obscure the "self" or block it or to twist it, so it won't be tagged "auto." What the hell's wrong with examining the auto and writing about it as an artist? Why all this delicate bullshit? Some of the greatest poetry ever written was intensely personal. Can it be that we no longer read poetry because it's gone obscure and nutty? Sappho, Pindar, Virgil, Dante, Goethe, Heine, Browning, all wrote from their heart, admittedly so. Why not in the field of prose? Of course. Besides, there is no harm trying something new. I am getting damned tired of having people apply the "rules of the novel" to books like *Boy* which are not novels. So off we go exploring something new. Sober critics are now pointing out that I am one of the first real "American writers" to have arisen here in U.S.A., not English [which is right; I don't write English], and they had better get ready for another shock: the first rumester in the history of the world. Well, enough for this parenthetical aside.)

Had a bad accident in March. Almost cut off my right hand at the wrist. Slipped on an icy and snow-covered outside step, plunged into a storm window below. Almost bled to death. Rushed to hospital, lay on operating table more than four hours while they sewed up tendons and veins and nerves and so, all the while, I was feeling it because by the time I got on the table I was so hyped up, the sedatives and locals wouldn't take. I felt terrible for a week because I was hot on the book and I don't like interruptions. After a week, I gritted my teeth and with one finger poking out of cast, set to work learning the peck system with my right hand and that, along with the usual touch system of the left hand, helped me continue work. Every time I hit the keys I had pain. I am writing that way now, that is, pecking, though the cast is off. Nerve won't be back for two more months. It is absolutely astounding how the human body adjusts. My left hand has never been very literate, but with the right hand inactive, it learned things in an incredibly short time. As if the know-how which runs the right hand just shifted channels and went down and made the left hand do it. Now that the right hand is coming back, it is curious to note how the left hand is beginning to put on that it no longer knows how to button pants and eat with a fork and embrace the wife and open door handles and urinate and turn keys.

Am sending these quotes or clips not in the hope of persuading you, or like a tract-bringer, but only to indicate the kinds of thoughts that pass through our heads. I can not vote Republican, and cannot vote Truman. All the new dealers are out of government, and Truman is little more than a tool for the military. And Forrestal and his millions. It's always a choice between two imperfect candidates, but now we are getting horrible candidates. With Wallace the only one, despite the Communists who support him, who speaks sense about science, atom destruction (if we increase radioactivity in the world by two or three percent—some 200 bombs dropped—your and my testicles become infertile—unless we can reascend them into the belly), about our oil interests, about our FBI, about our vast monopolies. He isn't going to win, but neither are we with Truman. I think we have reached that point that if we are going to have reaction in Washington, let's have it have the right name. When the ADA with Bowles, Humphrey, Henderson, Ickes, Reuther, et al, will not support Truman, you've got reaction in Washington. If the Dems can get Douglas to run, that's different. Then I drop Mr. Wallace. I am sitting back to see. In the meantime you boys can have your Missouri Jackass. I want no part of him. I absolutely refuse to have a hand in the destruction of mankind. Even if the Russians contemplate it, I personally as an American want my hands clean right up to the very last second of consciousness.

We all send you our love—our
very best, yours,
Fred

[margin] P.S. Are you coming this summer? If so, we have a bed and a home for you as long as you like.

[margin] P.S.S. I have been reading Steinbeck's *A Russian Journal*. It tells how ideas, governments, etc., come and go, but people remain people. Very good!

To Maxwell Geismar

[Minneapolis, Minnesota]
April 28, 1948

Dear Max:

Just a few days before your letter with review came I got another through the mail. So it's going back to you. Yours is a much more sober coming to grips and it hits pretty close to where it is

supposed to rank. At least so I think. One suggestion. Don't over-
look an innocent kind of irony in my things. It isn't central but it
plays along side like a flame, as if to give an extra light. My wife
misses it in my talk even, says I am deadly serious, and I am, but
at the same time I am having fun too with little off-to-side plays on
words or situations or intentions. It is just probably that that is
a form of northern European humor or irony. For when it comes
to making an ostensible witty remark, I can't. Whereas my wife
can. Well, just a suggestion. Of course you don't have the room but
someday I wish somebody would recognize my language. It is really poetry. It is loaded with semi-hidden alliteration, rime, with
an undulating rhythm. I am very conscious of why my sentences
do what they do. I study other poets and writers, and am aware of
why they hit me. For example, in describing a musician working
at white heat I wrote last week, "dripping pen in hand he *stabbed*
the notes on the *staff*." Or, from *Tree* "what is it that scuds us over
the sudsing maelstom." Or, from *Year*, "It sucked the succulent
soils etc." "A noodle in his nose." "The ear-ringing singing was as
sharp as a shriek. It was so near his teeth tittered together." To
do such things with the language for the fun isn't good, necessarily, but to do it to give an action an extra dash of power, and
to suggest by sound and by sight is to be the poet. "The squirrel's
needle teeth." When you say that, you are saying it plus letting the
reader see, almost without his knowing it, the individual sharp
teeth. The succession of "ee's" do it, particularly when the double
"rr" in the first word sets up the image background. This is a gift. It
is not learned, though learning will sharpen it. My early poetry,
of which I have an unpublished volume, is loaded with it, though
when I wrote it then I wasn't too conscious of it. My mind just
runs that way. I love clean tone-ringing words. I usually detest abstract words, words of Latin or Roman origin, and when I do accept them I make sure that they are simple and sharp, and very
similar in design to Anglo-Saxon-Frisian. I happen to love *Beowulf,*
and as a Frisian (from whom the Angles came) I have been trained
in alliteration. (This probably accounts for my love of Doughty!)
You should read my old Frisian books, the Frisian Bible, and a set
of laws that go back to 800rds. (All Anglo-Saxon law goes back
to this document, *Skeltana Riucht*. "This is riucht thet thi fria
Fresa ni thor fira hereferd fara... truch tha ned thet hi thenne ower
alle degan wera skel with thenne salta se and with thenne wilda
witsing, mith fif wepnem, mith spada and mith forka, mith skelde

and mith etkeres swerde . . ." "This is the law: the free Frisian need make no further foray . . . because he needs must guard the shore, day in day out, against the salt sea and the wild viking with five weapons: with spade and with fork, with shield and with sword . . ." The experience in the San made me. I might have just dissolved had that not come along. The reviews have been stunningly good. But they are wrong when they think it better than *Year*. I have finished first draft of *The Primitive*, will work until January polishing. Best, will write more soon.

Yours,
Fred

To Maxwell Geismar

[Minneapolis, Minnesota]
August 18, 1948

Dear Max:

Am taking a breather for a couple of days. Finished a readable draft of *The Primitive* and have sent it off to Doubleday to get some money on it, and then plan to finish it for the printers by next January. So far I am somewhat pleased with it. I can see already that it's going to be the best so far. Am most eager to get at volumes two and three. Am on pins and hooks wondering what the publisher will say.

Have had one bit of good news. When Newberry Library turned me down in July for fellowship (they were not inclined to help fictioneers), Emmett Dedmon, book editor of the *Sun & Times,* wired for all the application materials. He had been backing me. Some time later I heard from him. He talked Marshall Field into giving me a $1200 fellowship to be paid in quarterly installments. Comes from Field Foundation, Inc., which has been set up to help social ills, not literary at all. Vast exception, etc. Whatever it is, it is damned welcome. I sent them, among other things, some quotes from you. Thanks.

1. *The Naked and the Dead.*

Have been reading a little modern stuff. Mailer's book[1] was good and sharp until I hit the section where I learned Croft was to have the idea of climbing the mountain. That made me sick. Croft is not the vehicle. I've known millions of Crofts (well perhaps a couple hundred) and their reaction to such a project would be one of deep practical scorn. Such an idea or ideal requires education of some sort, either in college or in life, and a good imaginative mind. Croft has none of that. Red Valsen might have had, except that he is so burnt and bitter and turned in that he would have given it up in disgust. Curiously enough Mailer did have the right man there. He was Hearn. Hearn, who had a side turned to Cummings' odd-sexed aspect, could have shown his independence of that sex by climbing the mountain after discovering the pass was closed. And could have set himself free in his own mind. Once the pass was discovered as closed, Hearn would have been on his own, and could have engineered it. Besides, it might have been a brilliant tactic, as witness, Hannibal and the Alps, Chu-teh and the Himalayas in China, Merrill's Marauders in the reconquest of Burma, etc. Mailer is a bright boy and he knows a lot for twenty-five, but he just didn't sit down and think it out. Had he kept at that book until he was, say, thirty, he might have made it a colossal book. Young men can do brilliant short things, but very few can do the big ones until they've acquired some little age. Mailer's failure reminds me of Warren's *All The King's Men*. Warren missed the central challenge when he wrote the book from Jack Burden's point of view instead of Willie Stark's (Huey Long's). Oddly enough, I had this idea about a month after I read it, and now I see it reflected in an article by Eric Bentley in a book published by the Un. of Minn. Press this spring. (Side note: Ever notice the sex of Warren's men? Every seduction or intercourse is a rape or a harsh business. And his women are cruel.) [matter deleted by author] I had many conversations with Red when he was writing *King's*; he picked my brains so to speak of my knowledge of the Stassen regime, of Olson's and Benson's regime—I was once in politics up to my ears. (I should put this all down, I suppose.) But Red and I could never discuss his personal life. He sets up a shield. End of page and end of letter.

Cordially,
Fred

[margin] Hello to dear Brooks.

To George Shively

[Minneapolis, Minnesota]
October 26, 1948

Dear George,

I've written Curtis Brown to accept the financial terms. And for God's own good hurry contract and money. I'll have the book ready within two months. Thank God I've already had a good start

on cleaning it up on my own initiative or I would rebel at the idea
that I might clean it up for book clubs. If the book clubs take me as
I am, well and good: but I'll be seen in hell first before I *aim* to
please them. I live with me, not with book clubs. Even if I should
starve in the process of holding to this course of writing, it will not
be my loss but society's or the book clubs or the powers that be.
Book clubs and publishers etc., come and go, but Feikemas occur
but once in a world. I usually make it a point to ignore such self-
ideas but jungle situations make me show my teeth just like any
other human animal. There is absolutely no thought of going to
an other publisher. I am Doubleday's as long as you are there. I
despise authors who hop from publisher to publisher. I say, "Talk
tough if you have to, but *always* work it out with your partner."
So even if your boys had offered me a nickel advance I would have
agreed.

I think you're right about *The Stumbling Stone*.[1] Good, but not
big. I'll save it for that omnibus of shorts I'm collecting, to be published when the world at last recognizes me for what I am.

It's all very funny. My docs told me when I left the San that I
was to take off every six months. Now I'm asked to not only keep
up my present pace but go out and work to boot. And that after
my docs told me (within the last two weeks) that if I don't take a
vacation soon I'll have a nervous breakdown. Or go cracked.

No, I'm not going to take another job. I'm going to hold this
line of attack until either death or success. I'm dead right. My wife
has been threatening to leave me but not even that disturbs me to
the point of deserting literature. I know I'm "great" and I know the
day will come. (Again, I'm sorry to have to mention this, but the
jungle forces me to show teeth. I'm sorry, and apologize for showing the teeth. To that extent I am weak and not "great" and an ass.)

George, I know you are for me to the hilt. You know how good
I am. You have been wrestling, and have jumped and struggled for
me like a brother these last couple of days, like an older and wiser
brother trying to help his bright young brother. One of these days
your efforts will convince the rest there that, 1) they have a blank-
blank kind of writer in their midst, 2) that he won't do a Maugham
on them, 3) that he'll get better all the way up to seventy (some 35
more years of producing books).

What I've gone over in *The Primitive* looks very good.

Sincerely,
Fred

1. Later titled "Country
Love."

P.S. Send, immediately, your copy of *The Stumbling Stone* to Edith at Curtis Brown so she can present it to magazines and movies. *Please*.

To Kathleen Hoagland

[Minneapolis, Minnesota]
November 3, 1948

Dear Kathleen:

Such stunning news on the election returns! I hope every goddam editor of the Republican Press has the glorious shits this morning! I am usually fairly philosophical about elections but I have been burned up the way the editors and reporters and pollsters have picked Dewey's cabinet and Lady Dewey's crapper paper and so on. They knew. And yet, what did they know? The pollsters have not yet figured out how to take polls in the lower D class. I worked nine months on a public opinion survey outfit and that was the one section of the eight (high A, low A, high B, low B, high C, low C, high D, low D) that was a tough one to be accurate in. That lower class voted yesterday. And when you poll them they never give the right answers. Because they're afraid to talk. They're constantly being harried by inspectors, detectives, 36% loan shark investigators, FBI, delinquency experts, social workers, priests, preachers, slummers. And no one knows them. (I do. And I'd like to point out that no one in the history of literature, neither Tolstoi, Dickens, Steinbeck, Twain, Shakespeare, none of them knows them as well as I do, nor has any one put them down as accurately as I have, nor has any one written of them as poetically—that lower depth of society!) (And I know the other classes too!)

Doubleday has decided to take the first book of the trilogy, *The Primitive*. But for an advance of only $1000 because they are some $5500 in arrears on the other two books. They are keen on the new one but they want me to trim it down so that it'll have a chance at the book clubs so they can recoup and I can make some dough. I don't know if I have a chance at a monthly selection or not. In any case, I have said, flatly "No." When I'm done, I'm done. It's perfect according to Feikema as of the day finishing. What pressure they put on a guy! We're terribly hard up. I did manage to land a $1200 fellowship from the Field Foundation Inc. on the first book, and that plus the $1000 will take us to April. But no vacation and I need one so badly, Kathleen. And so does my wife. She's showing signs of strain. With my writing schedule and me. She's a good girl, it's that I and my career are inhuman. Doubleday says I have to take a job. That would end my writing. And so I've said, "No, I'm writing until I die. I've got a chance to scale Mt. Everest in letters before I die and I'm going to press on, even if it is with a bad pair of lungs and a country-trained mind."

Kathleen, I've not liked my jackets or the advertising. So, on signing the contract, I'm going to insist on a new type of jacket. I'm making up a list of quotes from reviews and from personal letters, and I want permission to use the material, signed, so that when I flash it on them they won't succumb to inertia and fail to get permission themselves. It looks like I'll have to do my own promotion. Thank God, my own editor is back of me. Can you, dear woman? My hand is slowly improving, but it seems I'll only get 50% recovery. A shame. Because now my music suffers. (But my writing gains?) I am terribly proud of my new book. I also wrote a novelette, a two-note affair, which Doubleday liked too but not enough to publish separately. That is now going the rounds of the magazines. I've worked terribly hard, and am very tired.

All our love,
Fred

To Clayton Hoagland

[Minneapolis, Minnesota]
November 14, 1948

Dear folks:

Just an hour ago the following conversation took place at our Sunday evening supper table (fire in the fireplace, sky in the west amber and rose in sunset):

She: And you wrote *that* letter to Clayton and Kitty?
He: Yes.
She: You dope you.
He: Why?
She: Clayton, my dear, works on a Republican Newspaper. As editor.
He: HomyGod!
She: Yes. And you're supposed to have brains. Literary brains.
He: OhmyGod! But I didn't mean . . . it was only that I got so sick of all the papers around here . . . you know how they're all Republican and how they always tell us how to vote and how we never listen to their advice and how sickening it is to be represented locally by people who do not express our feelings, who do not represent us at all, you know that.

She: I know. But Clayton still works for the *New York Sun*.

He: Aw, he'll understand. Besides, I never thought of him as a Republican editor. My idea of him is that he's a fine liberal man. He bothered to write about my strong stuff, didn't he? That makes him a warm-hearted liberal.

She: Aren't Republican editors warm-hearted men?

He: Well . . . but he'll understand.

She: And then that dirty word too yet. What'll she think?

He: Just that we use it occasionally around here.

She: That's what I'm afraid of.

He: You know, it must a been all that sulfadiazine I took for that bad throat. You know they say your judgment centers are affected by such.

She: Do you take it for breakfast every day?

He: (In righteous wrath) Now cut it out. Quit hen-pecking me. (He slams the table with his fist) No more wisecracks.

She: All right, father.

He: Well then.

She: Poor Clayton. I wonder what he thinks. 'I hope all the Republican editors have got the glorious . . .' uh, such a word. And Kitty to read it first yet.

He: Good lord, woman, she's a novelist.

She: What's that got to do with it?

He: Just that she has to know the facts of life or she's not a novelist.

She: But in a social communication.

He: Communication be damned. I just wrote my mind.

She: Instead of all the Republican editors in the country having the glorious uh . . . I think maybe you had it.

   (fadeout)

P.S. Dear Clayton, I am indeed sorry for that crack in that last letter. I just never thought, I guess. You see, we out here don't get anything to read but R. papers and we resent it so thoroughly we pop off about it.

   Yours,
   Feike

To Henry Zylstra[1]

[Minneapolis, Minnesota]
December 2, 1948

1. Chairman of the Calvin
College English Depart-
ment.

Dear Henry and Mildred,

After a couple of days of continuous sleeping, I'm gradually
emerging into consciousness again, and am able to realize that it's
time to catch up on correspondence. I've finally and at last sent
off *The Primitive*, the first volume of the trilogy, and am free from
now until Christmas. I've agonized over work before but not like
this one. In addition to the wrestle with words, and expression,
and so on, this time I also had the devilish wrestle between artistic
truth and chronological (or literal) truth. I was already running
short of energy back in the early part of November, but I hung on
despite some temperature and bone-achings and coughing, knowing that if I stopped I'd lose it all. I should take a half year of rest
. . . except that would increase the danger of losing the momentum
I need for the next volume.

What a devilish time I had! I had caught glimpse of what I
wanted to do, and I had to flagellate myself again and again to keep
glimpsing it. I no longer wanted the book to be about Calvin but
about secondary or non-university colleges in general. And that
against the culture of Christianity. And I wanted to show the provincial lad coming to the city and to learning, and young people
awakening to love and sex. I borrowed heavily on my Calvin experience, but also from what I knew of Hamline and St. Olaf, and
Nettleton Commercial College and Augustana and Carleton, and
the University of Minnesota. As far as I know you'll be able to spot
definitely the likeness of just four or five actual people. The rest
I blended together from many impressions (assuming, of course,
that we see each other with the same set of eyes . . . which I doubt).
The first draft ran to some 718 pages and this was pared back to
some 520.[2] I had three drafts and five readings. I think I've got it

2. FM later cut it more for
the *Wanderlust* edition.

down, at last, for beyond what I listed above, I've also got down
the story of the artist in society (or the artist versus society).

I'm not sure I'll please any one with it. But then, I have only this
to say. Wait until the whole sweep is done, and then see how well
the first third compares, in tone, to the whole. There is some denial
at the end of this one, but by the third, there is going to be considerable return to origins. One thing I do know; I could have been
ten times rougher, could have put ten times the strong truth that I
did put into it. (How I long for a time when man can say what he
really thinks. I'm not too sure but what that accounts for the great-

ness of Swift's *Letters to Stella*, and Hawthorne's newly discovered letters—the ones where the critic has filled in the inked out passages—such a dastardly trick, to hide the truth of the man!—and many another bit of writing never meant for the public eye!) (I am so suspicious of friends that I have already arranged with a library to take over my letters and diaries and journals intact so that no righteous or prejudiced relative or friend can go in and make a saint out of me. If people are to be interested in me in the years to come, by the beard of Moses, they shall be able to get at the truth. In the practical world of everyday carpentry or wood-cutting, and in the world of science, if man hides truth from himself or his neighbor, he is asking for destruction. As witness atomic fission. So why should we quiver about truth in fiction? Uplift is a by-product of literature. Description of humanity is the thing. So though Thackeray, Balzac, Swift (it makes me furious to think that some pale esthete has edited the "coarse" passages out of his work because I, reader of 1948, am too refined for it. Am I? And am I not? What does he know about my notions of art? Of refinement? Imagine, some bird with the I.Q. of 120 and with no creative instinct, is legislating my reading, a bird with an I.Q. far in excess of any measurement and with some creative drive. What crust!) My feeling is there should be two kinds of editions: one for the innocents (old women, aunts, children, youth up to 18 or maturity, eunuchs, queers) and one for grown-ups. (I write mainly for the latter.) We can say anything we want to in music, even describe intercourse in musical language as witness the Kruetzer Sonata, etc. Why not in literature? (It's the politicians, christian and communist, democratic and republican, that try to tell us that there is a time and a place for literature: when it is really the other way around, that there is in literature a time and a place for *everything*.)

It's been a rough year. First I almost lost my right hand in an accident so that I had to do much of my work with my crude left hand. Then the publishers decided to cut my advance from $2500 to $1000. (Because the account of Feikema is in general way behind. And rising costs generally.) Then I lose out on the Guggenheim for the third straight year. (I applied again.)

We had one fine thing happen. I was awarded a fellowship from the Field Foundation, Inc., some 1200 bucks. Special case, through the helping hand of Emmett Dedmon of the *Chicago Sun & Times*, lit. Ed. (For whom I do occasional reviews.)

Freya has been ill for a month and is only just now getting

around again, and once again has pink cheeks. She is slowing down in her growing according to a chart Maryanna keeps. I hope that worry of Maryanna does not carry over to the child. I want her to grow up like I did not: satisfied with what she is. (There is slight evidence that intelligence and height go together: and that despite the average-cutting incidence of cretins, gland-boys, acromegaly, etc.)

Hank, I agree with you that Greene's *Heart of the Matter* is significant writing. He is not only a craftsman, but he is presenting vital material. And what's least important about it is his point of view. It's the material. (Just as it was the material that won out for Chaucer and the point of view which lost out for John Gower, his contemporary.)

Tell me the news. What about Bird Vogel? Tim [Timmerman]? Jellema? (My true Christian hero!) Broene? (Another wonderful man!) Give them my fond regards.

And from us all, a very merry merry Christmas.

Yours,
F.M.F.

1949

This is a year of increasing indebtedness and the birth of Manfred's second child, Marya. As a consequence, he pushes for the completion of the first two volumes of the World's Wanderer *trilogy. Despite his appointment as writer-in-residence at Macalester College and a grant from the Andreas Foundation to write* The Brother, *financial dilemmas continue. During the year, Manfred completes the second volume, submits short stories for publication, and begins to collect manuscripts and letters for the archives at the University of Minnesota.*

To William Van O'Connor

[Minneapolis, Minnesota]
January 11, 1949

Dear Bill,

To continue our talk of the other night . . .

I find myself in sympathy with much of your point of view. For the full-rounded man as you outline it in the last chapter, for your insistence that what is written must have meaning, for your es-

pousal of "heightening" at the same time that you want it show
the author's irony, for your interest in tradition at the same time
that you want awareness of the present. All these things I like; all
these things I think have been a part and parcel of my own thinking
for a good many years. Though truth to tell, I had not worked them
out into terms, or into a statement. I had felt them out, but not
thought them out. One thing a fictioneer and a poet must watch:
not to get too self-conscious or too self-aware of what he is doing.
For I feel that no matter how great the intelligence or the brains,
there is a larger knowledge in all of us, in each of us. I always say,
train the brain the best way you know how and then let the larger
person speak out. The brain should be the medium, provide the
language, use the tools, but the Big Person should do the real talking. I have had, always, considerable suspicion of brains *per se*. And
of wits and intellectuals I have a distaste. The only trouble is that
when I begin explaining it sounds like I'm talking about spirits or
ghosts or God's voice. Of "mediums," or "seance masters of ceremonies." It's like having religion. You know it when you have it.
Only those who know it can see it in each other even though they
can't speak of it or prove that they have it.

I have only one real major quarrel with T.S. Eliot. (I can accept
his person just as I can accept other races or new planets.) And that
involves his emphasis on ostentatious learning or erudition. Long
ago I had worked out his idea of the "objective correlative." I called
it the "really real" when I was on the farm and reading the Bible
and Shakespeare. Lately I've called it the "new life."

I feel that the surface of the style of the new life should be clear.
It should be as clear a stream as possible, so that as it courses along
we can sometimes see, when the river-bed deepens, the terrible
rocks below, so that we can see, when the river-bed shallows, the
lovely stones in the fords. Take a good look at your consciousness.
It seems fairly clear, seems full of direction, seems to be plausibly
reasonable as you go along. The mind of the peasant thinks so, the
mind of the thinker thinks so—even though the real truth is that
the unconscious or the Big Person is very complicated and inturned
and convoluted and jam-packed with experiences and learnings
and forgotten loves and hates and hereditary mechanisms no longer
useful to us at this stage of our humankind-evolution and buried
uselessly but dangerously in our flesh and marrow. The assumption
we work under and the state of mind we have at any given moment
is that life is reasonable (chronological, etc.) So I say when you

create a book or a poem, make it, at least on the surface, resemble your ordinary state of mind. The symbols you can bring in, sure, and all the other techniques you have learned. But all should be seemingly held in leash by a sane mind or a sane plot.

It should all seem natural. Flashbacks, for example. We should have to want to flashback when the author gives them to us, just as, after we have met each other in the stream of things, we seek to know each other's origins. We seek them for some reason. Not arbitrarily. The author, like life, should invent the excuse for us to want to go back.

Eliot too often rams the stuff at us. And good lord, we are already such slavish imitators that I feel that after I've read Spenser, Doughty, Homer, Chaucer, the Greek Dramatists (cf. my *This Is The Year* in that connection), Dante, Melville, Camoëns, Goethe, Schiller, Grillparzer, Heine, etc., I should forget all about them. Deliberately so. And seek to be as original as possible. For I know, that no matter how far I run afield, I'll still be within hailing distance of the "boys." My erudition I want to come in quietly, stealthily, unobtrusively. The book must be able to stand on its own feet in case all other books and knowledge should die. Not the other way around. That I must read all books before I tackle Eliot. (Both positions, of course, are extreme. But they do serve to show where I differ from the duffer.)

Moreover, to go on about clear surface, even the brightest of us have about so much reading attention, say ninety points. If some fifty points of that must be concerned with the working out of the acrostic, or the trick, of the work, and also many remote and personal references, we have only forty points left for the "meat" (that "meat" being what you the new and original author has to say).

Here follow some tags, some odds and ends. Sometime when you feel like it, you might tip off your friends Heilman and Schorer that Feikema does not write only journalistically or "undigestedly." All the things that modern poets practise, symbolism, metaphysical representation, irony, inversion, paradox, humor, etc., are in my books. E.G. In *The Golden Bowl* (my original title for the book, *The Golden Bowl Is Broken,* was cut) there is an attempt at rebirth into the earth in the well scene; at the end, a foreshadowing of what Maury might have become had he not gone back to Kirsten in the boxcar scene, etc.[1] In *Boy Almighty* there are such things as the constantly changing meaning of The Whipper for Eric and his constantly changing attitudes to the women—he grows from Ma

1. The phrase "in the boxcar scene" should follow "a foreshadowing" [FM's note].

Memme to Martha to Nurse Berg to Mary—watch the talk about hands and eyes and breasts. In *Year* there was the symbol of earth-woman (an old one, I admit) and the form of the lot taken from the very panorama of the prairie itself. The reader was to feel the prairie from the style—even though he was not to be aware that he felt it. And so on. And of course, you should see my new book. I shouldn't have to mention this, except that, like Gide was with his, I am concerned with the direction that serious criticism is taking with respect to my work, for I know, as well as Gide did, that it takes a big critic to admit that he's blown the wrong note. More-over, just think of what happens to the thinking of all the lesser fry. Once you get the pack to stampeding, there'll be no holding them or getting them back in my lifetime. And you know, I'd like to feel that somebody appreciates me. The hot forty-year women don't like my books (though they like my body), *The New Yorker* hypersophs don't like me, the homos hate me, etc. I can't help what my publisher puts on my jacket. If he talks about all the journalist work I do, that's probably because, to win my argument with him, I have had to overwhelm him with "reasons." I want my book to go in as I write it. You should see my relatives, both learned and il-literate. They say, "why, what he writes ain't so at all," though they will admit that the incidents and the things did happen so. What they are thinking of is that I should be writing autobiography and biography. When I don't. When I was a little kid I was known, and I'm the only one known so in my family, as the Big Liar.[1] That Big Liar has become the fictioneer. The inventor.

1. Said teasingly [FM's note].

Finally, I believe that the artist must, in his creation, so con-struct and so create his book or poem that it will stand alone like Reality itself does. (Just look what your book did! Got me to write a long letter!)

Best, always,
Feike

To Senator Hubert H. Humphrey

[Minneapolis, Minnesota]
January 14, 1949

Dear Hubert:

I was very proud to see your picture on the front cover of *Time*. Both my wife and I read it at dinner last night, and talked about it for the rest of the evening and a good share of this morning. We had a fine time recalling many a memory. And as for that talk of your being a little reluctant to be introspective, let me say that I'll write a book or a testimonial to the opposite truth if you want. It happens that I had too many private conversations with you when the pressure was on to think otherwise.

Did you see, by any chance, the humorous and instructive article by Maverick in the *New Republic*? Don't rar' up when you see my underscorings. I was marking it up for my own purposes. You see, it is still my hope to write a political novel someday.

And in the same issue of *Time,* did you see that stuff about Americans pulling Nazi stuff on Nazi soldiers?[1] I love my country very much (I always say I use the American language, not the English, for example) but such things make me grieve. You can imagine what the Germans think of the Allies. For the Russians probably were rougher in their zone. Terrible business. The whitewash of civilization sometimes wears thin and the "beast" shows through, doesn't it?

Best regards to our friends Bill and Jean Simms.

And fond greetings to Muriel and the children.

Tomorrow I begin volume two of the big trilogy I'm on. I've got volume one, *The Primitive*, coming out in the fall.

Yours, always, a friend,

FF

Feike Feikema

1. Shooting the wounded.

To Mark Schorer
Harcourt & Brace, New York

[Minneapolis, Minnesota]
February 5, 1949

Dear Mark:

You're the bird who wrote . . . "in F.F.'s less able and much duller *This Is The Year*, a long midwest farm chronicle, there is nearly total failure to differentiate subject from experience, and a total failure to extract theme from subject. These are novels which seem to be about everything and nothing. Yet they are not poor books; they are merely wicked ones . . . Nearly all the novels in the present group are technically innocent and the reason is not far to seek. 'This Is The Year,' says Mr. Feikema's blurbist, 'is a novel, but it is a novel of life and of truth' "...and yet I must tell you what enjoyment I have been having lately reading *Criticism*. For that collection alone you deserve every writer's thanks. Much in it I remembered from college days, much in it I had already figured out, but a lot of it I had never seen before. I read a chapter or a section every night and mull it over as I go to bed. It will be interesting to see what effect it will have on my writing.

I am at present working on a trilogy, *World's Wanderer*, and the first volume, *The Primitive*, is now being set, while the second, *The Brother*, is in the making. This work, for the second time, will be heavily autobiographical, deliberately so. (The first one was *Boy Almighty*, and not *This Is The Year*, as you seemed to think.) I am finding all sorts of arguments, even in Aristotle (he says there is no harm in using literal events provided they will lend themselves to "plot") for such a work, and the fact that Maugham, Lawrence, Melville, Dickens, Thackeray (*Pendennis*), Goethe, Dante, Virgil, at one time or another wrote one, spurs me on. In fact, I feel that in addition to the fault you point out about such books (Lawrence, you say, achieved an effect he didn't intend because he did not get outside himself enough), there is the stigma the writer feels when he writes them. This stigma makes him shy away from what he should pursue. And I propose to help him by giving the auto-novel a new name, a coined word. This coined word I'll explain in a postscript to the whole trilogy. Had Wolfe, Maugham, and others not felt ashamed about writing auto-novels, we might have gotten better stuff. As it is, they blur to hide, not to create, e.g., Maugham's Mildred is in reality a homo dressed up in a woman's clothes, a terrible business, since the motives he gives "her" are not a woman's at all. Of course, this is not to deny that there are novels too. In fact, novels will always be far more prevalent. It all depends where it starts from: from within the author, or from the author's observance of life-in-general. Both have to be lifted into art—or they're still "wicked" books.

Anyway, my personal thanks for getting together *Criticism*.

Very sincerely yours,
F.F.

To Emmett Dedmon
Chicago *Sun & Times,* Chicago, Illinois

[Minneapolis, Minnesota]
March 23, 1949

Dear Emmett:

I feel awful to have to write you this letter but the Guggenheimers have turned me down again, for the fourth time. I can't understand it. And neither can Red Warren (and you know how he would stand in relation to my writing!). Maybe I got them excited in the wrong way with my parodying of T.S. Eliot in *The Primitive*, the first volume of the trilogy. (I had galleys and sent them in to Guggenheim.)

I feel all the more wretched since I have gotten some 200 pages into the second volume, and was going great until this noon. In fact, I think I am doing my best writing right now. It is even better than the writing in the first volume, *The Primitive*, a writing that my wife and I were very proud of.

Of course it is foolish of me to think of asking for further help from Mr. Field.[1] (In fact, as I recall it now, it was explicitly stated at that time that Mr. Field "would have no intention of renewing or extending the fellowship.") But I can ask you to send me books for review a little oftener if you will.

In a way it is presumptuous of me to write you this kind of letter because you too have ambitions of being an independent author. But I have to write my grief to someone.

If I had the least notion that what I am doing was not significant, I wouldn't feel so badly. But I know I have to write, and so the bitter feeling. I wish I could take it out of me somehow. I don't like to drink, I don't like to debauch, and so I have to ride it out with no anesthetic.

I only like to write.

Yours, wretchedly,
Feike Feikema

P.S. The last I heard was that *The Primitive* is to be published in September though books will be ready in May. As I said above, I have seen the galleys and they are wonderful.

f.f.

P.S. This whole thing is complicated by the fact that instead of giving me an advance of $2500 as I expected, Doubleday gave me only $1000. All because too much had been advanced on *The Chokecherry Tree*. It sold little better than diamonds sell in swineland. And that despite the good reviews I got.

[margin] —Who is going to get the Friends of Am. Writing Award this year?

—I know just how Melville felt when he quit writing at 36-37— my age.

—Dean Blegen tells me that he will write Mr. Field a "strong" letter in my behalf, if that will do any good, but I wonder.

1. Of the Marshall Field Foundation.

To Virgil Scott

[Minneapolis, Minnesota]
April 16, 1949

Dear Scotty and family,

By God, it's about time I wrote, not? So here goes in the way of news. Since around January 6, I've felt fairly good, at times wonderful, and have been writing steadily on volume two of trilogy, and am some 300 pages into it, and hope to be finished with a readable draft around the middle of June. Last year when writing volume one I discovered that my best sections were always those I wrote longhand first and then retyped. So this time, right from the beginning I started writing longhand, say the first three hours in the morning, and then later in the day retyped it so as to have a clean copy. It has worked spectacularly. And I firmly believe that that is due to the fact that as a boy I learned to express myself in writing through longhand and that the typewriting I learned at 24 served as a block, wasn't my natural or early-learned medium, for when I use typewriter it always seems as if two ways of expressing myself are wrestling with each other. Not so much when I write a letter, say, or some simple passage, but wherever I want to trail the old wick down deep. When I wrote first drafts on the typewriter they always were in such wretched shape I almost always had to rewrite them longhand in between the lines and then retype. Really, I've been simply amazed at the results of the new method. You see, by outlining each chapter the day before and then brooding on it at night and then the next morning writing it, I need not worry that I won't get it all down before I forget. My worry is instead to go slow enough to explore all the ramifications as I go along. With the new method of plotting and planning first, getting the path cleared first, I can now go slow and concentrate on the individual sentences, the multi-meanings. It will be interesting to see if you agree with me later. Certain sections in the new book are written in this way.

My wife has been very ill with the flu. In bed for two weeks and one week I had to take Freya away and take care of Maryanna hand and foot. I cooked, baked, cleaned, etc. Got pretty damned tired of it too. I think part of her illness was worry over money. That has now been fixed up somewhat and I can see my way clear through the summer, with maybe a vacation to the Rockies thrown in. I have been thinking too of teaching a writing seminar, and am approaching various nearby colleges. The University is all set, I find, for next year, though they were a mite interested. One thing, though. If I don't get a job in a college by this fall, I'll never get a job after, once they get an eyeful of the two books. What I have to say about T.S. Eliot and the New Critics (by inference) won't set so hot with them. The English not only brought over sparrows and starlings to infest the nests of our bluebirds and purple martins but they brought over Anglophile professor writers to stand in the way of our natural and native songbird writers. Pricks, bastards, cocksuckers. We honor a devil like Eric Bentley, a Bentley who would like to get into the Mayfair crowd in England but can't, and who then comes here and belabors us and becomes famous so he can go back there and at last get in as a footman to the Mayfair crowd. I'm going over to O'Connor tonight to listen to some more to the goddam twiddle. You know, I just don't understand their language anymore. To tell them I need to go to the bathroom I have to construct an elaborate and balanced and perfectly punctuated sentence like the following: "Uhhh, Van, I uhh would you mind awfully, old fellow, but I should very much like to ask you if you could tell me where your bathroom is situated?" What I should say is, "Van, I gotta piss. Where's the can?" I will say this for Van. I've given him a lot of hell lately and he has taken it all in stride, with a long hearty laugh. And he has lately admitted to me that he now reads the Sat. Rev. of Lit. (As if that were my ideal sheet!)

Dan Brennan is now secretary to the Mayor [Hubert Humphrey][1] and is writing a political novel. He is dealing with Harpers with another that Red Warren and I agree is just a step away from being "terrific." "It" as Red said.[2] Dos Passos was in town for a couple of weeks and all the literati got out and exchanged hellos with him over drinks at the Abbot Washburn's (he married Brennan's sister Mary.) Dos is coming back in the spring. Had a hair-raising moment or two at that party. Dos, Mabel Seeley, and Red Warren each have but one eye. Trying to find the right eye into which to talk gave me the willies. A little later Cinina Warren came by in her private iceberg-like fog and said, "But you know it's all in here. Personal. Deep. You know that. You can't get at it. Only he with the magic wang . . . I mean wand can." (Or something to that effect.) Mr. Seeley, just back from a nuthouse, kept interrupting (his psychiatrist told him to keep bearing toward facts, concrete facts, hard facts, lively facts) with his "Pick 'em up down field!" At this same party one of the respected professor wives admitted to another professor that she had come to the party without her brassiere. He asked her if she felt comfortable.

1. FM is writing of the recent past. Humphrey went to the U.S. Senate in January 1949.

2. *Honorable Estate*. Never published.

How's your work coming? I'm assuming you haven't written because you're hopping hard on *The Tower*. *The Primitive* will be published this fall, September. We've read proofs. My wife says it'll lose me the last few friends I have, both Christian and New Criticism. I told her I never had them as friends anyway, and that I now might win them over. She tries to tell me (anent something that's going to be in *The Brother*) that women take mensing as a matter of course, like weather, but by God try to mention it in a book and she gets on her hotwater heater. Two things a writer must avoid: criticism from professional critics and criticism from a wife.

Please write us, Scotty.

Yours old friend,
Feike Feikema

To John Huizenga

[Minneapolis, Minnesota]
June 7, 1949

Dear John:

Met your cousin down in Rochester last weekend and that prompted this letter. (Though of course I thought of writing often before.) What are your plans for the summer? Could you come up for a weekend during our July-August swimming and garden products season? We plan on leaving for the Rockies on June 15 and will be back around the 1st of July. (Maryanna has never seen them, and I've been lonesome for them for years.) Perhaps we can arrange something. I'd sure like it. It's been three years—too long.

About your comment that you have been trying to forget your experience at Calvin because of its disagreeable nature—that's perhaps why I wrote about it. To write about a happy placid time in one's life is to invite yawns. Moreover, I have great reluctance in the matter of admitting that any part of my life has been a waste. I have always sought to salvage something out of everything. To do so is to have a relatively easy conscience, is to have a generally optimistic attitude about life and people. I am pretty goddam rough on some types of people in my *The Primitive* but nowhere in it is there a hint that I did not *live*. The harness of the Christian faith inflicted many a gall and shoulder sore but I'll be a bastard before I admit that it killed me off. On the contrary, having survived it, I have a knowledge and a power that few have.

Your letter, of course, served its purpose too. It made me all the more determined not to follow the facts and events of your life in the character of Starring, but to make an artistic take-off on it—a something, by the way, that not many people are capable of understanding.

The book is already bound and a copy is here. It will be published in September. And in the meantime I've finished a readable draft of *The Brother*, the second volume of the trilogy. For the rest of the year I'll be checking facts, polishing, rewriting and revising, and so on.

To get a little extra income I've accepted a position as Writer-in-Residence at Macalester College, in St. Paul. I'm to conduct a two-hour once-a-week seminar in advanced writing in any fashion I see fit. For one semester. (We not only needed the money but next December we'll have an addition to the family.)

Howard Hoving was here. With wife and child. He acts queerly, sort of harshly, sort of as if he resents my having broken out of the mold he had set for me—the mold labeled "Feikema is a wastrel and will never make anything of himself." I thought at first it was my ego smoking that up, but when Maryanna remarked on it, then I knew that my "feel" about it was right. He spent a lot of the visit doing two things: showing that his Ma was wrong thinking that Feikema and Huizenga had perverted him, showing that he thought my last book pretty lousy (because Elof was a no-good). (Even brought a review to back up his point.) He didn't know what to make of my remark that I sort of agreed *The Chokecherry Tree* wasn't good. Can't you come?

Yours
Fred

To Maxwell Geismar

[Minneapolis, Minnesota]
June 9, 1949

Dear Max:

Just getting out from under a lot of work and fatigue. This morning I feel as though six diseases had their way with me last night. I think it's mainly that after a week of resting the real fatigue is at last smoking up out of my bones. I finished a readable draft of *The Brother* just before Decoration Day and have since written a short story and a batch of correspondence. Once I got going back there in January on the second volume of the trilogy, I drove and drove, some days light and some days hard, until I had it down. And now, after a two-week vacation in the Rockies (and possibly a few extra days in Aspen for the Goethe thing) I plan to polish it in easy stages until next Christmas. If I can get volume three next year in as good a shape as I got two, I've at last got something that will save you and Brooks and others from wincing when my name is mentioned.

You should be getting a copy of *The Primitive* any day this summer. Bound copies have come here. And the book has been scheduled for September.

To buttress the income I've accepted a position as Writer-in-Residence at Macalester College, St. Paul. It involves one semester of teaching a two-hour a week advanced writing seminar. I can run it anyway I want and probably will have only eight to a dozen students. Anything more and it would rob me too much of my work. In any case, I am still free during my first draft writing days, from January to June.

Do you see Uncle Van Wyck Brooks much? If so, give him our affection, the dear old man. I am to write him sometime this summer.

Have spent some four days with Dos Passos again. He was here on some magazine article thing concerning the milling industry. I like him. He is a gentleman and does not give himself too quickly. But when he does, he goes all the way. We talked books, life, women, steel industry, food, pains, joys, everything. Got along wonderfully. He wants us to visit him sometime. You know, Max, the best way I can tell I'm around a big mind is the way mine behaves. It suddenly feels free, takes off in any old direction and at any old time. Just goes. With Sinclair Lewis I always felt a strain. And Red Warren. But not John. He's quick to catch your least nuance, and you can let go all sorts of subtleties and be sure he'll get 'em, and you can tell the most embarrassing truth and be sure he'll respect it. He has only one drawback, so far as I can see. He doesn't pause long.

Do write me soon. As ever, your friend,

Fred

To Dr. W. Harry Jellema

[Minneapolis, Minnesota]
July 9, 1949

My dear Professor Jellema:

I don't know just what you're going to make out of a dedication from a fellow who was never an A student in your classes, who was primarily a poet and not a philosopher, and who, despite C pluses and B minuses, felt he got more from your classes than he did from those classes in which he got A's.[1]

1. FM received only one A in college, in art.

But that is just what I am doing, dedicating the first volume of a projected trilogy to you and to a mutual friend of ours (who took, for me, the modern human form of Helen Reitsema). And I do hope that it will not get you into trouble with touchy though well-meaning people there at Calvin.

In all my many various wanderings, I never forgot you. I may have forgotten your teachings but never your example, never your manner, never your air and attitude toward life and ideas and mental riches. I don't know if you know this or not, but you were our hero. The moment one found himself amongst better-than-average brains at Calvin, one heard the name of Jellema mentioned as if he were a god, a real and reasonable god.

As you go through the book, you will recognize, here and there, the traits of old friends. In a couple of cases, I modeled characters pretty closely after the real thing, much as Tolstoi did with immediate members of his family. I have also created, almost out of thin air (I say almost, since in the case of Mr. Menfrid I think I created what I think should have been and might have been my real father), various people and occasions. I have also moved incidents from other denominational colleges (Hamline, Macalester, St. Olaf, Hope, Augustana, Nettleton Commercial College, etc.) I have also purposely neglected stressing the Dutch or Holland aspect of Zion. (Or, Grand Rapids.) I did so because it is not important which Old-Country-Americans one writes about. I did talk about the Frisians, since I am one, and since I feel too they have been neglected by history, and since also they are a part of the Anglo-Saxon-American stream.

The trilogy tries to show that Creative Mind is larger than the things it creates, larger than Wodanism, Christianity, Hinduism, Brahminism, Marxianity, Scientism, etc. It also tries to show that that fact is both a good and a terrible danger, that perhaps, in the end, it is better that some sort of elastic system of thought or elastic way of life is best for the creature (the only creature which has it) with Creative Mind. The trilogy has a theme, I feel, that allows me to exploit many sorts of attacks on various troubles and advantages of our society, attacks (or provings) on labor unions, Communism, religion, sex, art, music, marriage, etc. I realize it is an ambitious thing, but my motto has always been, the more ambitious the better, the bigger the throw of imagination the better.

I hope you will not be angry with me for the dedication. I hope you do not get into trouble with it. In any case, so far as I am concerned, please remember that for me you have been one of the *good* Christians I have known.

> With love and respect,
> your stumbling student,
> Fred Feikema

P.S. The book will be coming your way sometime next week or the week after and I am mailing it to the college.

To Fred H. Baker
The *Grand Rapids Press*

[Minneapolis, Minnesota]
August 4, 1949

Dear Mr. Baker:

I'm sending this letter in care of Doubleday who, I hope, will send you book, pix, biography, et cetera.

One of the last things I want to do is hurt Professor Jellema. He was to me an inspiration in college. I got below-average marks from him. I wasn't particularly inclined toward philosophy, which he taught, and I don't think he thought much of me as a student. But it was his uncompromising sense of honesty, his great sense of debt to God and to society, his endless searching for a clearer understanding of God—all these—that led me to dedicate the book to him in part. He intended that such honesty should lead to a Christian way of life, in particular, the Dutch Christian Reformed way of life. Oddly enough, in emulating his honesty and his searching, it led me away from it. If there is any blame, it lies not on him but on myself. Or rather, to my type of thinking. History shows that ways of thinking, or processes of thinking, are always larger than the things thought about. Since I have left college I have learned there are all sorts of faiths on earth, Christianity, Socialism, Communism, Capitalism, Brahmanism, Mohammedanism, etc. They are all instances of the human brain asearch for a haven, asearch for the truth, and though each of these is at first very appealing and convincing, in the end they all fail. (It just happens that this is the subject of the trilogy, of which *The Primitive* is the first book.) It is an old story, that of Jellema the teacher and Feikema the student—he was a Hegel using dialectics to point to heaven and I was a disciple of Marx coming along using the same dialectic to point to earth. And I hope that the religious folk there at Grand Rapids understand that. They are inclined, at times, to be a bit touchy and proud (no doubt with reason) but they should also be inclined to be a bit understanding and gentle. The few times that I have felt a headlong impulse to embrace atheism I have found myself confronted by the image of Jellema the Christian.

The other part of the dedication was meant, mostly, to celebrate the fact that all young lads have ideal loves. It is closely associated with poetry and hope of life; it is the dream of youth. I don't want it to point at any one young lady in particular, but at the idea that young men have such young ladies.

As for Grand Rapids being Zion, your guess is as good as mine. I did not mean to point at Grand Rapids particularly, nor at Calvin College, say, but at the denominational college town generally. (Denominational colleges are quite distinct from universities. I wouldn't want to put one above the other since I feel that competition between the two is of benefit to the body politic.) I did use certain street scenes from Grand Rapids, but I also used them from other denominational college towns. As for the characters, well, there I tried with all my might to be as original as possible, there I tried to write a work of art and not a sociological report.

The Primitive does not point at any one religion, but to Christianity and faith generally. The second volume of the trilogy is going to point a finger at social-progress faiths. The third volume . . . who knows, except that I'll probably write that the problem is unsolvable in human terms. (At least so a scientist will admit in a church.) You can quote this letter but please make the tone of your story friendly because that's the way I feel toward Grand Rapids. And send both Doubleday and me copies of the story.

Sincerely,
Fred

To the Honorable Hubert H. Humphrey

[Minneapolis, Minnesota]
9-20-49

Dear Hubert:

It was very nice to find your letter at the Macalester College office as a sort of welcome. I have often thought of the times when I used to visit you up in your office when you were a teacher there.

I want to thank you for your kind attention. And by all means, when you do come home on vacation call me at SO8082 and I'll drive in and meet you somewhere as you suggest.

I would also like to call your attention to what seems to me a sad story of people wanting to live in our democracy. Elmer Kooiman brought me the story.[1] Elmer and I went to Calvin College back in the early thirties and we have kept contact ever since. Elmer has a business in Edgerton, Minnesota, and during the war he was connected with the OPA. Elmer would not lightly enter into this case unless he thought it had merit.

Could you take a little time and have a look at this and see if this could be brought to the attention of the Attorney General or the State Department? Perhaps the technical restriction which blocks Franz Gunnink's entry into this country can be waived, for it seems to me this man has committed a political misdemeanor and not a civil crime, and at a time when the whole world was in an uproar. Under similar circumstances I wonder what our actions would be.

This whole thing hits me where it hurts. I know these Dutch folk, and can feel it out as an issue worthy of your attention.

Very sincerely,
your friend,
Feike Feikema

1. Relating to the rescue of a Dutch Jew, a banker, and Humphrey's intercession on behalf of the rescuer, Franz Gunnink.

To David Cornel De Jong

[Minneapolis, Minnesota]
October 27, 1949

1. *Old Haven.*

Dear Dave,

Certainly by this time you'll be home from the Old Country. So I'll try hit you with a note. I've also just finished your book[1] and like it very much; the style is silken smooth and cuts in exactly and efficiently and the contents are surprising and, to me, eminently satisfying. I think you've put down the truth of that first pulsing time of young malehood, it could go either way in some instances, and I think too that you correctly paint what happens when a lot of old women, of various sorts, from the wonderful to the awful, stir up the young bloods. I liked every word of it, and since I've noticed that the *Chicago Sun & Times*, for whom I occasionally write reviews, has not touched it I've written a short notice and sent it in. It'll probably appear in their Christmas edition. (I got the book from Doubleday as a complimentary copy: so you get mine that way too.) I've been very busy the past month. Spent some time in

Omaha, Chicago, Sioux Falls, in an attempt to push the book and
to meet some of the writers living around. Everywhere I went they
were almost out of books but very cautious about buying any more.
So Doubleday, naturally, is going to be cautious too, since they
took quite a licking on *The Chokecherry Tree*. Had a most curious
but expected reaction at Calvin. First the local paper wanted me
to "admit" that "Christian was Calvin and Zion was Grand
Rapids," and then they wanted me to tell them about the dedica-
tions and so on. Then came a request from one of the students, a
nephew of Jellema, for information about the book (he can't understand why I should pick on the "christian poet Iliot"). Then later
I get hold of the *Chimes* review. He little understood that in the
days when you and I went to school Iliot was considered a bad
worldly poet. (Zylstra has changed this all; he thinks Iliot is a good
Christian.) Oddly enough, in those days I thought a lot of Iliot;
have lately come to the conclusion that he is pretty pale for my
money, that he is really the poet for those who are born in a library,
are raised in a library, and who die in a library—they crap eat forni-
cate the whole works inside walls. For those who are emaciated
and lifeless he is probably the perfect poet, just as Henry James is
the great novelist for the lifeless critics. Anyway that's what I feel
and t'hell with world opinion for the moment. (I did make one
mistake in the book, and I corrected it in the second edition: to play
on the names of authors I really like.) While in Frinjet[2] did you
meet any Feikemas? No doubt they were craphouse cleaners, since
I always suspect the grandiose stories the relatives like to spin here
in America about their origins. (Sometimes I'm guilty of it too.)
I've got the next section of the trilogy about done and hope to get
the other finished by this time next year. This whole project has
been hanging in my head for some thirteen years and if I don't get
rid of it soon will have an awful headache. It takes something to
keep such a thing hanging alive up there. Say, does Providence have
a reviewer whose initials are W. T.S.? What's his paper? I got a review with initials but no date and no name of the paper on it. Isn't
the atomic bomb business a mess? God knows what's next. I've
taken to sitting on the sidelines, saying they've got to win my vote
from here on in. Someone of us has got to holler out what he sees
and feels. Please do write sometime, Dave, and as soon as this
damned trilogy is done I intend to lay by a year and visit real
friends, which includes you and your wife. We are expecting
another child in December, our second, though my dear wife is not

2. Frjentsjer, in West Friesland.

too enthusiastic. Let's hope it's little Feike the rascal at last. Our first, Freya, turned out swell.

Affectionately,
Fred

To Mrs. E. Wolthuis[1]

Mrs. E. Wolthuis, 1030 Sherman Street, S.W., Grand Rapids, Michigan

[Minneapolis, Minnesota]
Thanksgiving Day, 1949

1. Formerly Jessie Zylstra.

Dear Jessie:

Of course I remember you. And very well. For one thing, as a member of my graduating class at Doon Christian School, and for another, as a Frisian.

Yes, I'm married, have one child, am expecting another in a few weeks. We live out in the country, on ten acres, though to be sure we have most of the city's advantages such as electricity, indoor bathrooms, and so on. We have a large garden, an orchard, and a pasture which we either rent out or pasture with grassers for our own locker.

About my writing, and living. Well, I look at that this way. 1) this is a democracy, and you are as free to pursue your religion and way of life as I am mine, 2) I can't use your conscience to live by nor you mine, 3) I wouldn't want to do wrong anymore than you and feel, like you, that I am on the right path, 4) I wouldn't want to be a hypocrite either, 5) I wouldn't want to get to heaven as a narrow-minded person since there will be many kinds of people there all the way from Chink to Arab to Indian to American to Dutch to German to Swede to Russian, 6) I don't write for children nor for adolescents but adults (we don't let children marry, nor do we let even the average man look into the private writings of scientists or doctors, and writers are as important as scientists, probably more so if you look at history), 7) I don't push my books on any one, 8) I try to write real history, as people live it, including all the things they say, (we go to Chaucer today to see how people lived in his day and not to Gower: Chaucer put a sample of everything in his things while Gower wrote elevatingly), 9) I have no objection to Sunday School writing or no objection to saving souls—it's that that doesn't appeal to me—let him who likes it go into it, 10) and finally I feel I have heard The Call to write what I write every bit as strongly as any minister has heard The Call to preach salvation.

If some of these things trouble you, bring them up to your husband. He's a scientist and he's had some exposure to an objective manner of thinking.

Sincerely,
Feike Feikema

To Malcolm Cowley:

[Minneapolis, Minnesota]
November 30, 1949

Dear Mr. Cowley:

I am writing this short note to tell you what a favor you have done me in getting up the *Portable Faulkner*. I had tried him a couple of times, but couldn't quite get in stride with him. I was probably a little like the women who fear pregnancy pains and then actually get them. I had been taught to think of him as incomprehensible, as difficult, and I found him difficult.

However, Warren's (Red) review of your portable made me buy it and this past summer I got into it.[1] And once into it I couldn't let go. Everything opened up for me, thanks to your careful selection, and manner of introduction. Since then I've read *Intruder in the Dust* and *Knights Gambit*. And shortly I shall get into his early novels.

He plays the great organ, with three or four keyboards, and he knows how to play all the stops. Or, to switch metaphors, he is a great jockey riding a greater horse. On occasion the horse gets out of hand a little, but he manages to keep it on the track and come in first. (Hemingway, by the way, is also a great jockey but he's riding a second-rate horse.) The main thing about Faulkner is the great droning sweeping music, with off to one side or the other little trills and runs and sparkling phrasings and twinklings of humor. I've always been more moved by a musical phrase than by a literary one, but here for the first time in Faulkner I almost found the situation reversed.

Well, anyway, I thought maybe you'd like to know what you did for a young writer.

Sincerely,
F.F.
Feike Feikema

P.S. I often see Red Warren, at his parties or at mine, or at lunch with other young writers in the neighborhood.

1. Warren also suggested I buy the book [FM's note].

P.P.S. Just for the heck of it I'm throwing in a clipping so as to give you a bit of a picture of this correspondent. You can throw it away when through.

P.P.P.S. I also know that I can't be reading Faulkner when I'm writing. Besides, I don't particularly want to find myself imitating him. My mind and life are quite different from his.

1950

Much of Manfred's attention in 1950 is on the trilogy and his financial troubles. Yet the letters are rich in literary theory. He completes the third volume, The Giant, *as well as his postscript defining the rume. He remains committed to absolute realism and writes of world peace.*

To Virgil Scott

[Minneapolis, Minnesota]
January 4, 1950

Dear Scotty and all,

It's early morning and I've just finished feeding Marya and changing her diapers (God, what a wad she deposited this a.m.!) and finished having breakfast and have come out here in a bitter cold morning and hearing on the radio that the cold weather is heading your way I decided that I would add to your bad luck by sending you a letter from the North too.

Marya is a very healthy little sucking-machine. When she isn't sleeping her one thought is to suck milk. She's geared for eating to a fare-thee-well. She's a little red-headed tyke like Freya, about as long, with lashes and brows a little paler than Freya's. Momma and Gramomma say she is another "little Poppa." She is very healthy, very vigorous, very hearty, and has already shaken a cold in a matter of hours. I can see it coming. When I'm a doddering 54, wondering if I have a few shots left in the old magazine, they're going to be rapacious she-hounds, tearing up the neighborhood and calling me deadbeat. I can see it coming. And I, of course, after a round of weak curses, will retire to philosophy.

Maryanna too is in fine shape. She had little trouble, a matter of but two hours in labor, and has pitched right in with the work. Gramma gave her one of those housecleaning machines that do everything including picking the housekeeper's nose and that has made it easier for her. (Maryanna just had novocaine.)

Somehow or other my last letter gave you a wrong lead. You
write that you do not agree with me that the James cult is dangerous. I can't recall having used the word dangerous, but I do recall having used the word deadly. It is my fault, of course, because I
meant deadening. They are deadening. Certainly they are not dangerous. They have no following to make them dangerous. And
they'll never get it. Even the Eliot boys are really not dangerous,
nor can they be ever, because you can get the number of Eliot de-
votees in under the thousand figure quite handily. That's why I
really don't give a shit whether they are out to get me or not. I'm
busy doing my work and as I go along I every now and then get
an impulse to spit in the bushes (it's better and more sanitary than
spitting on the public thoroughfare) and if I should happen to hit a
skulker hiding there, fine, so much the better, in the interests of
clearing my throat. You say I have to play the game according to
their rules. Wrong. They're not even in the game. It's my rules.
Moreover, they've been all their lives practising at being rapierists,
while I've been doing various things, including using an ax, and
in battle a swordsman doesn't have a chance against an axman. At
best the rapier leaves a little wound but an ax beheads.

As a matter of fact that little bit of parody has hauled a number
of one-balls up short. Including a few two-ballers. Before the book
was out such Eliot specialists as Unger and O'Connor used to give
me half-sneering greetings at parties I might meet them at, but now
they make a point of coming up to shake hands and so on. Quite
a different air. And O'Connor wants to know how much other poetry I've written. (I told him a whole lot but that I didn't bother
to have it printed, it wasn't worth much.) Best of all, students have
called me about it, and some student by the name of E.V. Griffith
(who is about done with a novel and who has signed a contract
with Little Brown, & Co.) wrote a long dissertation on the book[1]
and its passage[2] in the new *Minnesota Quarterly,* fall issue. He called
it a "murderous parody." So from where I sit the argument is not
altogether weighted in favor of those who think I made a mistake
to spit in the bushes. (There is no substitute for a kick in the balls.)

I sent *The Brother* off November 17 and I've heard about it and
they like it, as you correctly guessed, better than *The Primitive.*
Since that date I've loafed, helped with the baby, read, researched
a bit, brooded on the next one. I'm ready to write it now but I'm
going to wait until February before I start, sort of to let (as you put
it) the old well fill up a little. Also, to get to that point where I can't

1. *The Primitive.*
2. T. S. Eliot spoof.

resist writing it. (That's always the best frame of mind to write it in since then it isn't work.)

I notice that Hemingway really popped through for Algren. He wrote a little paragraph for the January Book Find Club news. Though I note a little air of patronizing. You know, I've come to the conclusion that it's bad to get remarks from older writers. They can't be objective. They can say they like you or they don't like you, yes, but they never make accurate estimates. They're too prejudiced. Besides, maybe Hemingway will die on you, in a literary way, and then where are you? Sunk with him. Best to work it out alone, to be singular. Different. To hell with schools and old pros. (I notice the same sort of thing goes on in baseball.)

It's true that for some guys the slow way of getting out a book is the best. Algren, I find, works very slowly, very painfully, sometimes a line a day. (Which accounts for the somewhat jerky narration in his books.) (But which also accounts for the "arresting" beauty of his metaphors.) He told me last fall he didn't have an idea for the next book. He asked me what my plans were and when I told him I had two more trilogies staked out, plus a duology and a decology, he shook his head and wished he could look ahead like that. I told him that I got most of those ideas while sick in the San, that I probably wouldn't get another one after they were off the boards, that, moreover, there is a danger in having an idea so definite in mind, because you might follow the idea and not truth, fictive truth. We agreed, and agreed also in the idea "Each man to his taste and inclination. There are no rules for creation." Algren is a nice fellow, inclined to crab a little with a twinkle in his eye. This air leads to all sorts of interesting conversational bits. (One more bit. I've been reading Faulkner some more and have to agree with you and Red Warren that he is our current best. I never thought I'd get around to agreeing with you but I have. I've also worked at Eliot again but he gets even worse in my head.)

Best,
Fred

To Helen Reitsema Vander Meer

[Minneapolis, Minnesota]
January 7, 1950

Dear Helen:

Yesterday I was 38. That makes it twenty years ago that I first met you. How much has happened since! And how little I dreamed

in those days that I would eventually be a man who has by now
written five published books and a sixth in manuscript and accepted
by the publisher! (Besides all the unpublished MSS in the files.)
And how little I dreamed that I would have by this time plans for
two more trilogies, a decology, and a duology! A regular headful.
It was awfully good to hear from you because I didn't know how
you would react to *The Primitive*. People have the damnedest reactions to finding a part of themselves in type; people just don't have
the wisdom to understand that no one can ever get another down
accurately, and that at best (or worst) he takes only what he needs
to get something said. (I discover that I'm already, in outline, in
two books. But it doesn't perturb me. Anything for the cause of letters.) As a matter of fact, consider what happened between me and
Jellema. I sent him a long fine letter plus a copy of the book. Never
an answer or an acknowledgment. As one man to another he
should have answered it. That's Christian, and human, and, in this
country, democratic. Is he afraid? Has he lost his teeth? (Or are
there some subtle private reasons that I can never know?) Of course
I shall inscribe a book for you. I'm ashamed now that I don't have
one for you. A week from Monday, January 16th, I'm going in and
I hope to find a first edition. A word about those future plans. In
three weeks I hope to begin *The Giant* and have it done by next
Christmas. *The Brother* is done and the publisher likes it better than
the first. (You'll probably not like it too well, because poor Thurs
gets himself into scrapes that I never dreamed of in similar circumstances—the more I contemplated living in this modern world
the more Thurs became separate and distinct from Fred Feikema.)
When this trilogy is done, I'll probably have to start writing the
next work, also a trilogy, without any rest. The next works are entitled like this, and you're the first I'm writing to about this, *Sons of
Adam* (I *The Frustrates,* II *The Outlaws,* III *The Pilgrims,*) *A Child
Is Born* (I *The Seed,* II *The Stalk,* III *The Ear*), Wings (I *The Fledg-
ling,* II *The Flight*), Siouxland Saga (*Pa, Ma,* etc., through eight
children, to make up the decology). If I live to get them all done,
why then maybe all that snorting and groaning back there in Calvin, and maybe my Mother's early death, may not have been in
vain. I also plan someday to publish my poetry, which I've always
kept, and some short stories (*Chips From The Chopping Block*[1]). And
then, in old age, I can get out my *Journals & Letters*. So I only need
to live to make living worthwhile. Thank God I got sick back there

1. Later *Apples of Paradise*.

in 1940. It gave me time to sprout all the above ideas. So many modern writers go charging to the publisher the first time they feel a little wiggle in their penmanship fingers. You ask about my reaction to reviews. Well, I'm pleased when they like my things, red-necked when they don't. But I'm saved by this attitude: that when a book leaves my worktable it's as done as it can be according to Feikema. After that, nobody can upset me. I'm sorry now that I let Doubleday scare me about T.S. Eliot, because I had him and those others, Fearless, Spinaway, in straight. I parodied to avoid libel suits, but went too far. In the second edition, all names except Eliot are straight again. Now that it's done the parody is too good to throw away. I tell you, I like those lists I find in Rabelais, Chaucer, Doughty. So, I write the kind of book I like to read myself. And now I must go to chop some wood. For the fireplace. Marya is a very healthy baby, red-haired like Freya, and almost her deadringer. Maryanna took this labor in stride, only two hours and I couldn't get out of my class fast enough at Macalester. Someday I hope for a little boy, a little Freddie, and of course if I could have quint boys, wonderful—a basketball team I could train. All the best to you and yours, and hello to M. and H.[2]

2. Mildred and Henry Zylstra.

It Beste,

Fred

To the Reverend Theodore Jansma

[Minneapolis, Minnesota]
January 12, 1950

Dear Ted:

I was pleased to get a letter from you the other day. I had not forgotten my visit to your church in Paterson some two years ago, and gave my wife quite a detailed account of it.

I don't know quite how to answer your question. I don't particularly feel unhappy, certainly not any more unhappy than a Reformed member. No civilization or way of life has yet been constructed in which people could walk from birth to death without any pain. What counts, I suppose, is the general frame of mind one has. Fundamentally I am interested in human beings. I like the idea that I am one, and I am glad I had this life instead of nothing, and I am endlessly curious about how others live their lives. I have also noted in passing that there have been all sorts of faiths and ways of life and attitudes, but that the human being persists

and outlives them all. This evidence we find in the Bible, in the
Hindu Scriptures, in the Upanishads, in all literatures. And it seems
to me that that literature which keeps its main eye on the human
being and his rutting and routings is the literature that lives.
Chaucer is alive to-day because he was human and kind and because
he put down people as he found them. John Gower, his contemporary, is pretty much dead. He was a faithful member of the
church, and wrote what the church heads wanted. His stuff was
propaganda, in a way, and of course served a purpose. But not the
purpose of literature. Now I have no objection to uplift writing.
That has its place. But to call that literature is quite another matter.
You say that from your point of view my talent is wasted. Well, to
the extent that I follow after my masters Chaucer, Rabelais, Shakespeare, Faulkner, Melville, Homer, Dante, Goethe, to that extent
is it wasted? If you say yes, you are condemning wholesale quite
a lot of what some people hold dear. (Oddly enough, and with
equal justice in this democracy, I could say that from my point of
view your talent is being wasted too.) Perhaps I'm too scientific
minded. I have an avid interest in What Is. I find I am much happier
when I know as well as I can What Is. I hate lies. I'd rather, if my
wife had stepped out on me, that she told me than that I should
find out later. It would be a shock, but not such a shock as the one
I'd have later in which I'd discover she lied to me. (Hey, I see I forgot to put down a lever on this typewriter. There.) I'm impatient
with literature that portrays people who rarely are natural. I keep
asking, doesn't this guy go to the can ever? Or don't they ever go
to bed? Or change clothes? Etc. I personally always find instruction
in the description of What Is. Certainly a physicist could never trust
a writer who put down things to please ministers, either those of
state or religion. He would blow us up. So he has to put down the
truth because he expects others in his field to do the same. It has
been this attitude that has given you a car, which you use, and modern acoustics in your church, which you use, and modern diet
habits, which you use, and modern postal systems, which you use.
Blind religion has given people nothing more but a certain kind
of numb safety. (You cannot control truth. It is everywhere. And
some look this way, some that way.) I tell you, I write mostly for
educated adults. I don't want high school kids nor the feebleminded to go digging through my books. We don't let our kids
marry either until a certain age. Or read doctor books. Hence, I
have no kick coming if I don't sell fast immediately. I'd rather sell

slowly, endlessly. This doesn't answer your letter, but at the moment it's all I can think of. My very best to you,

> your friend,
> Fred Feikema

To Nelson Algren

[Minneapolis, Minnesota]
January 25, 1950

1. Algren asked to borrow a ball for a week. [FM's note].

Dear Nelson,

The way to grow big is to order yourself a dish of sliced bull's balls[1] for breakfast, a dish of stallion's erector muscles for dinner, and a dish of elephant's balls for supper. Or better yet, and this was my recipe, be naughty and get kicked in the ass every night by the old man before going to bed.

But to get serious, I do thank you for telling Art Shay about me and my little baubles. I'm not sure I'll be along there until summer, unless somebody there thinks I should grace his banquet hall or pummel a rostrum somewhere. I'm about to begin a rough first draft of a book and always like to hammer and saw away until it's done, and that should be sometime in May. After that I can call up such cabinet-making instincts as I have to polish and finish the job at my leisure. But I would like to come very much, because the little I saw of you fellows pleased me much, and I in particular thought I would like to spend a lot of time with you on your haunts and rounds. Emmett [Dedmon] really held a small party, and yet, for my purpose, I like 'em smaller.

Of course, if in the meantime this Shay guy gets ideas he'd like to execute, why, I'd better let myself be available. I have three females to support now, and that's something. A fact almost as powerful as an Algren novel. So you might tell him what I say in this missive.

How did the Author-and-Luncheon (or whatever it was you were in) deal come off? I have now read Jane Ward's *The Professor's Umbrella* and I admire the insight and so but it seemed a bit talky to me. Though that might have been her intent since that's just about all college life is, talk.

I was guthappy to see the stuff in the *Book Find Club News*. Hemingway talks about your two fists, and he had better look out for them himself for reaching down to pat your head. Goddamn him. What I would like is a bull session some night with Ernest, you, and Jack Conroy. I think we might give the old boy a sore ball or two before the night was over. I was pleased, nevertheless, mainly because it sort of vindicated my own feeling about your work. I knew of it in the good old *Anvil* days, and literally forced the local libraries to buy your early books even when they had to pay outrageous prices for them. (Now they tell me they are glad they listened. The bastards, when my judgment might have been better then than now.) My own feeling is that measuring one guy against another is sort of common and silly, that anyone's brilliance is all our brilliance, and that if a Shakespeare lived next door to me I'd be that much the better. A man should have enormous confidence in himself but he should not carry a ruler in his pocket. Better that he should carry his friend's book. Or whatever it is that he offers.

If you should land in Hollywood, and should get near Warner Bros., ask a friend of mine, Ellingwood Kay, why the hell they haven't copped onto my books now when they're cheap-for-sale instead of later when they'll be rare-for-sale.

All the best, or, as the
Frisians have it, It beste,
Fred

[margin] Jan. 25, 7 a.m. 20° below and 10 inches of snow! But my cabin is snug and I work away.

To Eric Sevareid

[Minneapolis, Minnesota]
February 20, 1950

Dear Eric:

We too are a bit apprehensive that Freya and Marya will turn out to old-time Amazons, since Freya, the oldest, at five is already the size of one at seven. Luckily, she also has grown up mentally about as fast and if we're careful we can teach her to accept her giant proportions. When a tall woman is well-shaped she is practically incredibly beautiful and we're hoping that this may happen in part to them both. They're both red heads, both are long-fingered, long-legged like the old man. I suppose it'll be just my luck when a boy comes along that he'll resemble the more stumpy wife. Just when I'm dying to pass along, as any good father should, such knowledges as how to set a straight fence, dig a deep row, seduce the proper amount or number of women before marriage, pitch a fast-ball, and hook a good basket shot. But come what may, monster, giant, or minion, I'll love the little bugger.

I've been writing my guts out in a trilogy to be called *World's Wanderer.* The first volume appeared last fall (*The Primitive*) (it dealt with young manhood and ideals and college life against a Christian-Capitalist background), the second (*The Brother*) has been okayed in New York and is at Book Find (it deals with college graduates looking for work in New York and meeting labor leaders, assisting strikes, meeting Reds, artists, screwed-up New York brights, etc., against a general Marxist-Capitalist background). The third volume, *The Giant,* I'm writing now (it deals with marriage, nuclear scientists, the atom bomb, the war, etc., against a Scientist-Capitalist background). Quite an ambitious stunt. If it succeeds, it'll be a knockout; if it fails, it'll be a loud dud.

I think we're going down that last curve (in this age of curves rather than straight lines) and if we can make it without skidding, we're in as a species. If we don't, we, like the other giants, the dinosaurs, are out of it. Done. It all depends on the driver, and on the patch of ice ahead. It's fellows like you, and other journalists, and not so much the actual leaders, who have the thing in hand. You can make people write letters to McMahon. And knock Harry [Truman] out of his smug Missouri-kind of poker pride. We're not interested in pride right now so much as in a damn fine driver, and I for one am willing to call in a progressive Republican if need be. Just so he can drive. It is possible that our brothers, the Russians, are most at guilt in this situation but by God as a brother we have to act like a real brother to make them act like brothers. One slip and the family may vanish.

I'm for nuclear fission. We can use it. But we can use big human beings too. Write me sometime, and when you come in, let's have a cup of coffee or a drink.

Fred

To Howard Hoving

[Minneapolis, Minnesota]
March 12, 1950

Dear Howie:

When do you have your class on Thursday? What hour? I'm thinking I might make it April 13, since the rest of that week is shot for writing anyway what with a talk on Wednesday night to the Macalester faculty wives. (A talk kills any writing instincts in me for at least two or three days. I lose more damn chapters that way.

The act of talking and the act of writing, are for me at least, two totally different ways of expressing oneself. One is a public attempt to render and to please, the other is a silent and lonely business of trying to catch truth out of oneself.) But it will depend more on two other things: whether we get our car fixed in time (it now has two cylinders with no compression and it takes either a tractor to start it or one person cranking the other on the starter—this winter we've used the bus most of the time), whether we get a good contract on the new book which the publisher has accepted. However, give me the time of your class and then, sometime around the 5th of April, I'll let you know for sure. Oh yes, another factor involved is whether I get a certain section done before the talk April 12, since I'll be climbing toward a sort of climax in mood and hate to interrupt it. (If I'm not done I'll postpone the talk even.) I enjoyed your letter and got quite a kick out of your comments. The money business started a long chain of remembering going, and I came out with this, which I had forgetten: that Uncle Clarence (Eder] sent me 20 bucks in May of '34 for a graduating present, that in March of 1935 I borrowed twenty from you or your dad, that in January of 1936 when I was leaving Grand Rapids for a second time Huizenga loaned me a small sum (exactly what I don't remember), that the twenty dollars in the book, meanwhile, is to be used as part of a tripping of the plot in Volume III in which Thurs discovers his father and that the five bucks Huse gives Thurs is repaid in Volume Two now at the publishers. As Steinbeck says, it is difficult, once a book is done, to redefine what was once fact and what is now fiction. I also got a kick out of your reaction to the book's incidentitis. My worry was when I wrote it that the plot would be too obvious, that the bones of the skeleton would protrude too much. So I used every damn device I could think of to hide it, to make the book seem like life, a sort of aimless drifting though underneath a drifting steadily toward a definite climax. I have a theory that books should not seem too plotted. I like to think that art is the creation of the New Life out of the Old Life (reality). (Aristotle spoke of art as being an imitation of nature. But I don't like the word "imitation" and use the word New Life.) Also, if an author believes reality is an organized whole run by God he'll have organized art; if an author believes that fundamentally reality is chaos, and I incline to that view somewhat of late, then his art will reflect that attitude . . . though it must be organized enough to make communication, which, to the chaotic man, is about the only organization there is. So the best compliment I can hear now is that the books seem to drift a bit in the beginning. As you will note, the book does drive toward a climax in the final third. And each volume will drive a little harder and sooner each time. But I did deliberately use the long rambling wandering section in the first third. The first third of each book is to be a wandering aimlessly (seemingly) until he gets hooked into a situation, or "nexed" into it, in the second section. But toward the end of the second section and especially in the beginning of the third section the seeds of disruption, of breaking up of the placental connection, begin their festering so that by the end of the book he's ejected from the situation. Actually, of course, Thurs never stops wandering; first he does it physically and then he does it spiritually, as witness his remark, at the end of the first [section] The Chancing, page 77, "Here's where my body ends and my mind begins." The design of the tri-pointed attack, "The Chancing," "The Nexing," "The Rending," was the only one I could think of that would get anywhere near to doing the following: give an impression of the vastness of America, of the wandering population of America, of dissimilarity between the three kinds of lives he is to lead (the first in a world with the Christ-mood predominant, the second with the Marx-mood predominant (mostly), the third with the Scire-mood predominant, Scire being science), of the triple heritage we have of Christianity, socialism, and scientific attitude, etc. I don't pretend my attack will be complete, but it will suggest these phases. What, of course, I'm most interested in is the human being. If I have any religion at all it is that I don't mind being a human being, and that I like other human beings, and that I think that to himself he is all important, that only knowledge that is man's subjectively has much value with the rest interesting but mostly guesswork. I found it quite a problem to tackle college life, and considered various devices, and finally decided on the roll of time, the chronological one. That is the way it hits you when in college, a little basketball, a little sleep, a little eating, a little classwork, a little loving, a little crying, a little basketball, a little sleep, etc., around and around. I didn't particularly have Calvinism in mind and didn't particularly want to attack it point for point, but to suggest the mood of Christianity and how the artistic or the free-wheeling creative mind is not at home in it, no more than it is in any other kind of society. It is a peculiar irony, to me at least, that the very thing that makes man man is usually at war with all the rest of him. The creative mind of the scientist, the artist, the musician, the writer (basically creation is all the same fire, it only comes out of a different hole) has always been held in suspicion by the rest of man, and even by part of the artist himself. Mankind will take his benefits, his contributions, but wants nothing of him personally, certainly not the glow of his presence. And in a certain sense I can see where mankind is acting wisely, because I am suspicious of brains for brains' sake myself. Tradition and instincts are wiser. Complicated, that's what it is. So, yes, I thought it a compliment to be accused of incidentitis. By the way, you met Thurs's father in the book. Did you recognize him? And yes, you're going to have a lot of fun with the next book, though I warn you that you will not meet a single person or echo of a person that you and I both knew in Jersey. You never did know any of the people at U.S. Rubber where I worked (Eddie excepted and I never knew him at work), never did meet the Greenwich Village people I met, nor the little group of rich gals I ran into in one of my wanderings and of my adventures with them and of how one of the gals followed me all the way down to Washington in 1936, never did meet the unioneers I knew there. To make sure that there is little hint of the Hollander in the next book I never mentioned them as persons (once or twice the word occurs in a list of peoples). I had to move all sorts of models out of Minneapolis to the East, particularly those that Thurs knew from '37 to '39 since I was there myself but two weeks and that to see the World's Fair in '39. The landlady, Mrs. Babbas, was moved bodily to the spot of your house on Wallington along with her own house and married son and hired girl (in the book she is Mrs. Babbas' daughter), etc. And yes, there is no doubt that my quiet watching of you and hearing of you at the organ and piano, along with Warren Arnold, and along with my own private dream that I should have been a musician, go to make up Thurs. Thurs is already in my mind a separate man. I have dreamt about him, seen him as clearly as have I seen my own image in a mirror. He and I have the same problems, yes, but he and I are now different men. And of course I borrow from my life whenever I run stuck for ideas, since that is a lot hotter in my mind than is an intellectual abstracting or constructing. Well, your letter has stirred up quite a letter in return, though I do know that one's friends are the last to be good judges or condemners of one's work. What counts is what total strangers say. If they like it, if they're able to relive it, then perhaps one has hit common chords. The only trouble is, when does one hit those? Each of us makes a bold guess, and then plays, and hopes. Though I do think that the best chance of hitting such chords comes when one speaks from the heart as much as one can despite the possibility of hurt to others.

Yours,
Fred

To Virgil Scott

[Minneapolis, Minnesota]
November 15, 1950

Dear Scotty:

Your letter has just come and before I go into lunch and before I forget my first reactions to your letter, I think I'll quick write a little.

I'd like to clear up some misapprehensions on *Bowl* and *Year* for one thing. Some others have felt that those two were auto-biographical and this is as good a time as any to go on record that they are not.

Bowl: I have never lived in South Dakota, except for a few months of city life in Sioux Falls. I never lived in Dust Bowl times. I was in high school and college at the time, and during high school days lived in an area that was on the edge of it. I saw it in between school times. I did not stay at any farm house like Pa Thor's. I never met a girl like Kirsten. I never worked a day in South Dakota.[1] I never looked for work in the Black Hills, nor in Wyoming, nor in Montana. I never built a dam against water. But I did hitch-hike through it in '34 as a college student flushed with a diploma and a nice suit and eight bucks in my pocket to visit a friend in Belgrade, Montana, a friend named Don Houseman. I did meet a young bro-ken hobo for a few hours one night and it is on my memory of him that I built the story. I did see the dust drifts in '34, and I did see the hungry people, and I did see dead cattle. But I never lived it.

Year: I have never lived in a town called Starum or in a town located where Starum is set. There never was a Starum. The spot I set it in was a dead town and a filling station by the time I saw it. I never lived near the Hills of the Lord. I am not Pier. Pier is a combination of my father and my uncles and my neighbors, those among them who have great vigor and latent but un-developed brains and who behave like all male men have behaved in mankind's history. Teo is not me. I had five brothers and loved them and lived with them and never had the sense of being a single son. Teo is in part my brothers, and in part the boy with brains who

1. As a farmhand.

feels unused in the country, and to the extent that I have felt that I am in him. Nertha is not my mother. Nertha was a finely-strung not too strong female. My mother was a great rock of a woman, who died of heart failure and possibly cancer. My mother thoroughly and completely dominated my father.[2] I myself happened to dislike farming as a lad. I came to love the country *after* I had lived in the Twin Cities for a while, and went back to it, and studied it, and dug out all sorts of facts from my relatives and what little lay in my memory, and then wrote it and invested it with all the power of my imagination. (My trouble is I've got such an ungodly imagination I write about unseen things as if I've seen them. I was always called the Great Liar at home, once having described a snake so vividly I had a posse out for it.) Alde Romke, Teo's grandpa, was based on an uncle of mine. My own grampa Feike was another man entirely. My own father was highly religious; Pier was belligerently against it. I never fell from the barn, or fell into a manure pile, nor saw a coyote-rabbit hunt, nor a "penny sale," nor knew a county agent, nor got lost in a snowstorm with a heifer, nor had a neighbor like Kaia, nor knew a Blacktail, nor had a mother who had miscarriages, etc. Nor did my father end his farming broke; he wound up with some money.

But *Boy Almighty* and *World's Wanderer* are autobiographical. The only two. I've thought about a third for some day, but that'll be a long while from now. And I don't call them autobiographical novels. I call them rumes. Which is something else, and which I explain in my "Postscript." As to the question which is best, I don't know. I like trying both methods. The one helps me write the other. I learn from both attacks. There are many fine minds (see the quotes that will be given in the Postscript in *The Giant*) who like auto-writing the best, minds all the way from Gide to Thoreau to Maugham to Fitzgerald, and there are many fine minds who like objective novel writing the best (see also the quotes). In the case of Thurs, I don't consider him myself. I consider him a myth that grew out of my size and part of my life. Which is another matter. Which is precisely what a rume is, distinguished from a diary or a case history. (Also see the "Postscript" in this connection.)

But you are right to suggest that the big book is ahead yet, is always ahead. The moment you lose that little trick attitude in the head, you're done. Except, of course, that I haven't done too bad up to now. As good as anyone living in America. But the best is yet ahead. Always. And what is done, is still far short of what could

2. With her very kind demeanor [FM's note].

have been done. But no shorter than what has been done by some-one else.

You say it is tougher to write the objective. I find it is not. I find the *Bowls* and the *Years* and *The Chokecherry Trees* easiest to write. It takes more guts to write *W's. Ws,*[3] more insight; it takes more brains to look coldly on one's self than it does to view another. It takes bigness to laugh at oneself, to project oneself in such a man-ner that it is both serious and warmly ironic. And if I fall short with my rumes, it'll be not because the idea of the rume is wrong, but that I didn't quite have the brains and the bigness. Which, of course, I'm assuming I have . . . until we're done with it. When we'll have another look sometime. Besides, I'm probably the very first writer to deliberately set out to write a rume, to make a myth of a certain aspect of myself and to write about it. And the "first" guy usually doesn't do too well, as literary history shows. Except that I'm going to try anyway. Except that also I won't wail too much if I fall hopelessly short of the goal.

I have observed this much. And let's get it out in type right now. And that is that those who've not led a very interesting life, either outwardly or inwardly, are usually contemptuous of the rume-maker and his goals. The reason why critics are critics is because they didn't have it in them to become creators (that is, original cre-ators, since criticizing is a form of creation, though a secondary one). Or else, they lived such lives that they are ashamed of them and don't have the guts to write about it. And for that reason alone, I revere Gide, cocksucker that he was. He lived an odd and ostraciz-able life but yet had the guts to put it down on that sheet of paper. The question is, beyond art and style and finesse and taste, what are we? men with spines? or men without them?
Later in the day:

In so far as you review my work, that's another matter. What counts is what you really feel, not what I want. Because in the long run, if there is any value in what I do or what you do, either as critic or as writer, it is to what extent you told what you really felt. So I try to take with good grace almost anything said of me. And after a while will get to the point where I can ignore it. I have lately been reading Conrad, and have noted that one of his best is a rume, *Heart of Darkness*, and is marvelous in my eyes. I've also been read-ing Dickens and find him wordy, often thin, a poseur, very haphaz-ard—though he saw a lot and after 1000's of words finally said a little. Thackeray is much better. I'm also reading Ken Burke and he

3. World's Wanderers.

really says it for me as critic and thinker. I soon hope to get at *Don Quixote* and Faulkner's shorts (who is another rumemaker). Your theory about Butch intrigues me since I've always felt the Cubs made a mistake not to develop McLish as a two-armed pitcher (he's with Los Angeles now). With a good brain behind two good arms you could pitch to anybody. I am quite anxious to be getting at my next work, *Sons of Adam* (novel!), though I've much research to do. Had a long visit with Nelson Algren two weeks ago. No wonder he doesn't write more. He farts away his time writing movie scripts and *Holiday* magazine pieces and local newspaper stuff for no writing reason that I can see. I told him so too. There must be WORKS.

Write me, afft'ly,
Fred

To [Recipient unknown]

[Minneapolis, Minnesota]
[ca. November 15, 1950]

[Missing material]
and will send it off next week. So while we're in a . . . mood, let's get a few things off the chest about the rume, *World's Wanderer*. (You cannot take *The Primitive* or *The Brother* or *The Giant* as separate books. If you do they are only ninths, not thirds of an idea. Because everything has a place in the work. It's all tied together like an infinite infinite Chinese puzzle. There's not a word too much; not a word too little. I defy anyone to knock out a paragraph. I'll have at least three reasons up to a dozen why it should be in.) Now, First, there are many discrepancies between my life and Thurs's. I am not an orphan. I knew my father and mother. Thurs was, and spent his whole life being on the alert as to who they might be. This was done to represent mankind's continual interest in mankind's origin, witness his anthropology, etc. I never knew a Mrs. Brothers. Thurs did. Though I did know many tough Christian women. Live next to two right now, in fact. I went to Calvin College. Thurs goes to Christian College, a college that could be Calvinistic, or Lutheran, or Catholic, or Methodist, etc. (witness the many letters I've gotten from various denominational alumni who think I've written about their college). I did that deliberately because I wanted to point up as background a Christian-mood world. I knew Communist Party members, Lovestonites, Troskyites, etc., Thurs knew Marxists, which is a larger concept. I wanted, again, to use

Marxist-mood living for background as part of my theory that it is humankind that is eternal, if there is anything eternal, and not the theory or creed or religion that passes through humankind like waves go through the sea and leave the sea the same. I never knew but one Commy in New York. I myself left New York for good in 1936; Thurs leaves it in 1939. (I was there but six or seven months altogether in '35 and '36.) I never knew a Mrs. Babbas in the East. I peed over Roosevelt's evergreen tree in Hyde Park; Thurs pees over Chief Pecuspolis's tree. I did work in a rubber factory, but I never knew a Hammer family, or any part of the hierarchy such as I describe it. Didn't know a Palgrave there at all. I didn't meet any Rubber Worker organizers; had to dig that all up. There was no union at all at U.S. Rubber where I worked. (Though one came in later.) I never knew a Beulah Hammer, or a Rhoda Hammer, though I've met their type on occasion. I never visited a rich man's home in the East. I never lived on Manhattan Island, except for one night or weekend stays with friends. I never knew Cockeye Cutt. I never knew a Pece Roche there. Never in the world ever saw Miss Sabine in real life. Though I've met her kind. Never was on a strike there. Never knew a Rex there. Though I've met his type. Never went to any Commy meetings there; though I did to a few by invitation in the Twin Cities. I never studied art formally; though I did try learning it by myself. I never left New York City hating it. I left it still hating the West. Which I've come to love since, and see since, while I've come to despise the East. I never boxed in New York. Though I once did in Minnesota. I never was pinched by a motorcycle cop. I know my exact height; the reader never learns Thurs's exact height. And so on and on. What counts is that I am confessing my emotions, my general emotions in these times, in my rumes, not my individual sins. And so too now with *The Giant*. Eva is not my wife. Eva was created out of materials that came in part from a Lucie Lawson I knew, a Louise Thomas I knew, and in part from my wife whenever it would fit. I never knew a Helen Bernard. But, in looking at the evil and the good in my heart, and looking at the evil and the good in other hearts, yea, in your heart, I saw how Helen Bernards can come into married men's lives. As she probably has almost come into mine in various forms. Thurs finds his father and mother. I've known mine all along, though I've been interested in finding a sort of spiritual father. I don't create symphonies like he does. Nor compose for the Mpls Symphony Orchestra, like he does for the Cities Symphony Orchestra. I've known a half dozen scientists, but no particular Bruce Farrewell, atomic scientist. (I had to do a lot of sleuthing in Chicago for his life.) When I bring Thurs out here on the bluff, he finds the greathouse next door boarded up. For a reason. It has not been boarded up for me in real life. A Nancy never lived next door to us; though I've lived next door to her in real life. I never had twins; Thurs did. And finally, I never died in an accident; though I may, and mankind may. Now, goddam it, if that's case history, you can stick it up your ass, word for word, crosswise. I happen to think that's rumemaking.

Affectionately,
Feike

To Meridel Le Sueur

[Minneapolis, Minnesota]
December 20, 1950

Dear Meridel:

I shall answer your letter right away, while the responses are fresh in my mind. I've had a bad cold for about a month now, which I should have been able to shake, but didn't, perhaps due to all the work on my desk and at Macalester College. But this is too appealing to turn down. What has been upsetting to me is to find that, in my first life away from home in Iowa, namely in the Christian world of Michigan, the people whom I thought were warmhearted Christians should flinch when I suggested that I did not like the fanatic Christians. Invariably they identified themselves with the fierce boys. That stunned me. Because I wanted the warmness, the humanness, and did not think the ideology was important, at least not of first importance. Ideology was only useful as a way of getting a thing done, or of being a vehicle. But it was not warmness itself. And now I get letters from people like yourself, people I've always considered the Makepeace folk and not the Blutschwerts (the "bloody swords"). Oddly enough I do not hear from the Prexy Cees and the Blutschwerts. I hear only from the warmhearted ones. My mother believed in love, and my grandfather Feike believed in socialism, yet when I was ready to embrace a faith I found I had to take the tough boys with it, either in Calvinism or in Communism. Later on, when I turned to Science, to Scirism, I found the same dualism. And I backed away. If I could not have the warmhearted faith and the people without the fierce faith and the people, then I felt I should be careful. It was haunting. Because in my own life I had been trying to get away from violence, had been trying to be gentle, to be "the simp," "the infantile gullible" as certain reviewers are calling Thurs. I didn't want to hurt anybody, not even my enemy. I always felt that when a good boy got entangled with a bad boy, two bad boys were fighting. If goodness, or humanity was to triumph, it would have to be by a non-violent method. Perhaps I've been obsessed with it. Because I'm over-big, overstrong, overeager, overpassionate. But in any case I was sore sick of beatings and whippings and arrogance and "totally right" people. It was all that which started me off writing *World's Wanderer* (what you read was World's Wanderer, II) and I felt that if I felt like this I should put it down as a record because it was just possible that my oversensitivity about being big was somehow symbolic, suggestive, of the oversensitivity of big nations, big faiths, big movements. There was also the problem of being an artist, or a creator, or one who had gifts to bring to the swarm. It has hit me again and again that Mind in the human creature or in the human animal is a "world's wanderer." That is why the Christian and the Marxist and the Scirist is so terribly concerned about it. They want to make sure it doesn't run wild, become aberrant, become anti-social, anti-them. But when they control it too closely, it becomes an even worse entity, becomes either a Uriah Heep or a pompous Poet Laureate. So I thought perhaps it would be love, the love of a mother for her brood, the love of a man for his brother, the love of a man for his soil, that would save the Thurses, the artists, would save myself, you, Hemingways, Faulkners, etc. And the Einsteins, the Farrewells (he shows up in my next book), etc. And finally concluded that the real way to express this love was to find the one thing one was fitted for, in Thurs's case, musical composition, and to do it, and to hope that it would prove useful. Thurs caught a glimpse of this in *The Primitive (W's.W.I)* but was afraid when he saw what it might involve, that 51–49 or 49–51 it might be for hurt or for good. So he thought that an outright running out to "love" the people as "a brother" would do it. And of course it did not, as you have all too sadly noted. Thus in the next book, he comes back to the Midlands, to his roots, and does finally get into the music, but since he has not learned how to relate it to true Love, neither he nor Farrewell, and neither he nor all that constellation of intellects [find the happy life].[1] He has to pay the price, he is foredoomed. I have no happy endings in these days. If I knew them I would write them. I realize

1. FM's later addition.

that there must be some organization, and that some will create it, but I feel that those of us who see love and feel love should be on the side of those who are afraid of fanatic organizations, to preserve the human being who believes in being warmhearted. My mother never struck us, never lifted a hand against us, yet she was a most powerful female, and drove fear into us with a single look. She got her way by the sheer power of her love. My dad railed and roared, and we hardly listened when he did. When he tried it Ma's way, we did. So I don't like it that capitalists can tell me how to think, or Christians, or Marxists, or the Scirists. And, in future times, the Cosmics. I don't think myself better than anyone else. It is that I wish everyone my good, if such I have. In the writing game, I understand, there are fierce jealousies. That amazes me. Though, of course, knowing the human animal, it shouldn't. But yet it amazes me. Because personally I'd enjoy living in a society in which there were a dozen Shakespeares, Pavlovs, Tolstoys, Sholokovs, Doughtys, etc. Also, I am by no means done with the warmhearted ones who happened in the thirties to be Marxists. *Those I met in New York disgusted me, many of them.* Though New York people are Babylonites for fair.[2] But I knew many fine ones out here. In a new book I'm planning, to be called *Sons of Adam,* I intend to explore a boy known as Whitestone, reporter, who becomes a Marxist by choice, and who will open to all my respect for the many wonderful progressive folk I knew. And of course, even in *W's W. III,* the section called *The Giant,* you will find that Thurs recants some of his wild sophomorics, calls himself a Christian Marxist Scirist; because he can not call himself anything else having lived when these things were in the ascendant and were almost all-pervasive in society. If I have any faith it is that I like life. I like the seventy years I get. That is my only eternal truth. Faiths and beliefs and ways of living may come and go, may go momentumming through the sea of humanity, but the pleasure of having seventy years of living is the final thing. In other words, the people remain. I shall try to be persuasive about justice. Not necessarily shoot for it, or stab for it, or liquidate for it, or go to war for it. I feel that we have at last come to a time when all people, Americans, as well as Russians, must lay down all guns. All force must be laid aside. Even fists, though that is a harmless form of fighting, really. I was asked to sign a peace pledge once. I said that I would as soon as I was sure both sides had put aside all arms. Otherwise, one or the other might use the peace pledge as a way of winning over the other. It

2. See FM's note at the end of letter.

might be a trick. I want politicians to earn my respect, my vote, my support. I'm not going to chase after them any longer, and I shall teach my children to be wary of them all. And teach all my friends. The animal force that is naturally in us must be diverted from using destructive violence on the human flesh. It must be sublimated.

Funny thing is, I had been planning to write you. To tell you that I am dedicating my first real Minnesota book to you and to Helen Clapesattle. (Women!) You two turned open more doorknobs for me than all the rest. You told me long ago that I could write and that I had love in my heart. Helen talked herself blue in the face getting me two regional writing fellowships when I needed it most. (As she did getting them for you.) As for writing as I have so far, I have written as I felt, trying to offer as honest an opinion as possible. If the people decide that they don't want it, too bad for me. But I feel that for me to be "people" as much as anyone else is "people," I have to live with what I have in my heart and my mind, have to express it. Each person must say how he feels. Otherwise the human swarm will be a swarm of fakers, not truelivers.

Fred

2. [This if FM's note to the original letter.] It is probably true that in my endeavour to give the New York world "an unveiling" I also took down the veils of some of the "good ones." Though I was always impressed with the fact that most of the New Yorkers I saw coming through the Midlands, either Red or Black, were snobs, contemptuous of what we have here, even contemptuous of life.

There is also this problem in Thurs's case. And in mine. Neither he nor I were in jobs we liked or were fitted for, and so we were filled with discontent. I think it possible that some are not fitted for union work, or factory work, or politics, just as many are not fitted for music. I find just as many "arrogant" people among the Marxist politicians as I find in decadent artistic circles, people arrogant about the "power game" as contrasted with the "beauty game." To live love, to become the Brother, a man must work with and through the talent he was born with. Or else the very medium he is to use will embitter him before he gets going. Thurs, according to the plan I made, was to be a musician. Until he got back to it he could never get "on the beam." He gets back to it in Vol. III.

If the Reds say that they can create the situation where this will come to pass for most of us, I say, "Show me. I've been given the runaround thrice and have become wary. In the meantime, I'll till the soil, tell the truth, and resist reaction."

Also—what greater love could a male, a man, show than Thurs shows Roche? Who lied on at least four basic counts? And Thurs was willing to stay for more? It is this that causes New York critics to say that I am "naïve" and Thurs a "hulking juvenile" because he was such "an ass" as not to see through Roche. Thurs did hang on because he wanted to believe Roche each time. What greater love is there?

F.F.

To *The New York Times Book Review*

[Minneapolis, Minnesota]
December 21, 1950

Dear Harvey Breit:

I have no objection to someone who does not like my "work." I exercise the same privilege on occasion—I do not particularly care for Tom Wolfe, do not feel particularly en rapport with the Southern writers (I do, however, like Faulkner and have for some years now considered him a sort of Shakespeare of American fiction), and so on, though I respect them all. And many writers I do not like at all. Period. Hence I have to allow your reviewer (*Times Book Review*, December 17, 1950) the right to dislike my work and to allow him welcome to his own feelings.

But I would like it if next fall you folk there got someone to read the entire trilogy, *World's Wanderer*, along with the postscript that accompanies the third volume, *The Giant*. (I'm going to ask my publisher to make sure you get all three volumes.) I don't know who might do the job for you, Warren, Geismar, Van Wyck Brooks, Cowley, Mark Schorer (who has already expressed dislike for my things but who has been explicit about it in a fine scholarly way), Bernard DeVoto, etc. In any case it must be someone catholic in taste, someone interested enough to study the whole work, to see, for example, that this is a study of Love vs. Violence, that Thurs the hero will never come close to forestalling Violence until he has found the vocation he is best fitted for by nature. It is very difficult to exercise Love when one hates the work one is in. The very medium embitters one before one can get going.

I write this because I feel that I have something valuable to say, even something perhaps extraordinary to say. I think I am writing a real work of art because I think I (and not necessarily Thurs) am making the fundamental observation that ideas, faiths, religions, systems of living, may come and go, may go momentumming through the sea of humanity, like waves through the ocean, but the faiths and religions and waves are not the people.

I have been for some twenty years a faithful reader of the New York *Sunday Times* and it was a shock to find the misconception your reviewer had of *The Brother*, the second volume of the trilogy, in the latest *Book Review*. (I don't believe in clipping bureaus, by the way.) The whole point was missed—with no remarks at all about style, composition (*World's Wanderer* was modeled after a three-movement Beethoven symphony, what with Thurs being a Beethoven-like composer in the embryo, with themes and counterthemes coming and going as composition demanded), poetry, narration, etc.

Let us assume, for the moment, that someone had shown that I had failed miserably in executing my plan of showing just what a "world's wanderer" is these days, one who is not only a wanderer in the world but who is possessed by the world and can never escape it—it still would have made me happy to find at the very least that someone had read closely enough to see my intent. I have spent some 38 years (I am 38) brooding about my life and our lives, and at last, after great personal torment, have dared to put all this to paper. Surely the reviewer should have at least been conscientious enough to bother looking around a little after all that effort— and especially so since the reviewer does me the courtesy of saying that earlier I wrote "two strong novels about Midwest farm people and one highly regarded novel about life in a tuberculosis hospital."

Let me take just one paragraph of his to show what I mean by missing the point. He says about Thurs, the hero: "In the end he discovers that communism (and by the way I did not use that word but Marxism, which is a slightly different shot at the problem) has no more to offer than the Christianity which he has already rejected. He comes out with the same confusion he had to begin with, and with no more wisdom." It would seem to me that it would take a considerable wise man to reject a poor man's faith when he was broke and penniless, a time when "communism" is supposed to breed most easily as they say, to see that a particular faith does not solve the problem for either him or humanity, that the problem is larger, that if he is confused he at least knows what he does not want. Thurs does behave like a fool, but he is a good fool, since he would like to take people on face value. It is part of his faith, if he has any, that he must not only seek Love, but he must live Love. The reviewer did not see that "juvenile" Thurs persisted in taking up with the people he did because, once he had put aside his true vocation, music, he had to push his attempt at being the brother-to-man to the limit in an effort to find it. I have seen many brilliant people making fools of themselves over and over again, because they sought the impossible when they tried to reach their goal through a means not meant for them. These poor folk have worn hollows into the couches of confessors all over the country. Thurs will never find Love and live Love as long as he tries expressing himself in a work for which he is not fitted, no matter where he lives.

The reactions of the New Yorkers have been ferocious to *The Brother*. Perhaps because it does not deal too kindly with the New York scene. And perhaps it is just as I suggest—a good many of the most New Yorkish New Yorkers are provincial. Finally, let me say that I did not write *The Brother* as an expert on New York City. But I did write is as an expert on a Young Man Being Disillusioned in New York. That you have to grant me. I know that cold and hot both. And it seems very odd and very interesting to me that while the inferior provincial Midlander is supposed to act like an adult when the superior sophisticated New Yorker makes smart-cracks about him, the New Yorker meanwhile is allowed the privilege of resenting the smartcracks of the Midlander. (And for those who do not understand this sentence and its point, let me recommend the discipline of reading critic-philosopher Kenneth Burke.)

World's wanderer,
Feike Feikema

P.S. Mr. Breit, both my wife and I have enjoyed your little talks or interviews with authors, and we both have been pleased to note that you at least show the catholicity of being able to present clearly many different and opposite kinds of writers, from the real males to the pale males, from the Southerner to the Northerner, from the European to the American, from the motherly women to the masculined women. To a man like you a man dares to write a letter like this.

F.F.

Helen Margaret Reitsema:
"There isn't such a thing as
love for me anymore"
(photo in the Calvin College
Prism, 1936)

My lady,

Since I am not allowed to do nothing more than write a letter, may I here have two dates, Wednesday to the All-School party and Sunday again? I'll try to write a "real" letter. I shall have, by the way, some of your money.

Here's the joke I couldn't think of the other day. Why is a senator called a mugwump sometimes? Because he has his mug on one side of the fence and his wump on the other side!

My pretty one, I am more fond of you than ever. I feel as though I could be happy with things just as they are!

I read some poems, sonnets, in the May issue of Harpers. You must read that. Also the ~~S.S.~~ short story, ~~natural enough~~.

Isn't everything wonderful? Spring is coming! You're here! There is music!

You are always free to turn me down, you know. ~~Let me know~~ to-morrow.

Your, Fred

To Helen, Calvin College,
May 1933

Above: John Huizenga,
"confoundedly ill at ease"
(photo in the Calvin College
Prism, 1936)

Right: Peter De Vries, poet
and sophisticate (photo in
the Calvin College *Prism,*
1931)

Below: John DeBie, recipient
of "looking down" letters
(photo in the Calvin College
Prism, 1934)

Frederick Feikema, twenty-
two, about to graduate from
Calvin College, June 1934

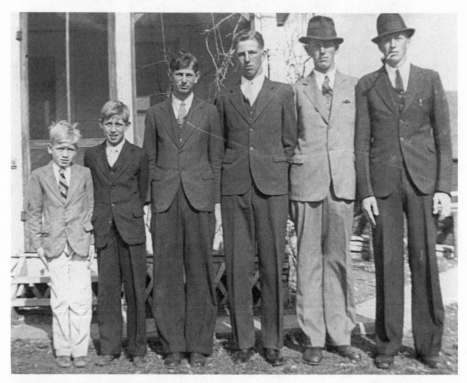

The Feikema boys on the
farm east of Doon, Iowa, fall
of 1934, after morning
church: left to right, Henry
Herman, Abben Clarence,
John Garrett, Floyd, Ed-
ward John, Frederick

Uncle Herman Van Engen
and Fred Feikema outside
Minneapolis when Feikema
was working for the *Journal*,
summer 1938

Above: The first autograph party for *The Golden Bowl,* at the Powers store: Maryanna, Laura Folsy (assistant buyer), Paul Hillestad (publisher, Itasca Press), Harold Kittleson (manager), Frederick, 28 September 1944

Left: At the sanatorium, February 1942, near release; weight, 279 pounds

Writing *Boy Almighty,* at 1814
4th Street, SE, Minneapolis,
1944 (photo by Don Berg)

Below: Frederick Feikema and Eric Sevareid, taken by Pat Knopf (Alfred's son) at the autograph party for Sevareid's *Not So Wild a Dream,* 1946

Above: Herbert Krause (*The Thresher*) and Feikema at the Sioux Falls Book and Stationery party for the bestselling *This Is the Year*, April 1947

Right: The Author of *The Giant* (1951) and six earlier novels at the time of his name change to Frederick Feikema Manfred (1952) (photo by Don Berg)

Manfred at Wrâlda in the
year of *Lord Grizzly*: Maryanna, Frederick VIII, Freya,
and Marya, December 1954

1951

This is a troubled year for Manfred, evidenced by health problems and continuing financial difficulties, the death of Sinclair Lewis, and disappointing reviews and responses from Doubleday. He receives rejections from Guggenheim and Fulbright. While trying to complete a final draft of The Giant, *which is published later in the year, he also begins work on* Sons of Adam *and completes* The Mountain of Myrrh. *The year's letters trace the discovery of and decision to adopt the name "Manfred" as an appropriate Americanized translation of "Feikema" ("Man of Peace"), which, he believes will place him more centrally in the American writing milieu.*

To Maxwell Geismar

[Minneapolis, Minnesota]
January 20, 1951

Dear Maxwell:

Brennan called to tell me about your letter to him and I'm very glad that you like his work. I was beginning to doubt my own judgment since I felt that he had It. He's a wonderful boy and loves writing. He's about the only one around here with whom I can talk Fitzgerald and Faulkner and Lewis and so on along with going hunting and partying with. That political novel[1] he's working on also sounds very good, but he should have another whole year to finish it and hone it into shape. What a wonder it would be to get his other two novels done first.

I've had the flu (the real influenza, that is, with fever, general malaise, and pain behind the eyeballs) which hit me when I was exhausted from finishing the new book and my stint at Macalester for the year, and it swatted me so hard I had extra systoles and a tight chest and a temperature that would not climb, after the fever left, to 98.6. Which left my brain in a cold frozen mass almost. I'm going to take it easy until next Tuesday when I give a talk over the University station on "The Rume As A New Discovery In Fiction," a talk that will be based on the postscript that is to follow the third volume in the *World's Wanderer* trilogy.

Have also been looking through my files of old stories and find that out of about fifty I have only six worth putting in a collection. Two of them are little novelettes. I have two new ideas I'd like to write this spring, one a story and the other a novelette, and so that'll go to make up the book. I'm also paging through my poems

1. A takeoff on Hubert Humphrey as mayor. According to FM, the novel was never published because of pressure from Humphrey's friends.

to see if I can work up a volume of them. What I want to do is to sit back most of this year before I tackle my next book, or work, since it too looks like a trilogy, *Sons of Adam,* a study in brotherhood against packinghouse and Siouxland country and Twin City intellectual backgrounds (University and newspaper and flour milling families). I'm also going to try a new tack, if possible. That is, keep myself as a person out of it as much as possible. Set up the characters and then let them go. They'll all be based on people I've known for years and so I have quite a knowledge of them. I once started this novel years ago, back in the very early forties, and had some 800 pages written. I read it while in bed this week and found but two pages worth saving. But I could see that I was learning to write in it, since when I was done I was affected by it, even though the style and the psychology and the plotting nauseated me and made me wonder why I ever persisted. I destroyed it because I did not want it around to be pulled to when making the entire new start with new characters, scenery, etc. (You know how a guy is, he thinks that the book he's on is the best ever written, which I thought a month ago about *World's Wanderer* . . . but now I'm not sure but what *Sons of Adam* will be. Such are the interesting, and needed, fictions in a writer's mind.) Saw your review of Pound in the N. Rep. today.

And now if you'll only like Willen I shall have passed on the help Red Lewis once gave me. He set me up in N.Y. (I'm to give the memorial address or whatever it is when he is to be buried next week at Sauk Centre.)

Ever,
Fred

To Harry E. Maule[1]

[Minneapolis, Minnesota]
February 2, 1951

1. Sinclair Lewis's editor
at Random House.

Dear Harry E. Maule:

I'm sending along my *only* copies of both the *In Memoriam Address* and the *Informal Portrait,* which you may copy, as you suggest. Be sure to return them because at the moment they really *are* the only copies.

A question of "taste" has come up with Edith Haggard. She said she would represent me on the *In Memoriam* but not on the *Portrait.* She felt that Red would not have liked all the reported dialogue, and she certainly did not like Red's mimicry of Dorothy his wife. About that I can only say, so help me, that is the truth as far as I can remember it. It happens that I have a particularly good ear, and an even better memory, a memory that my wife hates at times, a memory that caused even Red Warren to lift a brow. (Sometime ask him to tell you about all the information I recalled for him for his *All the King's Men,* information about the local governors when I was involved in politics.) *The New Yorker* has even commented on my gift of total recall. So I'll stand behind it. However, if *Holiday,* who has it now, doesn't want it, it'll go to *Atlantic, Harper's,* and the *Saturday Review.* If they say, no, then it goes into my private *Journals,* which I hope to publish someday à la Gide. Edith, to repeat, said she would not represent me, so I'm sending this out on my own.

But I will do something. If you strenuously insist that I should not send it out, I'll give it serious thought. But it is the truth, Harry, and anyone who knew Red would agree that I've caught him, really caught him. Moreover, as Hal Smith wrote last week in the *Review,* we must all pitch in with what we remember of him, even if he would not have liked it. Besides, while I wrote the *In Memoriam* and the *Portrait,* Red was looking over my shoulder and yelling angrily at all times, "Dammit, Fred, while you're at it, tell the truth. No lies, now. And to hell with me and everybody while you're telling it."

And of course, in case I should ever have trouble at Doubleday, I'm going to Random House. I've decided that long ago. I like you, now, and always did Bennett, and Warren who is with you. About the only thing I can suggest now is that, if you want to help me, you can plug for my novel, *This Is the Year,* for reprinting in the Modern Library. It is out of print (15,000 copies gone with the wind). I happen to think it one of the few great books since 1900. Doubleday is still getting orders, though not many. It is a mountain like *Moby Dick,* and like *Moby Dick,* it probably is starting slowly because so much of its power and beauty is locked in special information. There are not many who can estimate what I've done, because they have to know the farm like I did, *and* culture.

It was a real pleasure to meet you. Hello to Bennett.

All the best,
Fred

To Robert Penn Warren

[Minneapolis, Minnesota]
February 2, 1951

Dear Red Warren:

In talking to Dan Brennan last night over the phone (it's been too cold to drive in what with 20 to 30 below weather here for a couple of weeks) he mentioned that you were coming back to Minnesota next fall. Katie Beach has hinted too that she thought you were coming back. That is wonderful news because all of us have missed you. You should read the letters I get from some of the graduate or young writers (now scattered over the country) to hear what they say of the department now that Beach "that grandfather of letters and writing" and Warren are gone. They think the place has gone to the dogs.

As you know by now, North and Katie live next door to us. Katie makes a wonderful companion for Maryanna, who was beginning to show "being-a-writer's-wife" symptoms (some of them were strong enough to find an echo in me: spastic colon, disturbed gallbladder, extra heart systole, etc.) Katie seems to keep her going, smiling, challenging, etc. While Maryanna may have been good for me, I'm not sure but what I was bad for her, like marrying a petal to a shears. North and I have always been good friends, we seem to hit it off fine, talking about books, New England religion, birds, weather, even investigating an Indian grave some two miles west of here on a bluff. (He's still there, under glass. The owner built the case around him in front of his summer cottage.)

Saw Norman Katkov a few moments last Sunday at the Lewis rites up at Sauk Centre. Maryanna and I went up with a young newspaper man (he was in my class last fall) who was born and raised there. Heard many fabulous tales of Red's early life. Most of them parables, no doubt.

Have been thinking about the new project, *Sons of Adam,* which I asked you to comment on to Guggenheim. I hope to get at it this fall or early next year. Have some research to do. But more, some thinking. Talking to Joseph Beach about it, we both agreed it was a good story, but it all lay in "how to do it" without offending. We talked of *The Hamlet* by Faulkner. (F's best, perhaps.) I've just about decided to use the undertone, the understatement, and will probably never give a scene like F gave it, but will speak of Red Englen's (his name was Konstant Holman before but it didn't fit; besides Red seems to fit a family, a fabulous family, I know in Iowa who I want to use as models) burden of sin, or his unforgiveable sin, and only in the end, when he talks to his domeny, does he tell it, that he once played with a pet animal, "when I was an unknowin' boy." When you come back next fall I want a long talk with you about it, if you're willing. You've got the best critical mind I know of, which, along with your creativity, makes you someone to be envied indeed. Besides, talking to you makes a man key his mind up. Am finished finally with the last volume, *The Giant,* of the trilogy, *World's Wanderer,* and it now belongs to others. I am not worried about it. And the "Postscript" in it may be its best part. Well, Red, all our love, from Marya, Freya, Maryanna, and Fred,

Fred

To George Shively

[Minneapolis, Minnesota]
April 5, 1951

Dear George:

Got your letter just a moment ago and before the hottest thoughts about it vanish, will sit down and reply. I think you fellows are right that Thurs does not grow up as we'd all want. That is probably because he is an American. That is why too all American autobiographical or rumistic writing has been so embarrassing. The real truth about an American, way back inside him, is naïve, fumbling, boyish. We are a young nation and we do not yet have deep and abiding ways of living the American adult. He has not shown up yet. The standards that the New York savants and pundits talk about as being the adult goals or ideals are too much European and any writer with salt in his marrow knows it's better for him to react honestly as an American boy than to imitate a foreign notion of adulthood.

That is why, too, when Americans write objectively in novels about non-autobiographical elements, they can sometimes get a glimpse, and thus show us a glimpse, of what the goal should be. But too often too, because they are heavily influenced by the old masters, masters of another country, they get pulled away from the potentially true American behavior. So I say, that both rumistic and novelistic writing are valuable. The first shows how little we've learned, the second, after a look at the first, points the way ahead. Both forms of writing are valuable both to the society as well as to the writer.

The truth is, were we to write, say, the real nature of your life, of Ken's [McCormick] life, of Max Gissen's life, of Geismar's life, etc., it wouldn't be a bit more adult. For myself, I know what the good life should be, and strive for it, but I also know what the real lines of my life are, and I never let myself be kidded by my ideals. (My trouble is, I suppose, that I don't bemoan it, but celebrate it.) My wife thinks, for example, that I live too adult a life. She can't get over the fact that I just simply won't do certain things. Which she and others will. Which is true, perhaps. But at the same time, I know that such is striving. And I also know that the real truth of what goes on in my cells and head and nerves is something else. As a writer, once I know something, I have to put it down. Perhaps that is my calling: to show America how boyish it really is. Just as writers in Russia should reflect how goddam boyish they are too. We *are* children despite all those fiendish words Dr. Gesothzigger uses. So I am never angry when they say Thurs does not grow up. I don't take that personal. It only means to me that I have had great guts to put down the truth as I see it. *And at the same time that I must try to learn a lesson from my own preaching. And also at the same time hope that the rest of you will learn too.*

I have thought about the flour milling thing. But I don't know enough about it yet *as experienced*. As soon as I do, I'll start it. In the meantime I do know the slaughterhouses and the people they get as workers, both in South St. Paul and in Siouxland where it all starts from. *Sons of Adam* is going to be in the *This Is The Year* tradition.

As soon as Americans behave gooder, and that includes me, I'll write gooder books. And privately, I'm going to like the "boy almightys" a little better than those who stiffen themselves all up in manners and routines that are not native to America.

Rumes *are* confessions. Whereas novels are a little like public ceremonies, or public occasions, or sermons even, where everybody *tries* to be on his best behavior. (And the ones most likely to succeed will be a-sexed.)

I don't know what your new place looks like but I do like the looks of the new stationery. It looks almost as ancient and wonderfully hoary with book airs as do some of the British letterheads.

Meanwhile, of course, I admire you and Ken for speaking out. You know I don't get angry at you when you hit the bell. I always look at me first anyway to make sure I'm not guilty. Then I look out.

The remarks about being tired of Thur's fighting with women intrigues me. Because it allows me to get a fix on the people who make the remark. Let us look at Thurs's likes and dislikes in *W's*. *W*. Likes: Hero, Meridel, Flora, Mrs. Babbas, Ilse Levi, Bernadine, Mrs. Makepeace, Mrs. King, Eva, Eva's mother, Mrs. Lanweard who sells him the place, Roberta Bullhorn, and towards the end, Hancy. Dislikes: Mrs. Brothers, possibly Hero's mother, Rhoda and her mother, certain aspects of Sabine, Tollie Calveswell, Romelle, whores generally, the little tarts of Ohio, Orpah, the land-lady's daughter in Minneapolis, the early Hancy, and the dowagers of Summit Avenue. Basically, Thurs likes the woman the good doc-tor Gesothzigger marries. Looking that over, I'd say Thurs shows pretty good taste. But he *is* unwise to fight women. Because, in my book, women are more important to society than men. I think if you and Ken will look very carefully you'll find that Thurs's ideals and picks are something that American women could well look into. And of course both Thurs and I, however much we may think of women and put them above ourselves as men, we despise women who deny their womanhood and who every morning they wake up put on the imaginary peckers of the men they're envious of.

Would you please let Ken read this. Tell him I enjoyed talking to him the other night, as I always do, and that I apologize before-hand for any indiscretions I may have committed.

Sincerely,
Fred

To Maxwell Geismar

[Minneapolis, Minnesota]
April 7, 1951

Dear Maxwell:

Heard the bad news from Brennan and Willen the other night at Ann Chidester's at Stillwater where we gathered at the feet of Ken McCormick of Doubleday. Well, so it goes. It reminds me of those lonesome rejection years from 1937 to 1944. Good letters, near acceptances etc., but never quite. The thing to do is to push on. I think I go along with you that Brennan is nearer than Willen. At this moment. Brennan suffered a lot, went into deep depression. That boy went through a lot of hell in war. I think he's got it. I have another friend who really needs looking into. His first novel, *Cairo Concerto,* was published by Harcourt Brace & Co. He has now written a second novel, *The Angry Young Men,* which Harcourt rejected, for no particular reason except that the first didn't sell. His name is John Rogers Shuman. He is related to the local Walker family who were part of the old pioneer logging, railroading empires. He has his own money, has a country place on Lake Minnetonka, travels abroad every year, is around forty years old, very handsome, doesn't care much for girls, is a little on the over-sensitive side but by no means one of "the boys." He is extremely cultured, wise, well-read. It is the well-traveled, well-read thing that gets into his writing, and I'd say that he hasn't sold well because he is as difficult to read as Henry James. We get along very well, mostly because I allow him his world and he allows me mine. I think you should look into him. He is now at work on a third book. His *Cairo Concerto* didn't get good reviews but I liked it, thought it a "wise" book. His address: John Rogers Shuman, 400 Summit Avenue, Minneapolis, Minnesota. Brennan, Shuman, Willen, others (there's a lot of literary brains out here, by the way) have talked of starting a paperbound book publishing company, maybe even a magazine (eclectic, no coterie, just that the stuff has to be good), to get these good "unpublishable books and stories" in print and in the libraries. We thought of calling it The North Star Press and the magazine *The North Star Quarterly*. I think that my earlier books should be in reprints, by the way, and we might start with that, and say one of Red Warren's, etc. We got the printers, the binderies, brains, and the money. Somebody needs to put them all together and maybe the blocked Brennans and Willens and Shumans will do it. Well, this morning I am privileged! My daughter, Freya, 6, is paying me a visit and is drawing tulips on this same table, is looking into corners I haven't pried into for years (she found some old sketching pencils of mine and some sketching pads), and is paging through books and is looking at my manuscripts and has just now decided to publish an eight-page book herself right here in this den or "kiva." I've just given her a whiskery kiss and she has reacted by calling me Mr. Brush. Also, I want to thank you most deeply for pushing my *This Is The Year* in Britain. Such things help far more than we realize. We put "them" on the defensive. I've been reading Conrad, Indian philosophy or poetry (*Hymns, Upanishads, Gita*), am about done with *Quixote,* looking through Faulkner some more, also a book called *Eternal Eve* by Harvey Graham, *Genetics & Races of Man,* am going to have a look at Schweitzer soon, got a set of Fielding and want a look into him, and then of course I'm always reading Chaucer, who is really my great favorite.

Our trip to California and back occurred without mishap,

though there were the usual close shaves. We also spent a week at Ensenada, Mexico, which marked our first trip abroad. I read Mizener's book in between loafing on the beach and having an occasional Mexicali beer. We had a look in at the meteor crater, the painted desert, the petrified forest, the Grand Canyon, Hollywood movie-making, the relatives in Artesia and Bellflower, Laguna beach, ate seafood, drove through Carmel and Big Sur where Henry Miller and Jeffers hold out, and finally capped it by seeing the massive redwoods north of San Francisco. They were enormous Bach cantatas, or Beethovenian *Ninths*. They were all huge so that it was difficult to make comparison, so that they hardly seemed huge. But the dark shadows underneath, the red dark shadows, told you that you were in the presence of the mighty. I wished they had evolved with brains, those boys, what couldn't they tell us! 364 feet high. 25 feet in diameter. 4000 years old. Undisturbed by storms except for the last few twigs at the top. No groaning in the storm. Quiet and stalk-steady. They still possess me and from here on in there'll be no doubt that my books will take on the tone of them. Even the great snowfall we ran into on the way home, of more than 88 inches for the winter (and an all time record) seemed sort of natural after the redwoods. I make a proposal. All feeble writers, all B.S. Idioms should write their work in the dark red shadows of the redwoods. All U.N. conferences should be held in their shadows too. Truman and Stalin should meet there too. They built that UN center in the wrong place, removed from our roots and our brothers; they put it instead in a perpendicular desert. Where intellects are inclined to forget that three times a day the body makes acquaintance with killed or reaped things as food and where once a day the body makes acquaintance with the squatting position of excretion. No need to dwell on it; just have it there as a reminder of our origin and heritage and limitations, and especially our common attributes. Ah yes, American is great. That is, the land is. But the people are still children. We can easily house 400,000,000 folk here. We haven't learned how to turn the wastes into woods. It's all there. It just takes time and brains and peace. We must make the valleys green with grass, not red with blood. Lewis said that the great American novel will never be written. Because America is too huge, too multifarious. I think it can. One needs to catch its spirit, not all its various multitudes of facts. In fact, I think I've done it in *World's Wanderer,* on a boyish people trying to invest and to explore and to use a new continent. (My editor bawls me out for not getting Thurs into adulthood and he just won't understand that that's my point about him and his country. Also, that I don't want him to get his blueprint for adulthood from Europe, which worked out its own notions over the centuries, but he should work it out himself for himself. Doubleday feels uneasy about *The Giant* because of the violence in it, the sex in it, the roaring in it, the shots in it, and by God, Max, isn't that the true America so far? That's what it means to write the rume. And there are also in it hints of what adulthood should be for Thurs' America.) Well, end of the page. Guggenheim turned me down for I don't know what nth time, but will try again next year and will put down your name. I have a new plot, *Sons of Adam,* and will get at it. Meanwhile, am getting together a book of shorts, am writing two new shorts and a new novelette.

Love,
Fred

To Edith Haggard

[Minneapolis, Minnesota]
April 15, 1951

Edith Haggard:

Some time ago when you queried me if I would be interested in doing an article on the Twin Cities* for *Holiday,* I was almost tempted to latch onto the idea. But I was busy with the trilogy *World's Wanderer,* also I was not too sure I could do a good job on the Cities, also I didn't know enough about *Holiday*. However, the situation is now changed, even though Katkov has done the Cities thing. I am in between "big books," I have been studying *Holiday* carefully, and I have a project that I'm sure of. I've been thinking that someone should do a *Holiday* article on Siouxland.

It just happens that I shall be doing a lot of research on my own in Siouxland this summer. I won't begin my two-hour writing seminar at Macalester until the middle of September and even then I'll be free four days a week, and I won't begin *Sons of Adam* until next January.

To understand what I mean by Siouxland just take a quick look at the end pages of your office copy of *This Is The Year*. (I named that country. When I was writing the book, I first called it in my notes the Land of the Sioux, then Sioux-Land, then, at last, Siouxland. I now discover that the radio stations and the newspapers in both Sioux City and Sioux Falls are beginning to refer to the same area as Siouxland. "This is radio station XXXX serving greater Siouxland." That was one of my great thrills, by the way, the day I heard that on the Sioux City radio and then found out it came from my book.) It is the land drained by the Big Sioux River, the river that raised so much havoc in Sioux Falls recently. I rarely think of the state lines anymore in that area, nor do many other people when referring to it. I talked to some historians and librarians the other night and they agreed that state lines through that area are meaningless, but that the term Siouxland is wonderful. We don't think anymore of that area as a combination of Northwest Iowa, Northeast Nebraska, Southwest Minnesota, and Southeast South Dakota. We say Siouxland. Edith, that is my own native land and named by me. I love it. Always have. Three of my books have already been set there, also most of my short stories. And present plans indicate most of my future tales will be set there too. I could do an article about that land with love and affection, and bring to it the understanding and poetry that say an Algren is giving to his Chicago article for *Holiday*.

Think of what is in Siouxland: Pipestone where the Indians make the stone pipes of peace, Devil's Gulch, Gitchie Manitou, the Palisades, the first homestead site in U.S.A., the fine pheasant hunting grounds, the many parks and ski-jumps that dot the Big Sioux bluffs, the great fowl flyways, Devil's Nest where Jesse James hid out, where Lewis and Clark stopped, where the most ferocious Sioux pillaged, where the gentle Sioux Chief Yellow Smoke lived, where Rölvaag's *Giants In The Earth* and Ruth Suckow's *The Folks* were set, (plus my *This Is The Year, The Chokecherry Tree,* and *World's Wanderer*'s beginning and end), etc. I already have much soil conservation, geographical, racial, sociological data on hand, and need do only a very little more. Could you send a copy of this letter plus possibly your copy of *Year* (or maybe Doubleday has another left) to Ted Patrick of *Holiday*? I can begin May 15 and work off and on all summer. One thing: tell him that some of the town names in my *Year* map are fictitious since I fictionized about some of them. We could do a straight job.

Most sincerely,
Fred

*Checking the files I see it was the U. of M., not the Cities, you

queried me on—somehow in my mind the two became interchangeable.

F.F.

To George Shively

[Minneapolis, Minnesota]
June 13, 1951

Dear George,

I discover that Doubleday is publishing the Kefauver book
called *Crime in America*. Could you have that sent to me? I want
to make sure that I don't miss a trick in my book *The Mountain of
Myrrh*. I've been looking at such books, among others, of course,
Warren's, Dosty the Russian, Conrad's, etc., including the new
one by Field called *McDonough*.

I do hope too that you folks weren't too flabbergasted by my
last request for help. I hope it will be forthcoming. I came back
from town today where I signed my county pauper papers to get
into the University Hospital on June 24 where the following day
they'll go into my hand[1] to scoop out the tumors and also if possible
repair the damage done to the hand when I crashed into that storm
window three years ago. I'd like it that there would be some money
in the bank for us while I'm laid up that month. The last time I
went to the hospital I had some bad worry too and when I came
out of the anesthetic I went on a rampage in the ward. Two order-
lies, three nurses, and two interns couldn't hold me down and I
was swinging my arm with the cast on it like a club and was about
to get away (in my anesthetic dream, you understand) to "fix things
up at home." Fortunately, the hospital army made one more attack
with reenforcements and then they tied me down in bed until I
became conscious. When I came to my belly hurt awful and I was
strapped. By God.

Before I go in I'm going to write a story called "Treehouse" in
a last desperate effort to make money via the short story way. I
didn't like it at all that Alan [Collins] and Edith [Haggard] refused
to peddle "Sand Dollar," which I thought very fine. They have
lately given me the feeling that they push me in an apologetic fashion. They don't have to. It is a pity that I have been forced to give
my private feeling about how good I am. Maybe I'm wrong, but I
know I'm good, and I figure that if I have to talk up I'm not going
to blow a soft note when I think I have the right to blow a hard

1. FM also had Dupuytren's
contracture in his right hand.

note. Alan and Edith should feel grossly insulted and show it when second rate magazine editors (who can't write worth a shit themselves) don't rush to get my copy. But I'm afraid they are afraid of the New York literary steers, who, of course, have a right to run down a real bull from the prairie and his bellows. Anyway, be frank, George. You and I have always made that our first rule and so have always got on.

Sincerely,
Fred

To George Shively, Alan Collins, and Ken McCormick

[Minneapolis, Minnesota]
July 20, 1951

Dear George & Alan & Ken:

Today it was something else. I discover that I'm going to have to take whirlpool baths for my hand for some four to five months daily, along with some electrical stimulation of the muscles in the palm with a dingus, also daily. Well, if it isn't one thing, it is another. But I'll get a leg over that ridgepole too and later sit atop it. Thank God for pain.

More thoughts on Frederick Friskner as my new penname. I have noted and others tell me they have noted, that when names of writers are being mentioned, the tendency is to skip mine, even after they try pronouncing it. I have also noted how at parties where I met people like the poet Lowell, the critic Fowlie, etc., I will not forget their name but they will mine even though I have great height to use as an added catch. They will remember my body, and face, and even what I say. But will stumble trying to catch the name. Many times they'll talk to me about me without knowing it. And you should then hear them pronounce my name. E. G. Fee'kee Fee-kee'-ma, Fee-kuy'-ma, and so on. In fact I've often thought there might be six groups of people who speak of me as their writer, each one of them with their own pronounciation of Feikema, and not know each other. Consider Twain, and his reputation, however. When a Twain man talks to a Twain man about Twain, both are immediately en rapport. The name of Twain has a single and, ubiquitous attack. Feikema does not. I know how it is teaching. Whenever I give a list of writers for my kids, I tend to use those that I can pronounce without error. Also, when I'm casting about for the name of some student in my class who should re-

1. All of these were names of FM's students at Macalester College.

spond to one of my planted questions I usually pick such names as Amerson, Frye, Thornton, etc., and not Blanpied, Fornare, Nielitz, Piche, Peltzer.[1]

Now that Burke has spoken on the "lyric or Joyce novel," I'm almost positive that the little magazine and other magazine critics are going to chew over my "Postscript on the Rume." They are bound to in time. I want them to chew over a name that they can all pronounce, and pronounce pretty much alike, and a name that will feel and look brother to names like Faulkner, Stegner, Spenser, etc.

Why would it be disastrous to change now with *The Giant*? What would be lost? The librarians, I hear (I'm going in Monday to check the names of authors who changed their names with the library cataloguer), merely make double entries everywhere and write Friskner in under or over Feikema on the titlepage and on the spine as they did with all the Hueffer (Heifer, Heffer, Huffer) books. For the private buyers the problem will be one of suddenly owning a rarity, a collector's item. And finally, we are someday going to publish all three books under one title, *World's Wanderer,* just as Dos Passos did his *USA* trilogy. (He has the only slightly odd name in letters, and he, luckily, has his in two syllables, and pronounceable, whereas in my three syllable name the tendency is for the English-American tongue to hit the second syllable as they do on most three-syllable words, when we Frisians hit the first syllable. Also, we don't say Fei'-kee, but Fei'-ka, which the phrase I invented, "Feikean prose" helps spoil.)

July 21, *Saturday morning.* What a helluva storm we had last night. We're twenty miles out from town, so our house and grounds is all right. But in town, the Cities, wow! We happened to see the movie Kon-Tiki, and I was sure the moviehouse was coming down. The wind hit 100-miles an hour and then broke the windgage. Same with the raingage. The weather bureau estimated the wind went up to 120 mile gusts, with the rain probably hitting four inches in some places. I've never seen such devastation in a city. We drove home in the tailend of it and had to duck fallen trees, backwatering mains, etc. The water got into the ventilators in the movie and sprayed everybody inside. My wife's face looked just like a revolving barber's pole. While Freya slept on the backseat on the way home!

More thoughts on the subject of Frederick Friskner the author: We needn't worry what'll happen to those who are "Feikema"

conscious. They've stuck by me despite the tough name and will
be relieved to follow me with the new one. They'll be the first to
know about it. As for those who've already bought the first two
volumes of the trilogy under Feikema, the booksellers can tell them
to save the first two and the third under Friskner because in time
that two-named set will be a real collector's item .. Alan is probably right when he says there won't be much mention of the change
in names, but the little will be enough. And of course, in each review of *The Giant,* they'll probably use both names since we'll have
a sentence about it on the jacket. And in the short biograph in back.

About the health angle: one thing I know too. I've never looked
better. I weigh under 230 (when you saw me I was way over 250),
my blood and general condition is "pink," and I "feel" excellent. It's
just that I once had TB and have connective tissue that is showing
up bad at points of stress.

Back to Frederick Friskner. I've been calling up friends, seeing
friends, about it, and without exception they tell me to hurry up
and change to Friskner. And among them were those who thought
the oddness of "Feikema" was an advantage. I also discover that
they do not particularly care for Frisk.

We have to be hard about this. If the change is to be made someday, then we must make it now. And I'm all for it. Now. We must
hold our eye on the idea that *W's. W.* is one work, which eventually,
like *USA,* will be published under one head. The solid impact must
be *W's. W.* by Frederick Friskner. I have a sneaking feeling that *The
Giant* (because of its title, its smoldering volcanic contents, and the
essay on *W's.W.* as rume) will run away from us. What a pity that
will be when I'll want to change later on whether I sell under
Feikema or not. If it does go very good, so much the better when
we get out the whole-in-one. (*USA* was issued within a year after
The Big Money, the third volume, was issued.) If it doesn't go too
well, we're still all set, since the text of the first two will remain the
same and we have that all set in plates, and we take our chance again
in the whole. So far as we, you and I, are concerned, publishing
the books separately has served to pay, in part, for the plates, so that
issuing *WW's* as one book will be that much the more reasonable.
Again, let me repeat, that final goal is *World's Wanderer* in one book
(like *USA, Studs Lonigan* by Farrell, *Parade's End* by Ford Madox
Ford) above the name Frederick Friskner.

Sunday, July 22. In the interests of symmetry, I can see where
we should also publish *The Giant* under (or over) the name of

Feikema. But if we do so, I want to say right now that the next
book will be under Frederick Friskner, or some name very similar
to it. No matter how well *The Giant* sells, I still want *World's Wanderer* to come out over Frederick Friskner. This will not hurt the
text any. The only change will come in the front pages and the in
between pages, which I think should be condensed anyway. For
example, all acknowlegements, three, could be condensed into one
on one page, and so on. So this morning I feel that we should go
ahead under Feikema, so long as it is understood that I'd like *WW*
under Friskner sometime later next year. (Or whenever it seems
advisable to put the three under one cover.) And also, so long as
it is understood that my next new book, *The Mountain of Myrrh,* is
also to come out under Frederick Friskner.

I think you should immediately, in any case, ask the printers
to send back to you, then to me, the three page biograph. I don't
want any more Feikema dope put out as I have it there. In case we
do *WW* later, I can add it at that time, with Friskner corrections
in it. In case we do keep, by some strange quirk, the name of
Feikema afterall, I can add it when we do *WW.* In case we don't
do *WW* right away, then I'll use the biograph on Friskner-Feikema
at the tail end of *The Mountain of Myrrh,* since I feel that biograph
should go with the particular volume which carries the new name
of Friskner. When you ask to send it back, make sure they don't
send the "Postscript" back. That has to go as it is, except for such
errors as the copy editors find, and we find, later in galleys. Could
you have this done immediately, George, since there is no reason
to waste the money on it at this time? It's the last three pages of the
MSS.

It's going to be easier to teach with the new name too. As it is,
it takes the kids in my class some four weeks before they get it right,
and even then they hesitate to use it in my case. Also, there is the
case of my own children being derided with the name of Feikema,
like I was. I was called Frycake, Fuckema, Fuckeman, Fuck'em,
etc. All of which tended to make me think I didn't belong in America, when, actually, by accident, I am a real flesh-and-blood Anglo-
Frisic-American, having been born here, with a Frisian father, and
a mother who was of East Frisian descent,[2] the same peoples who,
years ago, when they went to England, were known as the Angles
(English). If anybody has a right to call himself one in the Anglo-
American tradition, I do. (If that is a signal honor?)

So my feeling is today, to let *The Giant* go through over

2. Actually, it turns out
she was of Lower Saxony
descent.

Feikema, with the distinct understanding that the biograph is to
go with the particular volume which is printed over the name of
Friskner (or some such name), with the distinct understanding
that the very next volume will be a Friskner production, either
WW as one book, or *The Mountain of Myrrh,* or *The Rape of Elizabeth,* depending on which we decide should go next.

I hope to begin work again next Thursday, and I have plans to
recast *Mountain* quite thoroughly, to set it "somewhere in
America," possibly hinting that it is in the Midlands.

(A weather bureau friend of mine estimates that the storm we
had gave the Cities the tit [the tornado] in seven different places. If
one of those had hit my place out here, I wouldn't be writing this
today.)

July 23, 1951. So be it then. We'll go along with Feikema on
the third volume of the trilogy. But, January 6, 1952 marks the beginning of the year when all further publications shall come under
the new penname.

Two other candidate names that I've looked at are:

Frederick Frisham

Frederick Freyson

Also, I've been looking at the longer ones, Frederick Freysham
and Frisingham. But they are odd. Frisham can be pronounced
at least two ways, Fris'ham and Fris'sham.

I had a long look at Ford Madox Ford's books at the library today. He published some twenty, with quite a number done by Doubleday Page. When he changed his name, they merely listed all his
old books under Ford, with a card in for Ford Madox Hueffer saying, "See Ford Madox Ford." The old books under Hueffer were
remarked on the title page, sometimes in pen, sometimes in pencil.
So in the change, nothing is lost. Same thing happened in *Who's
Who,* and would happen in my case, both names listed, with the
books under the penname and a "See" under the old name. It was
very heartening to see this. Nothing'll be lost in the switch.

July 28, 1951. Before I get to work this morning I want to ac-
knowledge George's letter of the 24th and Alan's of the 25th. For
the time being, at least through the publication date of *The Giant,*
I'll go along with the use of Feike Feikema. We'll see how *The Giant*
goes and also see how I feel next January 6, my birthday. One thing
is certain. Before, when I contemplated changing the name, and
it was often, I never had a candidate that was satisfactory to myself.
I've got it now. It has two aspects: it can be pronounced by

strangers and I like it for what it means for me. I know you're right, George, when you say that most people care only about how it sounds to them, wouldn't care what it means to me. Yet that private knowledge is important to me.

Also, I suppose it is too late to get back that biograph at the end of the MS, so let it go through, and if I decide I don't want it in *The Giant,* I can order it killed in the galleys.

Allen Tate will be here this fall at the U. He knew Ford Madox (Hueffer) Ford. I'm going to question him closely on why Ford took his final penname.

Have begun work on *The Mountain of Myrrh.* And doing some heavy rewriting and new writing in it. Am setting it in Algonquin country somewhere in Midland America, since there is where most of the information came from in the first place (except for one or two incidents that I ran into in Hudson and Bergen counties in Jersey).

Am also busy having brainstorms about *The Rape of Elizabeth.* Am planning to use that terrible July 20 storm as background, with its half dozen little tornadoes. Got the characters set too: Elizabeth (Else) Watke and Jack Nagel. Thanks for listening to me get rid of steam. It helps. And keeps other people from knowing what an ass I can be sometimes.

FF

To Alan Collins and George Shively

Frederick Manfred
[Minneapolis, Minnesota]
August 3, 1951

Dear Alan & George:

More about the new name. When I pushed my inquiry about the "Friskner" penname, I found that the further I got away from those who knew much about writing, the more I found they had trouble with it. They thought it odd, or objected to the "k" in it, etc., and some thought it just as tough as "Feikema" or least not too much of an improvement. In the meantime, even though I liked it much, I kept experimenting, looking around. One day, about a week ago, I lamented to my wife that it was a pity the literal translation of my name, Frederick Frederickman, was so long. (Note: Frederick, Feike, "friend," "freedom," and the Frisian word "frede" meaning "to love," "peace" all come from the same Aryan Root of "pri-tu" or "fri-du.") I next considered a short version of

Frederickman, namely, Fredman, or Fredeman. That still wasn't too good, so just for the heck of it, as a way of avoiding the "fr-fr" alliteration of the two names, I thought of flopping Fredeman or Fredman over. And, we got Manfred. Frederick Manfred. A translation of Feike Feikema. With Frederick being my christening name to start with. Maryanna liked this immediately, and is now a strong advocate for it. I've tested this name now, and of course nobody has trouble pronouncing it. I looked it up in biographical dictionaries and find that no one of importance, at least not in letters, has ever used it. Bryon once wrote a poem by that name and there is also a piece of music bearing that name. It is also a middle name for Thurs Wraldson in *World's Wanderer*. His father wears a variant of it, Menfrid. Manfred lends itself to "epithet"-making too, of a distinguished sort—"the Manfredean prose," "Manfredia," "the Manfredians or Manfredeans." This name has the virtue of being meaningful to me in a direct sense. It is Feike Feikema translated. I "feel" that name is mine. Which is sort of important. However, I think I'll wait until the year is out, say until my birthday next January 6 before adopting it (or some other still better name that might still come to me.) By that time *The Giant* will be out. Thus, let's go along with Feikema until January 6 in America at least. In case we sell books abroad we can then go into whether we want the new name on it. I think I'll make the legal name, in case I take Manfred, as follows: Frederick Feikema Manfred and publish under Frederick Manfred. How does this new one sound to you all?

Ford M. Ford did have trouble with anti-German feeling in England. Also, Ford was his mother's name and people were calling him "Ford" and he liked the alliteration of FMF, so he took it, according to the information I was able to dig out.

The deep X-ray treatments for the feet are over.[1] Now we wait and see for a couple of months. The hand, meanwhile, is responding marvelously, though the above is still poor typing, eh?

Best,
Frederick Manfred

Dear Alan: What chance is there of the Spanish advance from Callejo now that we're smiling at Franco? FFM

PPS. And just for the heck of it; how about having Edith send out my story "Treehouse" over the penname of Frederick Manfred? She can have the first page typed right there, perhaps. FFM

1. FM also had Dupuytren's contracture in his right foot.

1952

This year marks a shift in Manfred's literary focus, with the planning of a novel about Hugh Glass. Despite continuing financial discouragements, newly-named Frederick Feikema Manfred moves with enthusiasm on his Hugh Glass research. In the meantime, a number of rejections and disappointments with Doubleday cause him to leave the publisher. Further grant rejections intensify the financial problems.

To Alan C. Collins

Frederick (" ") Manfred
[Minneapolis, Minnesota]
March 8, 1952

Dear Alan:

After you've read George's letter to me (Naomi says you have a copy there), read the copy of my letter to George. Then as follows.

I've had two days to think it over now, to talk it over with my wife, and although I told them over the phone that I hated the idea of switching publishers, that I'd prefer to keep all my eggs in one basket at the market, that maybe I should lay *The Mt.* aside for a year or two and publish a "hotter" novel first. I've come around to thinking this morning that we should get another opinion or two on it before you send it back to me. With that in mind I've sent along some new front pages with the name Doubleday removed. See instructions attached. Where should we get the opinions? Well, I know that Bennett Cerf has always been interested, that Harry Maule has written me a number of times that if I should ever make changes in my publishing plans to let him know. Same for Houghton Mifflin, both through Geismar and others there. And how about Gold Medal Books? (In the latter case, can I stay with Dd and still let them print *The Mt.*? What is the ethics in the case?) Also, are we free to "quietly" get some other publisher opinions at the same time that I accept the March sum of money from Ken— if I return it when and if Random should give me a sizable advance? Cerf is coming out here this spring and wrote me that he'd like to get together with me. That was before this happened. I could at that time tell him of my next books, *The Rape of Elizabeth* (division titles are: "The Act of Lust," "The Act of Light," and "The Act of Love") and *Sons of Adam*. I absolutely hate switching publishers, but, if they won't publish, and I've got to live and get my books in print to make a record, then we've just got to shop around like Faulkner, Conrad, Warren did until we hit some jack-pots or popularity trends. (Here's a quote from Maule's letter to me on January 31, 1951: "I enjoyed meeting you very much indeed. Of course you know that I wouldn't for the world poach on any other publisher's preserves—much less, for personal reasons, on George Shively's—but if and when any change should come about in your publishing situation, please remember that I am, and will continue to be, interested in your work.")

I think too that Ken, George, Paul, others have a point that, 1) I should keep Feikema in the middle of the penname where it can stand as a "seen but silent insignia" tying the old with the new, 2) that the three together look very impressive, 3) that the public can skip over Feikema and grab hold of me by the easy handles "Frederick" and "Manfred". Will you tell Gertrude to tell Callejo, Garganti, Dobson, the Switzerland man, and any and all our agents abroad? And I think you people should address me that way too. It takes a while sometimes to get it all just right. If Bennett questions you about it tell him that the legal moves are on the way, that others of the Feikema-Manfred clan are already Manfreds.[1] My wife, children, brothers, friends, have all accepted it. My mail is all changed. I've even registered for voting under FFM.

Could you also give Arabel J. Porter a jingle to tell her that "the boys" think I should keep Feikema in the middle as a "seen but silent insignia"?

Write me soon, as always,
Frederick Feikema Manfred

P.S. *Winterkill* will be along in a day or so.

Later
P.S. Shively says they can send me $600 now plus $200 a month for April and May to coincide with the finishing of a rough first draft of *The Rape of Elizabeth*. This assumes that if they like that draft, they'll send more for me to finish the rough draft during the summer. That's a nice offer, very, very generous, but at the same time I feel so very bad that I can't get what I think is a fine book, *The Mountain of Myrrh*, published now. With no assurance either that even if they took *Rape* and it sold well that they would then take *Mountain*. Somehow, I feel I should get another opinion on *Mountain*. Suppose we could get $1500 from somewhere, could we return whatever I take from Doubleday since March 1, 1952? If I could only find some vague feeling in my mind that *Mountain*

1. Jake Manfred in Duluth, Minnesota.

was not good, that I privately felt it wasn't worth publishing, I'd feel better. (Ironically!) But I feel it's good. Do we owe Maule anything in case he likes *Mountain*? Could you, in behalf of the best interests of your client, get such an opinion on your own initiative? I don't know what's usually done in such situations. If I could feel that I could change one jot or tittle of *Mountain* in time to come, I'd say, let's let it cool off in the files for a few years and then I'll have another look at it. But it seems exactly as I want it. So far, I've worked so conscientiously that today I wouldn't want to change a line I've written in any of my books. I take my stand on them as is.

There's one question I should have asked them over the phone, and I thought of it, but I wasn't ruthless enough to ask it, to wit: suppose my books had been fair or good sellers up to now, would you have published *Mountain*? That question is a smoking-out question and I should have asked it.

If you do talk to Maule or Geismar about it, tell them that *The Mountain of Myrrh* is a sort of "romantic parable." I call it "a romance" but do so with a tongue just a mite in my cheek.

F.F.M

To Alan C. Collins

Frederick (" ") Manfred
[Minneapolis, Minnesota]
March 13, 1952

1. *Mountain of Myrrh*.

Dear Alan:

Of all the coldblooded businesses I've ever run into. Am I supposed to accept a rejection of a year's work, a book, without a struggle or an argument?[1] And that on the basis of a letter of four paragraphs totaling 27 lines? With just some flat statements but no explanation, no analysis, no attempt to show where a book might have been stronger, etc.? Could you write a new book, knowing your last, which you privately liked, was rejected without a fight on your part? I don't like working under a loaded gun. I can't. That's like asking a man to have coitus, with a man standing over him with a shotgun. It can't be done. If they can publish ads which compare me favorably with a half-dozen different authors one month and the next turn me down flat, something is wrong. (And by the way, they didn't by any means use the best quotes or the best reviews. There were other reviews which said I was better than half the guys mentioned. Not that that means anything to me. But it is merely a point to raise.)

Why can't they send on the money? We are two months behind in payments on our mortgage. We can't pay our income tax. Had they taken this book back in January, as usual, I'd've had the money and we would have been clear until at least the summer. I'm like a farmer who raises a good crop and then by God can't sell it at the market. He depends on that crop to catch up on his bills for the year.

Why can't Doubleday send that money? I'm already at work on the new book, and will use my spare time to read the *Mountain* to make sure that it is either publishable or not publishable. If at the end of two or three weeks I decide that it is, it goes back to them for one more chance at it, and then if they say No, then it goes out, and when we get an advance on it, I'll pay them back the $600: I did this once before. Reynal & Hitchcock sent me $100 on *Boy Almighty* (a couple of chapters) but when Hillestad wanted *The Golden Bowl,* an earlier book of mine, I sent that $100 back out of the advance Paul gave me. I want time to think over their rejection. Especially as they gave me no solid or valid or recognizable reasons. Just a blunt letter on a book that I think is "ten times better" than *The Chokecherry Tree.*

Or, can you send me $250 immediately until I have read this and have it back to you with a decision either way?

The point is, I have a deep hunch they are wrong on *The Mountain.* So wrong, that I feel that there is no point in going on since what I feel I'm doing I think is right and if it isn't right then anything I do is nothing.

Sincerely,

Fred

To Alan C. Collins

Frederick (" ") Manfred
[Minneapolis, Minnesota]
March 29, 1952

Dear Alan:

As the first paragraph of my March 22nd letter to you and as the first sentence or two of my March 22nd letter to George indicates, the version you now have of *The Mountain of Myrrh* is not the one Doubleday saw earlier but it is a copy which embodies author-initiated changes. And don't let them hold it too long. They knew from my January 7 letter that I needed money by the end of February for my mortgage payments. They have been goddam dilatory about a first-class book, old version or new version. I like being loyal to the same house, same wife, same goal—or I would

long ago have thought of making changes. In that respect I'm a
bullheaded American of Free Frisian descent. Publishers every now
and then give me a pain in the ass—just as no doubt authors give
publishers a pain in the arse. Publishers every now and then think
that authors are appletrees from which you can pick apples without
a squeak from the tree and then pack up the apples and sell them
at an apple market. But authors are human beings who need to be
fed and housed and clothed, and who not only write their things
out of terrible privacy of heart matters but also out of blood, from
blood, by blood, and for blood. Publishers package and peddle
bottled blood, not red apples. And peddle human blood. How can
anyone publish books until and unless there be authors? And how
is Doubleday or anyone to know if a Manfred is going to be someday a steady-selling author unless they invest money in a Manfred—especially when already a passel of necessary critics describe
him as being comparable to "Hamsun, Rölvaag, Dos Passos,
Wolfe, Steinbeck, etc.," and when a few of them say Manfred is better? (Not that I give a Chaucer's tord about such matters, except
as it may help pay for my bed and board and shingles. I know what
I am and God bless everybody else.)

I'm not forgetting these hard days.

Sincerely,
Fred

P.S. You might casually drop the hint to Dd (and others) that were
it not for the serious Manfreds, Algrens, Faulkners, etc., they
would never attract the "breast-and-ship" books they make money
on? First-rate though possibly poor selling writers attract second-
rate better-selling authors. A house collapses unless it has prestige
authors. Except for Maugham, which of their old authors gets
more attention of a serious nature than Manfred (Feikema)? First
runners, first explorers are never adequately compensated in their
own lifetime.

FFM

To Russell Roth

[Minneapolis, Minnesota]
Sunday, July 13, 1952

Dear Russell:

After reading your little book, *Slowly Toward the North*, I am sure
of your future as a writer. If you don't get the first of a lot of recog-
nition out this book, I'll be a mighty mystified man.

I don't believe this is a novel. It is too short, and not complicated enough. It is a novelette, or a short novel. Conrad wrote many such. Hemingway's new book which is coming out this fall sounds like it. I've written one too, *The Stumbling Stone,* as yet unpublished, which can be considered a short novel. To me a novel must have at least three main echoes, or arches, or layers.

To me your book told the story of civilized man's intrusion on the jungle. The road was the first intrusion, the man's attack on the woman the second. The slough the road vanished in was one face of the jungle; the woman was the other. Then there was a withdrawal or "man" would have succumbed, would have been swallowed by the jungle.

I have no doubt that you are preoccupied with what most real writers are concerned with. The jungle. Not only the obvious jungle, but the jungle that is within us, and upon which sits the human civilized conscious mind, sits almost like a cork on a huge ocean. Now there are two usual ways of reacting to the knowledge of the jungle: 1) retreat into the conscious self and this leads to puritanism, primness, gentility, etc., 2) surrender to the jungle. But there is a third. That is the route the artist, and the superior human, can take. To live mostly in the mind at the same time that he enjoys and lets live as much as is possible and even directs that part of the jungle he finds in himself. The whole trick, then, is to raise an ego (concentrated jungle) that other egos (jungle masses) will accept.

I thought the writing taut, deceptively simple on the surface, full of haunting disturbing echoes of something powerful, even fascinating, swift, and so goddam rich for all the simplicity that I couldn't read it more than 20 pages at a time.

All the best on it,
Frederick

To George Shively, Ken McCormick, and Alan Collins

[Minneapolis, Minnesota]
July 16, 1952

Dear George, Ken, & Alan,

I finished the first draft of *The Rape of Elizabeth* last Thursday evening at six, July 10. The book needs some cutting, some rewriting, some fleshing in, some fat removed, but in the main it's all there. I think this book will be a worldbeater. This book may even wake up the ossified old maids in the feebleminded institutions. The book is approximately as long as *Boy Almighty.* I began with the rewriting last Monday, July 14, and hope to have the first part,

"The Act of Lust," in your hands for a reading by the end of July.
This will be a readable version. I know this: if I can be allowed to
work at the rewriting without interruption, I can have it ready for
the printers by November 1st. Also, that I'll then be able to give
you even better writing than in *This Is The Year*. I propose that as
soon as the book is done, I take a workman's job for a couple of
months in the South St. Paul stockyards and slaughterhouses. I
need a little more background for my next trilogy, *Sons of Adam*.
While I'm at work there, both Alan and Ken, if they will, can be
working on getting me a good short time job in Hollywood, long
enough to earn money for the coming year and until *Rape* comes
out. After that I'll be in the bucks.

I've also just returned, today, from a long luncheon with Paul
C. Hillestad who has been reading *The Mountain of Myrrh*. He has
read it twice, once to get the swift story line, the second time to
read it in more detail. Today I got his second thoughts on it. I'd
earlier got his first reactions. Together, his reactions go something
like this: the whole thing is full of marvelous writing, some of the
best he's seen me do, which is particularly true if you take it sentence for sentence and paragraph for paragraph, but which is less
true when the project is considered as a whole—some of the writing is better than anything I've done so far, certainly far better than
the writing in *The Chokecherry Tree,* the book dedicated to Paul.
He thought the motion in it swifter, the writing tauter and more
lean, the symbolism more artistically executed. In some ways it was
again much like *The Golden Bowl,* which too had that off-center odd
light in it. He said there were the usual "Fred" bugs in it, such as:
sometimes the material is too microscopic, too particular; neologisms; attention-shockers which takes the mind off the story, etc.
The bugs, however, seem imbedded in my personality and readers
will have to go along with them just as people have had to take
Dreiser's crude syntax along with his other virtues. Some of his adverse comments: Polly uses too many nicknames for Ken; the first
meeting between Ken and Dolores needs a little tinkering to make
it more plausible; Dolores' dialogue needs to be examined again
to take out "Fred talk"; her father can be softened somewhat, made
more complacent in the sense that he feels "I've made it, to hell
with the rest of 'em"; Ken should have committed more moral lep-
rosy to deepen the tragedy. Paul thought that the book was as good
as any I've done so far, was eminently publishable (he let this slip!),
but that a reheating in the kiln might make it tighter, more a complete whole. Of course, I was awfully happy to get these remarks of

his, since he was the guy who, despite Random House, Macmillan, Dutton, Reynal & Hitchcock, etc., saw virtue in *The Golden Bowl* and published it—did so despite a night phone call from Mary Shipley of Franklin Spier not to publish it, despite advice from dozens of others in New York. Paul believed; & I lived.

Yours,
Fred

P.S. Had a wonderful letter from Van Wyck Brooks: "You are of course doing what no one is doing. You have great power . . . the key in which you write demands a tremendous emotional response from the reader."

P.P.S. Are you going to do *World's Wanderer* this fall? I can't win any awards for this year if you don't.

FFM

To Peter De Vries[1]

[Minneapolis, Minnesota]
September 13, 1952

1. A general editor at the
New York Sir or *New Yorker*.

Dear Pete De Vries:
    A neighbor lady brought over a copy of the September 6, 1952 *New York Sir*.
    Re your query on how to pronounce "Manfred": put the accent on both syllables—with dignity.

Always in warmest irony,
Frederick Feikema Manfred

P.S. My next book is going to be titled *The Rape of Elizabeth* so I suggest you buy a new batch of dental floss—plus a bottle of Chicago-hot sauce.

To George Shively

[Minneapolis, Minnesota]
September 24, 1952

Dear George:
    This is a hurry-up letter since I haven't much time if I'm to do what I have in mind. Could you send me $200 via Curtis Brown so I can make a research trip to the Badlands of South Dakota before the early fall season is gone? I have a project in mind which will take place about this time of the year and I want to get on the scene of it right away so I can get the exact right feel and smell and sight of it as it really is, along with knowing the exact state of fauna

which the guy will live off of. I also want to spend a few days at Pierre, S.D., as well as the Black Hills, to read relevant material at historical societies. My wife is going with me to help research. (She's an expert at this.) Also, to cart me out to a scene and later come and get me after I've walked over it, miles and miles, taking notes and collecting bits of fauna and dirt and rock.

I've had this story in the back of my mind for some years now, since the summer of '44[1] when I read about it in the *South Dakota State Guide* (as well as in the *Nebraska State Guide*) while writing the first draft of *This Is The Year*. But I never knew how to get at it, or how I should do it. Two weeks ago, while out walking, it came to me just how I should do it, all the way from the working out of the plot to the exact tone and drift of it. I also got the name or title for it at that time, *The Grizzly Bear,* and have since had brainstorm after brainstorm about it, have half-filled a new notebook with thoughts about it. My wife thinks the idea wonderful. [matter deleted by author]

It goes like this: Hugh and his buddy were out scouting ahead of a scouting party in South Dakota. The year was 1832. (I may move up the date because I want to include some legendary fellow from Siouxland itself.) (Say to 1860.) Hugh and his pal went up a draw. Hugh went one way, Jamie went the other way. Hugh explored a narrow coulee, came upon a great *horribilis imperator* grizzly shebear with two cubs. Before he could get up his gun, the shebear struck. He screamed for help; fought; was hugged almost to death; finally managed to get out his knife and stabbed her in the heart. Both he (a grizzly bear sort of fellow himself) and the grizzly shebear fell. When his companion came back, he thought him dead. Jamie waited four days for him to die; all the while scared the Ree Indians would get him. Finally his fears got the best of him and Jamie grabbed Hugh's guns and flint and fled. But Hugh didn't die. When he became conscious he realized from the ashes around someone had waited for him to die; then had left him. Hugh swore vengeance and despite a horribly crippled body crawled some hundred miles to the nearest fort. He survived, and then chased after Jamie for revenge. Meanwhile, Jamie, the coward, had a change of heart, and started looking for Hugh to ask for forgiveness. They circled each other trying to find each other. Finally they did meet. But instead of Hugh killing him, Hugh is reported to have said, after covering him with his gun and walking over to him and kicking him lightly, "Get up and wag your tail. I wouldn't kill a pup." And Hugh forgave him! What a sublime thing amongst the brutes of those days.

Now I have some interesting variations on this idea; and a novel conclusion. There'll be no sex in it. It'll be an out and out adventure story in the great tradition. I want to place it in the same area that most of *The Golden Bowl* was set, including the Badlands. I also want to keep it down to *The Golden Bowl* length and think I can easily enough. I've divided it into three movements: 1) "The Wrestle," 2) "The Crawl" (or "The Resolve"), 3) "The Showdown." I'm tremendously excited about this idea and feel I should do it before tackling *Sons of Adam*. I also feel that we can sell this to some magazine before publishing it in book form. Moreover, it'll also make a fine western movie I feel. I've always wanted to do a western, and here it is. A perfect plot for this particular author. And the reason I want to have the money now is that I've got to see the terrain now and do the research now in Pierre before the winter snows come and before the leaves fall. I can write it in the winter.

By the time you get this I shall have a readable draft, a good one, all done of *The Rape of Elizabeth*. Before I send it on to you, I want a lawyer and a young critic friend to read it. The lawyer especially since there's a lot of legal stuff involved. They can be reading it next week and the week after while Maryanna and I are busy researching in South Dakota. When I come back I intend to go over the whole book again for a final exhaustive reading and rewriting. I think the book is very fine, wonderful, a barn-burner like I said, even though I despair a little over a thirty or forty page section that is a little slow for me. The lawyer has already read the first third and part of the second third, and he says he can't lay it down. He wants to read the whole thing twice, once to get the story and the second time to catch the fine points of law involved.

What do you say to the $200? I need that much since I've only two good tires and should have at least three in that rough country. Otherwise the car is fine. (It's an old '38 Ford, but I've taken good care of it.) I can buy good tires second hand. I'd like to start out next Wednesday if possible. We've also got a sitter for the kids— Gramma.

Are you going to write out a new contract on *World's Wanderer* for the boxed sets?

In great haste,
Fred

To Alan C. Collins

[Minneapolis, Minnesota]
November 14, 1952

Dear Alan:

Please read accompanying copies of telegrams plus letters to Cerf and Maule of Random House.

I'm done with Doubleday. True, they've been good to me financially, but at the same time I can't let them take picks on my work, so that my files fill up with publishable books, some of which are sure to make their mark when the literary history of this century is written. They have turned down five projects of mine, now, and they are, to refresh your memory: *The Stumbling Stone, Winterkill, Sinclair Lewis: In Memoriam* (pamphlet containing funeral eulogy and personal impressions of Red), *The Mountain of Myrrh,* and now, the best yet, *The Rape of Elizabeth.* I hate divorce but here's a case where it had better be for all parties concerned. I note that they still want to see that western. This absolutely proves in my mind that they had me typed, as big companies often do, and when I departed from that type, they got cold feet, especially when they didn't make money on me. Had I made a lot of money for them they would have shut up. Alan, I have to follow my nose. Otherwise I'm a literary whore. I was warned by various people in the publishing world (I'll give names if you want them) that they were highly commercial and would try to push me around if I didn't make money for them. This fits in with my funny feeling that they seemed to be publishing me for one reason while I thought I was writing for another. And also fits my wife's feeling about them, to wit, "I've never seen a Doubleday man yet but what he didn't look and act like an account executive from an advertising agency. They don't have the air of being interested in literature." And actually, when I think of the royalties that Fitzgerald owed Scribners at one time, and of Dreiser with Lippincott (some $30,000), they haven't really been hurt too badly by me, not as long as they can publish all that junk they do turn out. (I'm still furious that they turned down *Mountain* while at the same time taking all that shit they've published since.) (My book was better than 90 percent of what they turn out.) So I'm done. Inform them that as soon as I get an advance from my new publisher, I'll return that $200 on *The Grizzly Bear* via your office. I want my new publisher to have a crack at that of course. So, I'm done. Perhaps just as well. I'm only stuck for three works with them, *This Is The Year, The Chokecherry Tree,* and *World's Wanderer,* and perhaps someday, when my day comes, we can have those plates bought up by The Modern Library. Inform Doubleday that they must not destroy those plates without informing me so I can borrow money from somebody to buy them.

To Harrison Smith

[Minneapolis, Minnesota]
November 17, 1952

Dear Mr. Smith:

I'm enclosing two things, the "Memoir" and a page of copies of letters. Two other letters and a note are in the "Memoir." As you probably know, the last years Red wasn't much for writing letters and continually warned me not to waste writing energy on letters which could become book paragraphs. He had a good point there because a fellow can waste a lot of time answering fan mail. However, in my own case, I like to write lengthy vernacular letters to dear friends, mostly because they often help me unlock or unloosen a word jam, as well as help me cut down on the polysyllabic style that likes to creep up on me.

I'm sorry the letters are so scanty. Their main interest probably lies in tying Red down to a certain place in a certain time. I wasn't going to include a copy of his autograph to me in his book but my wife said I should. I send it along modestly because I'm a long way from being a great man. That's still ahead, if at all. A man shouldn't look back too much to see how his furrow is coming along for fear he'll go askew ahead. Fix a point and bear steadily toward it, is my view.

I also note, in rereading the "Memoir," that it is rather personal. I've obtruded my person in it too much, even if it is from my journal at the time. I also note some boyish writing in it. But it is natural and it comes from the journal. There is a lot of conversation in it, but that I vouch for, to the word and letter. I have an excellent memory. And trust it implicitly in connection with remembering what I've heard people say.

I've often wondered about Red and his various lady friends. I felt that Lewis needed a woman who would not compete with him in his own field and who would be, truly, his wife and woman. He had the misfortune of many another writer who's married a woman with writing talent and whose wife becomes in part jealous, e.g., Thackeray, Warren, etc. Red wanted to believe and love with all his heart. But the women fell down on him. His instinct in choosing the right one for himself wasn't too good in the begin-

ning and by the time he was in his fifties he was becoming a little
too suspicious of them, even though he still desperately wanted
the true soul mate. I'm convinced only one in ten finds the right
woman. So perhaps there simply isn't such a thing. What we find
are women who bear our children and who try to be wives and who
shuffle on to the end like we do.

Red and I never had words (save for that close shave narrated
in the "Memoir"). He moved very carefully around me and I
around him. But we were hearty and frank, as sharp upright men
should be. There were times when he treated me as if he were my
uncle; sometimes as my older brother. He was a little worried
about my odd name, Feike Feikema, liked Fred and Frederick, and
I'm sure would have okayed my new and now legal name of Frederick Feikema Manfred (with Feikema being gradually dropped
out perhaps). I'm not sure he always liked my writing. It was a little
too masculine; or rather, bold for him. But then he forgave me
when he learned I was of Frisian stock. "They're a tough vigorous
people," he admitted. I often had the feeling that while he wasn't
exactly afraid of me, he didn't quite get me. He thought me singular, I think. He recognized the American in me, but there was also
something else.

But he liked me and liked to give advice right and left, including
the kind of clothes I should wear, the way I should space my MS.,
the way I should talk up to a publisher, the way I should fight for
my rights as a writer. He worried a little about the poet in me, he
once told me, but he had an idea I'd keep the horse under control.
(I don't know if I have, or if I want to, according to his lights.) I
called on him once at the Algonquin, and when he saw who it was,
someone from Minnesota, he threw his arms around me. "My boy,
my boy, I can still smell the Minnesota sun in your clothes. And
how are you?"

He and I were at a party one night, he in one corner, I in another. Somehow I got into an argument with a "broken prism egg-
head of the Kenyon School" and was going at it hammer and tongs,
using some pretty solid biological and agricultural type of arguments. He was smiling to himself. Later someone told me he had
whispered behind his hand, "Listen to him. Listen to him. And
I taught him all that."

Other people have told me they got terribly nervous around
him, worrying what he would do next. I never did. I'd had a tower
of a father who often got into towering rages. So Red couldn't

shock me, not after Pa. Also, I felt that it was the Head Bull's right to roar a little and keep the flock in line. I'm all for strong vigorous roaring males. (Too many timid males around and too many roaring females around to suit me, anyway.) A righteous rage is a fine thing to see. Especially when it comes from a poppa of many writers who is brilliant, honest, penetrating, dazzling. Such a sensitive nature, with all that power under it, is bound to tragedy. And his was tragedy at the end. While Scott F.'s end was, to me, hardly more than a pathetic drunken sot's end. Red's remark at the end there said it all, "Something terrible is happening to me." Death is terrible for one with his great great candlepower. All that light gone.

Yes, I know you have criticized my writing. But you did it fairly, soberly, and even kindly. So I can only feel sad about that, but never angry. I only get angry at that persnickety sophomoric stuff that shows up in *The New Yorker* and *Time* now and then. In my own mind I rest confident. It happened that I read *Don Quixote* after I finished *World's Wanderer*. And it hit me that I written another, in a way. With the same wild flights and strange faults, but yet, in all, a history of man and men. I wrote the book in warm irony, mostly. A hundred years from now that book is going to stand out by itself. To me it is one of the most complicated books ever put on paper. Well, the end of the page. If I have more thoughts on Red I'll send them along.

Fred

P.S. *Next morning.* More anecdotes as others tell it. Scotty McDonald (woman publicity director of the U. Press) says she was at a party here one night when suddenly in the midst of the talk, Red jumped up and whispered in the host's ear and the host thereupon led him upstairs with Scotty following. The host showed him a bedroom radio and Red turned it on and tuned in on Dorothy Thompson,[1] who was haranguing the nation on some issue or other. Red listened with rapt eyes and when she'd finished he hit his knee and said, "Atta girl, Dotty, give 'em hell. You can do it."

I was working at *Modern Medicine* as editor in the fall of 1942. One of the girls there was taking a course with Red Lewis at the U. She came back with countless tales, including the one where he asks how many of them there are serious about being writers and when they all raised their hands he says, "Well, why aren't you home then writing!" She also told the charming story of the time

1. Sinclair Lewis's former wife.

when Red singled out a story by a young man and read it in class.
Red went into ecstasies over it but confessed he didn't know why it
was good. He sat down, says this girl, he sat down on the corner
of his desk and read it over again and again raved about it but again
confessed he didn't know why it was good. This happened four
times, with the class getting more and more bored but with Red
getting more and more excited. After class let out, the girl happened to see the young fellow in the hall and he was turning red
and white and blue by turns like a revolving barber pole. Around
him stood Tom Heggen, Max Shulman, Bud Nye, urging him to
introduce himself as the young man who had written that "great"
work. The young man was too modest and escaped the adulating
group. His name was Russell Roth. Russell has since been to war,
taught at the U, rebelled against the Kenyon group, lectured on
Faulkner on the U. radio, written brilliantly on Faulkner in various
little magazines, has written a novel that my first publisher thought
wonderful. The novel is now at Scribners. Russ is also a fine drum-
mer and is an expert on jazz. He has one of the richest minds
around here. So again Red was right there with the finger on the
pulse.

At a party which Meridel Le Sueur attended (it was at Joseph
Warren Beach's house — you know him, teacher, poet, critic) Red
suddenly lashed out at Red Warren who had sat all night without
a word. Red Warren is a gentleman, and also at opposite poles liter-
arily speaking and so he wouldn't talk up. According to Meridel,
Red Lewis was pretty rough on Red Warren, scathing him for hiding under a faded old man's wings (Ransom) and being silent on
the Negro question. But Red Warren didn't bite or rise to the bait.
Later on, Red Lewis came to praise Red Warren's book, *All the
King's Men*.

At a party I attended someone happened to mention a survey
of his work by Max Geismar that was then appearing in *The Saturday Review*. The person reporting it seemed to indicate Geismar
wasn't friendly. (Geismar actually was, however.) Red muttered, "I
don't care what they say at this late date. I don't care what they say.
I write what I please. If I'd've listened to advice I'd right now
be in the old people's home south of town. The hell with 'em."
He threw a quick look at me as if to say, "Son, that's the way to
handle it."

Another story is told by Dr. Max Seham. They met him early

in the twenties when he was still married to his first wife. He was
electric, excited, ebullient, Max said, and foolishly uxoriously dot-
ing on his wife. When Red happened to leave the room for a little
while, his wife told everyone there that the reason Red loved her so
was that Red was grateful to her for giving him art. Red had the
power but she had taught him how to express it as an artist. Max
said he almost choked when she went on to say she was the daughter of a famous art dealer. Max knew what her father had really
been, some one who sold picture frames. The real point was, however, that she believed it because Red had talked her into thinking
just that. She had to be something "great" to Red and when she
didn't have it he invented it.

Maryanna my wife happened to spot a poem of Michael Lewis
in a national weekly. She clipped it out and the next time we met
at a party here she gave it to him. He gave her a resounding kiss,
embraced her like a father, read it a half dozen times. The first time
he said, "Wonderful. Wonderful writing." Then he cocked an eye
at the watchers, who were watching how he was going to take this
evidence of his son's talent, and said, the second time, "Good. It's
good." The next time he read it, "It's fine. Some sentiment in it
that's a little sloppy. But otherwise it's fine." Progressively he ran
it down a little, and said less and less. Red knew that people with
sharp little knives were sitting in the crowd waiting for him to show
his heart. And Red very wisely covered it over. My heart bled for
him.

At this same party someone asked Red if he'd noticed that that
Fred Feikema guy sometimes wasn't loath to talk about himself.
(I happened to overhear this: I have long ears trained on the
plains.) "Who doesn't?" Red shot back. And the Red added, "But
there's one thing he does that the rest of those who talk about
themselves don't do. Fred can talk about himself as if he were another person. He can take himself apart and his work apart better
than anybody else I ever saw. Just leave Fred alone if you don't want
to get into trouble. Just be thankful he don't take you apart like
he does himself."

At this same party one of the broken prism boys was complaining about how boring *The Saturday Review* had become, that it no
longer was the literary organ it once was. I took issue on this and
just for the fun of it argued that some of the best articles of the day
appeared in it, e.g., Ransom on Warren, Wm. Van O'Connor on

Stevens, etc. Red gave me a big wink and a little later said, "That was a real legpull, Fred. I couldn't have done better myself. You shut 'em up tight." He and I had a wonderful laugh then.

F.F.M.

1953

The letters of 1953 are dominated by the writing of Lord Grizzly *and its enthusiastic reception by a new publisher, McGraw-Hill. A generous advance from McGraw-Hill and a National Institute of Arts and Letters grant enable Manfred to pursue research in Hugh Glass country. In addition to tracing the conception of the novel, the letters detail other literary efforts such as the combining of* The Mountain of Myrrh *and* The Rape of Elizabeth *into one novel. In September, Manfred urges McGraw-Hill to buy up the rights on all of his books from Webb and Doubleday.*

To Maxwell Geismar

[Minneapolis, Minnesota]
January 2, 1953

Dear Max,

I know I've been negligent. Should have written you much sooner. I've been working hard; I've been fighting off the black thoughts; I've been plotting the new opus. And—I've been fighting with publishers.

When Doubleday declined *The Rape of Elizabeth,* I asked my agent to send it on to Harry E. Maule, Sinclair Lewis's editor. I had promised him next shot at any of my books. He has had it since November and I haven't had final word from him yet, though I've had a couple of letters, one to say that he was well into it and found that it had "tremendous narrative drive." Last year when Doubleday rejected my little *The Mountain of Myrrh,* I was furious. This fall I was merely numb. They don't like it that I'm departing from a formula called Wolfe-Dos Passos. I'm not supposed to write about the Cities at all. Just stick to the manure piles of Siouxland. I have as deep feeling about the Cities as I do about the country. In fact, I had both in *Rape.* Also I wrote about fellows quite different from myself. I think an author should if he feels impelled to. Funny thing is, some of the postwar boys who have read it think it the best book I've ever written. They keep telling me I've caught them and their lives exactly; in fact accuse me of writing about them personally (which I didn't). One young fellow,[1] who has written a lot of Faulkner criticism in the little magazines, says it's the best yet. (He is sending out a survey or essay on all my work so far; it has been at *The Saturday Review* and *Atlantic*.) I wouldn't worry about the books—except that I am so terribly broke. And in debt so far that even a good advance will just barely catch me up. In case Random House turns me down, I'm going to have it sent either to Houghton Mifflin or Ballantine.

But my dauber is not down. I am confident. Though it is hard work to first create one's own audience and then write for it. Which is what I am doing. (I haven't read the young critic's essay on me; but from his remarks when he went over my files he says the same thing.) The funny thing is: Doubleday, Simon & Schuster, others, have heard I'm thinking of doing a historical novel called *Old Hugh Glass*. And they want that, of course. Write me letters about it even and out of turn. It almost makes me want to drop it, because to me it isn't a historical per se. I just happened to be interested in the idea of it: from violence to revenge to love. (That is the subject of *Rape* too: the incitement to violence, the act of lust, the act of light, the act of love—in other words, "true justice is finally done.")
(*Rape*: married war vet during a violent storm finds potency returned to him; he climbs aboard a country girl in the same hospital he's in; a fire breaks out and he takes her to his home with his wife gone; he lets her go finally. She reports act to cops. Public defender enters after boy is jailed. He noses around; senses that girl lied a little; that she too has problems; drops a hint in her mind; she feels guilty and backs out of charge; his hint also relaxes her so she finally marries; justice is finally done when it is established boy is back on beam; book ends with boy driving family to another town for a fresh start and fighting snowstorm in which he roars at his car motor, "C'mon, baby, gimme some guts. C'mon, baby, gimme some guts.")

I too find that if I let my things lie around for a year or so I can then see what is fluff and dead skin and dead flesh and unnecessary scaffolding. I've done it with every novel I ever wrote.

I liked Steinbeck's latest[2] because he introduced a likable casual "I" note in it. Cuteness and coyness had been dropped for a direct-talking note. Also, the lines were wiser (though some were a bit boring for intellectuals). Also, he seemed to be giving "modern

1. Russell Roth.

2. *East of Eden*.

psychological wisdom" a stiff arm in it, and that is a good of a sort. Also, he seemed to be listening to that Leviathan that lies below in each soul, to the Voice.

There is an interesting dichotomy in this community as far as writers go: the group at the U with Allen Tate and Caroline Gordon and Wm. Van O'Connor and others versus Brennan, Roth, Manfred, Earl Guy, etc. (There is also a fine American Studies Program at the University.) Yet we all see each other and have our spats. I usually don't get into it; just sit back and listen. I let my books speak for me.

Oh yes. The young critic also sent the essay on me to John Crowe Ransom and by jaeggers if he didn't write a condescending note in return: to the effect that I was a "good man" but that I was guilty of hasty writing and that I needed advice badly. Which made me laugh. If it had been left to Ransom, fellows like Dreiser would never have been published.

I am very anxious to see your new book. Dan told me you had had it accepted. Which is good news indeed. And I bet you're now in that horrible state of in-between-books where you don't know if you should shoot yourself or jump out the window.

Write me when you have time.

Affectionately,
Fred

And call me what you wish, Feike, Fred, Slim, Shorty, etc. That is your privilege.

F.M.M.

To Lora Crouch

Frederick Feikema Manfred
[Minneapolis, Minnesota]
January 30, 1953

Dear Lora:

I've long ago finished the books, but was holding volume one because it had the best stuff on Glass and on forts Kiowa and Lookout. I've now copied out what I need and am sending it back to you, along with the other three, which I really don't need.

I have read Alter's *J. Bridger* and its footnotes were very fine. I haven't come across the other two references, but then I have some checking yet to do at the Minnesota Historical Library. The Minnesota Library had so much I'm just now getting on top of it. If I don't get those two other references you list, I'll drop you a note, and you can have them there at your office at some specific time when I'm coming through and I can read them right under your guardian wing.

The main thing, as I see it, is to make sure that whatever I happen to use is used right. Once I start writing I follow my nose (or instinct) as much as possible. This sometimes leads back to the notebooks, but not always.

I hope to begin *Old Hugh Glass* (my present title; though I also like *The Far Country*) sometime in early March and have two-thirds of the first draft done by June, when I plan a long excursion up the Missouri to look up the spots he'll visit in part three.

Many thanks for being so lenient with this one-time patron. My best to you. You're a dear woman and I send you my blessings and an empathic South Dakota kiss.

Sincerely, as always,
Fred

To William Carlos Williams

[Minneapolis, Minnesota]
February 20, 1953

Dear William Carlos Williams—

Sitting here in my kiva or workshop (better yet, just "the shop"), with a tearing backache from the flu, I can't help but write you that I'm at last caught up on a man named William Carlos Williams in his books. This morning I finished *In the American Grain,* having gone through the Autobiography and poems and novels earlier. The whole process has been one of coming to know and love an uncle. I have come to know the man; I have come to know the passion to find the American man and the American artist; I have come to know almost precisely what you mean by "the American line."

I was especially interested in *In the American Grain.* Every line became a slogan for me, it seemed. Not really, since it was real and powerful to me, awakening every chord in my being. I now understand more than I ever did just what it was I was always defending when I got into arguments with editors, critics, and my wife. They had a notion as to what they had got out of their reading and they felt that what I was doing had to be near or kin to it otherwise it wasn't "literature." They didn't know what I felt, what I saw, far inward. They didn't know I had to keep bearing toward that inner flame with blinded eyes, that only when I was facing it could I de-

termine if the light was there at all by a sort of vague red illu-
mination touching my eyes through my nearly closed lids. They
didn't know that when I deserted that vague but magnetic light I
was nobody, not even the kind of person who might possibly do
what they asked me to do, that if I did try it without that vague
blood light, I was worse than a second-rate traditionalist. It has
been hard. When I was first beating at the doors to get published,
editors kept telling me I wrote too episodic and that epics were out
of style (and why not when life on the plains is both epic and episodic?) that I should go look at Rölvaag, at Garland, at Steinbeck,
for attack, dialogue, and I kept saying I couldn't because what they
saw and what I saw were almost two different things, that in all
three cases the dialogue or "line" was false, that what I had heard
I had heard. Finally a western or midland publisher put out my first
two books. Then the eastern geldings got wise, seeing some of the
reviews. The "word" got around. I got telegrams from publishers.
If you're not happy, etc. Finally my western publisher, knowing
I needed money for a family, said, "Go to an eastern publisher.
Maybe they're ready for you." I got five published. (Actually only
three, because one was a trilogy.) Lots of critical noise, pro and
con, pro from the country (Boston, Los Angeles, the South, Midlands) con from Zombie City (New York City), poor sales, and
so now no more acceptances, not for four books, *Chips From the
Chopping Block* (tales), *Winterkill* (poems), *The Mountain of Myrrh*
(novel), and *The Rape of Elizabeth* (novel). And poor excuses. There
is no money in them; but they try to argue there is no value in
them. We're far behind in mortgage money, etc., may lose our
house. Well, I'm still right. Because you are right, as Poe was right,
Twain was right, Faulkner was right. (You have a real friend, by
the way, in a young Russell Roth.) (He knows your books by
heart.) I haven't been East since 1947. But when I come I want to
talk to you. I now understand the letter you sent me in 1946 about
Boy Almighty.

Yours,
Fred

P.S. My legal name was always Frederick Feikema. Manfred is a
translation of Feikema. (Fred=Feike; man=ma). I was tired of answering the question, "What an odd name—how do you pronounce it? What is your nationality?" I am an American. That

question was beside the point. I am an American just like a French-man is a Frenchman. F.F.M

P.P.S. Give my regards to the Hoaglands.

To Bernard DeVoto

[Minneapolis, Minnesota]
March 4, 1953

Dear Mr. DeVoto:

I'm confronted with somewhat of a puzzle. Since 1944 when I first came across the tale, I've dreamt of doing a short terse novel about old Hugh Glass. Since that time I've slowly been soaking up the Old West by reading your books plus Ruxton, Garrard, Lewis & Clark, Larpenteur, Clyman, Chittenden, etc., and lately Donald McKay Frost. Most of the things I've read have either awakened memories of old tales told by the natives of my home town, Doon, Iowa, near the Big Sioux River, or have tied them-selves to these old memories. (Only the other week an old trapper, just returned from the Dakotas, died in a shack on the edge of Doon. It burned down around him. He probably was having his first spree since last summer.) All this reading connected what I knew first-hand (as a farmboy and tramp and hired hand) with a usable past. Now to the puzzle.

Suppose, in this historical novel of mine, suppose I say that it was Jim Bridger and Tom Fitzpatrick who deserted Hugh Glass at the forks of the Grand River? Can I get away with it? Will histor-ical-minded reviewers kick my can for me? In all my reading I can find no concrete evidence that it was Jim and Tom, only hints. On the other hand, the names of no other men are mentioned in connection with it. And checking the movements of Jim and Tom it is possible they could have been the men. We do know that Jim was with Major Henry on the Yellowstone later in the year. And it is likely that Tom might have been sent back to Ft. Kiowa to Ashley with the news that Major Henry was moving from the confluence of the Yellowstone and the Missouri to the confluence of the Yel-lowstone and the Big Horn. And Tom might have got to Ft. Kiowa in time to accompany Jedediah Smith and Clyman when they took the overland route past the Black Hills to the Big Horn. Smith and company didn't leave Ft. Kiowa until late September. My feeling is that I can use the same literary license that Bill Shakespeare used. What do you think?

My plan is to show that Old Hugh made up that story that the boys "even had my grave dug for me," that he failed to realize the helluva spot they were in. Also, when Old Hugh at Ft. Atkinson sees Tom come in from across Nebraska in September of 1824, ragged, almost dead, he has sympathy for his plight. This, plus time, plus other considerations, help Old Hugh to forgive. Nobody is a villain in this case.

Sincerely,
Frederick Feikema Manfred

P.S. Here is what Houghton Mifflin said: "Frederick Manfred's novel, *The Rape of Elizabeth,* has now had several readings. As one of the readers said, 'There is no doubt that Mr. Manfred can tell a story. I only wish he had picked another one to tell.' He writes with force."

To Van Wyck Brooks

[Minneapolis, Minnesota]
(Spring, and a new season!)
March 21, 1953

Dear Van Wyck Brooks:

First, I want to thank you for having told Mr. Wreden about me. With this mail I'm sending him a long letter in which I am telling him he is going to get work or books to look at. Just yesterday I got the news that title to my "literary property" is free. I gave Mr. Wreden a list of books "done," books "in progress," and books "in plan." The list is as follows: *Chips From the Chopping Block* (tales), *The Mountain of Myrrh* (novel about politics and love and life around a weekly in a small village near a huge city-boss-run city), *North Star* (novel in which the crime is rape and in which the theme is justice: the hero is a returned war veteran who has trouble adjusting to reality around him), *Lord Grizzly* (historical novel about Hugh Glass and the grizzly bear), *Sons of Adam* (trilogy with subtitles, *The Frustrates, The Outlaws, The Pilgrims,* about a polar relationship between a city-bred boy and a country boy, with background in a newspaper and university as opposed to Siouxland and slaughterhouse, and, like *Lord Grizzly,* yet to be written), *Wings*[1] (duology with sub-titles, *The Fledglings, The Flight,* about my family, which I haven't tackled yet, mostly because I wanted distance between the "now" of writing and the days themselves, also to be written), *Siouxland* (decology with sub-titles, Pa, Ma, Tane, Thea, Dirk, Tressa, Lute, Johanna, Freya, Geoffrey, and all Freylings

1. *Green Earth.*

2. The Rape of Carla
Simmons.

living in my beloved Siouxland, starting with the year 1900 and on
into the present, still to be done), *Born*[2] (with sub-titles, *The Seed,
The Stalk, The Ear,* dealing with all the factors and influences at
work before a child is born, dealing with folk like my wife's family
who are of Slovakian descent), and *Miscellany* (poems *Winterkill*
and *Meltwater,* novelettes, stories, and a thing I want to call the
Journals & Letters of F. F. Manfred). I've staked out the continents
I want to explore and have an elastic and adaptable battle plan for
the attack. Much frozen tundra remains in my mind which has to
be thawed out and then farmed. But, God-willing, and with patience, and fortitude, I think I can do something that will weather
much time and chance. One thing I hope for: if Mr. Wreden
himself can't handle me that he assign me a young man editor, a
vigorous fellow who has some sympathy for a Midlander with Midland American themes and forms (mine are Upper Midland and
are every bit as valuable as Lower Midland Faulkner's), and who
knows that it will probably be the long haul in my case before I get
the large audience an author needs, though those who've seen the
little I've done on *Lord Grizzly* and who've heard me describe the
plot and problem believe I've got something profound which may
catch the popular fancy as well. Looking over the careers of Faulkner, Hemingway, Lewis, Steinbeck, I find that it was a close personal contact between editor and author which proved valuable
and lasting for both publisher and author. There must be faith,
trust, friendship, or there is nothing. That was one of the beauties
of my relationship with Hillestad at Webb's. Too bad they had no
distribution. They, Dutton, must look at my work as a whole, both
done and yet to come, to arrive at a true estimate of it. And the new
generation coming in will be the one to save me, just as the generation behind Faulkner saved him.

Most sincerely,
Fred

P.S. Could you tell Mr. Wreden some of these thoughts—better
yet, show him this letter?

F.F.M.

To Bernard DeVoto

[Minneapolis, Minnesota]
May 15, 1953

Dear Mr. DeVoto:

Humphrey *is* a damned good man. I'm his friend, have been ever since he first ran (when three of us sitting in his house decided he should run for mayor), have been even before that when he attended the University here. He is brilliant. In his youth his brilliance often caused him to lack thoroughness, depth. His brilliance would carry him over the obstruction, not through it. But lately he has shown great ability to research carefully, to think long and deep, and to be humble about it. He is going now and I'm very proud of him and am very fond of him. He and I can get into the damnedest confidential talks about love and war and politics and wives etc. He's a damned good liberal who never once was attracted to communism. I'm glad you like him. He was here over the weekend and I told him what you wrote me. He beamed all over.

About whether you like or dislike *Boy Almighty,* you're right: once a book is public domain the author can't do much about it if people like it or don't like it. And I don't give a rip either—except in those times when I'm desperately broke. When I'm broke I react a little like a storekeeper who hears people "unjustly" complaining about his produce. I tend to fight back then for the sake of my wife and kiddies and my "bosom friends the t.b. bugs" who depend on me for their support. Privately I have a notion that I'm doing some of the best writing going and nobody can touch that, but even if that were not true, so what? The truth of it or the lack of truth of it will not move mountains probably.

In any case I'm glad you like the books generally, that they are affording you some pleasure, emotional, aesthetic, even intellectual. To have you for my friend and in part an admirer is a most warming thing and it has fired me in my story about Hugh Glass. (I'm about half through the first draft. I've even dreamt about him, let alone feel sick when he feels sick, feel faint when he feels faint, etc., so that my wife thinks I'm a little off my nut—despite the evidence at the University where personality tests show I'm as solid as a rock emotionally.)[1]

Dutton's seems to be very very interested. Suddenly too I get letters from Scott Bartlett of McGraw-Hill that he is an admirer of mine and wants to publish me, as well as from Strauss at Knopf. Things are booming. And I hear that Herb Alexander at Pocket Books is sold on me and is trying to get them to reprint my earlier books. Good too.

1. Manfred took the Minnesota Multiphasic Personality Inventory, invented by his friend Starke Hathaway.

And I back you 100% in your notion about not telling the FBI anything except in an open court where the defendant can hear it with a lawyer present. And I back you in your battling with McCarthy. That man now and then shows evidence of paranoia.

Best, as always,
Frederick

To David Cornel De Jong

[Minneapolis, Minnesota]
June 6, 1953

Dear Dave:

Have been in the doldrums too. Doubleday rejected a collection of short stories plus a novel. No objection to content necessarily. Mostly that there are few buyers of this man's product. Have been at work on a novel about the Old Far West back in the time of 1823–24 and this has been very rewarding. Didn't know my bit of country had so much history. A white man by the name of Charles Pierre Le Sueur took a dugout down the Sioux River around 1680. Which makes Siouxland an old land indeed by white-man standards. Other fabulous things were uncovered. Will give me a sense of depth and of being rooted. Doubleday is interested in this book but so are Dutton, McGraw-Hill, and Knopf. McGraw-Hill by the way is not going in for fiction. Scott Bartlett is the man there. They have plenty of money, few novelists, and you and I might be the best they got instead of two among hundreds of entries.

That lancing of the throat business, how did that turn out? Wouldn't it be swell if it gave you back a normal voice? A fine joke on the Old Calvinists. I figure I'm a walking taunt to them. I should have died long ago from TB, but didn't. I run a ten-acre place here, write books which make them groan, have fathered two girls (by luck), etc., though I must also admit that I don't talk about the growths I have in the palms of my hands and feet which we must periodically take out (probably due to overwork on Dutch farms around Doon). But I enjoy the sun and the green grass of June and the black soil of my garden and my long lonely walks in the country and many visits to U campus where there are plays and music and friends and books.

Have been reading Conrad again. My mother-in-law found a leather-bound set of his works. Am about half-way through. At first I found his "line" or "sentence" a bunch of broken toothpicks pasted together again. I had to backtrack and backtrack to get sense. I had the vague feeling I was reading translation most of the time. Later on I noticed that either I got more used to him or Conrad got more used to using the English language. I'm now reading *The Secret Sharer* and that's rolling along swell on my tongue. Conrad had a lot to say, but he is curiously lacking in poetry, in fancy, is mostly an intellectual. He can build mood, and irony. He knows nothing about women, except when they're savage and I'm not sure he knows them since I have nothing to go by. Conrad is the hero of the New Critics (some of them) and I can see why. By gum, give me flesh, blood, semen, poetry, the bardic, and dramatic taling. Shakespeare didn't have the "brains" either but he was readable and alive and human and perhaps more profound. Me, I'm suspicious as hell about "brains." I've watched these brainy fellows and dames at parties and it always makes me laugh to see them rationalize their biologic drives into something "very intellectual." Write me about your operation. I'd like to know. Have you tried a Fulbright? I'm halfway toying with the idea. Regards to the good wife.

From us all, it beste,
Fred

To Scott Bartlett[1]

[Minneapolis, Minnesota]
July 28, 1953

1. Editor at McGraw-Hill Book Company.

Dear Scott:

I'm sorry our connection was bad. We've had some wind storms out here in the country and the lines were still makeshift.

I do hope you've found someone who'll read the book quickly and who'll also know his stuff. I do know DeVoto is on the road for the National Park Service, since I ran across trail of him at Scottsbluff, Nebraska. So I doubt whether you could reach him quickly enough. Also, I don't think he'd know as much as I or my friend Jim Howard about the Ree Indians. He might know the mountaineer better. Guthrie is good, but I might disagree with him. Stanley Vestal knows his stuff but I've become just a mite suspicious of his ideas because he sometimes gooses it up a little in his books. I may not have explained this to you, but I read hundreds of sources, digging out everything ever printed about Old Hugh. I'm probably the only expert in the world on Hugh. No one has ever put that together.

The trip turned out to be very valuable. I determined that a

number of the state guide-books are in error about the places or
locations of certain forts. I know because I walked to the spot and
kicked out the outlines of the forts, both white man fort and Ree
fort. Even my friend Jim Howard, the Ree expert, was in error on
some things. He tried to tell me that the Rees didn't wear a horse-
ear like headdress made of bones. I determined that they did (I
talked to an old Ree priest or medicine man), though it was not
a wolfbone headdress but an eagle thighbone headdress. And so
on. I think I've got the exact and final knowledge now and need
only to repolish and recorrect the book and we'll have the best goddam book ever written of the time. *Lord Grizzly* will be the model
for years to come. Not Guthrie's. Though he is good.

You asked if I've thought of doing more historicals. Well, yes.
But I've got to brood on it some more. But I also have my other
ideas of my own day and time. The truth is my first seven books are
far more creative and "monumental" than people suspect. Only
one reviewer has ever caught up with my books—a Christopher
Matthew of the Milwaukee *Journal,* an old professor-reviewer. I
don't say this in braggadocio—just as a matter of fact. I hope I live
to be eighty. I have ideas for at least two good men. Would like to
suggest you don't hold the book too long, because the book is in
me, and alive, and burbling, and we must catch the oil while the
well is blowing.

Isn't it odd to be introduced over a phone? A dozen questions
sit behind the least little remark.

Cordially,
Fred

Would it be worth either or both your or my time to talk face-to-
face before we join up?

To Scott Bartlett

[Minneapolis, Minnesota]
August 5, 1953

Dear Scott:

The offer you make is a good one and I'm telling Alan [Collins]
to go ahead. I am very happy about the new set-up. And I'm most
glad you're so enthusiastic about *Lord Grizzly.* Send it back and I'll
get at it pronto. It's all right with me if you have someone examine
it when it comes back—though I hope to make it so airtight nobody can quarrel with it. And yes, that trip I took was done solely
to make *Lord Grizzly* impeccable.

About *The Mountain of Myrrh*. The other day the thought occurred to me that that title fit the other book I've got a start on (the
one I called *The Blood of Grapes* in my last letter to you and which
I once called *The Rape of Elizabeth*). This led me to discuss it with
a friend of mine, Russell Roth, a brilliant young critic (see *Western
Review,* summer issue) and he agreed. From that I arrived at the
conclusion that I should completely dismantle both those books
and start all over, keeping the title *Mountain of Myrrh*,[1] a title I always thought a wonder. I might get a *This Is The Year* out of it.
Year I made two attacks on too before I finally got the magic formula for the third draft. In any case, send the present *The Mountain
of Myrrh* back to me express. You'll see a completely *new book* in a
couple of years (Locale here). And oh yes, could you tell me what
you thought were the better passages and scenes in it? That will
help a lot.

1. Later *Morning Red*.

Also send back *Chips*. It can just as well lie here in my fire-proof
filing cabinet. After *Grizzly* is published, we can see again, perhaps
publishing *Chips* in the spring of '55 if we have a great run on *Grizzly*. All I ask is that *Chips* just pays its way.

That's it then: *Grizzly* I'm to repolish as soon as possible, *Myrrh*
is to come back and be reborn again, and *Chips* is to take a rest until
after *Grizzly* is out. Okay?

Again let me say it: both my wife and I are very happy about
the new arrangement. And do send *Grizzly* on as soon as possible.

Sincerely,
Fred
Frederick Feikema Manfred

To Russell Roth

[Minneapolis, Minnesota]
September 21, 1953

Dear Russell:

Fall is coming in and I'm not yet ready to give up summer. I
haven't had my natural summer: have been gone all through it. I
didn't taste it every day. And too many of my summers are going by
like that. It's fine to be writing books, yes; but somehow I feel it's
a bit better to be eating and drinking the days more thoroughly day
by day.

Both Maryanna and I have read your long letter very carefully.
We are happy that you think the crops are getting better each year.
My own personal feeling is: it'll get better for the next fifteen years

and then level off into a plateau for a while. The trick will be to find the right seed. The land is there.

But neither of us feels that in the last while I've felt like a cripple. At least not that I feel it; or that Maryanna has felt it. Though maybe your keen eyes have seen it anyway. I have been weak in one thing: I've lamented that my family had to be deprived of some bread and some food, that we had to go to a relative to pay off our debts the last couple of years. This has eaten into me, not because of me, but because of or for my family.

There was a day when I did think I had to leave this part of the country to get the good life. That was before, during, and just after college. But I learned better by 1937, and by 1945, when I began writing *Year,* I knew for sure, when I had to relearn old lore about the farm which in my youth I scorned. Since then my quarrels with friends have been, or rather their quarrels with me have been (I'm thinking of the now dead Vic Williams, Mac Le Sueur, John Huizenga, Bob Grant), that my living out here is not a retreat but a natural course of events. These friends, and my wife at times, have wanted me to put on spats and liveried fronts, but I've always refused. I've always said, strongly, that anything I want to wear or anything I want to say my way, is the right way for me. (Just as I now wear a cap instead of a hat. I've always thought hats ridiculous.)

Which leads me to say that another reading of WW, especially the last movement of *Giant,* will tell you that that is my point about Thurs. He made the terrible mistake of thinking that he had to go to the East to be the full man, to live the good life. But he found out differently, finally, and came back and was about to become the full man, living the good life, in fact, did for a few moments live the full life (see page 380, *Giant*), when his fate caught up with him. That is, he lived for a time according to the "Devil's rules," and so had to pay for that when he returned to live according to "God's rules." It took Thurs a bit longer to learn that than it did me. But then he didn't stay in a San like I did where he could brood it out. That is why I had him cripple his hand a number of times in *Giant.* To show that he had a fatal tendency toward it. Like a deathwish.

My wife has often complained since we were married in 1942 that I looked down my nose at city folk. That I don't mean to, in my good-hearted way, but inwardly, far back, I still did it. She has complained about my high moral standards, about my high moral demands on her, on my friends, on life. She agrees that I have great

sympathy, but she thinks the other is greater. Well, I for myself
don't intend to be self-conscious about it. But I have been weak
in allowing debts and finances to get me aroused enough to throw
a lusty curse off to the East. Because Doubleday and the new
yorkers did rob me of money. Or rob my family since I don't need
much myself. (My wife can't understand how it is I'm not in the
least interested in money. But she's teaching me some little of it.
And, she has to. She is a shebear mother of two little cubs.)

I don't have to defend WW. It stands. One hundred years from
now it will carry its own world, self-explanatory, vivid, richly detailed, just as Chaucer's rambling *Tales* carries its own world for us
today. And now that I'm about to finish Bellow,[1] I know, with all
respect for Saul and his creation, that I wouldn't trade my sets of
rumes for his. His book is not very American (it is full of Old World
weariness, it has a rough Latinate difficult style for me); it is not
fiction but exposition. It is not very vivid; it is written like criticism
is being written nowadays in the *Partisan Review*. I have to work
at it like I have to work at reading Thackeray or Conrad. Good,
even great, but not natural to me. Difficult Faulkner reads very easy
compared to Bellow. (For me.) (Though Saul's book gets better
as it goes along.)

(I will say this: I may have had to write WW to prove to myself
that I did come home. And, once reassured, went out and wrote
Grizzly.)

What always makes me jump a little is that people find anger
in WW. That is, as a main theme. I don't see it. True, I did look
down my nose at the East like Cooper used to look down his nose
at the Westerners. But that's not anger. Oddly enough, the reviewers outside of New York spoke of the book's humor and comedy, of it being an Odyssey, of Thurs being an Ishmael, of Thurs
being a Werther, but never that he finally became a cripple. No,
they felt he won, in a measure, except that he had gone a little too
far to come back all the way. He went down a giant and in good
health.

I do intend to make the new *Mountain* a tragi-comedy. For one
thing I like the Twin Cities very much, mostly because it has not
as yet sunk into the evils of modern city massiveness. It is the massiveness of New York et al that hurts people. And I feel sorry for
them. But our Cities here still have lakes and trees and parks and
open lawns and access to the Wild nearby. (We are creatures of the
Wild, the natural Wild. When we become creatures of a Wild-

1. *The Adventures
of Augie March.*

made-by-our-selves, ah, God, then we got hell itself.)

Someday when you get a chance, read *Giant* again (and *Don Quixote*), especially the middle and last sections. In the meantime, and always, I like it when you get sharp with me. I may not always agree with it, but I agree with the intent. We both want things to be *good,* even if it comes from the Devil himself. There is no victory or life if one wins against pudding. That last paragraph of yours about "America is still a network of city forts" etc. is a great one. I'll fasten my eyes on that and make it my flag for the days ahead. I'll stick to that.

Fred

To Frank Feikema

[Minneapolis, Minnesota]
October 9, 1953

Dear Pa & Ma:

The last couple of times we wrote our letters crossed in the mail. Which probably sets us both wondering who wrote last and whose turn is it now. So I'll quick come in with another letter. We are all fine here. Finished hauling in the beets and carrots and squash and walnuts last week. Am winterizing my cabin, as well as the house and the car.

Last Tuesday Floyd and Freya and I drove to Hull, Iowa, to attend Gramma Longstreet's funeral. We drove down in Floyd's car, leaving early in the morning and driving back after the graveside service in Orange City. Most of the Van Engens we knew were there, besides some of the Slikkers. They held the first service in the house at Uncle Hank's, then to the church in Hull, and then to the cemetery in Orange City. Ed was pallbearer along with some of Gramma's other grandsons.

Many memories went through my mind that day. My first memory of her goes back to when I as a little boy wouldn't eat fet-met-stroop[1] because it was beef fat which hardened fast and stuck to one's teeth and was almost a hard ball before it hit one's stomach. At our home we always had hog lard, which didn't harden as fast. Grampa Frederick glowered at me, and looked terribly fierce, but Gramma said, "Ach, laat de kindt maar wesen. Hij hinderd niemand."[2] And then I remember one time when Herm and I crawled all through the new school they were building across the street. It was so fascinating I didn't take time to go to the toilet, with the result that I had a dirty pants when we got back. Gramma's nose

1. Hot beef fat with syrup.

2. "Oh, let the child alone. He isn't bothering anybody."

went up, and up, and finally when we went to bed, she spotted the blotch in my pants. "Fooi, fooi," she said, "en ik dacht het was maar een scheet."[3] Uncle Herm laughed so hard I thought he would die. I was mad at him because I was terribly ashamed of myself. I also remember the time when Herm and I crawled up into the apple tree in front of her old house in Orange City (the above tales took place there too) and we found the apples we wanted and came down and then Gramma said, looking at my long arms and my long legs and my height, "Jonge, jonge, je ben een reus!"[4] And then she went on to say Pa had better tie a stone on my head to keep me from growing up so fast. I also remember how stoic and calm she was when Grampa Frederick lay dead in the back room in his coffin, though I heard later she was quite broken up. Afterwards she told me that the man she really loved was Gerrit Stapert, her second husband. "I would gladly have jumped in the grave with him when he died," she said. I asked then about how much she liked Frederick. "Ach, jonge, je ben te jong."[5] But she finally told me he was too strict with her. It was always great fun to go to gramma's house. I remember a sort of big frame picture in which there was a portrait of one of her relatives, and there was a flag of The Netherlands in it, and a map I think, and it hung behind the door as you entered from the kitchen into the dining room. (I visited the old house this summer, but of course all those things were gone. Even the apple tree was gone.) Ah, yes, memories, memories, they ache, but they are the sweets of middle age.

The most haunting memory I have of her has to do with her remarks of the last years. "I'm ready to go. Why doesn't the Lord take me? I'm so tired of waiting. But my body just won't die." The minister mentioned this in his sermon.

I'm going to miss Gramma. She was emotional, easy to tears, sentimental, gushy at times, wasn't very practical, probably wasn't very bright, but she had a good heart, and she meant well, and she was my mother's mother.

Floyd and I also stopped to see Jake and Dora, and Jake's boy and his wife (she's pretty). We also saw Fred Zylstra at Sioux Center for a few minutes. Jake and his boy were busy cleaning up the new place they bought. Jake's a great fixer-upper. The county should hire him to revamp broken-down farms. He's an expert at it.

Uncle Hank said she passed away peacefully, quietly. She was pretty far gone. The strokes had left her almost unconscious. She

3. "And I thought it was but a fart."

4. "You are a giant!"

5. "You are too young."

was terribly thin, too, and I hardly recognized her. She weighed
only 135.

(Matter deleted by author.]

Freya and Marya send you their love. And best from Maryanna
and me,

love,
Fred

To Mark Schorer

[Minneapolis, Minnesota]
October 23, 1953

1. Of Sinclair Lewis.

Dear Schorer:

Perhaps this "glimpse" or "brief portrait"[1] will do. I'm not much
of an essayist. I have trouble formulating my thoughts in expository form; less so when I express them dramatically or poetically.
(I'm also enclosing copies of other letters he wrote me besides
those mentioned in the "glimpse.")

I was sick when the call came to do the "eulogy." I'd had a bad
case of virus pneumonia (a poor business for an ex-lunger). Moreover, I don't care much for funerals and was reluctant to accept.
But pressure was put on, and I was weak, so I agreed. So while I
was recovering I worked on the paragraphs of the *In Memoriam Address*. It occurred to me, as I composed them, that I should also
write a documentary or reportage piece, a piece done with clean
clear eyes, just as I saw him at the time. I thought it would make a
good companion piece. And I thought too to use it as part of my
journals when I should get around to publishing them as part of a
project called *The Letters & Journals* of F.F. Manfred. The
"glimpse" seemed to form an organic whole, like a short story almost, and then I decided to publish it immediately. I sent it off to
my agent, Edith Haggard. And I was astounded, as was my wife, to
have her reject it violently. Of course by the time it came back, I
was too late to get it into *Harper's, Atlantic, Saturday Review*. She
did like the eulogy, though, I must say that for her. Later on I read
where she inherited a third of Lewis' estate, and I also hear from
a spy (or gossip) that after her husband died Lewis became her
lover for a time, that to help build her prestige as an agent she got
him to give her his things. (Lewis, the shrewd one, got her to take
his things for the unusual rate of 5%!) Like a woman involved, she
was out to protect his "good name." The more I've dug into it
since, the more sorry it seems to me. I also think Edith was protect-

ing Marcella Powers' mother, who is mentioned obliquely in the "glimpse." Just the same, I still swear that this is the best picture ever given of Lewis in so few pages. Harry Maule, who read it, tells me this is Red's talk and manner to the letter, "almost 99% perfect!"

Well, with the pharisee crowd rejecting the piece, I next thought to send it to the sadducees. I gave *Western Review* first crack. Ray B. West had it almost three months and finally returned it, saying it was a matter of policy, since they'd taken on this project of examining the "new young writers." So instead of Manfred on Lewis they have "John Criticus" examining Peter Taylor. (Taylor isn't bad at that.) I don't know where to send it next. *Kenyon Review? American Scholar? Prairie Schooner?* I don't think Ransom would go for this kind of documentary (too damned American and dramatic for him). And I don't know about Hiram Haydn. And Wimberly and I've never got along. Yet it should be published since both Harrison Smith and Philip Allan Friedman have read it too and will use it. Friedman even asked me if I minded if he could use the kind of style and attack I've worked out in it. I mention all this to give you some idea of what happens when a man in all honesty and in considerable admiration sets down what truly comes to mind in a reminiscent mood. You are going to have your troubles, I can see that, mainly because you are an honest and clear-eyed man too. (Aside: I think your book on Lewis will be the best,[2] not so much because you have the best materials but because you have a mind that won't be stamped. Smith is writing his out of a mixed-up guilt complex— I hear he went around picking up the girls of geniuses after they were through with them, and sometimes before. Friedman is writing his out of too much admiration.

(Somehow, though, I'm going to publish both the address and the glimpse in some form. The two go together.)

So far as I've been able to make out, Red suffered from an inferiority complex early in youth. His father liked his brother Claude better than he did Red. Claude was going to be like the old man. Red was plainly an "odd child" right from the start. As a child, of course, Red couldn't know that being "odd" was a fine thing. As a child he would think that to gain his father's love was the be-all and the end-all of life. And I think that Red's greatest work, *Arrowsmith,* is the result of an "I'll show you, Dad" effort. That accounts for many deep things in it. Its passion, its love, its aura of awe for noble professionalism, its finality as a monument, as a Taj Mahal almost, to a loved one. It's one of the few books into which Red got

2. When Manfred read Schorer's book, he changed his mind.

his soul, even his viscera. It is full of the most profound psychological constructions. (Symbols, I think you say.)

Red also suffered from a lack of "mother's comfort" at the right times. So that he didn't so much seek his "mother" in his wives, as men are reputed to do in part, but the comfort of a mother that he missed. He tried to get such comfort from his first wife. And never got it. His notion of women was Victorian and small-childish. And he could not get used to the notion that they were flesh, and more, that they were more pervasively "beastlike" (not bestial necessarily) than men.

But Red overcame much of these two lacks. And became and was a man while he wrote the books *Main Street* through *Dodsworth*. He got on top of his turbulent fleshes and spirits, got on top of his game, during those years, as both man and artist.

Then he married Dorothy and he slipped back into the admiring role, and lost it. Dorothy became the man for him. That is, the director of his life. Of course he fought this. Resented it. And should have. But a good artist, no matter how much a bum or a drunkard he may be, is always his own boss in the act of creation, and to the extent that he is to that extent he'll create works that are "masterful."

There were still remnants left of this "man" and this "artist" in him when I met him. And he knew he had it when he felt it those times, and he recognized it when he saw it in others.

Red was very kind to promising writers. He was kind to me. Though I'm not sure he understood me. I wasn't particularly kin to him. And that, of course, is all the more to his credit. Red was a stabber, a stitcher, both in life and in art. He didn't weave friendships, or works of art. He was a rapierist. He didn't have much poetry in him, though he was full of deep and even great emotion. He couldn't brood. And rarely did. The nearest he came to brooding was seething. He was also incapable of a half-rambling, half-orderly philosophical examination of things. Conversation, if exchanged with him at all, was apt to dart all over the place. And a man went home frustrated with the evening. I think he sensed that I didn't work that way. But he tried to get his antennaes attuned to me. And I've always admired him for that. And I was quite surprised to find him playing Delius and other bits of music, and trying to like it. (I think he actually got to like it too.)

But I didn't care much for his fetish of liking or disliking a man at first glance. First glances, first intuitions, are often accurate . . .

if one is attuned to the thing or person in question. But so often one is not on the same wave length and terrible mistakes can be made with snap judgments.

I think Red heard "the voice" (the "voice" I speak of in my essay on the "rume" in the postscript to the trilogy *World's Wanderer*) while he wrote the books *Main Street* through *Dodsworth*. But he lost it after that. Why? Either he didn't know it for what it was or he didn't want to know it. He listened to Dorothy's "voice" instead of one he should have kept for himself. Civilization, materialism, is all too apt to dull the inner ear, and the only ear, that can hear that dark deep mental leviathan that lurks in our subconscious.

Well, such are my rambling thoughts. I think you should visit Sauk Centre. (Friedman did.) If you ever do, you can stay at our house for a day or so. I can probably tell you more face to face than this way. I'll help as much as I can. As for your feeling hesitant to write me, man, don't be foolish. What's a few rough words between friends in the arts? You've got a mind and you mean well and that's all that counts with me.

Do you ever see Henry Nash Smith? Or Stegner? Give them my regards. I see McGraw-Hill is publishing your novel. Good. And of course, later on, your Lewis study. My next is coming out with McGraw-Hill too.

Do you think Ransom might like to use my "Sinclair Lewis: A Portrait" (with its two parts: I, "Finger On The Pulse" (glimpse), and II, "In Memoriam Address")?

Most sincerely,
Frederick F. Manfred

P.S. If you should happen to refer to me anywhere, call me Manfred or Frederick F. Manfred, or Frederick Feikema Manfred, giving "Feike Feikema" as my former penname.

F.F.M.

P.P.S. Also—please return "glimpse" when you're done with it.

F.F.M.

To Senator Hubert H. Humphrey

Senator Hubert H. Humphrey, U.S. Senate Office Building, Washington, D.C.

[Minneapolis, Minnesota]
October 29, 1953

Dear Hubert:

I've a couple of requests to make of you. First, could you get for me a Soil Survey of Lyon County, Iowa? Some years ago I got almost all of those I needed from Representative Gale, but the one on Lyon County, Iowa, was out of print. Maybe it is back in print by now. As you know, many of my stories and novels (and poems, as yet unpublished) are set in Lyon County or Northwest Iowa, and the little booklet can be of real use to me.

Second, would it be possible to get a topographical map of northwest Iowa, in particular Lyon County? I want to know where all the bluffs, swales, hills, valleys, are in some detail. I go over them on foot as much as possible but it would be a fine thing to see it all on a map. If there is a charge for this map and for the soil survey mentioned above, be sure to send me the bill. (If there is such a map, is there also one which includes Lincoln County of South Dakota and Minnehaha County of South Dakota? I'd like them too please. I have the soil surveys for those counties.)

Meanwhile, I suppose you've heard that I've dropped using my nickname "Feike" in my penname and have gone back to using Frederick Feikema plus a surname, "Manfred," which is a family translation of Feikema. ("Feike" stands for "Fred" or "Frederick" and "ma" stands for "man.") Some of my relatives have already adopted this name. People can pronounce Frederick F. Manfred, whereas they always mangled "Feike Feikema." In my game, like yours, a man's got to have a readily pronounceable trade mark. In this connection, have I told you that I've discovered that Hubert means "bright mind" or "bright heart" and that Humphrey (comes from Hunfrith) means "giant of peace"? The "Phrey" in your name has the same meaning and has the same origin as the "freds" of my names. So Frederick (man of a peaceful house) Manfred (man of peace) respectfully sends greetings to Hubert (bright mind and heart) Humphrey (giant of peace) and also respectfully requests that when it comes time HHH might need some help from FFM in his reelection campaign next year *he ask for it*?

> In admiration and friendship,
> as always,
> Fred

To Scott Bartlett

[Minneapolis, Minnesota]
November 25, 1953

Dear Scott:

I've gone over your letter and the marks in the manuscript very carefully, and the following are the results:

About the Lafitte matter, I can't agree. I deliberately wove that in to set up the "dark shadows in Hugh's conscience" which, along with his "Christian training," account for his ambivalent attitude toward his deserters. On the surface yes, he rages against them. Far inward, however, it's another matter. Because of what he's been and what he still is. Who was he to cast the first stone? This comes to a head on pages 242–4, which is, to my lights, and to Russell Roth's too, one of the finest passages I ever wrote. All scouts have past histories, and in Hugh's case his life was a constant attempt on his part to get control of his hates and rages, to become, in the end, "the bigger man." No, to take out that Lafitte business, that buccaneer-killer business, is to take out one of the leviathans of his unconscious. (Cf. closing paragraphs in my essay on the rume in the back of *World's Wanderer*.)

I did try, however, to speed up the opening pages, particularly the detailed description of Hugh, pages 5-7. I put in an extra break, as a sort of warning to the reader a description is coming up, which he can skip all the way to the next break (if he is a hasty surface reader!), and I broke up the paragraphs into smaller ones. (When I was an old newspaperman, I often resorted to the old slogan: "When in doubt about dull passages, break it up into paragraphs!") I also did some cutting as you suggested, especially on page 13. I couldn't quite see pushing the description ahead to page 23, by the way. (See how Flaubert does the same sort of thing in his opening pages of *Madame Bovary*.)

I felt too, as you did, that there should be more of a fisting up when Hugh meets Jim. But I did not agree with you that it should be Jim's new strength entirely which daunts Hugh. It must also be that enemy within the gates, Hugh's black-and-white conscience. (Again, "Who is he to cast the first stone?") So I added a good two pages of "fisting and gouging and pinching" plus more material about "black regrets" and "old gray biles." This new passage should give the discerning reader both spiritual and physical orgiastic resolution of a sort.

However, I couldn't agree on taking out the arrivals of Dutton and Clyman. The reason I had Dutton and Clyman come stumbling in was to cut Hugh's exploit or crawl down to size, that is, to suggest that others were doing it and they were not demanding revenge or special consideration; to suggest also to the reader in subtle form that Hugh's subconscious nature realized this (besides realizing all the other facets that went into his thinking: "Who am I to cast the first stone?") By the time the book ends the reader is to understand that Hugh's incredible crawl wasn't, when fitted into context and the times, so incredible afterall, that it was within the range of human possibility, which immediately suggests that Hugh's notion of revenge is also reframed into human proportion and expectation.

All this, of course, leads right into the final scene where Hugh's troubled conscience takes over and keeps him from either striking Fitz or killing him. Underneath the surface growling and roaring, "the bigger man" has taken over. Another physical explosion would be too obvious for my purposes. The greater and more subtle climax comes in in just what he does.

I did do one thing, however. I made Hugh speak in slightly more forceful terms, when he scathingly says he can never accept "his own gravedigger's pay." But for the rest I want no more changes.

You will also note, as you page through it, that I have sometimes agreed with your marks along the margins, and sometimes have not. In most cases I've given my reasons in the margins.

Finally, let me comment generally on your job of editing. I liked it. You came to grips with the book just like my wonderful first editor, Paul C. Hillestad, did back in the old days. You put your best cards forward and left it up to me to accept or deny. That's adult editor-author relationship. So, I'm sending back the manuscript very happy about everything. No regrets.

As a general guide on how I operate, I think you should know on your side there that I've worked out a rule-of-thumb which goes as follows: when I react "hot" to a suggestion I try to follow it; when I react flatly or even only mildly to a suggestion I try to ignore it. What finally makes an author a great one is not how aptly he follows suggestions but how well he knows his own mind and his own intentions. The last and final step is self-criticism, and since it is a most delicate process, one that is easily killed or smothered from the outside, I always make it a real point to hear what my Old Adam or the Old Goat says about it. If he grins and shakes his head negatively, I'm negative. If he looks bored, I follow suit. If he grins and nods, I follow suit. In the final showdown only he knows. No one else. And I feel it my duty to keep him alive at all costs.

My Old Man Adam or the Old Goat was considerably disturbed some years back when I followed a suggestion I only half-heartedly agreed with, and he didn't rest until I'd talked the publisher into breaking up certain plates to get it right in his eyes again—*and I did this at my own expense.* As my books now stand, I have no regrets about my first five works (*The Golden Bowl, Boy Almighty, This Is The Year, The Chokecherry Tree,* and *World's Wanderer*) at this stage of my development.

The truth is, I was amenable to suggestions when I sent you the first rough draft, provided the suggestions fell within the range of my own intentions. But after I sent my final draft, I was done with the book, emotionally as well as technically, and any revision I might do would be carpentering not architecturing. Except for a little sanding here and there I was done. And I can't get excited about doing more. And Old Man Adam expressly forbids me to do more than I've now done. We sometimes are too interested in surface perfection. Look at the marvelous imperfections of Dickens and Thackeray. How often don't they, in their imperfect moments, express truths, side-thoughts, by-products, which illuminate life and the book both? And if it works for them, why should I take a backseat to them? I really don't get too excited about comments anent my slow beginnings. When I read Conrad, Hemingway, Faulkner, I'm constantly allowing them "slow beginnings", or whatnots, and I do not hold such against them, and, again, who are they that I cannot ask equal indulgence on the part of the discerning reader? (If there be any left.)

One final comment on the matter of Hugh's forgiving. The point of the book is, to my lights, that no one thing, or influence, makes Hugh forgive (or give up revenge). Hugh succumbs to the attrition of time, incident, self-guilt, good-hearted impulse. That is my philosophy and I intend that my books shall express my philosophy. (They will do it anyway.) To obey the rules of composition made up by others or for their own sake is opposed to what I believe. To obey rules of composition slavishly reduces my status as a man and as an artist. And on that score, if I can help it (in all humility) I bow to no man.

I've read the Lewis & Clark papers, the full version, though I intend to get DeVoto's book. I don't know just where I'll dip into that kind of thing again, but if I do, it will be related to work already done. As a matter of fact, far from being a strange book for me to write, *Lord Grizzly,* the novel, is part and parcel of a thing I call Manfred's Work. I have been busy digging into my hallowed land, my place of birth, which I call "Siouxland." It was inevitable as I went along that I would soon begin to wonder a little about both the past and the future of my Siouxland as I knew it. It is all connected, but it is always connected in a certain way. Old Hugh is the spiritual ancestor of Pier, Thurs, Elof, Eric, Maury. But I'm sure I'll need more such ancestors, and hence I am on the alert for some idea or person, perhaps a time before Hugh's time, but, more likely, in a time after. It would be very foolish for me to begin writing historical novels unless I had a "hot" reason for it. I'm a poor pretender. Both in love and in writing. (And I intend to stay a poor pretender and go on being a "live" liver.) And the history of Hugh's time isn't the thing either so much, as it is Hugh and his problem—just as it is Pier and his problem, as well as Thurs and his problem, which is, in the final test, the thing. So, before I get at another project about a time before I was born I'm going to finish a project begun some years back, none of which you saw, but which has me gripped compellingly. Russell Roth has seen part of it, half, and he has heard me tell the design of the rest of it, and he has said that if I can pull it off, The Work or The Rock I'm creating will outlast the washes of Time—if any book can outlast such attrition. Russell has the feeling that I've been writing all the other books to get ready for this new one. That is the next project now. The country I was born in (northwest Iowa) is very dear to my heart, but not half so dear as the "Siouxland" that I've created, both its past, present, and future. That is my The Rock. (Incidentally, the natives have taken over my name for the area drained by the Big Sioux River, "Siouxland," as witness radio stations, newspapers, posters, etc. One high school athletic league was named the Siouxland Conference *after* I coined the word.) (Incidentally, also, there was once a considerable mountain range just east and north of the Big Sioux River in Siouxland, and only the roots of it, huge flat quartzite pink spreads of rock, are left. I'm going to put that mountain range back up, so that no glacier, or glaciers, will ever wear it off again—by writing a literature of the country.)

Perhaps you'd like a copy of my earlier books? In any case I scurried around a bit and found copies of them all, most of them first editions. The second edition in the case of *The Primitive* is the final corrected edition, since that is the one I had corrected at my expense after the plates had been made up. And someday it is my intention to publish my first novel with the title I first had for it: *The Golden Bowl Be Broken*. And I'm also going to change all the "christs" in it to "cripes." I hope you'll like the books.

In the meantime I've looked at length into the Boswell book you sent me. I'm so enthusiastic about James (he's my kind of male) that I'd like the other two you've published too: *Boswell's London Journal* and *Boswell in Holland*. I don't suppose there are any first editions around any more. But could you send me whatever you have? And if it costs me, can it be billed me on author's discount? (What a magnificent job of binding you folk do!) I intend to collect Boswell, and someday want those "research" editions also.

Now for the galley proofs!

Most cordially,
Fred

1954

In this year, the publication and overwhelming success of Lord Grizzly *encourage Manfred to project the other books of the Buckskin Man Tales, which will cover Siouxland history from present back to pre-white times. Strong support comes from Robert Penn Warren and William Carlos Williams, and Manfred feels that he is accomplished in the real American language. The success of* Lord Grizzly *and the birth of his third child, Frederick, brighten Manfred's prospects both personal and literary.*

To Mark Schorer

[Minneapolis, Minnesota]
February 1, 1954

Dear Mark:

Sorry to be so late in answering your last queries. I've been trying to get in touch with a Mrs. Marvin Oreck who would know the name and address of Ace, Lewis' driver and chauffeur. She runs a dress shop in the ritzy suburb of Edina but she seems to be gone for the winter. Her husband died suddenly a few years ago. They're the couple I refer to in my portrait whom Lewis regarded as special because they were ostracized in Duluth for their nationality. He was Jewish. Her address, which will be good when she comes back in a month, is: Mrs. Marvin Oreck, 4450 West Lake Harriet Blvd.,

Minneapolis, Minnesota. In the meantime I've found out that if you'll address a letter to Ace, Ace Taxicab Co., Duluth, Minnesota, you should hit a flashing light. And if that doesn't work, write to the chamber of commerce. So far as I know he wasn't a secretary. He served as a sort of wise common man friend to Lewis. Lewis always had one or two of such friends around and it was from them that he pumped up such a seemingly inexhaustible supply of detail about the workings of the common world. He himself couldn't open a can of beans. I've met these Aces before. Without reading a book after grade school or high school, they seem to have a tremendous knowledge of the workable world as well as the knave world. (I almost said naïve world.") Were he to sum up Lewis for you, he'd either do it with a cryptic folksay comment (too short) or do it with reams of detail (too long).

I hear from one of my friends in the East that Hal Smith has given up the idea of doing a biography of Lewis. That leaves only Friedman. Hal Smith is now thinking of doing a collection of essays and portraits about him, much in the way like Unger's *T.S. Eliot: A Selected Critique*. But again I think he'll prove too lazy and that eventually you'll have to do it. You might keep that in mind as you work away on your biography: keep a list of candidate articles.

Hiram Haydn writes me that they want only the "glimpse" of Lewis. It will come to some 30 pages in his quarterly,[1] already too long. Which is a pity. (I read the galleys last weekend and added a few lines here and there—in talking it over with my wife I recalled a few more facts. I will send you an offprint for your files.) However, if I don't put the "In Memorium Address" in my projected *Letters & Journals* I'll include it in a projected sketch book to be called *American Notebook*.

You ask about my height. Yes, I'm tall. Six nine in my stocking feet, as they say. Weigh around 250. Am lean and broad (shoulders and hips) and knobboned. My brothers are tall too. All five are over six three, with only Ed, a farmer, coming to within a quarter inch of my height. Dad was six four (he had ancestors seven feet tall— West Frisians from the Netherlands) and Mother was six feet (she had ancestors up to six five and incredibly fleshy—East Frisians[2] from Germany). So it comes naturally. I've had to smile about some of the legends concerning my strength. But, as my wife says, more incredible even is the truth in a few cases. As for the t.b.—I've got that licked provided I get ten hours sleep a day. I can keep up with

1. *The American Scholar.*

2. Actually, Saxons from Lower Saxony [FM's note].

the best with that much rest. I burned too hard too fast some fifteen years ago, going along with little sleep and even less food while I wrote novels and took on physical labor. Plus having been exposed to two people who eventually died of "galloping consumption." If you're interested in part of the truth about that, read my "rume" or "novel" *Boy Almighty* some day.

We're expecting the third child any day now. In fact, "it" is overdue much to disgust of our oldest girl, Freya, 9. Maryanna for once feels fine. And this time she has shown real nesting instincts. (She denies it, of course, as all "educated" women must.) There never has been such a cleaning out of boxes and old files and shelves. The sounds are not unlike the sounds I used to hear in the cowbarn where the cows would scratch together new dry straw or where the sows would nose out a hollow in yellow straw. Rustling, rustling, rustling. While the old boar stands looking on with surly bloodshot bloodthick eyes.

Ah, which reminds me of a legend or story as told by Dr. Walter M. Simpson. He met Lewis at a party in New York. Some friend told Red that Walt was a famous doctor and researcher (he was chief of the Kettering Research Institute) and Red asked to see Walt alone a moment. They went off into the library and after hedging around for a few minutes, Red, using scientific terms, asked how much danger there was in a woman of some thirty years having her first baby. Walt knew what was up and said, Well, not too much if she isn't too close to forty. "Well," Red is reported to have said then, "Well, it looks I'll have to get on my bicycle and peddle." Doc Walt says it was nine months almost to the day that Michael Lewis was born. If you want to verify this, plus other stories Walt knows, tell him I said for you to write him. His address: Walter M. Simpson, Captain, MC USNR. Ret., 435 Cress Street, Laguna Beach, California.

Doc Walt also tells another interesting story about the Prince of Wales, now the Duke Edward. Doc got it from a royal physician in London at a medical conference. It seems Eddie (the Prince of Wales) was having trouble sleeping with girls. Couldn't get an erection in their presence. He tried and tried. Tried every sort of girl; every sort of aphrodisiac; every sort of situation. But no go. His father worried about it; his mother ignored it. His father, by the way, had a tremendous hold over him; towered over him. Eddie loved him "very" much. Eddie's mother had a terrible hold over him too.

You know the formula. Then Eddie ran into Wallie at a party. You know how even the most loyal wife won't miss a chance of contact with kingly blood. And it happened. She made a man of him for the first time. It was such a tremendous experience that Eddie decided he'd rather be man than king. This of course infuriated his mother the Queen. Wallie was at once her rival and her image. Doc Walt swears by this story. And curiously enough, recent disclosures by Edward himself and other biographers seem to verify this version. In any case it makes a good story.

The past three months I've been reading Conrad, Melville, Kinsey, among others. I've just about finished an entire set of Conrad (begun some three years ago). I find that while his material runs thinner, his style runs smoother as he goes along. At first he uses a highly Latinate and involved (even backtracking) style. This was probably due to his being a Pole who came at the English language through French translation. But toward the end, his style begins to spear forward, to run even, and the Latinate, thank God, drops away, and a pure swift Anglo-Saxon begins to shine through. I was especially aware of this because I've been on a campaign which says that a poet or a fictioneer or rumemaker should use as pure an Anglo-Saxon or Anglo-American as possible. Critical writing, philosophical writing, scientific writing, perhaps is more effective with Latinate sprinklings. The direction of the American Language, I feel, is toward a lively simple syntax, much like the Elizabethan language.

Reading Kinsey I had a smile or two. He brings forward some evidence which suggests that deep or loud sneezes have sexual content. I knew that for some years, having observed as a young man with a wild hair that many of my frustrated aunts (who'd never had orgasms) seemed to enjoy their great sneezes. So I gave it to Nertha in *This Is The Year*. And I went a step further. I also gave her sessions of hiccups, the last set of which leveled her. I think there is definitely some sex trouble behind hiccups. Funny thing is, I have some letters from women who wrote me solely about those sneezes and hiccups of Nertha. Farm women!

I'm going to sit back and see if I can't catch more stuff on that Lewis-and-his-father problem. And I'll let you know. You may be right. I may have to take off my own son-and-father-relationship spectacles to see the better.

Good luck. I think it will clear off from the West. My best.

Cordially,
Fred

Hello to Henry [Nash] Smith.
Scott Bartlett of McGraw-Hill seems to be very excited about your
Lewis Project.

To Frank Feikema

[Minneapolis, Minnesota]
February, 11, 1954

Dear Pa & Ma:

Well, like I told you on the phone last Saturday, Pa's first grandson, "it stamhâlder," finally came. I'll put the details on the baby's
card with this letter, but I better add that he has dark hair like Pa
had with an auburn tinge. He has big shoulders and chest and long
lanky arms and legs. Except for the ears and hair and nosetip, I'm
afraid he takes after me to the teeth, you might say.

You may wonder about his name. Frederick Feikema Manfred
the 8th. As you know, Pa was baptized Feike Feikema, but was
given the name of Frank, like his father Feike, when they came to
America. (Frank probably because they came from Franeker,
because Frank is not the right translation for Feike.) According
to the family tree that a cousin of Pa's sent me, a Henry Feikema
living in Hengelo, Friesland, Pa's name in the family really is Feike
Feikes Feikema, the 6th. Grampa is listed as Feike Feikes Feikema
the 5th and Pa's grampa is listed as Feike Feikes Feikema the 4th.
Since I'm taking the meaning of the name, "frede," peace, and since
Frederick or Fred is the correct translation for Feike, it makes me
Frederick the 7th or Feike the 7th, and it makes Pa's grandson Feike
or Frederick the 8th. He is 8th generation first son. So, he is named
for me and Pa and Grampa and Great Grampa, and so on, back to
1700 when it all first began according to court and church records
in Franeker, which this Henry Feikema of Hengelo dug up for me.
It isn't often that a line is continued for that long through the oldest son in each generation and we are proud of it and humbly
thankful to God that it came to pass. I had almost given up, I tell
you.

Maryanna is very fine. She took this one better than the other
two. She will be home next Saturday (they're keeping her a couple
of extra days to make sure her TB doesn't get started up again).

The girls are very anxious to see him. And I want to hold him
too. I sat in on the delivery like a doctor (with cap and gown and

mask) and I now fully appreciate what you girls go through, Ma. It is a great thing God has created in you mothers.

Well, I better hurry this off to the mailbox. I hope this finds you very well. You both sounded clear and fine over the phone. It was like talking to you next door. I think I'll use that phone more often.

We send you all our love,

Maryanna, Fred, Freya, Marya,
and Freddie The Feike

To Alice H. Palmer[1]

[Minneapolis, Minnesota]
March 2, 1954

1. Editing supervisor at McGraw-Hill Book Company.

Dear Alice H. Palmer:

By separate package I'm sending along the galleys and the manuscript. Both my wife and I read them. I've incorporated both her marks and mine with a blue ballpoint pencil. I hope we haven't made too much a mess of the galleys.

Both of us laughed outloud when we read the opening line of the Style Sheet sent to the printer along with the manuscript. "This book is definitely and intentionally non-Webster." My wife said, "At last a copy editor who understands that you're a Midland American author. Like Faulkner is." And truth to tell, I've had to insist in the past that my books be printed the way I write them. Had they edited Faulkner back to common grammar and dictionary usage and the English syntax, Faulkner would have to be de-Faulknerized. I've long felt that after Mark Twain, there were only two authors who were working "in the American grain," and they were Faulkner and Manfred, both of whom live in the Mississippi valley incidentally, as did their literary father. Critics, grammarians, etc., will never quite get us unless they are familiar with William Carlos Williams' *In the American Grain,* Constance Rourke's *American Humor,* D.H. Lawrence's *Studies in Classic American Literature,* and the dictionary by Mathews, *A Dictionary of Americanisms.* And possibly also George Frederick Ruxton's *Life in the Far West* and Lewis Garrard's *Wah-to-Yah* and Walter Prescott Webb's *The Great Plains.* Mathews' work should be on every copy editor's shelf. Because, I for one, do not think of myself as an American using English, but as an American using the American language, which Mencken so ably outlined in his monumental work *The American Language.* An acquaintance with the English dictionaries is all right, even Fowler (though he can be horribly wrong when it comes to American usage, which he'd be the first to admit were he alive today). Even the Webster-Merriam is okay to consult, provided it is remembered that the editors have an English-New England bias. But Fowler, Oxford, Webster, New England, they're going to lose. The new country and the new language is being molded right here in the great Mississippi River valley, and Twain, Faulkner, and Manfred are the first to record and solidify it. With all this in mind, that is why I cheerfully departed from Webster when I felt the need or inclination. Afterall, dictionaries are for clerks and letter-writers. It is the novelists and the poets who, after recording the neologisms of the people and of themselves, set the standards, with the dictionary grubs coming after. We are above dictionaries, even though we consult them constantly.

That is why I was so happy to see that the editor-who-used-green-ink tried to keep me up to the Manfred mark. I sometimes slipped back a little, or slipped off the track, but he or she hauled me back on it. I thought the editing very fine indeed. First rate.

My only quibbles were minor. For example, I couldn't see myself using the Spanish spelling of the word "compañero." I liked it the way I had it: "companyero". I put them all back in. Not only do I want to use it that way, but I notice that Ruxton spelled it that way in his book *Life in the Old Far West*. It looks like a foreign word Americanized. Nor did I agree about "popple." "Poplar" is fine. But out here in Siouxland we've come to use "popple" interchangeably with "poplar." Even the daily papers do it in conservation articles. I'm all for giving our language the human common touch and for ridding ourself of Latin-conscious grammarians. (The most terrible thing to happen to the English language was when Latin grammarians tried to impose a Latin logic on the old Anglo-Saxon base. Terrible. The two logics are not the same. There are all sorts of logical systems in the world.) (I happen to know the English language very well, all the way back to its roots even. I'm a Frisian, who knows Frisian, and Frisians can read a Chaucer with the greatest of ease. But because of that "main stream feel" for the Anglo-American language, I'm absolutely certain that its future is the American now being coined on the farms, streets, workshops, etc. We will win. And to the glory of language generally and to America specifically.) I also changed back all the "green bottleflies." "Bottleflies" are not "botflies." "Botflies" are a form of gnat who lay their eggs under the skin of animals. Bottleflies are usually found around dead carcasses.

A couple of questions. Was my "About The Author" sent to the printer too? Will it come along with the "front matter"? I had it placed at the rear of the book. It's always been my feeling that a book should have a note about the author inside the covers. Most people toss away the jacket. And libraries certainly do. And having it at the end of the book, as Random House now does, saves an author a lot of letter-writing. Reason I ask: I have a couple of items I want to check or change in the "About the Author."

Just to keep Scott [Bartlett] up on developments, I'm sending him a copy of this letter.

Once again, many thanks for helping Manfred stay Manfred.

Sincerely,
Frederick F. Manfred

P.S. The last three galleys are awfully dirty. I hope you can read them. But I just had to point up Hugh's dilemma a bit more.
F.F.M.

To the Editor[1]
[*Richfield-Bloomington Messenger*]

[Minneapolis, Minnesota]
March 13, 1954

1. Richard Higgin.

I note with some surprise Mayor H.E. Kossow's letter in last week's edition of your paper. Permit me to make a few remarks on it.

First, I'm not against industrial zoning as such. A fair argument can be advanced for it. Bloomington undoubtedly can use certain types of restricted industry.

Second, I will accept having a clean well-landscaped factory near my home once I'm convinced that the industrial zoning committee has sought advice from qualified experts. I attended one meeting of the industrial zoning committee last fall, and I studied all of their reports as given in the local papers, and I, for one, finally came to the conclusion that they had *not* sought competent advice concerning the overall health of our community: social, financial, educational, recreational, etc. When the health of one's family is involved one always gets the best doctor available. Why shouldn't this hold true when it comes to the overall health of our village? For example, for every acre we set aside as industrial, shouldn't we also set aside an acre as recreational? This is a big thing. It goes beyond just our generation. It involves not only thousands upon thousands of dollars, and thousands of acres, but also thousands upon thousands of souls, present and future. We are dealing with the future as well as the present, with the far future even, and we should get the best advice that money can buy. And this advice *is* available for reasonable sums of money. Let's not be penny-wise and pound-foolish. Let's not be ten-cent millionaires.

Third, I notice that the good mayor, in his letter, directed a few remarks at me personally. Let me assure the good mayor that I would not have recommended he read a few books on city planning if he had not revealed in his numerous appearances before the microphone (which had been set up to hear what we thought; not what he thought) that he had not made a thorough study of the matter. His remarks indicated that he had only a layman's opinion on the matter like our own. Furthermore, when the mayor saw that the tenor or drift of the meeting was going against his committee's recommendations and against his private wishes, he deliberately sought to rechannel the tenor or drift of the meeting by remarking that he was against hiring professional planners because, he said, they'd only recommend what his committee had already recommended and so the hiring would be only so much money thrown away. Had the mayor actually read the books mentioned, those by Lewis Mumford (*The Culture of the Cities, Technics and Civilization,* etc.) and Frank Lloyd Wright (*Autobiography,* etc.) he would have known this to be false. (The blunt truth is, in these complicated times, we must make sure that our elected city officials are well-informed men on the subject of city government and city planning. If they are not well-informed, then it is our next duty to keep a wary eye on them. Otherwise, in the case of Bloomington with its peculiar problems, they could just possibly make a mess of things for us. If we're not watchful, uninformed hometown boosters can make of the area south of Minneapolis another blighted nightmarish hellhole like South Chicago. Instead of our village being known as "Beautiful Bloomington" it can be known as the "Bloomington Slums." For instances of this kind of city official, see Sinclair Lewis' *Babbitt* and *Main Street,* both of which can be bought for a quarter at the corner drug.)

Fourth, the mayor also made some sliding remarks about my voting record. The mayor wrote: ". . . in all his years as a resident, this man had only voted once and that was at a presidential election, when party success must have meant a lot to some individuals." Mayor, what's that of your business? It is my American right to vote for whomever and whenever I please. But just to set the record straight, let me say that, with only a couple of exceptions, since coming to Minneapolis and vicinity in 1937, I have voted in every city, state, and national election, both primary and general, even including those years when I was sick in bed. (My wife, by the way has voted every time!) And those exceptions occurred when health and business interfered. I've had tuberculosis and my doctor has ordered me to curtail all outside activities. For the sake of my family, and for the sake of my neighbors, I've been, against my hearty inclinations, very conscientious about following his orders. Believe me, had I my health, I'd long ago have pitched in in local affairs. Also, let me inform the mayor (though it is really still none of his business) that in the last election I split my ticket. Let him make of that what he will.

As for seeing me at the next public meeting with respect to the problem of "indiscriminate industrial zoning" vs. "sound city planning"—yes, I'll be there, health permitting. And, I'll also show up again at the next village election, believe you me.

Sincerely yours,
Frederick Feikema Manfred

P.S. A paragraph in Richard Higgin's last column gave me quite a laugh. It read: "If plans of Bloomington's wide-awake, progressive village fathers materialize, this community will become the industrial center of the Upper Midwest." Really now, Richard, isn't that a bit grandiose? Bloomington to swallow both Minneapolis and St. Paul? Eventually? That's *sheer* babbittry.

FFM
(Except for Postscript also sent to Laura Baker, Bloomington *News*)

To Senator Hubert H. Humphrey

[Minneapolis, Minnesota]
March 18, 1954

1. Chairman of the Minnesota Republican party.

Dear Hubert:

Well, so they threw Val Bjornson in the ring against you. Good, perhaps, since he is a highminded man and will probably keep the campaign clean. He'll reject McCarthy, will keep a civil tongue in Etzell's[1] head, and will bring out the issues and in so doing help inform the public. The cleaner the campaign is kept, the better chance you have—mostly because newspapers in this state are more apt to print "dirty charges" against you than against "their side." But

I think you'll beat him handily, Hubert. You need but hold labor; hammer away at the Benson bungling to keep the farmers coming (who're already coming in droves if my relatives around Luverne aren't lying to me); and stress statesman issues like civil rights for Negroes, and the St. Lawrence Seaway, and the American way of life as opposed to totalitarianism. I've begun right now to collect things on Val, and will write letters later in the campaign when they'll tell most for our side. And by the way, those calm lectures of yours over KUOM and that witty, ironic, humorous collection of remarks you made to the *Minnesota Weekly* editors some time ago ("Remember that the money the Republicans pour into this state in their attempt to defeat me pay your bills") go over in a big way, even bigger than your rousing lectures. A change of pace makes big league pitchers.

Meanwhile, I've a request. I'm a member of the Authors League of America. Our League (which resembles the A.M.A. for doctors) has done much to improve the lot of writers. Yesterday I got this little folder from Rex Stout, our president. I've studied it carefully and I support it all. I'd like for you to read it and to consider it carefully. And then act as *your* heart and mind decide. One thing the folder didn't touch on: reciprocity in money exchanges. I've got money stuck in Spain and Italy for translations of my work. We can't get it out. This new Convention might help.

We had a baby boy here last month, Feb. 6. Weight, ten pounds, 23 inches long. We named him Frederick Feikema Manfred, VIII, since he's the eighth generation firstborn son named either Feike or Frederick (the names are interchangeable). We're so happy! And I will call you at the Nicollet the next time you're in town. I've got to tip you off about somebody who, sub rosa, has been causing you some trouble.

All my best,
Fred

To John Crowe Ransom

[Minneapolis, Minnesota]
March 20, 1954

Dear Mr. Ransom:

Thank you very much for your long note to me about my story "Free, White, and Twenty-One." Your good words and your interest are very much appreciated.

I have often felt though, Mr. Ransom, if you'll pardon me a

1. *Kenyon Review.*

mild reply, that your excellent magazine[1] could use what some people sometimes call stories and poetry written in the American Language. Warren is perhaps the only one who has got it into your pages, notably in that chapter taken from his novel *World Enough and Time* and then in the more colloquial parts of his long narrative poem *Brother to Dragons,* and every time I see it, I rejoice. Of course Faulkner has it too in his *As I Lay Dying, Light in August, The Hamlet,* and other of his work.

I suppose it is the old argument of: did Twain "write down" when he wrote *Huckleberry Finn?* At the time many of Twain's literary friends thought he did. But now, I notice, such elegant and formal fellows as Lofty-Nose Eliot, Beach, Trilling, consider it one of the great American masterpieces. The intellectual savants of today have caught up with his language of then. Shakespeare, too, made the formal boys frown in his day when he deliberately used street talk. And of course, my favorite of them all, Chaucer, used all sorts of talk and all sorts of dialect. The fact is, in my case, I can't help myself. When I find myself in the midst of proper city fellows, I use their idiom in their own talk and, to a lesser extent, in the narrative proper. When I find myself in the midst of hearty workers or hearty farmers, same. And I like to think that I am working from some profound, even tremendous, natural instinct, which causes me to do this willynilly, and which, if I didn't listen to, would be the killing of something rare and unusual. My ancestors were Frisians. I heard Frisian spoken in my family along with frontier American plus a little Schoolmarm English (my aunt teacher). Knowing Frisian, I can read Chaucer with ease and savoring delight; can even stumble through quite a lot of Beowulf without too much help. I also like Spenser very very much. And Shakespeare. And Doughty. And I find in me the living sound, the living utterance, of the entire sweep of a language that came out of Frisian-Anglo-Saxon roots, became Old English, then Middle English, then English, then American-English, which eventually will become American.

Because "they" will win. They'll outbreed and outlive the formalist English. I mean, the people living in the great Heartland of America. Our future writers and critics will come out of their families. And you can hammer and chaff them all you want with formal English, but the talk they hear around the family board and out on the yard and in the factories will outweigh, out-mood, outlast, all the English composition classes in the world. So I've decided that the only way to win is to take this language coming from the motherwort magma of our country and get on with the business of shaping it into the new instrument. I feel that Twain felt this. I think Faulkner knows this. "Tech my elbers," the old man said to Bookwright in Faulkner's *The Hamlet*. And that's what I'd like to say to people standing behind me as I use my witching-stick looking for wells and gold and hidden veins of wealth in the earth I've been given to live on. "Tech my elbers and you'll believe."

I've got a new book on the fire, *Lord Grizzly*. In digging around in my beloved Siouxland, I found myself also looking into the past of Old Siouxland, and I hit upon a tale or legend that opened upon a picture of the ancestors of my contemporary heroes Pier, Maury, Thurs, etc. Old Hugh Glass was a forerunner of Pier, and, of course, of my father, who, besides knowing Frisian and frontier American, was also, in boyhood, heavily influenced by Missouri air. I've asked the publisher to send you a volume and you can do with it as you will. It'll be ready in late June and will be published in the early fall. Russell Roth, my friend and critic, who has been (God bless him) most eager to see my cause advance, thinks it's the best I ever wrote. Which heartens me because Russ can be very rough on me on occasion.

Well, this has become a terribly long note. Give my regards to Peter Taylor. I think he's a fine, a very fine writer.

Sincerely,
Frederick F. Manfred

To John Crowe Ransom

[Minneapolis, Minnesota]
June 5, 1954

Dear Mr. Ransom:

I can't resist making a few comments about at least two phrases in your last note to me. "We're highbrow, I guess," you say. That remark set off a whole chain of reflections in my head, since I've always considered myself highbrow too. In politics a democrat, in aesthetics an aristocrat. And it was on the basis of my feelings or my demand for "the best in fiction" that I rejected almost every story you folk have published in the *Kenyon Review*. I'd read the KR stories carefully, sympathetically, because I felt we were all against the philistines, but for the life of me, I couldn't get excited about them. And I also couldn't help but think to myself, "Hell, my stories are far better than those." And so I sent mine on to you. But by reject-

ing the last three, I now know that the literary climate or literary
air mass you work in and the one I work in are literally worlds
apart, that you are England-South orientated, that I am an American—and that, curiously enough, despite the fact I perhaps instinctively know more about the true line of the Anglo-American
language than you do, what with my having been born in a family
of Frisians where American was spoken along with the Frisian (or
Old English). Maybe I can best illustrate my point by recounting
an experience I had while reading one of the KR stories. It was
published some three, four years ago. I read along, working at it,
determinedly deciphering the heavy latinate un-English style,
translating the cumbersome pachydermic expository syntax that
nowadays goes for English, and was beginning to wonder if the
few brains I had were nonexistent afterall—when suddenly I came
across the fine old Frisian-American word "beer." And seeing it,
I let out a shout of joy, and yelled across to my wife, "Ah! the story
is at last taking hold." And when I came across yet another "beer," I
declared it a success—as measured against all the other KR stories
I'd read. (As my pake, or grampa, used to say, there's nothing like a
good old plat Fries fart to clear the air.)

Mr. Ransom, I think the trouble is that our notions of classic
or highbrow are not the same. An English classic (or New Critic-
Southern classic) takes its meaning against the background of old
feudal concepts of justice, hierarchy, etc. while an American classic
takes its meaning against a background of democracy, the common
man, stress on individual responsibility, feeling for freedom, and
the like. The form and the plot of one will be different from the
form and the plot of the other. The two will never meet. Mostly
because a thing called America has never before been seen on earth.
Art products from a society with a rigid class structure will be one
thing; art products from a society with a fluid arrangement of peoples will be another. In another words, there are various literary
climates and there are various literary notions of what constitutes
a classic, of what is "highbrow."

If my story has a better chance of being taken by *The Saturday
Evening Post* than any of the stories published so far by KR, it will
not be because it is in a lower category than KR stories, but because
it comes closer to being an American classic.

But then, perhaps, you are not the final arbiter on KR fiction.
If you are not, permit me to suggest some reading matter for those
who are, as follows: *In the American Grain* by Williams, *American*

Humor by Rourke, *Studies in Classic American Literature* by Lawrence, *The Melville Log* by Leyda, *The American Language* by Mencken, *A Dictionary of Americanisms* by Mathews, *Huckleberry Finn* by Twain, *As I Lay Dying* and *The Hamlet* by Faulkner.

And don't for a minute think I reject English letters. I don't. English fiction for England is fine. Just as German fiction for Germany is fine. I admire it all, from their point of view, as much as I can see it. An English writer would be damn fool to try to write like an American. Just as an American *is* a damn fool if he tries to write like an Englishman. True, we are all a part of Western Tradition, but only with the Englishman as an Englishman, the German as a German, the Frenchman as a Frenchman, and the American as an American. And the more fully an American is an American, the more he will contribute to Western Culture.

I like to add that I love Old Frisian, and Chaucer, and Spenser, and Shakespeare, and Smollett, and Fielding, and Dickens, and Thackeray, and Doughty, and Conrad. I consider them noble people who became great writers. They are part of "the English line." At the same time, I feel that the Americans have broken away on their own from that line, both in their way of life as well as in their way of creation, just as the French once broke away from the Latin tradition. And it is a pity that such good men (fine talents) as found in yourself, Tate, Warren, have been the victims of bad advice. You fellows can't win because at best you are grafts. And grafted plants have only one generation of life, and little or no true offspring. The root and the head are not connected. The Cul-De-Sac School of American letters.

Sincerely yours,
F.F.M.
Frederick Roughneck Manfred

To Maxwell Geismar

[Minneapolis, Minnesota]
July 19, 1954

Dear Max,

Suit yourself about the quote. I wondered what you'd make of *Lord Grizzly*. No doubt others will wonder too what I *seem* to be doing writing Old West history. Truth is that in the process of digging down and back in my Siouxland country, I kept feeling that I should build foundations for my work to date, so that when I'm all done someday the reader of my Work will get an enormous

1. Later *Conquering Horse*.

2. Later a short story.

3. *Riders of Judgment*.

sweep of Midland (and USA) life, from its origins all the way to the last day of my life here. I'm planning to write a book called *Green Earth*[1] (from Arnold's "Who can see the green earth anymore/As she was by the sources of time?") which will describe a drama in the life of the Yankton Sioux before the coming of the whiteman. The Yanktons were one of the few "peaceful" tribes among the Sioux and wonderfully enough they had possession of the land where my ancestors settled, my presentday Siouxland. This will be set back to about 1800. Later on I want to write a book called *Wild Land*,[2] which will describe the first real toeholds the white man made in Siouxland. (I have a wonderful idea for that too: more of a psychological thing than historical, just as *Green Earth* will be and *Lord Grizzly* is.) I also have in mind a "cowboy" or ranch novel,[3] but this is not too definite. Of course all of this only after I've finished *Morning Red* and possibly *Sons of Adam*. I'm glad you like the Indians. The truth is that they were neither noble redskins, nor red devils. They were nomadic creatures still on the way up the "cultural scale" and my feeling is that the writer has to create honestly about them. I like human beings but I also have a sharp eye for his contradictory ways. ("Mind" emerging out of "the beast.") As for the "different" style, that could hardly be helped since the style had to go with the time within the area of my personal syntax. You see, Maury, Elof, Thurs, Pier, Eric, all, are descendants of Hugh Glass, including even the language they use. How did I get it all so accurate? Continuing interest, the taking of notes over many years, plus finally an old bachelor trapper named Willemstein who personally knew the spiritual heirs of Hugh Glass. As a boy I used to sit with him on a bench in front of the poolhall of a Saturday afternoon and listen to him spin yarn after yarn about The Old Days. There *is* a "warm" connection then. I also have seen Sioux Indians off and on these many years. Well, anyway, I had thought that if you did send in a quote it would somehow tie in my earlier books with *Lord Grizzly,* because to me it's all of a piece—the Work. I, too, wish that Pocket Books would do my earlier books, say, *Boy Almighty, The Golden Bowl,* and *The Chokecherry Tree,* but I hear that while Herb Alexander is all for me a man name Freeman Lewis is on the fence about me. I wish somebody would knock him over into my patch. Have been reading Twain, Poe, Balzac, Euripides. Plus some modern stuff (De Vries, Jarrell, Arnow—so-so compared to the others). Much of Twain is for me. He writes the American sentence, or line. Other-

wise, working steadily away on *Morning Red* (formerly *Rape*).
Brennan sends regards, as always,

Fred

To William Carlos Williams

[Minneapolis, Minnesota]
September 11, 1954

Dear Bill:

That letter of yours (and I write it unashamedly) about *Lord Grizzly* gave me one of the biggest thrills of my writing life. As you must know, I like you personally as a friend very much and at the same time I regard you one of our writing greats. We read all you write. And right in the middle of my collection of Western things stands your *In the American Grain*. (Next to it are: *Studies in Classic American Literature* and *American Humor*, the first by Lawrence and the second by Constance Rourke.) I wept over your letter. Because that was the way I felt I wrote the book. I felt, when I had finished with it, that no one had ever written as honestly and accurately, and at the same time poetically, about the frontiersman and the Indian and the Old Days. I plan to write another book, in two years, called *Green Earth*,[1] about a Sioux Indian family, of father versus son (along with a study of wild mustangs, also father stallion versus son colt, for subplot). When I get all done I hope to have written or painted a long hall of fictional history from 1800 to the day I die. Of the Midlands. Or the West.

1. Later *Conquering Horse*.

I can't help it, Bill, but I want to send your letter to my editor, Scott Bartlett, who had the guts to take me on when it looked for a while like I was through. Doubleday just didn't know what they had in me. He should know that a man like you liked *Lord Grizzly*.

How are Kitty and Clayton [Hoagland]? I often think of them. Give them my regards. I'm going to try to go to New York this winter, and will then look you up and Kitty.

Russell Roth, an admirer of yours, a critic too, and I hold the fort out here every weekend. He has one of the finest minds I've ever run into. And his friendship and counsel and cheer is invaluable. We often have fine bullsessions with some of the other writers around. We pretty much shun the U boys. Though now they're coming around to us.

Bill, again, thanks for the letter. I'm driving down the last pages of *Morning Red*, a whopper like *Anna Karenina* (and somewhat like it too). A word from you is a word from the best. You're just the man to appreciate what I'm up to generally, as well as the man to appreciate all the little phrases that well up from our subconscious selves, that motherwort magma of the race.

Sincerely,
Fred

To Harvey Breit[1]

[Minneapolis, Minnesota]
November 29, 1954

1. Of *The New York Times Book Review*.

2. Inez Robb.

Dear Mr. Breit:

The radio this morning says a snowstorm is on the way, so I'd better hasten and get this in the mail ahead of it. Yes, you may use whatever you wish from the previous letter, plus anything you find worthwhile in this one. And I want to compliment you, too, for asking me. I've had some bad experiences the last few years with reporters. One lovely young thing[2] for a national news service wrote a story about me that had an error of fact in every paragraph. My wife was furious: not only was her husband misrepresented, but she was too! Words were put in our mouths that were utterly out of character—let alone not having said them. It has always puzzled me why newspaper moguls will fire a poor secretary because she can't take dictation accurately, but keep a reporter at thrice the price when he is even more inaccurate. If I ever own a paper my reporters will have to be able to take dictation in shorthand plus have a photographic memory. (Impossible, of course.)

I'd like to add to the other letter, the following. Some have wondered how come I turned to writing historical novels. Now that is odd. I hadn't thought of it that way. What happened was this: in the process of looking at all sides, over and around and below, of this present day world I was describing in my novels, I got to wondering what might have happened before this present day—in fictionland of course. What sort of ancestors would Maury (*The Golden Bowl*), Eric (*Boy Almighty*), Pier (*This Is The Year*), Elof (*The Chokecherry Tree*), and Thurs (*World's Wanderer*), et al, have if one were to dig back. So while those boys were being born from one part of my brain, another bunch of boys were being hatched in another part. I caught sight of Hugh while doing Pier, for example. So you can see it's all of a piece in my head. No jump back without connection or in another field. I might also add that when I was a small lad I used to sit on the front stoops of stores on a Saturday afternoon and listen to the Doon, Iowa oldtimers talk. Among them was a gnarled old trapper. He trapped in the Dakotas in the fall and in the spring and came home winters and summers. He'd been trained by old trappers before him and he could trace certain knowledges of wily animals all the way back to the days of Hugh Glass. And what a haughty eagle he was. He had no time for paff talk. A young man was not expected to open his yap unless he had something weighty to say. I remember I once tried to tell him an impressive story. He looked at me with outraged amazement while I told it. That I had the gall! When I remember him I remember certain characters in Faulkner. Faulkner has got that haughty warrior of the Midlands down pat. One mighty snort and my story was blasted to shreds. They were great men and I regret their going. I know a half-dozen others like this old trapper and I hope to get their like in coming stories. Funny thing, I was about to start the first draft of *Lord Grizzly* when my trapper friend died in a fire. His shack by the railroad tracks burned down around him. Suffocated.

Some have also wondered how I dared tackle that Crawl section in *Grizzly,* since at first glance it looks like an impossible thing in fact, let alone trying to describe it and make it interesting in fiction. Actually, I never worried about that. I made myself a travois for a leg on my place here and crawled over the hillside to make sure it would work. Next I either drove my old '38 Ford over the route or got out and walked it, all the while collecting bits of sand, gravel, stone, ground, plus vegetation, plus pictures of animals. Next I did some reading to see what others had written on the subject and the area. As for the Indians, I went out to visit them, sought out the old boys, especially the medicine men. No, that part of it wasn't too hard. What was really hard was to make convincing the act of forgiving at the end. And it took me some nine years of waiting and watching before I caught a hint of how it should go. And something had to happen to someone I knew before I saw it. Also, I had to come around to doing some forgiving myself.

Mr. Adams speaks of the good portrait I gave of the Indians. Personally, I've never felt racial prejudice. My Mother loved all people and she taught us right from the start that it was the color of the soul that God looked at, not the skin. The color of the skin, she said, was the doing of the sun, not directly that of God's. I remember when a paving gang came to gramma's town, Orange City, Iowa, with some dozen Negroes. I stared at them a while and then ran in and asked, "Mama, can I have some blue skin too?" I'm a pink-skinned blond and I've always envied darkskinned folk. They not only keep longer, but they are more beautiful. My skin is already drying. After a bath I sometimes itch like the devil for an hour. Itching is as bad as a migraine headache in my book. Oh for dusky brown skin with an oily surface. I could swim all day long.

Well, I'd better get on with the book I'm doing. Which reminds me of a neighbor lady in the country I knew. She once told another neighbor lady, "Ya, it was a guud thing I got marriet. I was yust a chuckful a babies." Same here. It's a good thing I became a writer because I was just chuckful of books.

Sorry for the length. But I guess I got wound up.

Sincerely,
Fred

To Alan C. Collins

[Minneapolis, Minnesota]
December 16, 1954

Dear Alan (or Mrs. Byrne—I hope I'm spelling that right—if not please forgive—the telephone connection on my end wasn't too good—):

After my talk with you via telephone yesterday I had occasion to talk to the local correspondent of *Variety* and also for many years theatre and drama critic for a metropolitan newspaper. He told me: 1) that he knew of instances where authors got participation deals, that is, a sum of say $10,000 for an option and then a percentage on the gross-take (5% on down to 2%), 2) that many authors now sign on a seven-year lease basis at the end of which time all rights revert back to the author, 3) that he had read *Lord Grizzly* and thought it a timeless historical subject, that is to say, the idea in it would be as good a hundred years from now as it is today, 4) that it was his opinion that the book was all there, in the way of dialogue, incident, etc. He, too, felt that the book would climb up the bestseller lists and that I could wait a year and still have a very saleable product, that I'd be foolish, at this point, not to ask for say $10,000 down plus whatever percentage I could get.

Remembering the laments of Red Warren that he got but $7500 for his *All the King's Men* only to see it become a great movie, remembering the laments of others who'd sold too early, I know what I'd feel terrible someday if *Lord Grizzly* should turn out to be another *Shane*, which it could very well in the hands of such a one as Fleischer. Why isn't Fleischer willing to gamble at this point?

He's out only a small sum in case it flops as a movie. If it goes, then we're both in.

So as of now, I'd say to try to get the following: $5000 plus 5% of the gross-take plus a seven-year clause, or $10,000 down plus 4% plus clause, or $15,000 down plus 3% plus clause, or $20,000 plus 2% plus clause. I'm sure that we'll be getting offers for this book from now on till doomsday—so let's play "mean and tough" on this one so I can get all my work, my other books written and my family raised, done.

I'm so grateful for all you've done so far. You, all of you, are the happiest thing that has happened to me in the writing business. The name of Curtis Brown is the name of a household god in our house.

Most sincerely, as always,
Fred

P.S. When I talked to you on the phone yesterday we had but $2.00 in the bank. But I play poker tough and close to the belt. One dollar or a million in the pocket, I keep playing those %es.

P.P.S. Facts: the wonderful title is mine; the arrangement of the plot is my original idea; the working out of how come he forgave is my original idea; the research for background is enormous and very accurate; the speech is accurate down to a cough—no one can improve on it; and the material on the Indians, as J. Donald Adams says, is the best yet to appear in any book, Cooper's included. Whoever buys it is buying a masterpiece: flawless, solid, enduring.

To Scott Bartlett

[Minneapolis, Minnesota]
December 24, 1954

Dear Scott:

You'll never know how you touched me with your present— a copy of *Lord Grizzly* specially bound in deep red leather and trimmed with gold. It just happens that I have Smollett and Fielding bound in almost the same kind of leather (red or maroon) and the same kind of lettering. And I cherish them. And now here one of my books. My wife and I stared at it some minutes before she said, "Well, now I'm truly convinced that you were right to add Manfred to your name legally. Now I'm truly convinced it looks like the name of a classic writer." I felt the same way, of course, though I wasn't going to say so outloud, and I cautioned her, "Don't kill me off yet, dear. I've a few more I want to write yet." Aside from the blue folder I originally sent *Lord Grizzly* in, gold and maroon (and this particular shade too) are my favorite colors for books. Bound that way, the book becomes a hand against the erosion of eternity. Thanks, Scott, many thanks. I shall not soon forget it.

Yesterday at exactly 3:30 p.m. I finished the first rough draft of *Morning Red*. It comes to a massive monolithic 971 pages. And I think I did it.

Of course 971 pages is probably too long. I've paged through it a little since and I can see where it can be cut considerably. Perhaps back to some 750 pages. Just for the fun of it, I went back and checked the work schedule on *This Is The Year*, since *Morning Red* is about as long. I finished that book too in December, back in 1944. But it wasn't until the summer of 1946 before I had a typescript ready for the printers. It took me almost a year and a half to polish it into its present form. And I think I should have the leeway to take about as much time on this book. I want to cut away, with my new skinningknife, all excess fat and loose skin. I want to hone it up considerably. I want to make some of the features more prominent; tone down others. I want it to be as hard a piece of finished granite as *This Is The Year* is in my eyes. I can pick that book up today and read a ways and never find dross or slack in it. Every sentence in it still strikes fire. Still rings like a silver nickel.

1. *Morning Red.*

In many ways it[1] is a richer, and a more dramatic, book than any I've written. It is, like I suggested, not unlike *Anna Karenina* in design and execution. It came about this way, no doubt, not so much because I was influenced by that book, but rather that I was influenced by a milieu similar in kind to the one Tolstoy knew: the interminglings of country and city life on the midland plains of a continent.

So, Scott, I'd like to take all of next year to rewrite it and clean it up. I work best when I'm not pressured, when my mind is clear and rested in the sunny mornings. Also, Scott, I'm in that stage of my career when I can't make many more mistakes in my bigger books. They've got to be matchless. Especially these days, when the current intellectual fashion is to be suspicious of epics. I also think I should be allowed to go along in a solid steady leisurely fashion because of health. When I called my doc yesterday to tell him the news, he heaved a great sigh of relief. The major strain is off. There's still some left, of course, when a man rewrites, but at least the rope is across the stream and we know the bridge can be finished. Thus, if I may be so bold, I'd like to suggest that we publish *Northern Light*[2] first, to keep my hand in, so to speak, while *Morning Red* is being readied. It will help build the foundation upon which the bigger books get their point of spring. My dad used to say that a wagon wasn't full when a man had just filled it with pumpkins. "Look at the apples you can still fill in between the pumpkins," he used to say. If an author is good, and if he pretends to the heights, he tries more than just one formula. Who is to say that Hemingway got where he did solely through his long novels? or his short novels? or his short stories? They all help build each other. The more sides a prism has, the greater the variety of the refraction. For myself I'm convinced that *Northern Light* will make a great little book of novellas, that while it may not sell well, it will elicit a lot of comment from the barkers of letters, the critics and pundits, who are bound to remark that I'm good *too* in the shorter form and, perhaps, maybe, you-never-know, that man Manfred has more to say than we originally thought. All I ask from *Northern Light* is that it pays its way. No more. As for helping the name Manfred generally—there is absolutely no doubt of that in my mind. (By the way, recently I've noticed a couple of other books of trios: *Three* by Tey, *Trio* by Maugham, etc.) In fact, so far as I'm concerned you can cut the rate of royalty on it, and so on. Just so it gets into the libraries and works for me. So please, please, let's get that settled right away now. I think *Northern Light* should come out in early August to get the best breaks: better chance to be reviewed at that time ahead of the flood of fall books, hit the stands a month before Pocketbooks comes out with *Lord Grizzly*, and so on. If we are to hit in August, then by gum we've got to get it into the works immediately.

I might also tell you that Richard Fleischer of Disney Productions made another offer, one of $10,000 and another of $12,000 (there were two methods of giving me the money) but that we turned it down. And I turned it down with less than $2.00 in my bank account!!! (I got ten bucks yesterday from *The Times* for participating in their symposium and with that we're buying a jug of wine and some special meat for Christmas dinner tomorrow.)

I think I shouldn't sell for less than a flat offer of $25,000 or an option of say $5000 plus a percentage of the gross take (if I can get it—and I want that if possible because then I can claim capital gains exemption in taxation later on). But to hold out until I get what I want, I'll need some money in a few weeks. I wonder if I can't have $750 against the account. I'll ask Alan to contact you. After we get that "right" movie contract, we won't bother you again. Won't it be fun to be lackadaisical about a publisher's biennial statement? Or, perhaps, we can get that amount against *Northern Light* by way of an advance. In any case, don't wait too long because *I don't want the electricity shut off here.*

Scott, just hang with me and you and McGraw-Hill will have a property of no mean value on your hands. Since getting rid of that crust of a penname, Feike Feikema, I've exploded like an American volcano. Islands, continents, all of them new, have been aborning in my head. I once scared a publisher[3] away by listing plot ideas in the form of titles, but if you don't mind I'd like to tell you what I want to do in the next few years, and give a hint of things to come beyond even that. So far I've already had published *The Golden Bowl, Boy Almighty, This Is The Year, The Chokecherry Tree, World's Wanderer,* and *Lord Grizzly.* You have in hand *Northern Light.* I have a first draft of *Morning Red* in hand here. After that I want to do a novel on the Sioux Indians of Siouxland just before the white man arrives, 1800, to be called *Green Earth.*[4] After that comes *Sons of Adam,* a modern study of brotherhood and mutual guilt and mutual redemption. (I've got some of this written and in a fat notebook. I can almost see it in print already.) I had hoped to write after that *Wings of Love*[5] (main character modeled after my mother with my brothers in it too), then *Eden Prairie* (main character modeled after a striking distant relative of a previous era with a marvelous plot and twist, also in Siouxland), then *Wild Land*[6] (cowboy novel and the *real* one for once), and after that *Heartland Fury*[7] (in Siouxland during Civil War times). But by golly it looks like I'm going to have to do one called *Paul Bunyan* right after *Sons of Adam.* I got an idea on how to do Paul the other day just as I finally got it on Hugh Glass. (You see what's going on here: I'm making *USA* heroes out of Hugh and Paul and so on, and using those legends for art just as, pardon the presumption of this please, just as Aeschylus, Sophocles, Euripides did of their heroes, Heracles, Oedipus, Agamemnon, Achilles, etc.) (Christ, I hope this ebullience and planning and optimism doesn't scare *you* off!)

Well, let's get on it. Let's hear from you soon on *Northern Light.* I want those three little fellows, or novellas, to get to work for me. And again, many many thanks for the wonderful Christmas pres-

3. Mr. Wreden of Dutton.

4. Later *Conquering Horse.*

5. Later *Green Earth.*

6. Later *Riders of Judgment.*

7. Later *Scarlet Plume.*

ent. With that red book, and the red wine and red meat, I'm having me a time this Xmas.

Best,
Fred

To Helen Reitsema Vander Meer

[Minneapolis, Minnesota]
Christmas Day, 1954

Dear Helen,

There wasn't much to go on. The longest account of Hugh Glass runs to some five pages in *A Treasury of Western Folklore* by B.A. Botkin, which in turn is a reprint from Hiram Chittenden's *A History of the American Fur Trade of the Far West*. I think you can find either book in your downtown library and I think too it'd be a good idea for you to read that.[1] It'll give you some idea of how much I really had to invent. [Matter deleted by author.] You get but the barest outline, like one of the book reports we used to turn in to Jakie. On the crawl, for example, there is but a paragraph. And as for his letting them off, the reports conflict. One says Fitzpatrick was in the army and this kept Hugh from shooting him since then he'd have the army after him. I decided to make my own ending, that is, invent the frame of mind and the kind of guilty soul that would feel like forgiving them at the end. "We boys. O them haunt companyeros." It's all in those two phrases at the end. My first goal was a plausible work of art, and if history fit, fine; but if it didn't, out. I probably went about using the story of the legend much as the Greeks, Aeschylus, Sophocles, Euripides, did the legends they had to hand in their day, of Heracles, Oedipus, Achilles, etc. The whole trick was to seize on a dilemma and make of that a dramatic work. I had in mind to write it for a long time, some ten years, but it wasn't until I had to do a little forgiving of my own that it suddenly was ready to write. (Right now I'm passing the legends of Paul Bunyan through my head: so far I haven't found that key, that dilemma, which will illuminate not only all the legends but also, generally, human drama. Give me dilemmas, conflicts, and I'll write books.) Once I had the *real* ending in mind, I knew the book would write easily. And it did. It came off almost perfect in first draft (longhand) and after I'd retyped it I needed but a blue pencil to clean it up. Looking back I remember the writing of it as both a daring ride and also an exhausting one. (By the way, let me recommend your buying *Western Folklore* by Botkin. It should be

1. Helen was reviewing *Lord Grizzly* for the Calvin Literary Club.

in every family's library for everybody to read.) I can't say that being bound by fact was limiting. Rather that once I had that ending worked out I drove for that like a blind man for food and light. (Some claim, for example, that Hugh died on the banks of the Platte in Elk Tongue's tepee.) To give you an example of what I added: I made up Bending Reed; filled in the figures of Ashley, Henry, Fitz; made up Stabbed and his mother; made up the two encounters with the grizzlies after the first incident; made up the death of the old mother Ree; made up the dogs; made up the horses (actually there were fewer wild horses in those days than I lead you to believe); made up the walk through the Bad Lands; made up Hidden Springs; made up the entire ending in the fort; and so on. The account in Botkin will tell you. How did I get the talk? I took down every recorded remark of the day. You know how some historians like to sprinkle quotes to liven up the texts? Coyly? I took these all down. The best sources were *Life in the Old Far West* by George Frederick Ruxton and *Wah-to-Yah* by Garrard. Their pages were filled with it. When I was ready to write I had some twenty pages of very carefully pruned and edited "talk of the day" and these I read over every morning to get a certain "talk" and rhythm going. I made it a point to resist letting them get into the conversation and the narration because I didn't like the way Guthrie went out of his way to get 'em into his *The Big Sky* and *The Way West* (much overrated). Then, to make sure that it would be my way, not anybody else's, I tried to conceive of myself as a sort of Homer doing an *Odyssey* of the American Civilization, a first book of a primitive time in a culture. I don't know why it is, but I can't do things the way other people do 'em. It's got to be new and my way, or nothing. I guess I'm a natural born lawbreaker lucky enough to be working over in a safe area, letters.

Tell Ray [Vander Meer] that in looking over my annuals of *Prisms* the other day, I ran across a wonderful prophetic note from him. He was making comment on a poem of mine in the annual for 1933. He signed himself as Ekmor, which I take to be an anagram for his Fries name of Romke. Right? I got the same thrill out of it that I did the first time I read it back in 1933.

Yes, we have three children: Freya, 10; Marya, 5; and Frederick F, 10 months. All of them seem to be bright children. For which we thank God since that assures us of endless preoccupation with lively growing folk. Frederick is going to be a tremendous fellow. He was 23 inches and 10 pounds at birth. I sat in on the delivery and the doc conducting the symphony turned to look over his shoulder after F's head had come into the world to say, "My God, this one's got shoulders!" He could raise his head immediately upon birth, from one side to the other. He was a couple of weeks late and probably got an extra dose of growing out of the long sleep. He will have my size and Maryanna's looks, plus a little of my brother Henry's. By the way, that birth was the greatest thing I ever saw. They all had to laugh because I kept alternating between profound silent observing and noisy cheering. I just fell in love with my wife all over again. For days I was filled to the eyes with emotion.

I've written books. But give me children every time. I wish we were both healthy enough to have a dozen.

We send you our very best. I didn't know your new address or you'd had a card from us. If things go right I'll probably come around to the homecoming next June. (Disney has made movie offers for *Lord Grizzly* but he isn't high enough. When he comes up, I can afford to come.)

Sincerely,
Fred

BOOKS BY FREDERICK MANFRED

(From 1944 through 1951
Frederick Manfred
published under the name
Feike Feikema.)

The Golden Bowl. 1944.

Boy Almighty. 1945.

This Is the Year. 1947.

The Chokecherry Tree. 1948.

The Primitive. 1949.

The Brother. 1950.

The Giant. 1951.

Lord Grizzly. 1954.

Morning Red. 1956.

Riders of Judgment. 1957.

Conquering Horse. 1959.

Arrow of Love.
Short stories. 1961.

Wanderlust. A one-volume
trilogy incorporating
revised versions of *The Primitive, The Brother,* and *The
Giant.* 1962.

Scarlet Plume. 1964.

*The Man Who Looked Like
the Prince of Wales.* 1965.
Reprinted in paperback as
The Secret Place. 1965.

Winter Count. Poems. 1966.

King of Spades. 1966.

Apples of Paradise.
Short stories. 1968.

Eden Prairie. 1968.

Conversations. Moderated
by John R. Milton. 1974.

Milk of Wolves. 1976.

The Manly-Hearted Woman.
1976.

Green Earth. 1977

The Wind Blows Free.
Reminiscence. 1979.

Sons of Adam. 1980.

Winter Count II. Poems.
1987.

Prime Fathers. Essays. 1987.

Index